A 'Belle Epoque'?

Polygons: Cultural Diversities and Intersections
General Editor: **Lieve Spaas**, *Professor of French Cultural Studies, Kingston University, UK*

A 'BELLE EPOQUE'?

Women in French Society and Culture 1890–1914

Edited by
Diana Holmes and Carrie Tarr

Berghahn Books
New York • Oxford

First published in 2006 by

Berghahn Books
www.BerghahnBooks.com

© 2007 Diana Holmes and Carrie Tarr
First paperback edition published in 2007

Library of Congress Cataloging-in-Publication Data
A "Belle Epoque"? : women in French society and culture,
1890–1914 / edited by Diana Holmes and Carrie Tarr.
    p. cm. -- (Polygons ; v. 9)
    Includes bibliographical references and index.
    ISBN 1-84545-021-3 (hbk.) -- ISBN 1-84545-094-9 (pbk.)
        1. Women--France--History. 2. Women--France--Social conditions. 3.
    France--Civilization--19th century. 4. France--Civilization--20th century.
    I. Holmes, Diana. II Tarr, Carrie. III. Series.
HQ1613.A24 2005
305.42'0944'0904--dc22

                                                            2005049339

British Library Cataloguing in Publication Data

A catalogue record for this book is available
from the British Library.

Printed in the United States on acid-free paper.

ISBN-10: 1-84545-021-3   ISBN-13: 978-1-84545-021-2 (hardback)
ISBN-10: 1-84545-094-9   ISBN-13: 978-1-84545-094-6 (paperback)

This book is dedicated to all the women of the Women in French networks – WIF-UK and WIF-US – and in particular to the memory of Claire Duchen (1955–2000) and Jill Forbes (1947–2001).

Contents

PART V: COLONISED AND OTHER WOMEN

Acknowledgements

The starting point for this book was the Seventh Weekend International Conference of *Women in French UK*, held in Leeds in April 2002, on the theme of 'A Belle Epoque? Women and Feminism in French Society and Culture 1890–1910'. The success of that conference owed a great deal to the enthusiasm, energy and organisational skills of Maggie Allison, to whom we owe warm thanks.

Thanks, too, to the staff of the Bibliothèque Marguerite Durand, where many of the scholars whose work appears here conducted parts of their research. The Bibliothèque has kindly given us permission to reproduce several of the book's illustrations.

Finally we would like to acknowledge the invaluable insights and assistance provided by Lieve Spaas, editor of Berghahn's Polygons series, and the support of Leeds University, particularly its French department, which has allowed the work of editing to be shared equally between us.

Diana Holmes
Carrie Tarr

List of Illustrations

Introduction

Diana Holmes and Carrie Tarr

If the decades around 1900 were remembered in France as a
'Belle Epoque', a golden age of affluence, security and frivolity,
that is because they were cast in this light from beyond the
trenches of a war that killed well over a million young French
men and wounded three million more, disabling many of
them for life (McMillan 1985: 77). Viewed retrospectively, the
years before 1914 were suffused with the prelapsarian glow of
an era blissfully unaware that the most 'civilised' nations on
earth could thus choose to butcher their sons in a struggle for
power and territory. The term 'Belle Epoque' is nostalgic, and
also somewhat elastic. If the historian Eugen Weber defines it
as 'the ten years or so before 1914' (Weber 1986: 2), Charles
Rearick in another influential study of the period has it cover
'the three decades before World War I' (Rearick 1985: xi), and
Jennifer Waelti-Walters and Steven C. Hause also imply the
broader definition in their anthology of Belle Epoque feminist
writings (Waelti-Walters and Hause 1994). In this book we
have also adopted the longer time frame, with our central
focus on the decades that close one century and open the next.
Although the continuities of history and the artificiality of
periodisation should not be forgotten, the years between the
consolidation of the Third Republic and the outbreak of war
do seem to correspond to a particularly colourful, dramatic
and to some extent self-contained period both for French feminism and for French women's history.

A term born of nostalgia needs to be treated with a degree of scepticism. After all, this era of modernisation and the consolidation of democratic republicanism was also a period that opened with the massacre of the Communards, accentuated the material inequalities between peasants and towndwellers, workers and bourgeois (McMillan 1985: 48–56), saw the country deeply divided over the Dreyfus affair, and pursued a policy of ferocious colonial expansion. The fact that the Belle Epoque straddles the 'fin de siècle', with all its connotations of decadence, degeneration and cultural crisis, intensifies the need to ask in what sense and for whom the lived experience of the era was 'belle'. Avant-garde intellectuals of the period identified themselves with what they depicted as the decadent spirit of their age, 'a mortal weariness with living, a bleak recognition of the vanity of effort',[1] though this elegantly languid pose tended to go hand in hand with reactionary, elitist politics, and to be a way of expressing rejection of an emerging mass culture. 'Decadence' in the context of the Belle Epoque designates the malaise of a certain cultural elite, disgusted by the materialism and republican democratisation of the era, and convinced that they were witnessing the decline of civilisation and imminent victory of the barbarians. It also refers, more specifically, to an artistic trend in both painting and literature, characterised by these same sentiments and hence by an aesthetic retreat from reality into artificiality and imagination.[2] In its recoil from the perceived democratisation of society, decadence in both these senses seems to confirm that the Belle Epoque was an era when social hierarchies were loosened, and the quality of life began to improve for the mass of people. Nonetheless, the France of 1900 was very far from being a homogenous society, and any attempt to define the age must take account of the fact that in terms of material living conditions, degrees of leisure and social and spatial mobility, the lives of individuals differed radically according to class and indeed – given the concentration of French economic and cultural life in the capital – geography.

But cutting across all other lines of difference there was gender: French women did not enjoy the status of free citizens in the new Republic, and the complex weave of expectations, education, family and social pressures that shape identity were utterly different for a woman than for a man. At the same time, women felt the impact of living in a regime that glorified freedom and equality, and their lives were altered, too, by technological progress and the cultural changes that constituted the new modernity. This book, then, asks to what extent the period 1890–1914 was a 'Belle Epoque' for women, against the background of a regime that at once proclaimed the freedom and equality of all its people, and denied both of these to the female half of the population. Its five sections correspond to five broad perspectives on women in Belle Epoque culture and society.

Part I, 'Feminism and Feminists', explores the variety of ways in which women claimed political and social agency. The Belle Epoque is the period of what came to be known as the 'first wave' of feminism, and saw the articulation of feminist issues that would run through the next century, as well as their translation into political action and protest. But women also contested restrictive definitions of female identity in other ways, through their behaviour and style, through women-centred cultural initiatives, through individual entry into what were assumed to be male-only domains. In the first chapter, we (the editors) examine the fundamental contradiction between on the one hand the extreme gender conservatism of the Belle Epoque, and on the other the impetus towards women's emancipation provided by both republican principles and socio-economic progress towards modernity. We assess the relationship between political feminism, and that more diffuse and ambiguous form of feminist opposition to patriarchy represented by the 'New Woman'. In the following chapter, delving beneath later feminists' alternately idealising and deprecating views of the 'first wave', Máire Cross finds evidence of a vibrant, multi-issue feminism from the 1890s on, albeit one divided by class, positions on anticlericalism and views of motherhood. One of the achievements of the Belle Epoque was the remarkable phenomenon of the feminist daily paper *La Fronde*, and Maggie Allison traces the ways in which it provided a platform for political causes whilst steering a delicate path between feminine gentility and feminist militancy. The paper's founder editor, Marguerite Durand, emerges as an astute manipulator of her own and the paper's image, whose legacy to French women lasted well beyond the Belle Epoque. Despite its strategic deployment of a traditional femininity, *La Fronde* lent its support to many radical feminist causes and figures, among these the remarkable activist Madeleine Pelletier. Anna Norris charts Pelletier's early career, pointing out how her feminist tactics involved infiltrating male domains in her capacity as doctor, scientist, freemason and socialist, and arguing for the symbolic force of these (often unsuccessful) challenges to male authority and misogyny. Finally in this section, Melanie Hawthorne takes as her starting-point the map of Natalie Barney's literary salon, published in 1929, in order to demonstrate how it constituted a (literal and virtual) place where national, generational, cultural and sexual boundaries could be crossed, from the Belle Epoque through to the 1920s. By tracing the links between, for example, writer Renée Vivien and painter Romaine Brooks through their connection to Barney, she establishes the significance of Barney's virtual salon as the site of an imagined international lesbian (and, by implication, feminist) community.

As at any other period, women at the Belle Epoque did not form a homogenous group but were divided by class, income, age and many other factors. Their ability to profit from the technological developments of the time was constrained accordingly. In Part II, 'New Technologies, New Women?', Siân Reynolds' discussion of how developments in transport affected women's mobility emphasises the differences between working-class and bourgeois women, but also demonstrates how the period saw a general enlargement of opportunities for women to travel both within and beyond the city. These opportunities were widely promoted in the advertising posters of the day and, as Ruth Iskin points out, the advertising industry addressed the New Woman as the consumer of a range of exciting new products. While the posters she discusses may appear on one level to offer conventional images of women as objects of the gaze, Iskin argues that their representations of New Women actively enjoying the pursuit of freedom, pleasure and achievement must have had an impact on women's identities and subjectivities

Among the women who themselves contributed to the development of science and technology – the most famous example being Marie Curie – is the enterprising American dancer, Loïe Fuller. Naoko Morita draws attention to the ways in which Fuller's innovative performances drew on the technological, aesthetic and spiritual implications of the 'Electricity Fairy' as well as on Art Nouveau, and made her one of the most celebrated women of the Belle Epoque. However new technologies did not necessarily mean new representations of women. The Belle Epoque saw the birth of the cinema industry and, with it, the pioneering role of Alice Guy, employed by Gaumont from 1896–1907 (McMahan 2002). But, taking as her starting-point the late nineteenth-century phenomenon of the medical operation film, Elizabeth Ezra demonstrates how the films of Georges Méliès, better known to film historians than those of Alice Guy, utilise the tropes of the cutting up and (re)making of women. Her discussion of cinema, gender and technology suggests that these early cinematic representations of women may be generated by a desire to 'gain control over an elusive and threatening femininity' (Showalter 1992: 134).

The question of the representation of women, of women as fascinating yet disturbing spectacle, is crucial to the Belle Epoque, with its enthusiasm for fashion, theatre and the music hall. But if women were frequently the objects of spectacle, they also learned to manipulate their images to their own advantage, Loïe Fuller being a case in point. Part III, 'Woman and Spectacle', focuses on women in the arts – theatre, dance and sculpture – and the different ways in which they express their subjectivity. Kimberly van Noort assesses how women playwrights contributed to making women the subjects of the gaze. Drawing first on little known plays by the internationally celebrated actress Sarah Bernhardt, she shows how Bernhardt critiques the specularisation of women and makes women the subjects of action and desire, while highlighting the ways they are limited by their social roles. Her subsequent discussion of *La Halte*, an association which promoted women playwrights, exemplifies how women writers at the beginning of the twentieth century turned to the stage, as elsewhere, as a platform for the expression of their artistic and political views. In the field of dance, certain well-known dancers of the period were able, like Sarah Bernhardt, to accept and exploit their roles as objects of the gaze, albeit at a cost. Hélène Laplace-Claverie focuses on the issues raised by the writings of Cléo de Mérode, Liane de Pougy and Isadora Duncan, and assesses the contradictions and paradoxes of their decision to opt for a career in dance at the expense of more 'normative' lives as wives and mothers. Citing Colette, however, she also points out that the majority of young women who sought a career on stage to avoid traditional feminine roles were often forced instead to accept starvation wages and sexual exploitation.

The career of sculptor Camille Claudel provides an example of a woman determinedly working in a field of representation and spectacle which was conventionally a male preserve. Angela Ryan analyses two of Claudel's key sculptures and suggests that, despite the constraints on Claudel as a creative artist, both through her association with Auguste Rodin and later through her family's ability to have her sequestrated in a psychiatric institution, her work challenges the hegemony of

masculine ways of seeing and forges a unique vision of the
human condition undistorted by gender stereotypes.

If the plastic arts were a particularly closed domain for
women, this was less the case in publishing. The Belle Epoque
was a period of huge expansion in literature, and saw a proliferation of women writers, many of whom (like the women
playwrights) have since been lost from literary history. Part IV,
'Women, Writing and Reception', explores the ways in which
gender shaped both the production and the reception of literary texts. By writing within traditionally feminine genres,
women writers could more easily gain access to publication;
but this did not prevent some female authors from appropriating the higher status 'masculine' genres, including the often
misogynist discourse of decadence. Critical reception was often
patronising or downright hostile, in line with the prevailing
doctrine of artistic creativity as an essentially masculine pursuit. Juliette Rogers examines popular 'middlebrow' novels of
the period that deal with the conflict between women's new
professional ambitions and their personal lives. Though few of
these have been read as oppositional feminist texts, Rogers
argues that in fact they gave popular currency to important
feminist ideas. She shows that what might seem to be cau-
tiously conservative plots are often simply acknowledging, for
their readers, the real difficulties of becoming a professional
woman at this period. In her discussion of the best-selling
work of Daniel Lesueur, Diana Holmes demonstrates how the
popular romance, a 'feminine' genre with little cultural status,
was an easier point of entry for women writers than the more
prestigious literary categories, and how the romance could
serve as a space for women to explore the constraints on their
lives and imagine utopian alternatives.

Jeri English turns to a writer who made her name by flouting hegemonic assumptions about the relationships between
sex and gender, and between gender and genre. In her analysis of two prefaces to novels by Rachilde – one preface written
at the Belle Epoque, the other in the 1980s – English demonstrates how the highly ambiguous work of this decadent
woman writer has been legitimised in entirely opposing ways
for very different reading publics. The lesbian writer Renée
Vivien also worked within a genre associated with hostility to
women, but Tama Lea Engelking argues that Vivien, rather
than internalising the misogynist discourse of decadence,
appropriates this very effectively for feminist ends. Rebutting
the many biographical readings of Vivien's work, Engelking

points to a crucial difference between the poet's short, sad life and the positive creative charge of her texts.

Catherine Perry is also concerned to show how the critical reception of women writers and their place in literary history have been shaped by an excessive attention to biography, and by derogatory images of femininity. In her discussion of the work of that Belle Epoque publishing sensation, Anna de Noailles, Perry shows how assumptions about both gender and ethnicity determined the interpretation of Noailles' work, and how Noailles actively resisted this process. Angela Kershaw looks at the phenomenal success of *Marie-Claire*, the first novel by the working-class writer Marguerite Audoux, and the more muted reception accorded to the postwar sequel, a novel which provides an illuminating perspective on women's working conditions at the Belle Epoque. She finds that a bourgeois readership was more able to accommodate proletarian fiction before the First World War than in the more conflictual climate of the 1920s, but also attributes the critical and commercial triumph of the first novel to Audoux's finally conservative stance on both class and gender.

The final section, Part V, 'Colonised and Other Women', highlights the fact that the Belle Epoque was a period of reflection on women's lot in other cultures as well as in metropolitan France, thanks in part to women travellers who reported on the condition of women in France's empire as well as in other exotic climes. Pioneering feminist Hubertine Auclert travelled to Algeria in the late 1880s and drew attention to the contradictions of the Third Republic's attitudes towards Algerian women, particularly in articles in her broadsheet, *La Citoyenne*. As Edith Taïeb points out, Auclert underlines the hypocrisy of the ways in which the values of the Republic are refused in the treatment of Algerian women (especially with regard to arranged marriages, polygamy, rape and the lack of education for women), and insists that it is only by according women equal rights with men, in France as well as in Algeria, that a 'democratic Republic' will be assured. Travel writing by women was also able to demystify some of the myths of the Oriental woman to be found in mainstream French culture of the period. For example, in the two male-authored novels analysed by Jennifer Yee, one addressing the situation of women in Turkey, the other women in Tunisia, the case for progress and modernisation is undermined by a continuing nostalgia for, or imperialist acceptance of, an exotic and tragic vision of the Orient, embodied in women who are victims of Islamic oppres-

sion and require liberation by the West. In contrast, as Margot
Irvine demonstrates, Marcelle Tinayre's travel writing subverts
dominant visions of the Orient. Her account of her visit to
Turkey explicitly challenges representations of 'disenchanted'
Turkish women and highlights similarities in French and Turkish women's struggle for emancipation. If Tinayre chooses not
to address cultural differences, as Auclert had done, her concern for solidarity with women of other cultures is nevertheless
indicative of the international perspective which informed the
writings and politics of Belle Epoque feminists.

As these various approaches to the Belle Epoque suggest, a
significant number of French women sought to express and
disseminate their different, gendered visions of a changing
world. In doing so, they asserted their right to an active place
in the political, social and cultural processes that would determine the nature of the new era, and thus laid the foundations
for the self-determined emancipation of women, one of the
most significant developments of the twentieth-century Western world. The nature of women's changing experience during
the Belle Epoque, the limitations but also the inspiring extent
of their achievement, form the subject of this book.

Notes

1. 'une mortelle fatigue de vivre, une morne perception de la vanité de tout
   effort' (Bourget 1883: xxii).
2. For the gender implications of decadence and women writers' relationship
   to the decadent aesthetic, see below, Chapters 15 and 16. Henceforth, following majority practice, we have used 'decadent/ce' with a lower case 'd'.

PART I

FEMINISM
AND FEMINISTS

CHAPTER 1

NEW REPUBLIC, NEW WOMEN?
FEMINISM AND MODERNITY
AT THE BELLE EPOQUE

Diana Holmes and Carrie Tarr

The New Republic and Political Feminism

Postwar nostalgia played its part in constructing the Belle Epoque as an optimistic, confident and colourful era, but this image is not made of myth alone: the Third Republic did usher in what, for France, was an unaccustomed period of stability, relative prosperity and (qualified) democracy. Born out of national defeat in the 1870 Franco-Prussian War, and the resulting demise of the Second Empire, the new regime survived the bitter conflict of the Commune and the opposition of the monarchists to restore national pride and consolidate a democratic republic that, on 4 July 1880, was able for the first time to celebrate the anniversary of the fall of the Bastille with a national fête. Political stability was accompanied by economic growth, above all in the technological and tertiary sectors (McMillan 1985: 47–48), and by imperialist expansion: between 1880 and 1895 the size of the French colonial empire grew from one to 9.5 million square kilometres (Magraw 1983: 235). The expanding empire fuelled a growing mood of national self-confidence, and added a touch of safely contained exoticism to the great Expositions or World Fairs held in

Paris in 1878, 1889 and 1900, such as the 1889 reproduction of an Arab street with its fountains, cafes and belly-dancers.[1]

The Republic's founding principles of liberty, equality and fraternity were never intended to apply to women as they did to men – or at least to white, metropolitan-born men. Male authority and privilege were built into the political, legal and economic fabric of this regime, just as into all the preceding ones: 'universal' suffrage meant male suffrage, the husband was legally the sole authority in the family, women workers – by 1906 38.9 percent of the female population and considerably more than a third of the country's workforce (McMillan 2000: 161) – were automatically paid lower salaries, and a married woman's earnings were in any case the property of her husband. Inequalities such as these were so familiar that they had come to appear natural. But the Republic's commitment to the ideals of democracy and equal rights produced a very visible contradiction: how could these be defended while half the population was excluded from civil rights and subjected to the authority of the other half? As would occur later with the nations France had colonised, the Republic provided the ideological basis for contestation of its own practices. The development of state education for women,[2] designed to wean them away from the influence of the Catholic Church and create a generation of good Republican mothers, also strengthened the social confidence and the intellectual armoury of women inclined to question the assumption of male supremacy.

Feminism was a minority activity in France at the Belle Epoque but, fuelled in part by belief in those very human rights from which the Republic excluded women, it was highly vocal and received a good deal of attention in the press, so that feminist ideas were 'in the air'. There were numerous campaigning groups that varied in political shade from conservatively Catholic to radically socialist, with the largest organisation, the *Conseil national des femmes françaises,* led by Protestant and pro-republican women such as Avril de Sainte-Croix and Sarah Monod. Though small in relation to the British or American movements, feminist campaigning groups could count about twenty to twenty-five thousand members in 1901 (Hause and Kenny 1984: 42) and well over one hundred thousand by 1914 (Waelti-Walters and Hause 1994: 6, 167). Regular feminist congresses – at least eleven between 1878 and 1903 – provided a very public forum for discussion of the major issues: the suffrage, reform of the profoundly sexist legal code (the *Code Civil*), equality in education, employment and equal pay, the recognition of maternity and domestic labour as socially important functions, the reform of the laws on prostitution. Though female membership of the trade unions remained low (5.26 percent of total membership in 1900, McMillan 2000: 183), not least because of the traditionalist hostility of male unionists, women workers demonstrated their capacity for a fierce and imaginative militancy on many occasions, both alongside men and in women-only strikes such as those of the sugar workers,[3] textile workers, tobacco workers and *sardinières* (McMillan 2000: 182–84). Those women who worked in the most traditionally feminine sectors – domestic labour and the fashion trade – were significantly absent from such protests, for their isolation and often harsh working conditions made the development of a politicised sense of collective identity particularly difficult.[4] For many working-class women gender and class identities conflicted (Sowerwine 1982: 8), so that on the whole even the most militant of female workers would probably not have recognised themselves in the label 'feminist'. At the congresses and through shared campaigns, however, middle and working-class women moved towards a collaboration based on the recognition that, as the socialist feminist Hélène Brion put it, 'women are even more exploited as women by the male community than they are as producers by the capitalists' (Waelti-Walters and Hause 1994: 148).

The most radical thinkers proposed arguments that would be central to the post-1968 second wave of feminism: Hubertine Auclert not only adopted a series of imaginative strategies to campaign for political rights, but also denounced the subordination of women within marriage; the popular public speaker Nelly Roussel argued for women's right to choose maternity, hence for contraception and at least implicitly for abortion on demand; Madeleine Pelletier made this demand explicit, and argued the constructionist case for gender as made rather than born; in defending prostitutes from the harsh system of regulation that operated only in the interests of their clients, many feminists made the connection between political rights and sexuality, and saw that patriarchy operated at the most intimate levels of behaviour.[5] Feminists won a series of small but important victories that extended women's legal rights and, by 1914, when the outbreak of war led them to suspend the struggle, they seemed very close to winning the right to vote.

The Anti-feminist Backlash

The existence of male 'experts' on women's nature, health and
potential to make trouble was a very marked feature of the
Belle Epoque. Despite the small scale of the feminist movement in France, a crisis in men's confidence in the solidity of
the patriarchal order seems to have occurred, at least among
intellectuals.[6] In essays, novels, lectures, plays and press articles men exhorted women to be what they claimed (with some
lack of logic) they inevitably and essentially were: kind, more
concerned with the good of (male) others than with their own,
gracefully passive, chaste, the guarantors of a humane society
not through any active political role but indirectly, by taming
the brute that was one aspect of masculine strength. They
waxed vehement on the dangers of any other course of female
behaviour: women who wrote, voted, pursued their education
too far would become sterile, hysterical or mad, while their
men folk would become feminised and French civilisation
would decay. Henri Marion, Professor of education at the Sorbonne, devoted a lecture series (1892–4) and a book (Marion
1900) to the 'Psychology of Woman', arguing, in a manner
that typified the anti-feminist discourse of the age, that science
had proved women to be ill-adapted to rational thought or
intellectual enquiry, and that the hallmark of an advanced
and progressive civilisation was the maintenance of firm gender boundaries (Marion 1900). Medical science pathologised
both the female body (for mental illness in women was widely
attributed to the effects of the uterus and the menstrual cycle)
and 'feminine' qualities; for if women's emotional and intuitive 'nature' was praised as a useful complement to male reason, it was also seen as the source of the second sex's mental
instability and propensity for hysteria.[7] At this period an ideology of gender difference that had long been largely uncon-
tested came to be articulated insistently and emphatically, not
to say hysterically.

There is an apparent discrepancy here between the small
scale and limited strength of the French feminist movement,
and the virulence of the backlash against the 'blue-stocking',
the 'emancipated woman', the 'Man-Woman',[8] who according
to so many male authors was threatening to abandon to men
the tasks of 'making jam and feeding the children'.[9] Annelise
Maugue identifies a crisis in male identity around the turn of
the nineteenth and twentieth centuries, and interprets this as
a reaction to a modernity that many men perceived as

empowering for women, but as profoundly destructive of virility. During forty-four years of peace, as work became gradually more mechanised, spectacular consumption took
precedence over production, and sedentary white-collar jobs
(the lower-paid ranks of which rapidly became feminised) proliferated in public and private sectors, men – at least some
men – felt 'deprived in the social sphere of the means to satisfy
their demiurgic aspirations and will to conquer'.[10] New social
conditions that seemed to hold liberatory potential for women
were experienced by many men as a threat to their virile identity. The small but noisy feminist movement undoubtedly
fuelled male fears, but the intensity of the backlash and the
wave of rhetoric defending an essentialist view of gender
expressed a reaction not just to feminism, but to more widespread and less explicitly political shifts in women's behaviour
and sense of identity. There was a widespread fear at the Belle
Epoque that the 'New Woman' had arrived in France, her-
alded by Ibsen's Nora – *A Doll's House* was first performed in
Paris in 1894 (Ibsen 1965 [1879]) – and already a stock figure
to be celebrated or (more often) lampooned in the British and
American press. She filled the pages of reviews like *La Revue*
and *La Plume,* the subject of articles and cartoons, dressed in
bloomers, abandoning husband and children to cycle to a
feminist congress, abrogating male rights and forcing men
into domestic servitude. The New Woman merged in the public imagination with feminism, but she represented a more
ubiquitous and insidious manifestation of some perceived
shift in gender relations. The question is, how far was she the
mythical projection of male fears, and how far the emblem of
real forms of emancipation?

Modernity and the New Woman

The perception of some significant change in female identity
came in part from changes in the fabric of everyday life, or at
least everyday urban life. Feminism in the political sense was
not a concern for most French women whose lives were situated, practically and by centuries of tradition, in the private
sphere. But changes in the material infrastructure of the everyday also had their effect on the scope of women's activity and
on their possible senses of identity. Belle Epoque France was
proud of its own modernity – its new technologies, its cutting-
edge fashion and design, its capacity to master and integrate

the exotic cultures of the colonies – all of which it celebrated and displayed in the three great Paris Expositions (1878, 1889, 1900). In France as a whole, urbanisation was still advancing slowly: in 1899 only 35 percent of the population lived in a town of more than five thousand inhabitants (Weber 1986: 51). But as the railway network expanded and travel time reduced, it became much more feasible for people to visit the larger cities, just as it became more possible for affluent city dwellers to depart for a seaside or rural retreat at the height of summer. And life in the cities – Paris especially – felt increasingly different from that static, inherited lifestyle, ruled by the natural rhythms of seasons and sunsets, that still prevailed in rural France. Electricity put an end to dependence on natural light, and further altered the relationship to space: the Eiffel Tower (one of the star attractions of the 1889 Exposition) could be ascended in seconds thanks to the electric elevators, and electrified trams made much of Paris more easily accessible even before the 1900 opening of the Paris underground. Nature – also the bedrock of arguments for gender difference – was clearly able to be changed by human intervention, and the new forms of transport in particular quite literally opened up the public world to women. From the 1880s on, the design and mass manufacture of the bicycle gradually progressed until by 1914 France counted three and a half million cyclists (Weber 1986: 200). For men, but still more for women, as the advertisers emphasised, the bicycle represented a liberating sense of mobility, independence and freedom to roam.[11] The soon generalised fashion for less constricting clothing – divided skirts and culottes, masculine-style tailored suits (the 'tailleur') – took its initial impetus from the need to pedal and to move around more generally whilst adhering to contemporary standards of female decency.

More markedly in Paris than elsewhere but, thanks to new forms of media and transport, in a way that had its impact across the country, this was already becoming the sort of fast-moving world that would be entirely recognisable a century later – a world of competing images and narratives, of a collective imagination both stimulated and distorted by the power of marketing and of modern urban bustle.

New modes of consumption in one sense situated women still more firmly in their roles as managers of domestic life and objects of desire: household goods, made-to-wear fashions, beauty products were all designed and displayed to appeal to female taste. But the transformation of Paris into the 'emblem of the consumer revolution' (Williams 1982: 12), begun under the Second Empire, also favoured women's personal mobility and a new sense of the self as a legitimately desiring, pleasure-seeking subject, free to travel around the widened streets with their colourful posters advertising products and leisure pursuits, the *grands magasins* with their mouth-watering merchandise, the dreams and fantasies propounded by the Expositions themselves. For bourgeois women, the propriety of staying close to home and venturing out only when chaperoned conflicted with the economic imperative to seek and purchase. In the city, the female body was on public display to an extent hitherto unknown, as advertisements for new commodities and entertainments eroticised the offered pleasure by embodying it in the person of a beautiful, inviting (and often minimally clothed) young woman. The deployment of women's bodies as spectacle reached its apotheosis with the twenty foot high stucco figure of *la Parisienne*, a statuesque creature gorgeously dressed by a leading couturier, above the entrance gate of the 1900 Exposition. But the pose of *la Parisienne* suggested movement, not passivity: she was clearly on her way to explore what the city had to offer, the consumer as well as the object of consumption, hence subject as well as object of new ways of looking.[12]

The new consumer-oriented city had the technology and the will to feed the imagination of its inhabitants, selling them dreams, and mobilising fantasies to sell them merchandise. The Belle Epoque, armed with effective mass-printing techniques, supported by a liberal, anti-censorship regime, also fed the demand for stories and images. Mass-circulation daily newspapers captured modern life as it happened and turned it into colourful tales, as well as offering fiction proper in the form of serialised novels or *feuilletons*. The publishing industry thrived as an increasingly literate population devoured the new low-cost novel collections, many of them deliberately aimed at a mass, popular audience. Stories and spectacles were also available at the theatres and music-halls, to which half a million Parisians flocked at least once a week throughout the 1880s and 1890s, and increasingly from 1895 through that more modern medium, the cinema. The insatiable demand for the printed word created openings for women (many of them now state-educated to secondary level) as well as for men: as this book demonstrates, journalism and the writing of mass-market fiction, as well as more conventionally literary careers, attracted many women at the Belle Epoque.

Women were also an important element of the market for stories – indeed experts on female criminality maintained that
their excessive reading of *faits divers* and novels corrupted
women's feeble minds and led to crime (Shapiro 1996: 34). The
dangerous potency of fiction and other media was perhaps not
entirely a figment of an anxious male imagination, for in the
pages of novels addressed primarily to a female market
(romances, stories of female lives, family dramas), in advertising posters appealing to female consumers, or in postcards of
female celebrities whose transgressive lives challenged conventional expectations of women's roles, women did find a space
outside any form of feminist campaigning where they could
explore the contemporary world from a female perspective, and
in some instances identify the causes of their dissatisfaction.

Public Lives

Without necessarily identifying themselves with any political
movement, then, or relinquishing those signifiers of authentic
femininity that were elegance, seductiveness and maternity,
women were able to dream of and even to appropriate certain
rights and roles hitherto reserved for men. But beyond private
experience, this era with its love of the stage, stories and spectacles witnessed the public playing out of transgressive 'new
womanhood' by a certain number of iconic individuals:
actresses, writers, journalists, scholars, and artists in particular. Mary Louise Roberts argues that in France what characterised most of these figures, and what distinguished them
from the feminists proper, with their (on the whole) sober and
rational style, was a capacity to combine scandalous appropriation of male prerogatives with the maintenance of very
'feminine' forms of behaviour. Rather than seeing this as compromise, Roberts (2002: 129) interprets it as a particularly subversive form of 'cultural illegibility' that seriously undermined
the gender essentialism that the Belle Epoque backlash tried so
hard to defend. It was not too difficult to caricature the militant feminist as simply outside the circle of seduction, an inau-
thentic or hybrid woman (an *'hommesse'*[13]), an effective way
both of neutralising the threat of feminism and of expressing
male anger, for the accusation of 'not being a real woman'
was designed to hurt. But the 'New Women', whose lifestyles,
careers and behaviour implicitly contested the dominant ideology of womanhood, could not be simply dismissed as 'man-

nish' feminists, for however much they trespassed on territory defined as 'masculine', they also displayed many of those qualities that their culture defined as truly 'feminine'.

Thus Marguerite Durand, owner-editor of the entirely female-staffed, campaigningly feminist newspaper, *La Fronde*, was renowned for her elegance, charm, beauty and gracious entertaining, and the whole tenor of the paper and its staff confounded the idea that feminism meant the adoption of a masculine style. In far less flamboyant mode Marie Curie, wife and mother, became a celebrity with her co-discovery of radium in 1898 and still more in 1903 with the award of the Nobel Prize in physics, shared with her husband, followed by a second Nobel prize in 1911. Successful women writers such as Marcelle Tinayre were regularly featured in the press, fascinating readers with the spectacular contradiction between their professional celebrity and their private lives as wives and mothers, while Rachilde combined the writing of dark and sulphurous erotica with the public persona of (in the 1880s) an innocent provincial virgin and (thereafter) a wife and society hostess. Adulated figures such as actress Sarah Bernhardt and dancer Loïe Fuller managed spectacularly successful careers on stage whilst remaining subject to a male (as well as a female) gaze. These public faces of the 'New Woman' tended to display key signs of the authentically 'feminine', of the 'real woman': an (at least apparently) heterosexual seductiveness, charm, domestic and personal elegance, and in some cases devoted maternity, even as they flouted the rules of gendered behaviour. They provided role models for women privately negotiating the frontier between emancipation and femininity, many of whom no doubt were heterosexual and anxious not to renounce love and motherhood. They also acted strategically, aiming at survival and success in a culture that made gender differentiation and the game of heterosexual seduction so central to social identity. But their highly visible fusion of contestation and conformity both disarmed male opposition to feminism and at a deeper level fed the fear of gender anarchy, for it surely undermined the neat binary model of complementary difference on which the Third Republic's economy, legislation and hegemonic sense of personal and national identity depended.

Some 'New Women' clearly did not remain within heterosexual norms. The artists, writers and society women who frequented Natalie Barney's famous salon were in many cases 'outed' lesbians like Barney herself, and of the women dis-

cussed in this book several (among them Bernhardt, Liane de
Pougy, Fuller, Colette, Rachilde as well as Vivien and Brooks
who were both Barney's lovers) had significant emotional and
sexual relationships with other women.[14] Whilst public awareness of the 'Sapphic community' at the Belle Epoque may well
have added fears of sexual redundancy to male anxieties, the
powerful hegemony of a heterosexual culture was largely able
to recuperate Sapphism, and accommodate lesbian sexual
activity as a titillating image for the male voyeur, presumed to
be merely a secondary pleasure to the main heterosexual
event. Lesbianism was not illegal in France, and though working-class lesbians often found themselves ridiculed and
harassed (McMillan 2000: 159), those who moved in the circles of high culture – protected too by Barney's own non-sepa-
ratist accommodations with mainstream culture – were not
unduly persecuted. They nonetheless added a further layer to
the accumulating sense that women were stepping outside
their prescribed role and identity.

The New Woman and Feminism

In Mary Louise Roberts' agreeable image, women's resistance
is a diverse language of which political feminism is merely
one dialect (Roberts 2002: 9), and the New Woman is another.
This distinction usefully highlights the difference between the
organised campaigning movement, and the wider shift in
women's sense of identity and rights, but it also covers up a
great deal of overlap. The New Woman dialect, we might say,
is so closely related to that of feminism as to be incomprehensible without it. Firstly, there is an overlap of people: the archetypal New Woman Durand, despite her reservations about
involvement in the movement itself, was nonetheless editor of
a newspaper feminist both in its methods of production and in
its editorial stance. Tinayre, a public New Woman who wrote
best-selling novels about New Women (such as La Rebelle,
1905), was also a regular contributor to La Fronde, and the
author of uncompromisingly feminist articles. Political feminists such as Nelly Roussel (like Durand, trained as an actress,
and a brilliant speaker whose persuasive rhetoric – the tran-
scriptions of her speeches are scattered with the word
'applause' [Waelti-Walters and Hause 1994: 18–37] – carried a
thoroughly radical message) could surely also be described as
New Women.

Secondly, the themes addressed at a theoretical and strategic level by feminists were also those that were being lived out by women in private lives and on the public stage, as well as being explored in best-selling 'women's novels' and the women's press. How far did a woman have a right to self-expression, to a voice in the affairs of the community, to individual self-fulfilment, and how could these things be reconciled with her emotional need for love and social endorsement? Were male and female sexualities fundamentally different, and how could the 'double standard' be changed so that it no longer worked to frustrate middle-class wives and criminalise poor working-class women? Was paid employment a liberation or a grim necessity? How did women in other cultures live, and what did a comparison with their situation reveal both about French society and about colonialism? Thus both as the source of the male backlash against women that was so central to Belle Epoque discourse, and as the fabric of women's collective self-awareness and search for new identities, feminism and the New Woman need to be seen as a diverse but integrated whole. Without the underpinning presence of an articulate political and social theorisation of women's cause, it is hard to imagine that the New Woman would have been taken so seriously, by her detractors or by her supporters.

Conclusion

Women's lives and identities underwent an accelerated change as the new Republic established itself as a legitimate and durable regime, and as France developed into a more urban, market-oriented, internally and externally permeable society. Women of all classes benefited (to differing extents) from better education provided by a Republic anxious to win and keep the hearts and minds of its citizens. Modernisation altered the fabric of daily life: the urban, middle-class woman became the newly mobile, individualised consumer of goods, fashions and literature that had to be designed to please her, and her proletarian and peasant sisters also felt the impact of these new forces as social and geographical mobility very slowly increased. Yet Belle Epoque women remained deprived of political rights, of some basic human rights (rape and violence in marriage remained legal), and of anything approaching equality in French society and culture. Indeed, it was the contradiction between the impetus towards emancipation and the reality of gender discrimination that both fuelled the growth of organised, political feminism, and produced that creatively hybrid mix of femininity and feminism, the New Woman.

Notes

1. Belly-dancers must have appeared thrillingly sexy to a public accustomed to different, more stylised and concealing forms of eroticisation of the female body.
2. 1880: law establishing free state secondary education for girls and female *lycées* (secondary schools). 1881: free, compulsory state primary education established for both sexes.
3. The feminist daily *La Fronde* provided sympathetic reporting of such strikes. See below, Chapter 3.
4. See below, Chapter 18.
5. See, for example, the articles under the heading 'Prostitution and the Double Standard' in Waelti-Walters and Hause 1994: 165–88, including Ghénia Avril de Sainte-Croix on prostitutes as female serfs (1901) and Madeleine Pelletier arguing for 'One Morality for Both Sexes' (1911).
6. This Belle Epoque backlash has been well documented and analysed by French feminists. See for example Groult 1978; Maugue 2001 [1987], Bard 1999, Chapters 1–6.
7. See below, Chapter 9.
8. *L'Homme-femme* was an essay by Alexandre Dumas fils published in 1872. Dumas was also the author of a later essay with an equally revealing title: 'Women who kill and women who vote' ('Les femmes qui tuent et les femmes qui votent'), 1880.
9. 'Soon it will be us, my friends, who will have to make the jam and feed ('allaiter' in French is closer to 'suckle') the children'. ('Ce sera bientôt nous, mes amis, qui serons obligés de faire les confitures et d'allaiter les enfants'.) (Cim 1891: 33).
10. 'privé(s) des moyens d'assouvir dans le champ social des aspirations démiurgiques et conquérantes' (Maugue 2001: 88).
11. See below, Chapter 6.
12. See Part III of this book, 'Women and Spectacle', and Naoko Morita's discussion of Loïe Fuller in Chapter 8.
13. Term employed by one G. Valbert in the *Revue des Deux Mondes*, 1 June 1889, to describe emancipated women who refused to play the game of seduction (Rochefort 2001: 218).
14. Melanie Hawthorne's chapter discusses the importance of Barney's lesbian network.

CHAPTER 2

1890–1914:
A 'BELLE EPOQUE' FOR FEMINISM?

Máire Cross

The proclamation of universal suffrage has
exacerbated the appalling nature of the unfair
exclusion of women. Before the end of the
nineteenth century, we will see the triumph
of this act of reparation and equity. Britain will
lead and France will follow.[1]

The term 'Belle Epoque' is a retrospective construction that is
suffused both with belief in the vibrancy and innovation of the
period in question (the moment when the nineteenth century
passed into the twentieth), and with a more generalised nostalgia. On the one hand it evokes the style, glamour and
sophistication of modernisation and multiple avant-garde
movements. On the other, it is associated with exceptional
political stability since, even with the Dreyfus affair raging,
the parliamentary processes of the Third Republic demonstrated a certain maturity. As Michel Leymarie (1999: 9)
argues, 'What would come to be called the Belle Epoque was
one of those stages in history which Péguy described in *Notre
Jeunesse* (1910) as temporary periods of calm'.[2] In both cases,
it is tinged with regret for the passing of a glorious bygone era,
glorious, that is, for the privileged classes in France.

The hallmark of the way in which the Belle Epoque has
been interpreted by succeeding generations is the focus on the

creativity and modernisation of the period, seen through the filter of nostalgia. For example, political confidence at home is seen to have fostered France's elegant poise in the world as a colonial power. The great international exhibitions in Paris, occasions for the display of technical and scientific progress, combined with innovations in art, music and literary output, meant that in 1900 Paris enjoyed world capital status. Ongoing economic expansion would eventually create improvements in living standards, at least for some. Knowledge was becoming more democratic through compulsory schooling. Under the liberal laws regulating the press and censorship, and thanks to new inventions in transport and communications, writing and publishing flourished.

The Belle Epoque is also seen as a precious time for women's aspirations, as many were to benefit both directly and indirectly from change. It was, indeed, a golden age of the feminist press with the appearance of *La Fronde*, the first newspaper entirely staffed by women. With new opportunities for paid employment, middle-class women became more assertive and broke new records of achievement in removing barriers to women in public life, at university, in the professions, as writers and as artists. They formed associations in a wide number of fields including the political. The feminist movement that grew during the period from 1890 to 1910 was thus part of the changing, modernising world of the Belle Epoque.

However, interpretations of Belle Epoque feminism have been complicated by the fact that feminists of later generations have oscillated between an aggrandising nostalgia that inflates the period's achievements, and a tendency to minimise feminist gains and the efficacy of the movement by comparison with later periods. On the one hand, the fast-living artist, journalist or writer has been idealised as a representation of feminist achievements. On the other, given the failure of the French suffragists and the lack of women's progress in politics, the alluring images of Art Nouveau posters and fashionable women dressed in Parisian chic have enabled Belle Epoque women to be interpreted purely in terms of style and glamour, as compliant objects of the gaze. What I am suggesting, then, is that the Belle Epoque invites both a nostalgic desire to overestimate its achievements, in feminism as in other fields, and a deflationary desire, apparent for example in second-wave feminism (at least in France), to play down the radicalism of early feminists by a self-enhancing comparison with post-1968 achievements. As many recent studies have shown (Waelti-

Walters and Hause 1994; Bard 1995; Smith 1996; McMillan 2000), the Belle Epoque has both positive and negative implications for French feminism. However, above all it was an era of innovation, both for women's emancipation and for French society as a whole, which laid the foundations on which future generations could build. The aim of this chapter, then, is to assess some of the issues raised by the Belle Epoque for feminism in a way that is neither idealised nor deprecatory.

Interpreting the Belle Epoque

Many innovations of the Belle Epoque that seem at first unconnected to the political emancipation of women, especially economic developments, in fact had a major impact on women's experience, and also form a useful parallel to feminist achievements in the way they have subsequently been interpreted by historians. The story of the French automobile industry is a case in point. In the 1890s there were several car inventors in France – manufacturers working in artisan conditions; by 1910, they had already been merged into a smaller number of companies; after the Second World War, the industry expanded to become one of the strongest in Europe. Its success had begun with the remarkable engineering feats and economic restructuring that took place during the Belle Epoque. Yet it was not until after the period known as *les trente glorieuses* (the thirty years of unprecedented economic growth from 1945 to 1975) that the economic importance of the Belle Epoque was recognised as such (though the French economy still compared less favourably with the British experience in terms of output and expansion).

The same applies to the reputation of the suffragettes. Compared to the British suffrage movements of the pre-war years, French efforts are considered rather feeble by some (Waelti-Walters and Hause 1994: 1–3). Nonetheless in May 1919 the Chamber of Deputies voted to grant an extension of the suffrage to women by 329 votes in favour and 95 against (Sowerwine 2001: 123), even if, due to the conservative nature of the second house, the bill never got to the statute books. Thus the pioneering efforts of the women's movements in Belle Epoque France, including the formation of small-scale associations, although scattered, had far-reaching implications. The period laid the foundations for women's social progress and for a more sustained political development of feminism.

Although the impact in France of change in the political, economic and social sectors at the end of the nineteenth century has been well documented by contemporaries and by subsequent historians (Kuisel 1981; Asselain 1984), it took the new generations of feminist historians to focus on the gender dimensions of this period (Hilden 1986, 9–32; Salin 2000: 25–72). Even so, among feminist writers of the period such as André Léo, Hubertine Auclert and Madeleine Pelletier, there was an informed opinion and an awareness of how economic changes affected the situation of all women; many articles on women's working conditions appeared in the columns of *La Fronde* for instance. A record number of women were employed in the secondary sector and more significantly in the nascent tertiary sector, both public and private. This put pressure on the state to modernise the civil laws on women's earnings and employment rights and legislators paid considerable attention to the subject of women during this period (Accampano et al. 1995: 1–27).

However, beyond a gender analysis, 'traditional' political historians have usually been more preoccupied by the fragility and paradoxical stability of the Republic (Rioux 1991). Rémond (2002: 12–13) prioritises the themes of crisis and durability in the Third Republic thus:

> Are we right in thinking that after wandering in search of the best regime for France, the French had the feeling that they had finally found the Promised Land? [...] The Third Republic had just as much opposition determined to fight it and overthrow it as the other regimes. The theme of republican consensus that is taken for granted nowadays is a friendly legend: until its last days, the Republic had ferocious enemies.[3]

As the Republic was born out of military defeat, with politicians nervously remembering previous crises, politicians and historians of the Belle Epoque have devoted much attention to the question of the definitive establishment of an enduring republican consensus. Very often this has been undertaken without a single mention of the exclusion of women from this so-called consensual process (Rioux 1991; Rémond 2002). Democracy in France has been viewed as synonymous with the Republic and women were not excluded from the Republic even if they were excluded from the democratic process. Though legislation defined their lives as pupils, daughters, mothers, writers and workers, by far the majority of women in feminist organisations willingly accepted republican culture. Indeed their desire to become wholly integrated into the Republic galvanised their efforts to will a gendered egalitarianism into democracy. Their desire for the suffrage stemmed from their desire to play a full role in republican democracy. Hence the fact that, despite the growth of feminism and the many burgeoning women's associations – women were active in Catholic women's motherhood leagues, as socialists and republicans, as suffragettes, nationalists, syndicalists, anarchists and freemasons, and as libertarian writers and artists – women were not considered a threat to political stability.

The Development of Belle Epoque Feminism

The reaction of Belle Epoque women to their subordination in French society was not a new phenomenon but it was a break from what had preceded it. Since the 1789 Revolution, women had been formally excluded from politics because of the gendered definition of citizenship. At the same time, the Revolution provided the egalitarian discourse with which to challenge this exclusion. According to Geneviève Fraisse, the Revolution and the subsequent separation of the sexes into distinct public and private spheres throughout the nineteenth century made possible the development of feminism but also set up a double problematic: the equality of the sexes could be established by reference to human rights, but the 'Rights of Man' lacked an acknowledgement of gender difference (Fraisse 1998: 8). The French feminist movement in particular was (and still is) characterised by this problematic. This is evident in the variety of the causes for which movements were created during the Belle Epoque, from sexual abstinence to equal pay. Women demanded a voice in the Republic both on the grounds that their female difference would have a civilising influence, and on the grounds that they were workers and citizens in exactly the same way as men.

There may have been earlier emancipatory women's movements in France, but Belle Epoque feminism was the first sustained movement under contemporary republican institutions. Indeed the political term 'feminism' was firmly established during the Belle Epoque (Rendall 1985: 1–3; Offen 1988) and signified the demand for women's equality in public life. Resistance to these demands gave rise to an anti-feminism based on pseudo-scientific arguments (Bard 1999).

However, a minority of women and some men believed women were entitled to become agents in politics, even if many simply wanted better home and working conditions. Feminism had become common currency by the 1890s.

Like all social movements, feminism can only flourish when there is an opportunity for expression. Already in the late 1860s, before the end of the Second Empire when political censorship was relaxed, arguments in favour of gender equality had appeared in print. In 1869 feminist campaigner André Léo (1824–1900) had responded vigorously to Proudhon's claim in his *De la Justice dans la Révolution* (1867) that women were inferior physically, intellecually and morally to men:

> Anyone opposed to women's demands for freedom and equality, who wishes to establish a code of conduct for the family whereby the first rule is for women's subjugation and material dependence, is living in the spirit of the past and is a champion of the old order against the principles of the new one.[4]

A focus of attack for feminists was the Napoleonic Civil Code of 1803 that had formalised women's subordinate role in familial relations. Together with their exclusion from politics, the *Code civil* was seen as the greatest injustice to women in France in the nineteenth century. With or without the drive for emancipation from feminists, a degree of financial independence was imperative for women to play a full part in the changing world of the Belle Epoque.

In the 1860s, demands published by individuals had been modest enough. Arguments in favour of equal treatment of the sexes in matters of education and civil law were more numerous than demands for political suffrage, not surprisingly as parliamentary democracy had been suppressed by Louis-Napoléon in 1852. Political crisis and war limited opportunities for broadcasting feminist demands. The military defeat by Prussia in September 1870 and the collapse of the Second Empire caused political upheaval in France, including the Siege of Paris in the winter of 1870 first by enemy troops, then by the French in the spring of 1871 when, in a bloody episode of the Franco-French war, Thiers' conservative republican government defeated the left-wing Commune of Paris. The resulting suppression of the insurrectionist movement ensured the loss of a generation of militants to lead the left wing in the new Republic. Much attention has been devoted to the disastrous impact of the Commune on the Left (Tombs

1999: 184–216). It is true that the execution or exile of left-wing Parisian leaders eclipsed the radicals from the national picture for several years. Those silenced were not clamouring loudly for sexual equality at work, in marriage or for women's political rights; yet the repressive atmosphere reduced opportunities for social reform, stifling even the most moderate demands that had been heard in the 1860s. The accumulated effect of the socially conservative Second Empire and the 'flash flood' of the Paris Commune revolt was the same: in that climate of repression women's protests were stifled and feminism was depicted as a threatening virago, associated with previous threats of revolution (Gulickson 1996).

The defeat of the Commune delayed the creation of a socialist organisation and made the ruling political elite fearful of political instability. Feminist demands for what are now considered basic rights were scarcely heard in the cacophony of monarchist versus republican debates from 1871 to 1877. The ideological power struggle among republican factions dominated politics, overshadowed interpretations of French history and dwarfed accounts of feminist struggles. However, the development of women's studies has provided the incentive to probe beneath the prevailing narrative of republican discourse in Belle Epoque France. Once into backstairs politics, scholars have discovered that the end of the nineteenth century is particularly rich in material for studies of demography and social policy (Ronson 1980; Cova 1997). The relationship between the French state and its citizens had been gradually changing before the advent of the Third Republic. Its political stability in the period 1890 to 1914 meant that there was opportunity for the formulation of new policies on birth, child-drearing and family structures:

> ... legislators' preoccupation with the negative impact of women's work on both the family and the nation led in 1892 to the first comprehensive French law to protect women employed in factories and ateliers, child labourers having already received some protection from laws passed in 1841 and 1874 (Clark 1995: 129).

These reforms derived from the thinking of men anxious to secure the future of the French state, under threat both externally, from wars and invasion, and internally from the enemies of republicanism. The regulation of women's lives was part of this defensive strategy (Accompano et al. 1995; Fuchs

1996). The relationship between republicanism and feminism during this period can thus be seen from two points of view: government policy-making targeted women as socio-economic subjects according to men's interpretation of women's (different) role in society; feminists attempted to acquire full citizenship for women according to their interpretation of equality.

By 1890 public associations burgeoned, leading to the creation of political parties, trade unions and women's rights organisations (Waelti-Walters and Hause 1994). For the first time since 1848, men and women were granted the right to political activism and thenceforth were exhorted to participate in public life as good citizens. All men over twenty-one were allowed to vote and stand for parliament. Women were not allowed to vote but many were to avail themselves of every other opportunity to voice their opinions. They acted through the medium of the liberalised press and the now permitted collective associations. The majority of feminists were republican and anxious to play a part in public life. They were passionate about matters pertaining to the inequality of the sexes but also about the burning issues of the day, not least of which was the Dreyfus affair.

The feminist movement was thus very far from being a single-issue pressure group around the vote. Most studies suggest that anticlericalism made suffrage a complex issue, but there were also other issues to divide feminists. Many saw the vote as less urgent than the scourges of prostitution and infant mortality. In this instance, consensus was difficult because of prevailing attitudes to the birth rate, considered to be of national interest. French politicians were obsessively conscious of the demographic superiority of their troublesome neighbour Germany. However, although appalling housing and factory conditions had affected the health of mothers, motherhood was not a unifying issue among women and feminists, even if the issues surrounding it inspired many to join organisations. In general, membership of campaigning organisations rose at this time as the stark inequalities among the French spurred many to join trades unions and take industrial action. The 1890s saw the brief existence of an anarchist group that took direct action against the state in the form of isolated acts of terrorism. Extreme right-wing groups also formed, championing nationalist sentiments. Desire for state intervention to alleviate poverty existed and, as part of this, practical social and economic feminist demands began to be heard. Alliances of unlikely bedfellows to achieve the suffrage were formed, a pattern that has continued until the present day with the issue of parity. Because of the multiple layers of ideologies and political families not yet formed into coherent parties, feminism of the Belle Epoque is a mosaic of French politics.

The Achievements of Belle Epoque Feminism

Earlier in this chapter it was argued that interpretations of the Belle Epoque have varied and that this may have affected the way we view the developments of the feminism of the time. The reputation of first-wave feminism (an expression coined in the 1970s by feminists who designated themselves second-wave) is that it was a more moderate precursor to contemporary feminism and thus by implication incomplete. It is true that the majority of vociferous feminists were republican and for the most part liberal, and that though they believed there should be greater equality between the sexes, they did not wish to overturn the status quo. Anxious to avail themselves of the freedoms enjoyed by men, the majority of women who sought greater emancipation did not question the rules of a man's world. Most shied away from the term 'feminist' and wished for moderate reform rather than a total rejection of patriarchy. For a small number of women in 1900 abortion and contraception rights were of paramount importance; but these were considered by the majority to be revolutionary demands. However, neither this tendency to moderation, nor the many divisions in the feminist movement, alter the fact that a host of important issues and demands were articulated, discussed and defended at this period, and that they would set the agenda for the twentieth-century women's movement. As a result of the development of women's studies, feminist historians in France, Britain and the United States have documented the evolution of the feminist movement from the 1880s onwards. A more inclusive story of the evolution of social relations between men and women has become possible, though it has yet to be fully integrated into what is referred to as mainstream history or the grand narrative of French politics (Offen 2000: 1–17; Reynolds 2002).

Unlike previous generations of women militants, activists and writers of the Belle Epoque left substantial archival evidence of collective action in their publications and association papers. Waelti-Walters, Hause and Bard have presented evidence of women's enthusiasm in forming public associations. Out of the seventeen tabled by Waelti-Waters and Hause

(1994: 5) seven were founded between 1870 and 1893, with ten founded between 1897 and 1901. Of these the biggest by far was the *Conseil national des femmes françaises* with a membership of over 21,000. Fifteen of the 103 associations supporting women's issues directly or indirectly cited by Bard (1995: 463–5) were formed before 1910.

Historians have tried to disentangle the divisions among the numerous feminist groups (Bard 1995) by defining them as moderate, reformist and radical (Klejman and Rochefort 1989) or as Catholic and anticlerical (Smith 1996). Arguably feminism followed a similar pattern to that of the socialist movement in the nineteenth century. Individual and shared awareness of oppression led on the one hand to the publication of personal theories of oppression (Pelletier 1978; Roussel 1979; Auclert 1882a; Léo 1990) and on the other to the creation of a movement to fight against it. One of the toughest lessons of second-wave feminism has been to recognise that heterogeneity is a critical feature of feminism. This recognition is essential for our understanding of the feminism of the Belle Epoque period when, as with any period, opinions differed as to the priorities for change. Divisions over tactics and ambitions led to splits and a multiplication of associations.

The most moderate feminists and those most prolific in forming organisations sought improvements in women's condition as mothers and as spouses. This was mainly the remit of the many Catholic women's organisations founded during this time. For some, Catholic support for women's concerns was living proof of the Catholic Church's determination to resist the secularisation of family values through the state provision of education and health services; but it must be recalled that the Vatican had proclaimed its approval of female suffrage before the establishment of the Third Republic. Many of these moderate organisations expressed their demand for political emancipation, like the *Union nationale pour le vote des femmes* (Smith 1996: 13–62). Yet the centrality of the clerical-anticlerical debate in the early decades of the Third Republic meant that inevitably a wedge was driven between Catholic and republican feminism. At the same time, the existence of such a debate provided a forum for the articulation of ideas. Politics became a vehicle for women to engage with their fellow men and citizens and, as they became more articulate, to gain in confidence and experience.

On the Left, there was the question of the relationship between class and gender. Women workers in factories became potential party members for socialists campaigning for the working-class trades unionists. The problematic issues surrounding this question emerged very clearly during the Belle Epoque and have been hotly debated ever since (Frader and Rose 1996). Evidence shows that women were more reluctant than men to take industrial action and that some men resented their presence in trade unions as they were keen to promote the idea of a family wage. However, this must not be taken as the universal pattern. There is also proof that women did become unionised and that the Guesdist socialist party did address female-related struggles. Women's concerns were debated in meetings, and they were prepared to take strike action (Hilden 1986; Salin 2000). Inevitably, however, class divisions between women frequently took precedence over their shared subordination as a sex. The greatest division among women at the International Congresses arose in relation to the question of time off for workers in domestic service. The suggestion that employers should perform their employees' tasks while they were off duty once a week was met with a stony refusal. The tension between the (possibly feminist) mistress leading the life of a *femme mondaine* (Plott 2002) and an overworked servant or seamstress, usually from the country, lodging in the cramped accommodation of a *chambre de bonne*, neatly articulates the conflict between class and gender of the period. The architecture of apartments in the grand districts of Paris specifically catered for this class division of labour and allotted domestic social roles that disappeared dramatically after the 1914–18 conflict. Education and employment opportunities for women at the Belle Epoque were gradually beginning to expand, to some degree in response to feminist pressure, so that eventually they would provide alternatives to the drudgery of domestic service.

In the more radical discourse of some Belle Epoque feminists can be found many of the ingredients that were at the heart of the vibrant feminist movement of the late twentieth century. Radical individuals wrote passionately, condemning the lack of freedom for women outside the home and condemning inequality wherever it existed, in politics, at work or in school. Nelly Roussel argued that alcoholics and illiterates could vote, so why not women:

> If you were to tell me as I have been told, that devout religious women are not ready for the vote, I would reply that they are just as capable of voting as are drunkards from pubs![5]

Madeleine Pelletier campaigned for the vote inside and outside political organisations, gaining a place on the executive of the SFIO and getting the party to agree in principle to vote for women's suffrage when it came up in parliament. She argued for the right to abortion and contraception, insisting that women should take control over their own destinies in personal and in public spheres: 'It is solely up to a woman herself to decide if and when she chooses motherhood'.[6] Hubertine Auclert declared the political system was inadequate so long as women were absent from it as voters and as elected representatives, and argued vehemently that the double standards of morality were equally evident in the colonial situation in Algeria.

So was the Belle Epoque a millstone or a milestone in the history of feminism? The fact that without the vote women's political identity remained elusive should not detract from recognition of the success of other aspects of the feminisation of the public sphere, including that of politics itself. Feminism of the Belle Epoque denounced the structures of women's subordination, and women participated in political associations and industrial action whenever opportunities arose to do so. It became commonplace for women to publish and create voluntary associations. They articulated their search for identity or sense of self in the fast-changing world of education, communications, transport, technology, state pensions and maternity care, mass publishing and women's national and international associations. The period saw the beginnings of the modernisation of the economy and of cultural and social relations, and feminism played its part in this. Divided, often derided, beset by the opposition even of those whose commitment to human rights should have made them allies, Belle Epoque feminism nonetheless made women's voices heard on a public stage and set the agenda for a struggle that would continue throughout the following century.

Notes

1 'La proclamation du suffrage universel a encore rendu plus choquante et plus injuste l'exclusion de l'élément féminin. Le XIXe siècle ne se passera pas sans voir s'accomplir cet acte de réparation et d'équité. L'Angleterre commencera et la France suivra' (Deraismes 1980: 140).

2. 'Ce qu'on nommera Belle Epoque est un de ces paliers dont Péguy dit, dans Notre Jeunesse (1910) qu'ils apaisent tout pour un temps plus ou moins long' (Leymarie 1999: 9).

3. 'Faut-il penser qu'après avoir longtemps erré en quête du meilleur des régimes les Français ont eu le sentiment d'avoir enfin trouvé la terre promise ? [...] La IIIe République n'a pas connu moins d'oppositions, non moins déterminées à la combattre et à la renverser, que les autres régimes. Le thème, aujourd'hui banalisé, du consensus républicain, d'une adhésion quasi unanime au modèle républicain est une aimable légende: jusqu'à ses derniers jours la République a eu des ennemis féroces' (Rémond 2002: 12–13).
4. 'Lorsqu'on s'oppose à la revendication pour la femme de la liberté et de l'é-galité, lorsqu'on veut formuler une constitution de la famille dont le premier article est l'assujetissement de la femme et sa dépendance matérielle, il faut s'avouer du moins que l'on vit encore dans l'esprit du passé, qu'on se fait le champion de l'ordre ancien contre les principes de l'ordre nouveau' (Léo 1990: 118).
5. 'Si vous me dites, comme on l'a dit, que les dévotes des églises ne sont pas mûres pour la Liberté, je répondrai que les ivrognes des cabarets ne le sont pas davantage!' (Roussel 1979 [1906]: 102–3.
6. 'C'est à la femme seulement de décider si et quand elle veut être mere' (Pelletier 1978 [1914]: 127.

Figure 3.1 Portrait of Marguerite Durand by Jules Cayron,
1897. Courtesy of the Bibliothèque Marguerite Durand.

CHAPTER 3

MARGUERITE DURAND AND *LA FRONDE*: VOICING WOMEN OF THE BELLE EPOQUE

Maggie Allison

The publication run of the newspaper, *La Fronde,* and the life-time of its founder-owner, Marguerite Durand (Figure 3.1), both sit well and truly astride the turn of the century, in the middle of a period which was rich in opportunities for women's development and self-expression, but not without its hazards and ambiguities. The newspaper ran from 9 December 1897 to 1 October 1903, and Durand's life extended from 1864 to 1936, providing perfect symmetry; yet Durand and her relationship to *La Fronde* and the world beyond it also gave rise to asymme-tries and contradictions which are arguably symptomatic of their time. For, if founding an overtly feminist publication was a bold step for a woman, that woman herself reflected the mul-tiple facets of feminism, femininity and the 'New Woman' prevalent during the Belle Epoque. This chapter looks at the ways in which the newspaper acted as a tribune – or platform – for women's voices, while at the same time reflecting the ambiguous role and striking public persona of its founder.

Origins, Aims and Ethos

It is recounted that Durand, having attended the Women's International Congress of 1896 with a view to obtaining an amusing piece of copy for *Le Figaro* where she was a journalist at the time, found herself instead rather convinced by the debates, determining her to set up her own newspaper to further the cause of women (Dizier-Metz 1992: 7; Rabaut 1996: 24). The aims, printed in the third issue on 11 December 1897, were as follows:

> *La Fronde.* A major daily newspaper. Political and literary. Managed, administrated and compiled exclusively BY WOMEN. In the French population women are in the majority. Millions of French women, unmarried or widowed, live without the legal support of a man. Women pay taxes which they have no say in approving; their manual labour and intellectual work contribute to the wealth of the nation and they claim the right to be allowed to voice their opinion on all questions affecting society and humanity, of which they are members on a par with men. *La Fronde* is a faithful reflection of their approval, their criticism and their rightful demands.[1]

The title of the paper is significant in itself, 'la fronde' being the name for a catapult and also that given to the period of revolt during Anne of Austria's regency of Louis XIV in the seventeenth century. The verb, taken from that time, means to attack the respected establishment by means of satire, mockery and other forms of impertinence. The message was clear: Durand's newspaper was to take on the male establishments of France, both in terms of criticism and campaigning and, just as importantly, on equal terms with other quality press of the time. This was not to be either a 'feminine' newspaper nor a more confrontational 'feminist' publication. Such a position is not without its ambiguities, but Durand's overriding concern was that her newspaper should be measured by its professionalism as well as its message.

This concern set the scene for the overall discourse of the newspaper, which foregrounded educated women writers, prominent in their fields, but not necessarily experienced journalists, apart from Séverine (a pseudonym for Caroline Rémy). Séverine was a staunch social activist, only the second French woman to obtain a *carte de journaliste* and still a byword for French woman journalists to this day.[2] Her regular first page column, 'Notes from a Frondeuse', spearheaded the feminist content of the paper, and provided a link between the fashionable orbit of Durand and the world of the less fortunate. However, tensions of interests are revealed in the paper's range of copy and rubrics, and the implications this has for the readership. If the writers are highly articulate professionals, the advertisements on page four open the door to a varied, albeit literate clientèle, since they include not just incitations to buy the six volumes of the *Nouveau Larousse Illustré* dictionary or to venture through the doors of the *La Samaritaine* department store, or buy a piano, but also to receive a reduced price Singer sewing machine (regarded as the sine qua non of any well-organised household) in return for an annual subscription to *La Fronde*, or to purchase the 'ferret', a wasp-waisted corset, supposedly good for preventing a bloated stomach. These all imply a certain aspirational purchasing power, which contrasts with the paper's acknowledgement of many of the social issues affecting women workers, as discussed below, but chimes in with the edifying, educational thrust of much of the journalism. As Durand herself wrote in the edition of 14 September 1900, the target readership was educated women – the paper offered cheap subscriptions to women primary school teachers, for example – for Durand was clear that her 'overriding concern [was] and always [would] be to awaken interest in the feminist cause among those women who are knowledgeable and reflective, who are capable of spreading the word in those sections of society where it needs to take root'.[3]

Content, Concerns and Complexities

La Fronde existed for six years as a four-page broadsheet, page one of which was a mixture of general information as to political events in Paris and elsewhere, together with regular columns, such as that of Séverine, taking a specifically feminist stance on current affairs. The inside pages could be devoted to lengthy accounts of parliamentary debates or current legislation, but page two always bore the 'Tribune' section, that is, a space for women to write over a period of three days on an issue either of social and topical importance, or an historic topic from a feminist perspective. In contrast, page three carried a specifically literary section, in the form of serialised romantic short stories or novels, including, for instance, those of Daniel Lesueur, whose novel, *Lèvres Closes* (*Closed Lips*), was serialised as of the first issue.[4]

Maria Pognon, who had presided at the 1896 Congress, and Clémence Royer, scientist, translator and pacifist, were among the many eminent contributors. Regular features geared to women's social and legal position include columns such as:

'Women's Work', recounting the many difficulties women faced in industrial surroundings; 'Women Local Councillors', debating current issues and urging women to see themselves as civically responsible and to claim the same representational rights as women in England; 'Feminist Chronicle', providing an update on debates and achievements of women in France and other countries. In addition to this, and the high level of mainstream content in the paper with daily accounts of parliamentary debates, proceedings in the lawcourts and full financial reports, cultural events were also covered, as were visits of international significance. Page four, alongside the advertisements, tended to include more domestic items such as the 'Le Home' column, with, slightly incongruously, at the very bottom, the closing stockmarket figures. At times of intense political activity whole pages of the paper could be devoted for many days to particular political events, such as general elections and, most notably, the Dreyfus Affair.

If *La Fronde* set out to be a serious, generalist newspaper like any other broadsheet, its difference lay in its being controlled and staffed solely by women (with the exception of the night watchman) and its championing, among more general causes, of issues concerning women. However, its feminist slant on affairs was compromised inasmuch as Durand, for all her entrepreneurial skills and intellectual acumen, went to great lengths to exercise her feminine charms, over which much ink has been spilled, to avoid the stigma suffered by earlier, more militant feminists such as Hubertine Auclert (1848–1914). Durand preferred to adopt a 'genteel feminism' (Cross 2000: 109) and, indeed, her newspaper was nick-named '*The Times* in petticoats' ('*Le Temps* en jupons'). The renowned beauty of the woman became conflated with the journalistic enterprise and the feminist cause, such that she herself said: 'Feminism owes much of its success to my blonde hair [...] I know it thinks the contrary, but it is wrong'.[5] This did not, however, prevent her from welcoming a whole range of outspoken women writers and journalists, including Auclert, into her columns.

Durand's Theatre of Ambition and Ambiguity

Although *La Fronde* was born of Durand's rather sudden conversion to the feminist cause, there are plentiful reminders of her preparedness to use her femin*ine* attributes to obtain her femin*ist* objectives. These involved a grand lifestyle, a social circle which included her flattery of key political figures of the day, and a taste for the theatrical, derived from her earlier experiences as an actress. Moreover, at the headquarters of the paper, elegant premises in the Rue Saint-Georges, things were done in style and sophisticated soirées took place alongside the nitty gritty of the printing press. One example of *La Fronde's* highlife was the banquet held at the Château Madrid in the Bois de Boulogne in honour of Durand on her saint's day, 20 July 1898, for which the sumptuous menu involved nine courses.[6] The extravagance of 'the blonde lady' sits uneasily perhaps with the newspaper's championing of the plight of poorer women, and led to questions as to her own independence, with implications that her many male admirers financed her newspaper venture. She was a woman in favour of liberty, but was she also a libertine? She was not averse to marriage, but led a free personal life; she was in favour of women's independence, but pro motherhood; in favour of divorce (she herself divorced her first husband, Laguerre), but advised it be used with caution. She was a member of the elite but on the side of the underprivileged and the poor. In spite of these ambiguities she sustained an active and arguably influential paper on a daily basis for six years, with infrequent and sporadic appearances subsequently, giving it her own stamp, although not writing for it regularly herself. In short, *La Fronde* and Durand were a class act.

Indeed, the paper could be seen as a tribune or platform for Durand, for, as Mary Louise Roberts points out, prior to being a journalist and newspaper proprietor, Durand had been an actress, entering the Conservatoire at the age of seventeen, and becoming a member of the Comédie Française some three years later in 1881, where she remained until her marriage to Laguerre in 1888 (Roberts 2000: 171–217). She braved the ambivalent attitude to actresses of the time when they were seen as little more than seductresses, and her background enabled her to add theatrical seduction to professional enterprise and to combine the seduction of power to her feminist politics, from the staging of her extravagant premises in Rue-Saint Georges to her privileged position as the only woman in the press box at the Chambre des Députés, and her notorious photographed appearance with a pet lioness, named Tiger, as publicity for her candidacy in the elections of 1910. If one agrees with Roberts that Durand was 'an "actor" in a double sense – a key agent in the transformation of gender identity –

as well as a performer on stage', and that her example 'reveals the volatile cultural stage of the fin de siècle' (ibid.: 199), one must read into this the will on the part of Durand to use the theatrical attributes and overtly feminine aspects of her persona to subvert the traditionally more disempowering construction of femininity, recuperating it for feminist ends.

Front Page 'Causes Célèbres' and Mixed Messages

Given Durand's taste for theatrics, little wonder that the arrival of *La Fronde* was as much a *coup de théâtre* as a media production, and that the cover page was both a showcase for the literary talent of top women writers of the day and a billboard for the polemics of the period. As to its political stance and its position in media history, more cynical observers might suspect the timing of the newspaper's launch, 9 December 1897, coinciding conveniently with the Dreyfus affair which became a *cause célèbre* for the paper and received ample coverage, including a full account of the later trial in Rennes, 7 August–9 September 1899. The verbatim report, running from 13 August to 10 September, displaced most other news and features for several issues. As a result of this, and despite its secular principles, *La Fronde* was accused of adopting a pro-Jewish stance, but justified its position by drawing parallels between the injustice done to an individual, a man, Dreyfus, and the many injustices suffered by women. Hence Durand showed that she was not afraid of 'acting up', as Roberts would put it, by coming out on key issues and contextualising them in feminist terms.

One could also foreground the explicit anti-clerical stance of *La Fronde*. Jean Rabaut describes French feminism of this period as 'republican, anticlerical, socialist and subversive' (Rabaut 1996: 33), and Máire Cross has pointed out that, in spite of an all-embracing approach to the diversity of women's opinions at the beginning of the newspaper, by 1900 'preference was given to activists with anticlerical sentiments' along with the turn of the century concern to 'end the oppression of centuries, if not a particular century' (Cross 2000: 108). Indeed the rubric 'Tribune' proper ran a series of some ten episodes (way beyond the usual three) of a 'Letter to the French Clergy', by Maria Deraismes at the end of January and the beginning of February 1900. Taking the Catholic Church to task in presuming to be indispensible to the prosperity of France and the nation, Deraismes refutes most of its practices and tenets and asserts the justification for a secular state.

A further cause of *La Fronde* was its pro-peace stand. On 3 January 1900, in one of the very few articles to refer explicitly to the new twentieth century, Clémence Royer inveighs against the ills of the previous century, in particular excessive military zeal, and urges a change of philosphy, concluding, 'Only then will 1900 be a good and useful year, encouraging progress, developing humanity and paving the way for a twentieth century which will repair the errors committed in the nineteenth'.[7]

In contrast to this strong feminist approach to the political and social issues of the period, a major issue for women, the right to vote, was not one which Durand championed particularly vigorously, thus raising another striking ambiguity. Although she herself was living the life of an independent woman, she felt that women of 1900 were not yet sufficiently educated to handle the vote. Earlier Maria Pognon, too, on the front page of the 26 January 1898 edition, had run an article on the question, arguing that women should have the right to vote, but not that they should be candidates, maintaining that women were still needed to provide the stability of the male-female domestic relationship. That did not, however, mean that others were not welcome to write in favour of women's suffrage, to wit a front page article on 13 December 1897 (issue No 5) by Hubertine Auclert. Auclert reiterated demands she had made more than a decade previously in her own paper, *La Citoyenne*, namely that, in accordance with The Declaration of the Rights of Man and the Citizen, those who pay taxes, and that included women, should have the right to vote and decide their level and how they would be redistributed. She concludes: 'If women are thwarted in society it is because they do not have the right to vote. It is important that women participate in the management of human affairs in order to cease being stooges in human relations'.[8] In fact, both Auclert and Durand stood for election in 1910, but Durand's was a rather late conversion.

The 'Tribune': Making Way for Women's Voices

In 1789 Olympe de Gouges complained that women had the right to climb the scaffold, but not to attain the public platform, or 'tribune', in order to voice their views. Nearly a century on, *La*

Fronde's regular rubric entitled 'Tribune' provided a platform
where a wide range of women writers could, usually for three
successive days, develop a particular theme. These were many
and varied, reflecting the aims of the paper to be feminist, political and literary. Those for the first three weeks of publication not
only cover social issues, such as the role of women in education,
the problems of child rearing, including the unhealthy aspects of
the 'the long-tubed babies' bottle', and the poor conditions of the
women in Saint-Lazare prison, but also provide exposés on German feminism or nineteenth-century women writers. Later con-
tributions pick up on issues already aired in the main columns,
such as women prisoners, with 'The story of the organisation of
women freed from Saint-Lazare Prison', a rehabilitation organisation for women ex-offenders (24, 25, 26 February 1898). Here,
too, the international awareness of the newspaper is reflected,
particularly in terms of comparative feminisms. The editions of
27 and 28 February 1898 see two 'Tribunes' devoted to 'Women's
clubs in London', and later in that year three concerning 'Servants in England' (14, 15, 16 March 1898). Interestingly, news
production being what it is, these articles conveniently coincided
with the visit of Queen Victoria to France. But other topics of
immediate significance also figure such as 'Employment on the
railways' (1, 2, 3 April 1898), 'The right to know the identity of
one's father' (4, 5, 6 April 1898), in response to a piece of legislation which had provoked considerable polemic in the pages of
the newspaper, 'Planned motherhood' (27, 28, 29 April 1898)
and 'Women voters' (7 and 8 May 1898) at the time of the general elections, followed by 'Universal suffrage: the right to full citizenship' (15, 16, 17 June 1898).

Women at the Workface

In contrast with the daily 'Tribune' section, reflecting in a relatively leisured and theoretical manner on pertinent topics, the
tribulations of women as they appear in other columns in *La
Fronde* are more immediate, focusing on areas concerning
women's work and the conditions associated with different
trades. The less frequent rubric, Aline Valette's 'Women's work',
brings to light a range of issues, from working hours to male
aggression and inequalities in the workplace, to the opening
up of more seemly careers for women. All emphasise women's
solidarity and determination: the women sugar workers, on
strike on 20 February 1898, 'take up the fight every time the

oppression of the employers produces fresh, unacceptable demands'[9] and complain by striking when 'the bosses want to hire women factory workers for a lower wage than that of the men they are replacing'.[10] This was the climate as they tried to reorganise their working time following the law reducing the working day for women over the age of eighteen from twelve to ten hours. There was solidarity again in the case of the gold beaters, striking in support of two women dismissed since the boss took exception to their comments against employers and capitalists: 'In a recent union meeting they had been even more violent than usual, he sees them as two ringleaders and to avoid a strike he dismissed them'.[11] This backfired, since not only the women but also their male colleagues all took strike action. Male aggression, however, is highlighted in the 20 March 1898 report on the abusive language of the employer in a sewing factory who addressed the women workers thus: 'Be off with you, you load of oysters. Go and get yourselves opened'.[12] The journalist adds that 'many of the large Paris factories are run by gentlemen of this ilk'.[13]

Reflecting the supposedly middle-class readership, Valette does not, however, restrict her attention to the grim problems of lower-class factory workers: at a more genteel level (6 February 1898) her rubric hedges its bets as to the nature of work suitable for men and for women of certain means but who wish to move with the times and acquire greater mobility and independence outside the home:

> It is due to our serious concern over this that we decided to indi-
> cate, alongside back-breaking occupations, others which offer
> women sufficient means to support themselves and at the same
> time provide relatively comfortable working conditions [...] A
> woman stenographer in Parliament? This would not be without
> precedent. Many women, including the talented writer, Miss E.
> Crundtwig, work as stenographers in the Danish Parliament
> and nobody to our knowledge has thought to complain.[14]

In fact this profession, linked to journalism, is one close to Durand's heart and she was proactive in setting up, starting with her own workforce, a women's typesetters' trade union, given that women were excluded from the existing (male) one. In addition she was actively supportive in the setting up of other women's trade unions for florists, accounts clerks and midwives.

One of *La Fronde*'s greatest successes was its ability to pro-vide for a wide spectrum of interests and struggles, being informative and supportive, as well as acting as a platform for feminist views. A note from *La Fronde*'s offices, dated 1902, confirms the paper's commitment to enabling needy women to work, and on terms equal to those of men in a new industrialised workforce, saying: 'Given that lower-class women can no longer make a living from feminine trades [...] it is imperative to allow women access to men's workshops [...] This is what *La Fronde*'s feminism is about [...] in their daily struggle, women, poorly equiped with an outdated education and barely literate, need support and someone to defend their interests. Such is the aim of *La Fronde*'.[15] Putting this into practice on its own territory, the newspaper also achieved its key aim of operating professionally with a totally female workforce, ranking alongside other recognised newspapers of the day (Figure 3.2). However, the success was not financial, for Durand admitted that there were never sufficient subscriptions to cover running costs for more than fifteen days and her own tribulations became those of the paper in 1903 when, due to cash flow problems, it was decided to cease daily publication on 1 October of that year.[16]

Launching Women's Voices: an Accomplished Mission?

Through *La Fronde*'s pages and its reputation, the 'voice' of Durand made space for other women's voices and, above all,

Figure 3.2 Women workers at *La Fronde*. *L'Illustration*, 15 January 1898. Courtesy of the Bibliothèque Marguerite Durand.

led to action, in various forms, from supporting the creation of women's trades unions, to cultural and intellectual development via the columns of the paper. However, these 'good works' were always framed by her own imposing persona, for Marguerite Durand had a prominent position in Parisian society of the time and, thanks to her enterprise, so did women's issues, great and small. For if, as Rabaut says, it was the 1896 Women's International Congress which prompted the creation of *La Fronde*, the paper and Durand underpinned the Congress of 1900. She was always ready for new ventures and on the setting up of a Labour Office, with the possibility of funding for a Women's Labour Office, she herself organised a special congress, which in part backfired. For the clash of styles between her own flamboyance and the down to earth attitude of male trade unionists caused her and her associates to be heckled and criticised. Said one: 'You could smell the opopanax these people were wearing at fifty yards'.[17]

It would thus be tempting to conclude that the courageous, feminist political venture which *La Fronde* represented was in some way compromised by the mixed messages emanating from its founder: on the one hand her fearless commitment to coverage of the most contentious issues of the day, be they feminist, religious or political, and on the other her reliance on her femininity to maintain her place among those of influence, predominantly male. However, it would be more realistic to say that Durand's attitudes and actions illustrated many of the constraints, contradictions and opportunities affecting women of the Belle Epoque period. Although her more forthright contemporary, Auclert, gained respect from male politicians and commentators of the time, she was also regarded as straight-laced and too 'aggressively' feminist by others, a pitfall Durand was keen to avoid. At the time of *La Fronde*'s closure in 1903, when she was about to launch an anticlerical newspaper, *L'Action*, Durand optimistically stated that: 'Feminism has achieved, or is on the point of achieving, all it could hope for in the current circumstances'.[18] Arguably, the means she employed justified the end: there was a general and ultimately positive interweaving of the paper's personal promotion of Durand and its providing of a voice to many other women through a form of journalism which, while 'mainstreaming' its coverage, always allowed a range of female voices to prevail, in a strong and often acerbic discourse.

Durand's legacy is great, not least through her feminist library, housed initially in *La Fronde*'s premises, Rue Saint-

Georges, later in the Town Hall in the fifth Paris arrondissement, and now in the Bibliothèque Marguerite Durand in the
thirteenth arrondissement. Beneath the portrait of this complex woman many feminist scholars still sit and work. Just as
important is the example she gave to successive generations of
women who, over the past century, have continued, with some
success, to address the contradictions which beset Belle Epoque
feminists.

Notes

1. LA FRONDE: Grand Journal Quotidien. Politique et littéraire. Dirigé,
   administré, Composé exclusivement PAR DES FEMMES.
       Les femmes forment, en France, la majorité de la population. Des mil-
   lions de femmes, célibataires ou veuves, y vivent sans le soutien légal de
   l'homme.
       Les femmes paient les impôts qu'elles ne votent pas, contribuent leur
   travail manuel ou intellectuel à la richesse nationale et prétendent avoir
   le droit de donner officiellement leur avis sur toutes les questions intéres-
   sant la société et l'humanité dont elles sont membres comme les hommes.
       LA FRONDE est l'écho fidèle de leurs approbations, de leurs critiques,
   de leurs justes revendications (Durand 1897).

   This notice appeared framed and in advertisement layout, positioned
   among those for sewing machines, etc., on the back page of the newspaper.

2. It is not for nothing that the annual prize awarded by the *Association des
   femmes journalistes* for the most positive French non-sexist advertisement
   is named after Séverine.
3. 'Ma constante préoccupation a été et sera d'intéresser à la cause féministe
   celles qui savent, qui raisonnent [...] qui sont capables de semer la bonne
   parole dans les milieux où elle doit germer ...' (Rabaut 1996: 50).
4. See Chapter 14 for a discussion of Lesueur's fiction.
5. 'Le féminisme doit à mes cheveux blonds quelques succès [...] Je sais qu'il
   pense le contraire: il a tort' (Dizier-Metz 1992: 20).
6. The menu was as follows: Melon; Salmon trout with Nantua sauce; Fillet
   of beef, renaissance style; Cyprus wine sorbet; Hot and cold duckling
   Madrid style; Romaine salad; Medley of beans; Peaches royale; Dessert.
   Wines by the carafe: Saint Julien; Tigane. (Dossier: Daniel Lesueur, Bibliothèque Marguerite Durand).
7. 'Alors seulement l'année 1900 sera une bonne année; alors seulement elle
   fera oeuvre utile, servira le progrès, fera avancer l'humanité et nous pré-
   parera un vingtième siècle qui réparera toutes les fautes commises durant
   le dix-neuvième' (Royer 1900).
8. 'Si les femmes sont si lésées dans la société, c'est parce qu'elles ne votent pas.
   Il faut que les femmes participent à l'arrangement des choses humaines,
   pour cesser d'être dupes dans l'association humaine' (Auclert 1897).
9. 'engagent la lutte chaque fois que l'oppression patronale témoigne de
   nouvelles et inacceptables exigences' (Valette 1898a).

10. 'les patrons appellent la femme dans l'usine pour un salaire inférieur à celui de l'homme qu'elle remplace' (ibid.).
11. 'Dans une récente réunion de leur syndicat elles avaient été encore plus violentes que de coutume, il les considère comme deux meneuses et pour éviter une grève il les a renvoyées' (Dissart 1898).
12. 'Allez donc, tas d'huitres. Allez vous faire ouv...' (Valette 1898b).
13. 'nombre de nos grands ateliers parisiens sont dirigés par des gentilshommes de cet acabit' (ibid.).
14. 'C'est hanté par cette préoccupation que nous avons pensé signaler, à côté des métiers 'destructeurs de moelles', certaines professions pouvant offrir à la femme des moyens d'existence suffisants en même temps que des conditions de vie relativement douces [...] La femme sténographe parlementaire! Le fait ne serait pas sans précédent. Plusieurs femmes, parmi lesquelles Mlle E. Crundtwig, écrivain de talent, remplissent des fonctions de sténographe' (Valette 1898c).
15. 'Les femmes du peuple ne pouvant plus vivre de métiers féminins [...] il a fallu ouvrir les ateliers d'hommes aux femmes du peuple [...] Mais pour la lutte de chaque jour, les femmes, mal armées par une éducation d'un autre âge, à peine instruites, ont besoin d'être soutenues et leurs intérêts défendus. Tel est le but poursuivi par "La Fronde"' (Dossier: *La Fronde*, Bibliothèque Marguerite Durand).
16. The paper underwent stages of less frequent appearance until 1905, with a few reappearances in July and September 1914, and from May to July 1928.
17. 'Ce monde fleurait l'opopanax à trente pas' (Rabaut 1996: 100). Opopanax was a resinous gum drawn from certain plants growing in the Mediterranean area and from which a perfume was made. Today, in addition to being the title of the prize-winning novel by Monique Wittig, it is also marketed by Dyptique as a sophisticated air freshener.
18. 'Le féminisme a obtenu, ou est sur le point d'obtenir tout ce qu'il pouvait prétendre en l'état actuel des choses' (ibid.: 80).

Figure 4.1 Doctor Madeleine Pelletier (1874–1939), candidate at the 1910 legislative elections. Courtesy of the Bibliothèque Marguerite Durand.

CHAPTER 4

THE UNCOMPROMISING DOCTOR MADELEINE PELLETIER: FEMINIST AND POLITICAL ACTIVIST

Anna Norris

> I think that I've always been a feminist;
> at least since I've been old enough to understand.[1]

Nothing seemed to predispose Anne Pelletier (1874–1939), born in the dingy back room of her parents' fruit and vegetable shop in the rue des Petits-Carreaux in Paris, to become Dr Madeleine Pelletier, anthropologist, physician, psychiatrist and feminist theoretician (Figure 4.1). Pelletier's later writings on sexuality, the right to abortion, the education of girls, and the questioning of the traditional nuclear family were to carry the most weight in the analysis of women's condition, but her achievements during the Belle Epoque were crucial in French women's itinerary toward equality. Focusing on the period from 1898 to 1910, this chapter examines her rise and success in spheres where no French woman had previously succeeded, from her attempt to enter a deeply misogynist milieu, the scientific arena, to her involvement in several feminist and political groups, most importantly *La Solidarité des Femmes*, the freemasons, and the *Section Française de l'Internationale Ouvrière* (SFIO). Through her life and actions, which are inseparable from her feminist and political activism, she became the first Frenchwoman to serve as a physician in the public health system, the first woman authorised to take the examination for physicians of mental institutions, the first woman to refuse to wear feminine clothing and to theorise the reasons for doing so,[2] and the first to gain an important position in the freemasons and in the Socialist Party.

Pelletier and the Scientific Arena

Madeleine Pelletier left school at thirteen, frequented anarchist circles, prepared for her baccalaureate exam on her own, and then enrolled at the College of Science in 1898 when she was already nearly twenty-five.[3] To understand how unusual the course of her education was, we must remember that she was born a poor woman in a period when, in spite of the Jules Ferry laws, it was extremely difficult for children from modest backgrounds to pursue advanced studies, a difficulty that increased tenfold when a young girl was concerned since higher education for women was not encouraged. Though the law did not forbid women from sitting the baccalaureate, it was not until 1861 that Julie Daubié became the first woman to attempt – and gain – this important qualification. As for women's rise in the medical profession, Madeleine Pelletier's course was arduous, and sparked several polemics since it was only in 1868 that the American Mary Putnam had become the first woman permitted to enrol in the Paris School of Medicine, in 1882 that women were granted the right to take the competitive externship exam, and in 1885 the internship exam, and that only after a series of petitions, counter-petitions, and legal quarrelling. As Felicia Gordon emphasises in *The Integral Feminist*, 'In a country where the Napoleonic Code defined what could or could not be done in almost every sphere of life, no one had had the foresight to forbid medical education to women' (Gordon 1990: 27).

Madeleine Pelletier attracted public attention in 1902 when she demanded the right, until then forbidden to women, to compete in the internship exam to qualify to work in mental institutions. Marguerite Durand's newspaper, *La Fronde*, took an interest in her cause, publishing several articles in her favour, notably, 'Toujours l'hominisme', relating the audacity of the young woman who stood up to the bureaucrat who refused to let her take the exam because, as a woman, she did not enjoy the same political rights. 'She retorted, "I have made a firm decision to ensure the triumph of my rights. I am openly protesting the injustice being done to me"'.[4] Having finally won her case, she passed the exam and thus became the first woman authorised to work as a physician in mental institutions. While she completed a series of internships in psychiatry at Sainte-Anne, Ville-Evrard and Villejuif, Pelletier wrote a thesis in psychiatry that was well received by her professors and later republished. She thus appeared well integrated into the academic and scientific milieu. Pelletier has written little about her personal experience as a psychiatrist, but in *Doctoresse Pelletier: Mémoires d'une féministe*, an unpublished manuscript presumably written in the early 1930s, she reveals the unquestionable distrust toward her in these circles, whether on the part of the nursing staff or her fellow students: 'The male interns fought me constantly'.[5] Having established links with the school of anthropology, notably through the intervention of Charles Letourneau, she pursued a career as both a psychiatrist and an anthropologist.

It may seem surprising that Pelletier turned to anthropology, a discipline that was far from open to women and was, for the duration of the nineteenth century, marked by misogyny. She sought prominence not only in a profession nearly closed to women (although nothing stopped her) but one that 'justified' anti-feminine theses by developing theories that aimed to prove the innate inferiority of women from all points of view: physical, intellectual and moral. Multiple examples could be given, but take for instance Auguste Comte's statement in his 1877 *Cours de philosophie positive*: '[O]ne cannot seriously question today the obvious relative inferiority of woman, who is less suitable by far than man for the necessary continuity as well as the high intensity of mental work, be it because of her lesser intrinsic intelligence or because of her greater moral and physical susceptibility'.[6]

As Gordon notes, this school of anthropology, originally founded by Paul Broca, maintained very close ties to the medical world (Gordon 1990: 32–33). It was also, at its root, anticlerical and republican, elements which doubtless attracted Pelletier in spite of the flagrant misogyny of the environment and of the discipline. Nevertheless, she must have found work at the School of Anthropology extremely difficult. She relates the sexism of her professors, who permitted themselves to offer her outrageous advice. 'One of my professors advised me to commit suicide, since without family support or money, it was certain that I would never succeed at anything [...] another time I was advised to flirt since that was the only way a woman might succeed. "Be the mistress of a politician. When he's finished with you, he'll find you a job"'.[7]

From her earliest work, Pelletier adopted a tactic she would use several times within the freemasons and political parties and that she would theorise a few years later in 'La Tactique féministe': enter the man's world, fit the mould, excel in one's work and inspire men's respect (Pelletier: 1908a). Thus she seemed to conform totally to the masculine world of science by following the course laid out by her professors. However, she rapidly began to use her research to call into question the inferiority of women, conducting anthropological research just as 'scientifically' as her predecessors had done – questionable as this method may have been – but with this as her central aim. Thus, by appropriating its method of analysis, Pelletier uses this 'science' that was both misogynist and racist to prove fervently that women were not inferior to men. In her first studies on Japanese skeletons we can already see traces of feminism, since her research includes comparative studies between men and women (Pelletier: 1900). One senses throughout these texts the burning desire to prove the equality of men and women, or at least the desire to prove that women were not physiologically inferior.

'La Prétendue infériorité psycho-physiologique des femmes', which first appeared in *La Revue socialiste*, could be considered Pelletier's first purely feminist work (Pelletier 1904). It is interesting at several levels, first because the author questions the pseudo-inferiority of women in scientific terms, but even more because she lays the groundwork for her later writings on the feminist education of young girls by showing that all the reasons put forward to prove the intellectual and moral inferiority of women were due only to an education that was itself inferior. She especially refutes the genetic critique that attributed an inferiority to women due to their biology. As for moral questions, even though she insists on the fact that all men are not endowed with a moral sense, she explains that it is once again the difference in education between men and women that inculcates the first with courage and a sense of honour while women are made into passive beings who 'have an extreme need to be loved, cherished, protected, and even directed and who very willingly trade their independence to acquire this protection which is, moreover, very often illusory'.[8] Schooling as well as the influence of the family and of society rendered a woman's education inferior, dooming her to weakness and submission.

Pelletier abandoned her career as an anthropologist and psychiatrist after failing her examination. No one knows if her failure was totally justified. She herself admits to having had little time to study, being occupied by her feminist activities. However, she also received a fairly poor grade for her scientific writing even though she should have received a higher one, since her work had been well regarded by her instructors. This alone should have sufficed to pass. But Pelletier was not a meek woman. She was already actively participating in feminist leagues and her wearing of masculine clothing was probably not welcomed by her professors and examiners. One could thus hypothesise that the academic milieu did not look favourably upon her rise in the academic world, and that these elements contributed to her failure. Charles Sowerwine holds this opinion, as is evident when he points out another woman, Mademoiselle Pascal, who passed the exam that Pelletier had failed and became the director of the Maison Blanche psychiatric hospital, but who 'took care to remain a woman' (Maignien and Sowerwine 1992: 50).

If Pelletier thus abandoned a career she had set her heart on, her first scientific works served as a theoretical springboard: they already contained the essence of her most important feminist writings, notably *L'Education féministe des filles* (1978 [1914]) and *L'Emancipation sexuelle de la femme* (1911b).

Pelletier and French Feminist Groups

Through the autobiographically inspired works she has left us, notably *La Femme vierge* (1996) and *Doctoresse Pelletier: Mémoires d'une féministe*, Pelletier revolts against the feminine condition and the limitations her society and era imposed on women. Though she seriously doubted the efficacy of French feminist groups, she became, at Caroline Kauffmann's request, the secretary of *La Solidarité des femmes* in 1906, and then founder and editor of her own feminist journal, *La Suffragiste*, during the winter of 1907–1908, all the while becoming more and more influential within mixed freemasonic lodges and then within the SFIO.

The French feminist movements of the Belle Epoque were still very much influenced by the *Société pour le droit des femmes* founded in 1869 by Léon Richer and Maria Deraismes. Pelletier felt little sympathy for the feminists, aside from Hubertine Auclert, founder of the group *Le Suffrage des femmes* and the

review *La Citoyenne*. She saw more weaknesses than strengths
in their organisations, and reproached them for their lack of
extremism and their middle-class nature. She felt a great deal
of antipathy toward Marguerite Durand, whom she considered
a socialite and not an authentic feminist, even though *La
Fronde* had defended Pelletier in her fight to take the interns'
exam a few years earlier. As for Caroline Kauffmann's group,
La Solidarité des femmes, it included too few women and was too
much on the margins of the larger leagues. Nevertheless Pelletier, who became the secretary of the organisation somewhat
in spite of herself, led several historic actions in its name and
solicited its support on several occasions. In *La Femme vierge* she
humorously relates the encounter between her heroine, Marie
Pierrot, and Kauffmann, whom she describes with sometimes
cruel irony as a slightly crazy old woman, enamoured with
spiritualism. She recounts with the same acerbic pen meetings
during which 'everyone talked at once and one only heard a
brouhaha in which it was impossible to make out anything',
and looked severely on this 'lamentable group of old women'.[9]
She never felt at ease with the French feminist movement, often
praising the actions of British suffragettes while deploring the
lifelessness of the French, the fragmentation of their groups
and their lack of ambition.

   Aside from her work as the secretary of *La Solidarité des
femmes*, Pelletier organized several memorable actions in the
history of French feminism. During the legislative elections of
1906, she, along with members of *La Solidarité*, joined Auclert to
form a procession of ten hackney cabs carrying banners that
read: 'Women must vote'. In June of the same year, aided again
by members of *La Solidarité*, she threw tracts claiming the right
of women to vote into the gallery of the Chamber of Deputies:
'Women must vote: they are subject to the law and pay taxes.'[10]
During the candidacy of Jeanne Laloë in the municipal elections of May 1908, Auclert and Pelletier took action again, this
time of a slightly more violent kind. During the first round of
balloting, Auclert overturned a ballot box, while during the second round, Pelletier broke the window of a voting office, was
arrested and then charged with trespassing. In June 1908,
shortly after her arrest, she and Kauffmann attended the large
demonstration of British suffragettes that included 500,000
women, whose discipline and organisation Pelletier both
admired and envied. However, if her actions were important on
a symbolic level, reflecting further the frustration and anger of
Pelletier and other feminists, they brought no tangible results.

Pelletier and the Political Arena

Pelletier's affiliation with *La Solidarité* and the feminist groups was not enough to achieve women's emancipation. She also turned to political activism within the mainstream political parties themselves. In her view, 'If there is a place for the women's cause, there is not a place for women's groups' (Maignien and Sowerwine 1992: 78).

The first male group Pelletier targeted in her attempt to advance the cause of women was the freemasons. She entered a mixed lodge while still a public healthcare physician, encouraged by her professor, Dr Paul-Maurice Legrain. She was drawn to the freemasons' progressive, social and anticlerical values, which appeared to her the ideal springboard for the cause of women. Though women were excluded in principle from the large Masonic lodges like the *Grand Orient de France* and the *Grande Loge de France*, mixed lodges were tolerated, notably the *Grande Loge Symbolique Ecossaise* (GLSE), founded in 1893 by Deraismes. Pelletier chose this lodge in joining *La Philosophie Sociale* (LPS) in 1904 and also introduced the famous anarchist and heroine of the Paris Commune, Louise Michel, there in the same year, shrewdly intending to make use of her notoriety. Her first goal was to secure the admission of women to the regular orders.

Pelletier envisaged the opening of the freemasonry to women as a first, symbolically important victory for the women's cause. In addition, their admission to the freemasonry would give women the chance to enter the political sphere, providing access to a political education that was until this point forbidden. The issue of education was a governing idea for Pelletier, who felt it was essential to emancipation. She rapidly became an important and visible member of the GLSE, becoming secretary, and engaging in debate by leading lectures on social subjects such as the eight-hour day, but especially having as a target feminist preoccupations like women's suffrage, abortion rights, marriage and sexual freedom. She also collaborated on the Masonic review *L'Acacia*.

Her involvement and success in the Masonic setting gained Pelletier numerous enemies. Her activism in favour of women was undoubtedly troubling for most male masons, and she began to lose control of her freemason venture due to an unfortunate but symptomatic incident. A freemason brother wanted to admit a prostitute to LPS with the goal of discrediting the mixed lodges. Pelletier opposed this plot, but failed to gain support. Thus, she left LPS and affiliated instead with the *Diderot* and *La Nouvelle Jérusalem* lodges. At *Diderot*, she once again rose rapidly to an important position as the first woman to be elected assistant secretary-treasurer of the commission of the *Bulletin Hebdomadaire des Travaux de la Maçonnerie*, a report including all the orders, large and small, mixed and exclusively male. Becoming more and more influential and appreciated among the new members she brought into these lodges, notably feminist activists, anarchists and socialists, she seemed to have succeeded in creating an important place for herself within the freemason movement. It was exactly this that began to displease the large orders that remained closed to women. They reacted by demanding in March 1906 that mixed lodges be excluded from the writing of the *Bulletin*. Although the proposal failed, it illustrates the mistrust of the mixed lodges by the large lodges, as well as their refusal to open the freemasonry to women. This mistrust of Pelletier continued to solidify through an accusation that was taken up in a general assembly. She was reproached for, among other things, overly violent remarks, and was accused of threatening a brother with a revolver, a fact she did not deny. Suspended from *La Nouvelle Jérusalem* for a month, the incident resulted in the exclusion of women from this lodge, which rejoined the lodges of the regular order. In September 1907, Pelletier, like Kauffmann, was definitively excluded from the GLSE, but continued to believe in Masonic principles and called herself a freemason until her death.

Pelletier's activism within the freemasonry ended in failure, illustrating contemporary intolerance toward women and their pariah status. So she turned elsewhere for her political activism, still having the improvement of the social status of women and the gaining of their right to vote as her objectives. Although Pelletier felt many affinities with the anarchist milieu, she chose to join the Socialist Party to make the voice of women heard, while continuing her involvement with *La Solidarité*.

As indicated above, Pelletier had ambivalent feelings toward the feminist leagues: 'I joined the Socialist Party [...] feminism is too small and the atmosphere of gossip disgusts me'.[11] She was persuaded that, parallel to 'the creation of vast feminist organisations, the existing political parties had to be penetrated'.[12] She judged, too, that one had to make oneself noticed and respected in that environment, and be ready to keep quiet about one's feminist aspirations: 'As for feminism, one speaks of it little, and one especially doesn't speak of it at an inopportune time. A feminist should commit herself above all to being a good activist, a member whose opinion counts. She can only gain more authority to defend the claims of her sex as a result'.[13] Pelletier probably wanted to profit from her unfortunate experiences in the scientific milieu and with the freemasons, thus her strategy is totally defensible. However, here too, she endured bitter disappointments, in spite of an impressive political career with the SFIO.

Pelletier joined the SFIO in 1906, where she took an interest in the Guesdist faction of the party, which tended towards Marxism and was clearly more leftist than the Jaurès faction. A few months were enough for her to build a platform. She had a resolution on women's suffrage voted on, which she took to the national Guesdist congress of Limoges in November 1906. There she made a case for the women's vote, challenging the inferiority of women and refuting the influence of religion on them. The proposal was passed by the congress. Ready to do anything to ensure the success of the resolution, she went to the Chamber of Deputies, accompanied by Kauffmann and seventy members of *La Solidarité*. This intervention in the Chamber, during which Pelletier and Kauffmann spoke, seemed to bear fruit. Jean Jaurès promised them his support, and the deputies announced the creation of a sub-committee on women's voting rights. In a signed article in *L'Humanité*, she reported on the demonstration at the Chamber of Deputies and enthusiastically announced the support of Jaurès and the Socialist Party for women's suffrage. 'Jaurès assured the delegation that the necessary steps would be taken in the very near future. It is time to make the women's vote a reality and the Socialist Party will not fail at it ... *feminism is no longer isolated; it has the support of the Socialist Party*'.[14]

Unfortunately, the sub-committee was not soon formed and once it was, it never met or produced a single bill. This was Pelletier's first disillusionment with socialism. But she would not allow herself to be easily discouraged. She invited and welcomed a delegation of her British counterparts from the *Women's Social and Political Union* (WSPU) and demonstrated at their side at the Ministry of the Interior, the Chamber and the headquarters of *L'Humanité*. In addition, when the next two federal congresses met in July 1907 in Paris and Nancy, she presented the same resolution proposed at the Guesdist congress. Her proposal passed in both cases. But, frustrated by the moderation of the Guesdists, she moved to the left wing of the party with the Hervéists, the most radical faction of the socialist movement with little sympathy for the women's cause but which, for Pelletier, had the merit of being more revolutionary, more antimilitarist and more militant.

One may wonder again at her motives for allying herself with a group so hostile to women and feminist ideas. Was she once again applying her 'feminist tactic' of making herself known and respected by men, vainly hoping to thus win them to the feminist cause?

At the international level, Pelletier made her voice heard by participating that same summer of 1907 in the first international socialist women's conference in Stuttgart. At the time of the submission of a resolution on the women's vote that risked failure when voted on by both the male and female delegates, Pelletier was indignant about the amendments some wanted to make, and it was thus passed by the Congress. But she did not espouse the same views as the German socialists, notably Clara Zetkin and Rosa Luxembourg, on the creation of women's sections in each country. Clearly, Pelletier's view was that: 'the bourgeois woman is tangled up in prejudices that hinder her actions or render them useless',[15] that proletarian feminism was the future of the feminist movement and that it was absolutely necessary 'to create alongside bourgeois feminism a proletarian and socialist feminism'.[16] However, Pelletier was against the dominant influence of the Socialist Party that meant privileging the battle against the bourgeoisie over the battle for feminism: in a sense she was far more in favour of an international congress of women than of socialists. 'German women have rejected what they call bourgeois feminism with an ostentation that truly lacks dignity. Our women's movement is profoundly socialist... but it must remain slightly separate from the party'.[17] She considered herself above all a feminist, an allegiance to be conserved at all costs, even if all feminists joined political parties. 'Under no pretext must a feminist prefer the party she has joined over feminism itself since if she *serves* the first, she *belongs to* the second, and to nothing else'.[18]

Having become a frequent contributor to the Hervéist journal *La Guerre sociale,* she wrote articles in which she espoused the revolutionary sentiments of the group, going so far as to advocate violence and even assassination. But she did not hesitate to confront the collaborators of the journal who were hostile towards feminists, especially toward British suffragettes. In spite of the opposition of numerous Hervéists to feminist causes, through her debates and her articles in *La Guerre*

Sociale Pelletier became once again an important figure at the centre of the faction, and practically its leader. She did not hesitate to stand up to Jaurès and Vaillant during the course of numerous debates and succeeded Hervé at the *Commission Permanente Administrative* (CAP) in 1909. But her association with the Hervéists would not amount to anything as she left the group in 1910, justly accusing Hervé of swerving to the right; likewise, he had little appreciation of Pelletier's feminism, not to mention her short hair and men's clothing. Thus she lost the leadership of the CAP and returned to the Guesdists.

An important event took place the same year. In 1910 Pelletier, Kauffmann and Elisabeth Renaud ran first in the legislative elections, then in the municipal ones. But Pelletier, who hoped to run in the fifth arrondissement, found herself reprimanded by her party and given the reactionary district of the Madeleine. As Gordon notes, 'Socialists were not to be accused of refusing to endorse women candidates; instead women were given candidacies in hopeless constituencies' (Gordon 1990: 125). After a campaign during which she came to preach the ideas of the Jauressians she despised, Pelletier's efforts were crowned with a small success: she received only forty votes, but it was a better result than that obtained by the SFIO candidate four years earlier. As a candidate in the municipal election in another conservative district, the seventh arrondissement, she obtained a similar outcome. After this, Pelletier distanced herself more and more from the socialists to turn toward the anarchist movement, an evolution but also a logical return to her personal convictions. Though her political career ended during this period, in spite of a short return to the SFIO, Pelletier remained very active among the anarchists.

Conclusion

Although Pelletier was always ultimately disappointed by her association with the feminist leagues, the freemasons and the SFIO, her achievements were of considerable symbolic importance, as they had been in the scientific arena. Pelletier succeeded in making her voice and the voice of women heard in domains not just essentially masculine, but actually hostile to women. Through her setbacks, her disappointments, her successive refusals to be brought into line and her controversial remarks and writings, Doctor Madeleine Pelletier held to her views on the condition and the cause of women.

Unfortunately for her, they eventually led her to the Perray-Vaucluse asylum, where she was incarcerated in 1938, accused of having performed abortions. There she died alone. Clearly the abortion charge may well have hidden the real charges, since the psychiatric evaluation concluded that, 'she could still be a cause of trouble to public order and a danger to others'.[19] These are probably the same sentiments she inspired in those with whom she battled from her beginnings in the scientific and political arenas during the Belle Epoque.

Notes

1. 'Je pense que j'ai toujours été féministe; du moins depuis que j'ai l'âge de comprendre' (Pelletier undated: 1).
2. Pelletier discussed her choice of wearing masculine clothing in various articles in *La Suffragiste* (see, for example, the issues of July 1912 and July 1919), as well as in her unpublished autobiography.
3. Pelletier was one of only two surviving children of the twelve her mother gave birth to. Named Anne Pelletier, a name she shared with her mother, she took the name 'Madeleine'.
4. '[...] je suis fermement décidée à faire triompher mon droit. Je proteste hautement contre l'injustice qui m'est faite!' (Pelletier 1902).
5. 'A l'asile, les internes mâles me faisaient une guerre incessante' (Pelletier undated: 15).
6. 'On ne peut sérieusement contester aujourd'hui l'évidente infériorité relative de la femme, bien autrement impropre que l'homme à l'indispensable continuité aussi bien qu'à la haute intensité du travail mental, soit en vertu de la moindre force intrinsèque de son intelligence, soit en raison de sa plus vive susceptibilité morale et physique' (Comte 1877: 4, 406–7).
7. 'L'un de me professeurs me conseilla de me suicider, car sans appui familial et sans argent, il était certain que je ne réussirais jamais à rien [...] une autre fois on me conseilla de flirter car c'était le seul moyen qu'une femme réussisse : « Soyez la maîtresse d'un politicien. Quand il en aura fini avec vous, il vous trouvera un emploi »' (Pelletier undated: 11a).
8. 'a un besoin extrême d'être aimée, choyée, protégée et même dirigée, et très volontiers elle fait bon marché de son indépendance pour acquérir cette protection, qui est d'ailleurs bien souvent illusoire' (Pelletier 1904: 49).
9. 'tout le monde parlait à la fois et on ne percevait qu'un brouhaha dans lequel il était impossible de rien distinguer [...] ce groupe lamentable de vieilles femmes' (Pelletier 1996 [1933]: 60).
10. 'La femme doit voter; elle subit les lois et paie les impôts.'
11. 'Je suis entrée au Parti Socialiste, [...] le féminisme est trop petit et puis cette atmosphère de ragots me dégoûte' (Maignien and Sowerwine 1992: 70).
12. 'la création de vastes organisations féministes, il faut pénétrer les partis politiques existants'(Pelletier 1978 [1914]: 145).
13. 'Quant au féminisme on en parlera peu; et surtout on n'en parlera pas hors de propos. Que l'on s'attache avant tout à être un *bon militant* un membre dont l'opinion compte; elle n'en acquerra par la suite que plus d'autorité pour défendre les revendications de son sexe' (ibid.: 152).

14. 'Le citoyen Jaurès assure la délégation que le nécessaire sera fait et dans un avenir très rapproché. Il est temps en effet, de réaliser le vote des femmes et le Parti socialiste n'y faudra pas [...] *Le féminisme n'est plus isolé: il a un appui dans le Parti socialiste'* (Pelletier 1906: 1).

15. 'la femme bourgeoise est empêtrée dans des préjugés qui entravent son action, ou la rendent vaine' (Pelletier 1907a: 2).

16. 'créer à côté du féminisme bourgeois un féminisme prolétarien et socialiste' (Pelletier 1907b: 2).

17. 'Les Allemandes ont rejeté ce qu'elles appellent le féminisme bourgeois avec une ostentation qui manque vraiment de dignité. Notre mouvement de femmes est profondément socialiste [...] mais il doit se tenir un peu à l'écart du parti' (Pelletier 1908b: 329–30).

18. 'Sans aucun prétexte une féministe ne doit préférer le parti dans lequel elle est entrée au féminisme lui-même car si elle *sert* le premier elle *appartient* au second et rien qu'à lui' (Pelletier 1978 [1914]: 152).

19. '[...] qu'elle peut encore être une cause de troubles pour l'ordre public et de danger pour les personnes' (Maignien and Sowerwine 1992: 231).

CHAPTER 5

CLANS AND CHRONOLOGIES: THE SALON OF NATALIE BARNEY

Melanie Hawthorne

Gendered Internationalism

While modernism may have reached its apogee in the inter-war period, and while the First World War is generally viewed as one of its most important formative events, this chapter explores how women's experience of modernism was shaped – at least in part – by events that preceded that conflagration. Modernism was a famously international movement, but men and women have had a different relationship, historically, to what it means to be internationally or nationally situated. For women living in France, the Belle Epoque was a time when questions of national affiliation were brought to their attention in a number of ways, including debates about suffrage, and legal reforms about how women's (and seldom men's) nationality was affected by events such as marriage and expa-triation. Shortly after the end of the Belle Epoque, American and (some) British women had been ratified as citizens by being granted the vote. Not in France. In all three countries, women's provisional relationship to nationality was still an issue for many years to come. Certain forms of expression, particularly artistic expressions by women invoking national or international community, only became 'legible' in the interwar years but have their roots in the Belle Epoque. This chapter traces some of those genealogies.

It has long been acknowledged that there was something empowering for modernist women about the internationalism of that movement. Whether it is Virginia Woolf's famous statement of statelessness (in *Three Guineas*): 'As a woman, I have no country, as a woman I want no country, as a woman, my country is the whole world' (Woolf 1938: 125), or whether it is the correlation between expatriate status and literary achievement that seems to characterise the work of the so-called 'women of the left bank' (Benstock 1986), the crossing of national boundaries – literally or figuratively – seems to have been empowering for women in the early twentieth century, particularly for women whose sexual expression also exceeded traditional boundaries.

Consider, for example, the case of Natalie Clifford Barney (1876–1972), a rich American heiress who chose self-imposed exile in Paris where she established a salon famous for bringing together (among others) women who blurred both national and sexual boundaries. Barney herself referred to 'these little gatherings in this little international salon' ('ces petites réunions dans ce petit salon international', Barney 2002: 93; see also 134), while others refer to 'the famous lesbian salon established by her in 1909' (Elliott and Wallace 1994: 20). What seems remarkable about Barney's salon, then, is that it appears both international and marked by sexual transgression, a synthesis captured by Joan Schenkar, biographer of Dorothy Wilde, in her description: 'It was, quite simply, the most subversive literary salon that ever existed' (Schenkar 2000: 12).

Situating Barney's Salon

Barney's salon has taken on a kind of mythical status, with the result that there often appears to be a perception that this salon was a fixed and unchanging entity that lasted from the turn of the nineteenth century – when Barney's name was linked to that of the poet Renée Vivien – until well after the Second World War – when Barney had become a legendary figure. This static image is perpetuated by some of the materials that circulate about the salon, including materials sanctioned by Barney herself. A notable example is the cartoon that appeared as a foldout leaf at the front of Barney's *Aventures de l'esprit* in 1929 (Figure 5.1). It seems at first glance an

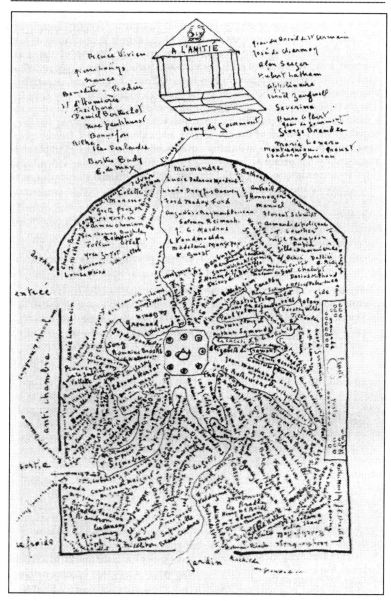

Figure 5.1 'Le Salon de l'Amazone'. Frontispiece to *Aventures de l'esprit* (Barney 1929).

innocuous résumé of Barney's salon, with the caption 'le salon
de l'Amazone' at the side. In the table of contents of *Aventures
de l'esprit*, it is clearly presented as 'Map of the Salon of the
Amazon between 1910 and 1930' ('Carte du Salon de l'Amazone entre 1910 et 1930', Barney 1929: 277), the more ampli-
fied title making it clear that it charts only a twenty-year span;
yet it is often taken as a more ambitious (if simply rendered)
document. In their discussion of it, for example, Bridget Elliott
and Jo-Ann Wallace suggest that 'it collapses attendance during the *six decades* of [Barney's] salon into one crude rendition'
(Elliott and Wallace 1994: 156, emphasis added).

The sketch is both superficially simple and hard to read (and
not only because some of the names themselves prove hard to
decipher). At the top of the picture is a sketch of the famous
'temple of friendship' ('temple à l'amitié'), while below we
have what seems to be a floor plan. In the centre of the room
is a square (presumably a table), with a teapot, and an aerial
view of what appear to be cups or plates set around it. To the
right is a buffet, with a large oval labelled 'fruits,' and little circles representing the glasses containing 'orangeade', 'porto',
and finally 'whiskey'. To the left are breaks in the outline
marked 'entrée' and 'sortie', and another at the bottom called
'jardin'. Within are the names of all the notable people associated with Barney and her salon, as though the artist had taken
a snapshot, but with a pencil rather than a camera, of one of
those legendary Fridays when Miss Barney received her famous
and infamous guests at the rue Jacob.[1]

Running down the front steps of the 'temple of friendship'
and winding through the crowd is a line labelled 'l'amazone'
(the Amazon), a punning reference to the nickname given to
Barney by Remy de Gourmont based on her horse riding (and
also a coded reminder of her sexual preferences). This twisting
line in the cartoon suggests the route taken by Barney as she
circulated among her guests by representing it as the course of
a river (the Amazon), descending from its hidden source high
(at least on the page) among the columns of friendship's temple, and winding through the plains of the salon before flowing
out into the garden. The cartoon is thus also a sort of 'carte du
tendre', an allegorical map that summarises a sentimental
narrative with Barney as the heroine whose travels provide the
link connecting the various visitors in attendance at the salon.

This allegorical quality should alert the viewer to the fact
that, far from being a snapshot, this cartoon is more of a mon-
tage, a composite image that should not be read too literally.

Like a 'carte du tendre,' the map is cavalierly oblivious of real time. In the real world, not everyone represented on the map was present at the same time, but the carte/chart manages nevertheless to effect some impossible encounters. Thus, just to the right of the teapot at the centre of the room is the name of Elisabeth de Gramont (a.k.a. 'Lily,' the duchesse de Clermont-Tonnerre). To the left of the teapot is the name of Romaine Brooks. And in the top left hand corner, just to the left of the inscription 'à l'amitié' on the temple, is the name of Renée Vivien. All three were major love interests in Barney's life at one time or another. This staging creates the false impression that Vivien came to the rue Jacob, when in fact Vivien died in 1909, just before Barney established herself there (and just before the parameters of the chart – 1910–1930 – begin). It suggests that Vivien met Elisabeth de Gramont, when in fact the latter states explicitly in her memoirs that she never met Renée Vivien (Gramont 1928: 213). Finally, it suggests that Natalie Barney was somehow responsible for bringing together the poet Vivien and the painter Brooks, when in fact, Brooks met Vivien but knew Barney only by reputation until after Vivien's death.

The chart seems wrong, then, at least in one sense. But while the chart distorts the literal truth, it nevertheless presents a different truth by showing that the thing that really brought the painter and the poet together (albeit posthumously in Vivien's case) was Natalie Barney and her salon. While Brooks and Vivien did not interact at Barney's literal salon, they interacted in a way in her virtual salon. As depicted in the sketch, the conduit of influence, the current linking one to the other, is the Amazon running between them, as it were, Natalie Barney.

Romaine Brooks met Renée Vivien before she ever met Natalie Barney, though in hindsight her acquaintance with the former seems barely to have left any impression, while her relationship with the latter marked her for life. Brooks describes visiting Vivien in her self-imposed 'exile', in the early years of the twentieth century, but Brooks found Vivien too affected to do more than simply 'drift along' with her for a while: 'Though I know that she is a very gifted poetess it is difficult to detect other than a seemingly affected and childish personality', reported Brooks, and 'her melancholy child-like self amid such a show of affectation never ceased to embarrass me and to keep me silent' (Brooks undated: 238).[2] While Brooks recognised Vivien's talent in retrospect, she was unable to appreciate it at the time. It was only after she met Natalie Barney a few

years later, that Romaine Brooks realised she might have had
something in common with Renée Vivien, a mental connection
that seems to have required Barney to act as current.[3]

As the example of Vivien and Brooks shows, Barney succeeded in bringing people into relationship with one another
even when the people themselves remained unaware of it.
Thus, the chronological inaccuracies are not the only problems that arise when the chart is read too literally. The sketch
of Barney's salon is also misleading on the literal level in its
indiscriminate mingling of Anglophones and Francophones, a
picture of international entente that seems to go against the
grain of testimony by those who witnessed some of the rival-
ries and clashes that fractured the social circles.

The image of an integrated international salon in the
sketch does not fit with some of the evidence that has been
gathered by scholars about Barney's salon. On a general level,
for example, Barney's housekeeper Berthe Cleyrergue has told
interviewers (including Gloria Orenstein and Michèle Causse)
that Barney's salon fell into two 'clans,' the French and the
Anglophone, and that despite Barney's attempts to bring them
together, they often did not interact all that much.

Other, more anecdotal evidence suggests that personal ani-
mosities sometimes fractured the image of a happy international band of sisters. Romaine Brooks was somewhat
reclusive and antisocial, and by no means a 'regular' at Barney's Fridays. Moreover, she developed a hatred for her some-
time rival in Barney's affections, Dolly (Dorothy) Wilde, whom
she referred to as a 'rat' hiding in Barney's skirts (quoted in
Schenkar 2000: 32), so that simply being on opposite sides of
the room, as the two are in the sketch of Barney's salon, was
not enough: Brooks would simply stay away or leave town
when Barney was expecting a visit from Wilde.[4] This was not
the only personal disagreement that kept members of the
salon apart, but it illustrates the fact that if some encounters
suggested by the sketch were downright impossible for chronological reasons, others were just as unlikely for personal ones.

The image of Barney's salon as represented by the sketch is
in some senses, then, all wrong, at least on some descriptive
level. Why, then, does the image of Barney's salon as a coherent entity persist?[5] What does it mean to call it a 'lesbian' salon
(as Elliott and Wallace [1994] do), when over half the names
on the sketch are neither women nor gay, and how is that
linked to the perception that it was 'international' despite the
gulf that continued to separate the national clans? What made

it so 'subversive'? Perhaps the answer to these questions lies in the fact that what seems inaccurate on some factual level is in fact somehow accurate on another, wholly imaginative, level.

It is true that, in some senses, Vivien never attended the 'same' salon as Romaine Brooks. By 'same' here I mean not only in the strict sense of being present at the same time and place, but I mean to suggest the larger sense, all the elements that go into making up an event: the people, their conversation, the interactions and atmosphere. Yet Vivien and Brooks share certain features: both were 'international' women who also crossed sexual boundaries.

International Women of Mystery

Renée Vivien (1877–1909), the daughter of an American mother and English father, chose to live in France and write in French, though she travelled widely and constantly throughout her abbreviated life.[6] In her sexual expression, she consistently preferred women, and Natalie Barney was arguably her one abiding passion, though not one without difficulties on both sides.

Romaine Brooks (1874–1970) was a similarly international figure: she was born Beatrice Romaine Goddard in Rome of American parents, but married an Englishman. This meant that in 1907, under the US Expatriation Act of that year, she would have been stripped of American nationality and considered a British national under US law. While continuing to travel widely, Brooks spent most of her time neither in the country of her birth (Italy), nor the country of her parents (the USA), nor the country of her citizenship (Britain), but a country to which she had no claim of affiliation: France. Although Brooks' relationship with Barney was not exclusive, the two were each other's primary partner in a relationship not legally recognised by any state, and remained so until late in life, when Barney's infidelity finally brought about a definitive rupture (see Secrest 1974: 377–80).

Renée Vivien and Romaine Brooks do not only embody internationalism in their own lives, however, but they create it in their work. Vivien's poetry shows a preoccupation with national types, whether it is her invocation of cold northern beauty or her appeals to Hellenic culture and Sappho the lesbian (a term she uses as much in a geographic as a sexual-taxonomic sense). Romaine Brooks explores transnational identities through her portraits, particularly those painted in the years after she became involved with Barney, which are striking for the way they effect a sense of collective identity among women whose only other commonality was their membership – loosely defined – in Barney's salon. An analysis of how Brooks achieved this sense of community will be the focus of the remainder of this chapter.

Barney would inspire some of Brooks' best mature work, either directly, by serving as the model for Brooks' portrait of her titled *The Amazon* from 1920, or indirectly, by offering her social network as a way for Brooks to meet others she might wish to paint, such as *Una, Lady Troubridge* (1924), *Peter, a Young English Girl* (a portrait of Gluck, 1923–24), *Self-Portrait* (1923), *Elisabeth de Gramont, Duchesse de Clermont-Tonnerre* (ca. 1924), and *Baroness Emile d'Erlanger* (1924). Brooks' famous, iconographic top-hatted self-portrait also dates from her mature years with Barney (1923).[7]

Yet Brooks' formative years during the Belle Epoque preceded her acquaintance with Barney and she was already an established portrait painter when she met Barney. There are a few exceptions – landscape paintings and numerous non-portrait sketches – but portraits were her speciality and her ability to capture what was perceived to be the essence of the sitter in her painting earned her the nickname of the 'burglar of souls' ('cambrioleur d'âmes').[8] The earliest work she chose to exhibit (such as *The Charwoman, The Black Bonnet* and *Maggie*) dates from 1904. A 'middle' period around 1910–1914 includes the striking self-portrait *At the Edge of the Sea* (1912) along with *Jean Cocteau at the Time of the Ferris Wheel* (1912) and *The Cross of France* (1914).

Another factor from the Belle Epoque that influenced Brooks' style was her relationship with the Russian dancer and actress Ida Rubinstein, who had come to Paris as part of the Ballets Russes (Depaulis 1995). The revolutionary new dance company had taken Paris by storm and introduced a whole new aesthetic associated with the launch of modernism. To begin with, Rubinstein suggested a new model of female beauty with her thin, androgynous body that contrasted strongly with the curved voluptuous ideal of female beauty that had prevailed until the turn of the century. Rubinstein served as the model for a number of paintings by Brooks during this transitional period (her last portrait of Rubinstein was in 1917). Brooks had also begun to explore representations of female sexuality, for example in the paintings *La Jaquette rouge* (*The Red Jacket*, 1910), *Azalées blanches* (*White Azaleas*, 1910), and *Le Trajet* (*The Crossing*, ca. 1911).

Brooks had also established her palette of mostly neutral colours before she ever met Barney. One self-portrait by Brooks from 1912 is almost entirely in black, while in an earlier one (ca.1905) Brooks' face is completely obscured by a black veil. While the overall tone seemed to lighten considerably in her post First World War work, Brooks continued to use the neutral colours, along with just a touch of dramatic red here and there, in her mature work.

There are many aspects of Brooks' work, then, that show a continuity between her work during the Belle Epoque and the mature work she produced after becoming involved with Barney, and critics such as Lucchesi (2001) have noted Brooks' indebtedness to Belle Epoque iconography in her later work. Yet it is nevertheless striking how Brooks' sense of situating her subject changes when she begins to paint predominantly women whose sexuality violates social norms. As late as 1910, Brooks was still painting in the style illustrated by the portrait of Princesse Lucien Murat (Figure 5.2).[9] In less than ten years, her style would be transformed.

Figure 5.2 *Princesse Lucien Murat*, ca. 1910, Romaine Brooks. Whereabouts unknown.

By the 1920s, Brooks had broken with the kind of realism that pervades the Murat portrait. By 'realism' I do not mean to suggest that her later portraits cease to be accurate. On the contrary, the lesser attention to rendering the background within the conventions of realism amplifies the psychological realism of the portrait. Thus, the background may still be grounded in a specific, recognisable place, so that a portrait from the earlier period may depict, say, the Longchamp racecourse, while a later portrait, say that of Natalie Barney, also shows the subject's own milieu (Barney's apartments and the temple to friendship, for example). But in the later portraits, no attempt is made to present the increasingly stylised background within the conventions of realism. In some portraits, the subject is also given attributes that function symbolically. Thus in the portrait of Barney, there is a little statue of a black horse in full gallop that works on several levels. It reminds the viewer that Barney is a rider of horses (an 'amazone,' in French), and evokes the nickname given her by Remy de Gourmont in his 'lettres à l'amazone' as well as the lesbian connotation of the name. At the same time, Barney resembles the galloping horse (rather than a rider) in that she enjoyed a certain 'freedom to run', both as an independent woman of means and as someone who refused monogamy. As if in recognition of this, a highlight draws attention to the horse's prominent and rounded rump and echoes the colour of Barney's fur coat. In the portrait of Una Troubridge, the two dachshunds playfully remind the viewer of the importance that Troubridge and her partner Radclyffe Hall attributed to breeding, in every sense of the word.

The most significant development, however, is that in her mature work, Romaine Brooks developed a visual vocabulary for expressing simultaneously a sense of sexual difference and of an alternative community. Many of her sitters were women whose sexual nonconformity was notorious: they included not only herself and Barney, but also Gluck, Radclyffe Hall's partner Una, Lady Troubridge, and Lily (Elisabeth) de Gramont.[10] What is striking about the (imagined) community that emerges from these portraits, though, is that it is not a national community, but one that crosses national boundaries, an international one that places women with links to Britain, France, Italy, Russia, Switzerland and the United States in a new relationship to each other. In *Aventures de l'esprit* (in which the map of the 'international' salon appears), Barney comments that Brooks 'has not had the enemies she deserves' ('elle n'a pas eu les ennemis qu'elle mérite', Barney 1929: 245), explaining that someone declared, meaning to insult her: 'She is a foreigner (or an outsider) everywhere' ('C'est une étrangère partout').[11] Barney, however, finds this quality in Brooks reassuring. Not belonging to the imagined community of the nation, being a foreigner, is seen as an asset rather than a disadvantage.

One of the ways Brooks creates a sense of alternative community in her portraits lies in her use of a visual language that cuts across national boundaries while constructing a transnational sense of an alternatively gendered community expressed through clothing. Katrina Rolley has emphasised the importance of dress for self-expression – particularly the expression of a 'deviant' sexual identity – in her analysis of the dress of Radclyffe Hall and Una Troubridge (Rolley 1990), the latter also one of Brooks' subjects.

Some critics have read this aspect of Brooks' work simply as cross-dressing and see it as a form of masculinisation and even self-hatred. Benstock sees in these 'cross-dressed' portraits evidence of 'misogyny' and argues that 'the portrait reveals the painful results of self-castration' (Benstock 1986: 305). Chadwick sees in the 'pinched faces' of most of Brooks' female portraits the exposure of 'self-divisions', and, in particular, the *Self-Portrait* of 1923 (Figure 5.3) appears 'tense and secretive'

Figure 5.3 *Self-Portrait*, 1923, Romaine Brooks. Courtesy of the Smithsonian American Art Museum.

and 'in uneasy relationship to the rhetoric and commodification of the modern woman' (Chadwick 1990: 262).

These portraits are less cross-dressed, however, than they
are portraits of women wearing a different 'national costume',
as it were. The costumes may de-feminise, but they do not necessarily masculinise. Few of the portraits show women wearing
a costume in which they could realistically pass as a man, for
example. (Exceptions might be the portraits of Renata Bor-
gatti and Peter, but we only see these sitters in profile and
details of the clothing are harder to discern.) While Brooks
might appear to be dressed 'like a Coachman of the period of
Pecksniff', as Djuna Barnes once put it (Barnes 1992: 36), it is
a superficial effect based largely on the appearance of the top
hat and belied by greater attention to the details of Brooks'
clothes. A number of photographs show Brooks hatted and
unhatted, draped in cloaks and undraped, in various costumes that announce their transvestism through the inclusion
of pants, but seldom constitute any outfit in which a man of
her day might have appeared in public without attracting a
considerable amount of attention.[12] Some of these photographs, for example one of Barney and Brooks in Geneva,
ca. 1915 (reproduced in Chadwick 2000: 29) in which Brooks
is draped and wearing a top hat, also serve as a reminder of
Brooks' numerous border crossings and of Barney's role in
encouraging such dressing up (Barney also liked to be photographed in a range of costumes, and her role playing with
Renée Vivien in particular is well known). The photo suggests
that it was with Barney that Brooks began experimenting with
costume, linking cross-dressing to border crossing and sex-gen-
der boundaries, elements that characterise her later depictions
of sexually nonconformist women.

The kind of gender-blurring clothes that Brooks specialised in
depicting creates a sartorial style that links her subjects to one
another and takes them out of – and beyond – the specific time
of composition. The portrait of Lucien Murat, for example,
seems to bind the subject to her culture by its invocation of fashion through the showy feathery hat, whereas the non-specific
clothing of the self-portrait and the perennially fashionable
garments of the portrait of Gramont (such as her lacy jabot)
place the subjects outside a specific time (see also the photograph of Barney at the beginning of Blin et al. 1976). Occasionally the clothing is less gender neutral and more
masculinised, as in the portrait of Troubridge, but the monocle
and the severity of the tailored clothes must be read against the

Byronic neck scarf with its asymmetrical collar tips and the pearl earring. In the portrait of the baroness Emile d'Erlanger, the subject appears to be wearing only a dark overcoat and a panel of animal skin. She can hardly be said to be cross-dressed, and yet she clearly escapes conventional representation as 'feminine'. In each portrait, the lack of specificity in the costume serves to place the subjects of these portraits more in relation to each other and less in relation to their national and temporal context. The subjects thus come to seem part of a community of their own, a community of individuals who cannot be understood through reference to a national typology. The imagined community of the nation is replaced by a different imagined community of chosen affiliations, what in 1970s feminist parlance was called 'the lesbian nation'. As Bertha Harris puts it in her description of the women of Barney's salon, their 'father's nationality' was 'wiped out by the more profound nationality of their lesbianism' (Harris 1973: 79). Although the French and the Anglophones may not have mixed well as 'clans,' some of their members came to form a different 'clan' of their own thanks to their affiliation with Barney and Brooks.

Barney's salon may not have literally done certain things. Certain Belle Epoque figures such as Renée Vivien never came to the rue Jacob. Yet, as the diagram suggests, Barney played an important mediating role in creating links through her salon between women who may never have met or who met but did not sympathise. The salon stood for an escape from national identity and offered a way to explore alternative sexual identities. While modernist women may not have perceived the benefits of such internationalism until the interwar years, the experiences of expatriation, the questioning of what it means to belong to a nation, and the literal crossing of national boundaries were experiences that characterised the formative years of this movement, the years of the Belle Epoque.

Notes

1. For further discussion of this sketch, see Elliott and Wallace 1994: 156–60 and Chalon 1979: 144. Here, authorship of the sketch is attributed to Natalie Barney, though other sources attribute it to the cartoonist André Rouveyre (including Cody [1984] and George Wickes in a personal letter to the author).
2. Quoted with the kind permission of Mr Richard Schaubeck.
3. While there seems to be consensus that the star-crossed meeting between Brooks and Barney took place at a tea given by Lily Anglesey, the date is less

well documented than other encounters, and various sources place it at different times: Vivien's biographer Jean-Paul Goujon places it in 1913 or 1914 (Goujon 1986: 178), both Benstock (1986: 304) and Chadwick (1990: 261) in 1915. The oldest letter we have between Barney and Brooks dates from somewhat later, 25 September 1917 (Blin et al. 1976: 20). Jean Chalon claims that when asked, neither could recall the exact date of their meeting but placed it around 1912 or 1915 (Barney 2002: 23). While they might well have forgotten the date of the encounter by the time Chalon got around to asking them in the 1960s, Brooks' autobiography was drafted in the 1930s when memories were still fresher, and although the memoir contains few dates, it strongly suggests that while Brooks knew of Barney's existence long before, she did not actually meet her until being introduced by Lady Anglesey after the outbreak of the First World War (Brooks undated: 277).

4. See also letters exchanged between Barney and Brooks that are now part of the University of Tulsa collection.

5. The idea of Barney's circle as forming a *single* salon is perpetuated by some of the recent interest in Barney. In his 2001 novel *Un soir chez l'Amazone*, for example, the Italian novelist Francesco Rapazzini imagines the interactions among the figures that gather at a 'Scorpio Club' party held at rue Jacob to celebrate Barney's fiftieth birthday on 31 October 1926. The work never pretends to be anything other than a fictional recreation, but it perpetuates the myth of a single, unified salon by bringing together (among others) Barney, Djuna Barnes, Romaine Brooks, Colette, René Crevel, Paul Morand and his wife, Liane de Pougy and her husband, Rachilde, Gertrude Stein, Alice Toklas, Dolly Wilde and Thelma Wood. It *is* a fascinating exercise to try to imagine how all these strong personalities might get along if thrown together (just what *would* Liane de Pougy and Gertrude Stein find to chat about, for example?), and I am not suggesting they never in fact faced this situation, but the fascination with literary celebrity gossip in Barney's salon sometimes obscures the more subtle ways that participants resisted being seen only in relation to Barney.

6. For a discussion of Vivien's writing, see Tama Lea Engelking's chapter in this volume.

7. Many of Brooks' paintings can be seen on websites such as www.satanic.org/~succubus.romaine.html.

8. The phrase is usually translated the 'thief' of souls, but the French 'cambrioleur' is more specific than the general 'thief' ('voleur' in French). Unlike a thief who steals anywhere he can, a 'cambrioleur' invades private space (the word is linked etymologically to 'chambre'). The 'crime' of the 'burglar' is not just the loss of property, but the violation of privacy. At the same time, France during the Belle Epoque was delighted by the exploits of Maurice Leblanc's Arsène Lupin, dubbed the 'gentleman-cambrioleur,' so that burglary also could be construed as more aristocratic than common theft.

9. The location of this work now is unknown.

10. Brooks did not paint only women. Male sitters included Gabriele d'Annunzio (1912, 1916), Jean Cocteau (1914), Paul Morand (1925) and Carl Van Vechten (1936).

11. The French word 'étranger' does not distinguish between being a stranger (someone unknown) and being a foreigner (someone of another nationality).

12. See Elliott and Wallace (1994) and Chadwick (2000: 29, 34–35) for reproductions of some of these photographs.

PART II

NEW TECHNOLOGIES, NEW WOMEN?

Chapter 6

Vélo-Métro-Auto: Women's Mobility in Belle Epoque Paris

Siân Reynolds

How easy was it for women to move about freely in the city, during the age later known as the Belle Epoque? The much-written-about figure of the *flâneur* has perhaps accustomed us to assume rather readily that freedom of movement was a male prerogative in the nineteenth century.[1] This is at best a half-truth, but examining the point at which half-truths break down can be instructive. This chapter concentrates on a few modes of transport which saw remarkable expansion during the Belle Epoque years, and on the degree to which they were available to women. For a sense of what was and was not possible for Frenchwomen in the period between the 1880s and 1914, however, we need to bear a few general parameters in mind, and be wary of easy assumptions.

The first parameter is diachronic, over time. How did these decades compare with the years that preceded and followed them? This period was certainly an age of change compared with the earlier nineteenth century, but it witnessed nothing like the major transformations which were to follow. One should however exaggerate neither the constraints of the past nor the freedom of the present. Women can move about alone today in ways that were not dreamed of in 1900, but they are still vulnerable, whether backpackers in the bush or teenagers walking home from city clubs. Women travelling in the past had fewer

options, but may have been less at risk. And there were plenty of
so-called exceptional cases, including intrepid female travellers
such as Isabelle Eberhardt (1877–1904), Jane Dieulafoy
(1851–1916) or Alexandra David-Neel (1868–1969) (Perrot
1991: 483–86). Women have *always* managed to get about if
they really wanted to. Historically, this chapter considers the
everyday norm rather than the no doubt numerous exceptions.

The second parameter is synchronic, over place. Was France
different from other countries? A French academic, teaching
summer school in Edinburgh in 1892, was most surprised by the
degree of mobility and freedom allowed to the 'jeune fille' in
Scotland – not usually regarded as a permissive society. He was
astonished that young women came from other cities to attend
courses: 'our young ladies do not yet venture so far, even accompanied by their mothers'. In Edinburgh, 'a young girl can come
and go, unaccompanied, and that surprises us. What aston-
ishes [people here], to an even greater degree is the cloistered
regime *we* impose on our young girls, and which they accept'.[2]
We know from many sources that American and British young
women in Paris were seen as having much more free and easy
behaviour than the French 'jeune fille'. Without exploring further the comparative dimension here, we might reflect that
'freedom' could mean different things in different places.

Finally, it hardly needs saying that the category 'women' is
not very helpful: within France, it could refer to the young girl,
the married woman *en famille*, the professional woman, the
student, the old woman, the rich/poor woman, the prostitute,
and so on. In each case, women's relation to mobility was varied and could alter over time. Social class was of course a great
divider. In a pioneering article on 'the woman of the people' in
the nineteenth century, Michelle Perrot drew a distinction
between the bourgeois woman – 'la femme comme il faut', as
Balzac describes her in the 1830s – and the 'femme du peuple'
(Perrot 1979 and 1998). The former had to be careful going
about in the city: she was 'encased' in corset, tailored clothes,
gloves and hat, and liable to be observed by neighbours and
servants. The unmarried girl had to be chaperoned, and even
the married woman was held within a confined space. To justify going out of her way, she needed to resort to subterfuge,
like Madame Bovary. By contrast, Perrot describes 'la femme
du peuple' as follows:

> The woman of the people had more freedom of movement. Her
> body was unfettered by a corset; her ample skirts were handy

for concealing items ... the [working-class] housewife went out
hatless, indifferent to the dictates of fashion ... hardly even
troubling with cleanliness, something hard to achieve anyway
because of inadequate water supplies. She was quick to gesticu-
late and answer back. For this constant picker-up of trifles, the
city was a forest in which she tirelessly roamed, always in
search of food and fuel.[3]

In exploring French women's mobility then, we have to distinguish from the start between who could, and who could
not, move about freely. In the early nineteenth century, the
constraints were more perceptible for the respectable woman
than for the 'femme du peuple'. 'A woman must not step out
of the circle drawn around her', wrote an avant-garde Saint-
Simonian woman sadly in the 1840s (quoted in Perrot 1991:
467). In 1855, the year of the Bovary trial, Mme Marie Rocher-
Ripert, an inspectress of nursery schools sent on official business by the French state, was travelling alone, by train, and
pregnant. The mayor of a small town in the Sarthe mistook
her for a prostitute, refused to look at her official papers and
kept her in the cells overnight, terrifying her with his crude
language. He had to let her go in the morning (Clark 2000:
32). A real prostitute would, paradoxically, have had somewhat greater freedom of movement.

Had this situation changed by the time of the Belle Epoque?
If we leaf through a Baedeker *Guide to Paris* dated 1900, it
would seem as though little was different. A series of warnings
is delivered in the section on cafés, shops and restaurants:

> Cafés form one of the great features of Parisian life ... Most of
> the Parisian men spend their evenings in the cafés, where they
> partake of coffee, liqueurs and beer, meet their friends, read the
> newspapers or play at billiards ... The best cafés may with pro-
> priety be visited by ladies, though Parisiennes of the upper class
> rarely patronize them. Some of those on the N. side of the Bd
> Montmartre should however be avoided as the society there is
> far from select (Baedeker 1904: 23 ff.).

Safer places were patisseries or teashops: 'the customers who
frequent them in the afternoon, to enjoy their *goûter* (cakes &
pastry) are chiefly ladies and children'. The Bouillon Duval
restaurants 'are very popular with the middle and even upper
classes and may without hesitation be visited by ladies'.
Department stores are much visited, since they retail 'all kinds
of materials for ladies' dress'. Even so, foreigners were advised

that it was best to enter them with another woman as companion. Cabarets in Montmartre however were 'hardly suitable for ladies'. As for the *bals publics* (such as the Moulin de la Galette or Bal Bullier dance halls), 'it need hardly be said that ladies cannot attend these balls' (ibid.). A local guidebook, *Paris-Parisien*, published in 1898, informs us additionally that the right-hand pavement of the boulevard Saint-Michel was reserved for women only (Prochasson 1999: 58). There was obviously still a gendering of space for 'respectable society', and the Baedeker *Guide* of 1913, on the eve of the First World War, repeated exactly the same warnings.

My argument is therefore quite simple: the historical development of women's 'freedom' has been extremely uneven, depending on who or where the women were. We should not be misled by the appearance of the New Woman of the Belle Epoque (and she certainly did exist, as discussed below) into thinking that this meant a step change in all Frenchwomen's mobility.[4] In this brief survey, I hope to contextualise some changes that did happen and to avoid lumping all women together. This account focuses first on the *vélo* (the two-wheeled bicycle), then on public transport, particularly the *métro* (the underground railway), and finally on the *auto* (the petrol-engine motorcar), a means of transport which became particularly important during the Belle Epoque. The Parisian example affords plenty of illustration.

Le Vélo: Bicycles 'Devouring Space'

Ride a bike and reach for the stars. Turn-of-the-century poster artists found the combination of young women and bicycles irresistible. There were more poster advertisements for bicycles than for any other product, though they are more remarkable for the fantasies they seem to have encouraged than for any practical demonstrations of cycling (Rennert 1973). The regular pedal-powered two-wheel bike began to take off in the 1880s, especially after the invention of pneumatic tyres (by Dunlop, later patented by Michelin). In 1891, the Paris-Brest-Paris cycle race, for men, was partly responsible for launching cycling as a fashionable sport. By 1892, there were '30,000 happy owners'. By 1899 there were about 186,000 bikes in Paris alone, rising to 277,000 by 1904. The bicycle was the mobile phone or designer scooter of the day perhaps, being available chiefly to the young and athletic, and at first only to the fairly rich. An average bicycle cost 500 francs, three months pay for a primary school teacher (quoted Laplagne 1996: 86). As a form of transport, it was only one step above walking: more a sport or pastime than a serious way of getting from A to B, except within a small radius – a ride out of the village, through the *quartier*, or round the park. However for women it marked a breakthrough, since from the start it was available to both sexes.

There is plenty of material associating women and bicycles during these years, but much of it falls into the category either of decoration or of prescription. As suggested above, poster art launched a series of suggestive images. Bicycles coincided both with Art Nouveau curlicues, and with the invention of the colour litho poster, an art form attributed to Chéret who pioneered it in the 1870s and later exploited it with success, as did Mucha and Toulouse-Lautrec. Cycling maidens were sometimes referred to as 'les Chérettes'. Posters encouraged not only sexual but emancipatory fantasies: one shows a young girl in white on a Griffiths bike representing freedom, while an old woman struggles in the brambles of the past. They paraded an image of freedom necessarily far in excess of realities.[5]

At the other end of the spectrum came the prescriptive warnings. There was much medical head-wagging over the possibility of masturbation, defloration, or damage to women's internal organs by this somewhat shocking machine. (Despite fanciful posters suggesting otherwise, cycles could not be ridden side-saddle as horses could.) 'For women,' wrote one doctor, 'the velocipede will always be a mechanism not to be recommended, a sterility-machine' (quoted Laplagne 1996: 83). In 1896, in response to a questionnaire, no less a person than Sarah Bernhardt replied: 'The bicycle is on the way to transforming our way of life more deeply than you might think. All these young women and girls who are devouring space are refusing domestic family life' (quoted Thompson 2000: 9, a rich source of quotations). A famous cartoon from *Le Grelot* entitled 'Off to the feminist congress' of 1900 (Figure 6.1), shows a pert young woman in a tucked-up skirt, smoking a cigarette and wheeling her bicycle out of the home, where a harassed husband is left amid a scene of domestic chaos.

Bicycle manufacturers sought to break into the female market, so they tried to associate women and bicycles in their advertising. In reality, women constituted a small proportion of bicycle owners: only 1 percent of cyclists in the 1890s. One summer Sunday in 1893, a survey of the bikes going out of

Figure 6.1 'To the Feminist Congress!', *Le Grelot*, 1896.

Paris on the Saint-Cloud road reported 5653 cyclists, of whom only 192 were women (Thompson 2000: 28). Women were specifically barred from cycle racing, which became a major spectator and participant sport – the Tour de France started in 1903 (ibid.: 31). Nevertheless, young and go-ahead girls persuaded their parents to buy them bicycles, learnt to ride in velodromes (often former horse-riding stables), and the new invention was soon figuring in popular romances.

That relatively few women actually rode cycles did not prevent men viewing the bike with some fascination as the stage prop of the New Woman. Among many literary references, the most celebrated is perhaps in Proust's *A l'ombre des jeunes filles en fleurs* (1919, but referring to a time twenty years or so earlier) where his narrator sees the sporty Albertine for the first time, wheeling a bike along the sea-front at Balbec, a moment constantly returned to throughout *A la recherche du temps perdu* (Proust 1954 [1913–27]). Bernard Shaw gives New Woman Vivie a bicycle in *Mrs Warren's Profession* (1898, see Reynolds 2001). New women did not always look like the posters however. They did not wear floating garments, which would have caught in the spokes. A Scottish art student in Paris in the 1890s wrote home: 'I bike *à l'américaine*, as the nicest French people do: a short skirt about 4 or 5 inches below the knee and long gaiters which go right to meet the knickerbockers in case of one's skirt blowing up. I always strap mine down'.[6] Photographs show soberly clad women in similar skirts, or sometimes early versions of trousers or breeches. Bloomers, which became famous, were originally meant to be worn under skirts. Costume played a part in the alarm occasioned by women teachers riding bikes to school. The director of education for the Seine *département* in 1897 issued a statement saying that, while it was permissible for women primary-school teachers to cycle at the weekend, they should not 'turn up at school on a bicycle at the start of the day, not only because we do not allow them to take classes in the special costume, but because they might have some accident within the sight of their pupils, which would not add to their authority'.[7]

Public Transport: Trains, Trams and Metros

The bicycle was a private means of escape. But this was the age when public transport, especially inside the city, was in a phase of unprecedented expansion. Paris was late with its subway, as France had been late with rail travel. The major expansion of railways under the Second Empire is well known, but it was during the Third Republic that rail travel came within the reach of most French people. There were about 20,000 km in 1879; 26,000 in 1882 and 65,000 in 1910, including 12,000 km of the 'petits trains d'intérêt local' referred to by Proust. Even so, French people did not at first take the train a great deal, unless they had to. There were 443 million journeys in 1900 (1142 million in Britain). And most of these journeys were taken by Parisian commuters – 77 percent of the traffic went to and from the Gare du Nord and the Gare Saint-Lazare. Third-class passengers accounted for much expansion in the Belle Epoque, because of cheap day-returns for families, introduced in 1891 (Zeldin 1977: 639). It became a regular outing to go to suburbs like Asnières for the day, as in Seurat's somewhat earlier famous painting (*Baignade, Asnières*, 1883). The other stimulus came from the great Paris exhibitions (1878, 1889 and 1900), which encouraged investment in transport by entrepreneurs.

Long-distance trains were now more comfortable – when on-board lavatories were introduced in the 1890s, it became easier for women to travel by train (otherwise one had to get out at the stations). But trains were still only lit at night, so tunnels remained hazardous – and the subject of risqué jokes. Apropos the Batignolles railway tunnel on the outskirts of Paris, one commentator remarked: '[O]nly those condemned to death, or women who are sitting face to face with a ruffian in darkness, know how long a minute can be' (quoted Evenson 1979: 115). Even for men, a guide in the 1870s advised travelling with a revolver. Perhaps only *after* the Belle Epoque did trains become reasonably safe for unaccompanied women, despite the provision of ladies-only compartments, a feature that survived in several countries until after the Second World War.

Within Paris, public transport was not hazardous, provided the vehicle was under control. There was a bewildering variety of means of transport. Horse-drawn omnibuses with two decks had been in circulation since the 1830s. When these acquired staircases later in the century, the top deck became accessible at last to women. Previously men had climbed up a ladder to smoke on the *impériale*, the setting for Maupassant's sad story of treachery, *La Dot*, written in the 1880s. Guidebooks nevertheless advised foreign visitors to take a cab (horse-drawn until the 1900s), since one had to know the routes well to get about by public transport. But during the Belle Epoque, first electric trams, which appeared from the 1880s, and then motorbuses (1905), provided a more regular and predictable service than the omnibuses. We probably underestimate the extent to which this opened up the city for women: it was easier to take a tram than to call a cab, find an omnibus, or own a carriage. The mother of the painter Paul Sérusier wrote to him in June 1891: 'When I left you on Sunday, I found a tram which took me to Bastille and then to the Madeleine, with one change. I was much better off with that than in these wretched cabs which I do not like at all. I was home by 10.30'.[8]

In fact public transport developed so fast and so chaotically that by 1910, Paris had virtually every kind of traction equipment one could imagine. Motor engines, steam traction, electric vehicles and horses all coexisted. In addition, the river provided yet another means of transport and one that could safely be used by anyone. Regular passenger boats could be boarded at several points from Charenton to Auteuil, along the right bank, and from Austerlitz to Meudon, along the left bank. There was a regular fleet with about eight departures an hour and ten on Sundays. In the 1890s, 22–24 million tickets a year were sold on the riverboats. In the 1890s, the sculptor Rodin used to take the boat from the Quai d'Orsay, near his studio, to Meudon, where he lived. During the 1900 exhibition, boats plied in a steady stream up and down the Seine to the main site near the Grand Palais. Thereafter however the number of passengers declined.

One reason for the decline was the coming of the metro. Safer than the long-distance trains, this enlarged all city dwellers' horizons, widening the circle of possible journeys within Paris, and crossing the river both under and over ground. The Paris subway was long overdue by 1900. The London 'tube' was started in the 1860s, New York had a subway in 1868 and Chicago in 1892. Glasgow had an underground railway in 1897, Berlin in 1871 and Budapest in 1896. The metro had been delayed not because France did not have the technology but because the city authorities and the state were at loggerheads for about twenty years after the 1870s, over strategic decisions. Briefly, the state wanted the metro, for military reasons, to link the main railway stations and to have the same gauge as railway trains, so that troops could be moved quickly. The big railway companies agreed, but the Paris council wanted a service of dense networks for commuters to serve local residents. In the end it was the imminence of the Paris 1900 exhibition which broke the deadlock: in return for the city making available funds for the *Exposition universelle*, the state conceded that the metro could be built in the city's preferred mode. The city paid for infrastructure (tunnels, engineering, and so on) while a private company (CMP), run by the Belgian baron Empain (though not under his own name), invested in the line laying and rolling stock. At first the rolling stock was rather crude: wooden carriages and large gauge, but small width of train. The tunnels were rumoured to be glacial in winter, hot in summer, though in fact eyewitnesses at the opening of Line 1 on 19 July 1900 said it gave welcome relief from the very hot weather that day. Following a bad fire at Couronnes station in 1903, the only serious accident of the time, safety measures were introduced which have made the metro to this day a very safe means of transport, with a hugely increased network, now in a single publicly-owned company, the RATP (*Régie autonome des transports parisiens*).[9]

The metro became popular very fast. Even in 1900 there were 48.4 million journeys (Paris had two million inhabitants); by 1910, there were 251.7 million. Alas, we have no way of knowing how many of those were made by women. The network expanded during the first four years from 13,000 metres to 30,000. The connections were the key to the success: even a dog's leg meant a faster journey than the tram or bus; trains left every six minutes. Trains had three carriages at first, expanding to eight in 1902, which sent up the number of passengers. A first-class carriage was available in the centre of the train (until the 1970s) and this may have been used by those middle-class ladies who ventured below the street. The problem from our perspective is that the point of view of women travellers is impossible to ascertain, since the reference works do not mention them at all in the early years. The Baedeker guides warned that the whole idea was possibly 'rather untempting for the susceptible', which presumably meant women, and remarked that the non-first-class carriages were very crowded. The metro was not a woman-free zone however, since about a tenth of the total staff of about 1000 were women. They were all employed as ticket sellers, and in most cases were married to the ticket punchers at the barriers.

In the long run, the metro was to make a difference by extending the distance Parisians could live from school, place of work and central sites. It does not however seem to have been the preferred means of transport of women, who were more likely from the pictorial evidence to be found on buses and trams; even today, many women prefer to take buses.

Automobiles: Travellers into the Future

Motorcars were only produced in any numbers after 1890. France was the scene of several pioneering experiments in the field before that, and the earliest women associated with motor travel were often wives or daughters of inventors (Mmes Lenoir, Bollée and Levasseur for example). The subject has attracted little serious attention. One of the few studies of women and the automobile in France reports that during the early period they were more likely to be passengers than drivers. Alexandre Buisseret has surveyed 200 posters advertising cars, concluding that two thirds had a picture of a woman passenger (Buisseret 2000: 44). It is always well to approach iconography with caution. The woman passenger no doubt played the decorative role later to be taken by fashion models in the Salon de l'Automobile, but in this case the posters may have been a reasonable reflection of majority behaviour.

Few Frenchwomen seem at any rate to have taken the wheel themselves in the early years: two pioneers who received media attention precisely because they were so rare were the Duchesse d'Uzès (1847–1933, *grande dame*, sportswoman, feminist and suffragist) and Camille Gast (1868–1942, sportswoman, explorer and racing driver, an activity in which she was long the only woman). The former was the first woman fined for speeding, in the Bois de Boulogne in 1899; the latter spent much time fighting prohibitions and prejudices in her efforts to compete on the same terms as men. But these exceptional cases were extremely isolated. Statistics are not easy to find, but one set of figures for driving licences for Paris issued between 1911 and 1914 tells us that only about 300 were taken out by women, for a population of 2.8 million (1.5 million women). Almost all came from the well-off districts of the city and the number was in any case small: 'a microphenomenon' (Buisseret 2000: 49–50).

It is true that compared with the simple mechanism of the bicycle, the technological specifications of the early motorcar, not to mention the noise, smoke, oil and general mess surrounding it might deter women, few of whom had any background in engineering. The *Guide Michelin* for 1900 (the first ever, sponsored by the tyre firm) contains pages of technical information about tyres and the need to change them. It also lists something like forty items the well-prepared motorist should always carry (including every conceivable kind of spanner). As one elderly aristocratic lady is reported saying, cars were 'dirty, disgusting, evil-smelling and they don't work' (Buisseret 2000: 51).

One development, for this very reason, was supposed to be aimed directly at women: the electric car. Developed both in France and the United States, at a time when the petrol engine had not yet triumphed, the electric-powered vehicle (the British milk-float is a present-day example) had both advantages and drawbacks. It was quiet and clean, and extremely easy to manipulate. But it was also slower than a petrol-powered car, and had a limited radius before it needed re-charging. This particular dead-end development was briefly considered by manufacturers as particularly appropriate for ladies. It was a city runabout, a 'shopping car', perhaps, but restricted its driver to a small radius and did not allow her to reach what were for the time high speeds of 20 mph or more. The electric car, usually enclosed rather than open, has also been described as 'a boudoir mouvant' (quoted Buisseret 2000: 61). One can glimpse something of the appeal from an advertisement for the electric Columbia carried in the *Guide Michelin* for 1900: 'Columbia cars have already conquered the motoring public in Paris, both by the elegance of their bodywork and the simplicity of their mechanism, which is controlled with ease by the hands of the least experienced of drivers'.[10] I think we can guess who that might be.

The electric car never really caught on, but some of its associated refinements and comforts did. These included the enclosed cabin, with side doors and luxurious upholstery, all of which increased the comfort of the motorcar, but also required technological changes, as they were gradually incorporated into the standard models. This development is generally supposed to have been influenced by women customers, who were not usually themselves drivers. The very well-off lady employed a chauffeur, the bourgeoise usually travelled as her husband's passenger, the rare enthusiast drove herself, and of course the vast majority of Frenchwomen never had the remotest chance of driving a car before the First World War. During that war, a new generation was drafted into roles which included driving motor vehicles, though women drivers remained a minority. Even in the 1950s, the association of women and speed appears to have been capable of provoking scandal, *vide* the publicity given to Françoise Sagan's exploits: driving a sports car at speed in bare feet was considered daring. In the long run the private motorcar carried the greatest promise of individual mobility, and Frenchwomen, after an interval, took virtually as much advantage of it as men.

Conclusion

The Belle Epoque was undoubtedly a time of technological change. But those best placed to take advantage of the new world were those who already possessed social, material or cultural capital. Even so, the degree of freedom available was relative and variable. The Paris metro may not at first have made a great deal of difference to working-class women who rarely needed to go outside their *quartier*, or to middle-class women who probably preferred surface modes of transport. But new technology did make it possible for young women to ride bikes and for bourgeois women to get to department stores, while titled ladies who previously rode horseback or drove victorias through the Bois de Boulogne might occasionally be spotted in an electric car. While she did not always have the freedom of the streets, it was in the long run the wealthier woman who would break through to longer-distance travel in a way the less well-off would normally not achieve – apart from the exceptional circumstances of emigration. Thus in a reversal of Perrot's typology, the 'femme comme il faut' became more mobile than the 'femme du peuple' after all.

Let me end with an anecdote about cycling which runs counter to the prevailing imagery and points towards other kinds of emancipation, again in a privileged context. Newly arrived in Paris from America in 1895, Romaine Brooks went cycling in the Bois de Boulogne. Her bicycle broke down, so she stopped for a lemonade at the Pavillon chinois, a favourite halt for women cyclists – and was immediately picked up by a 'beautiful woman, fashionably overweight and covered with jewelry'. Thanks to this encounter, she eventually became aware of the alternative lesbian networks of Paris, including the circle round Natalie Barney (Hawthorne 1997: 165–66).[11]

Notes

1. For references to the 'flâneuse', see Hawthorne 1997.
2. 'Nos jeunes filles ne se hasardent pas encore si loin, meme accompagnées de leur mère'. [Ici] 'la jeune fille va, vient, sort seule, cela nous étonne. Ce qui les étonne bien plus [les Ecossais], c'est le régime claustral auquel

nous soumettons nos filles, et qu'elles acceptent' (Demolins 1892: 103). The writer, Edmond Demolins, was the disciple of Le Play who went as a guest of Patrick Geddes to Edinburgh and reported on his impressions in *Le Mouvement social*.

3. 'La femme du peuple a plus d'indépendance gestuelle. Son corps demeure libre, sans corset; ses amples jupes se prêtent à la fraude ... la ménagère va 'en cheveux', indifférente à la mode et à ses commandements ... à peine soucieuse d'une propreté que compliquent ... les difficultés d'avoir de l'eau. Elle a le geste prompt, comme la repartie. Pour cette glaneuse éternelle, la ville est une forêt où elle déploie son inlassable activité, toujours en quête de nourriture ou de combustible' (Perrot 1979, reprinted 1998: 166).

4. For a recent discussion of the New Woman, see Roberts 2002, especially Chapter 1.

5. Though see Ruth Iskin's chapter on advertising posters for a more optimistic view of their impact on women's sense of identity.

6. Ottilie McLaren, letter in Wallace Papers, National Library of Scotland, MSS 21535, 27 November 1897.

7. 'Nous conseillons [aux institutrices] de ne pas se présenter à bicyclette à l'école au moment de l'ouverture des cours, non seulement parce que nous ne les autorisons pas à faire la classe dans le costume spécial, mais parce qu'il pourrait leur arriver en présence de leurs élèves assemblés telle ou telle mésaventure qui n'augmenterait pas leur autorité' ('Les institutrices et la bicyclette', *La Fronde*, 25 December 1897, unsigned).

8. 'Dimanche en te quittant, j'ai trouvé un tramway qui m'a conduite à la Bastille puis à la Madeleine par correspondance, j'y étais beaucoup mieux que dans ces méchantes voitures qui ne font pas du tout mon bonheur. A 10h 1/2 j'étais à la maison' (Clémence Sérusier, letter of 8 June 1891, in Getty Archives (860131), reference kindly provided by Belinda Thomson).

9. On public transport, see Zuber (ed.) 1998. For a brief history of Paris transport, see Margairaz 1989. Many publications and archives are to be found in the RATP library, rue de Bercy, Paris.

10. '[Les] voitures Columbia ont déjà su conquérir la faveur du public automobiliste à Paris, autant par l'élégance de leur carrosserie que par la simplicité de leurs organes mécaniques qui obéissent docilement à la main du chauffeur le plus inexpérimenté' (*Guide Michelin* 1900, no page number, advertisement).

11. See also Hawthorne's chapter in this volume.

CHAPTER 7

POPULARISING NEW WOMEN IN BELLE EPOQUE ADVERTISING POSTERS

Ruth E. Iskin

Critical studies of advertising have tended to focus primarily on the objectification and sexualisation of women, and thus on the representation of women as passive objects of the gaze.[1] While insights drawn from this approach have been central to feminist critiques in art and visual culture, they do not address an important aspect of advertising, namely, the extent to which it addresses modern women as agents in its attempt to attract them to the products they advertise. This study focuses on selected Belle Epoque advertising posters and suggests that they offer possibilities of identification for modern women of the time by portraying them as the active consumers of a wide range of products and activities. It analyses examples of posters that depict a mainstream 'New Woman' ('la femme nouvelle') enjoying freedoms such as walking in the city, participating in leisure and sports, occupying public spaces with ease, projecting her sexuality well beyond bourgeois constraints, or practising professions opening to women at the time.

The fact that some Belle Epoque posters portrayed not merely the seductive or passive woman, but also the active modern woman, must be understood in the historical context of the late nineteenth and early twentieth centuries. The fin-

de-siècle and the Belle Epoque were marked by fierce debates
in the press about changes in the roles and identities of
women, their opportunities for higher education, new professions, salaried work and demands for legal and political
rights. Modern women's lives were changing. The heroine of
Louise-Marie Compain's 1903 novel *L'Un vers l'autre* (*One
Toward the Other*) writes that 'We are preparing a new race of
women ...[we are] beings in transition' (Waelti-Walters and
Hause 1994: 94). Some Belle Epoque advertising posters depicting women capitalised on this development and flourished by
popularising the New Woman as a desirable icon. By dissemi-
nating such images they themselves helped shape the changing images and identities of modern women.

It is important to recognise that, as a new and highly effective form of mass communication, posters occupied an
entirely different role in the culture of the Belle Epoque than in
our own twenty-first century media world.[2] However, the contemporary idea that media images influence the identities of
the subjects they portray had its precedent in the nineteenth
century. Several decades before posters became a major force
in Belle Epoque advertising, Baudelaire recognised the power
of illustrations in the press to influence the men and women
whose 'type' they portrayed. He noted that Gavarni's litho-
graphic illustrations 'had a considerable effect upon manners'
(Baudelaire 1965 [1863]: 183),[3] and observed that students
and *lorettes* (the term invented in nineteenth-century journalism describing young women who consorted with artists, students and journalists) actually modelled themselves after such
illustrations and fashion plates:[4]

> Not a few of those girls have perfected themselves by using her
> [the *lorette*] as a mirror, just as the youth of the Latin Quarter
> succumbed to the influence of his [Gavarni's] *students,* and as
> many people force themselves into the likeness of fashion-
> plates (ibid.: 183).

During the Belle Epoque, advertising posters, even more than
press illustrations earlier on, most likely influenced the subjects
they represented, since their advertising function depended on
evoking associations and identifications. The 1911 volume *La
Publicité suggestive: théorie et technique* articulated the goal that
'advertising shapes the consumer and educates her, transforms
her tastes and habits' (Tiersten 2001: 76). One of the ways in
which posters attempted to achieve this, as this essay demon-

strates, was by portraying an attractive 'type' of New Woman and appealing to the gazes of female consumers.

The normative assumption that advertising images present women as spectacle to attract men's gazes has overshadowed the fact that many Belle Epoque posters were aimed primarily at women because of their role as consumers. While this, of course, did not exclude men from looking at such posters, it does demand a different approach to interpreting the images, their mode of address and their likely impact on women. It helps explain why some Belle Epoque posters considered women as spectators with a measure of agency. Zola dubbed French women a 'nation of consumers' in his 1883 novel, *Au bonheur des dames*, which was based on extensive research on the development of the department store in nineteenth-century Paris. Describing the display and marketing strategies used by the emerging department store, he writes, 'it was for woman that all the establishments were struggling in wild competition' (Zola 1970 [1883]: 69).[5] The fact that many women spent money they did not earn themselves did not deter advertisers, who were well aware that earner and spender were not necessarily the same person, just as today's advertisers spend large budgets catering to children and teenagers although they are not in charge of the family income. Furthermore, changes in laws in France and Britain during the late nineteenth century made it possible for some women to control their own money. At the same time, a growing number of women were entering the wage-earning work force, constituting 26.6 percent of the total female population in France by 1891.[6]

Feminists and Femininity in Posters and Press Caricatures

Most of the posters discussed here are French (some produced by artists who emigrated from other European nations), and two are from French-speaking Brussels and Geneva.[7] They feature images of middle- and upper-class French and other European women as well as working-class women. However, none of them are outright feminist posters like, for example, Clémentine-Hélène Dufau's *La Fronde* (Figure 7.1), an 1898 poster advertising the feminist newspaper *La Fronde*. Dufau, a feminist associated with the *La Fronde* circle, was primarily a painter rather than poster artist. In this poster she represents a

Figure 7.1 Clémentine-Hélène Dufau, *La Fronde,* 1898. Charles Verneau, Paris, 137.1 × 97.8 cm. Courtesy of the Bibliothèque Marguerite Durand.

group of mostly lower-class women of diverse ages. The higher-class figure portrayed in a leadership position probably symbolises *La Fronde's* dynamic founding editor Marguerite Durand. Portrayed showing the way to a group of women less fortunate than herself, she embodies *La Fronde's* role toward its female readership, pointing to a feminist horizon that stands for new possibilities and a better future.

By contrast, the other posters discussed here advertise consumer products and are not overtly feminist; any feminist message they may contain is implicit. Marcellin Auzulle's ca. 1903 *Auto Barré* (Figure 7.2), for instance, promotes a car by portraying daring and adventurous women. Overtaking another car chauffeured by a man seen in the distance, these spirited women are proclaiming their own success as well as the superiority of their car. Part of the implied message is that this car is better than others because it is so easy to drive that (even) women can win a race. However, it also quite explicitly conveys the women's great enjoyment of their performance and their thumbing their noses at the competition as well as at convention.

The affirming effects of posters portraying the independence of the New Woman in attractive terms can better be

Figure 7.2 Marcellin Auzulle, *Auto Barré*, ca. 1903. Th. Dupuy & Fils, Paris, 150 × 111.7 cm. Courtesy of the Poster Photo Archives, Posters Please.

understood when compared with the scathing visual discourse of press caricatures. While hosts of press caricatures tended to portray the New Woman through negative stereotypes as unfeminine and unattractive, advertising posters presented images of modern women as integral to consumer culture and as fashionable participants in modern life. If the aim of these posters was to forge an identification that would lead women to buy the products, flattery was surely a better strategy than assault. Read within the broader field of print culture of the time, in which caricatures played an important role in expressing hegemonic viewpoints, posters introduced a differ-ent note into the visual-culture discourse on the New Woman.[8] The dominant culture's objections to the New Woman is expressed, for example, in Alfred Le Petit's 1880 caricature of a feminist in *Le Charivari* (Figure 7.3). The dark, menacing image visually assails the viewer. It portrays the feminist as a dominant, overbearing figure looming over innocent maidens to whom she issues a call to arms. Her ungainly figure is thrown into relief by her juxtaposition with the petite, stylish young woman standing below. The words she utters from the

Figure 7.3 Alfred Le Petit, caricature, *Le Charivari*, 1880.

podium appear in the caption, 'Citizens, since men persist in refusing us our civic rights, let us refuse them our (sexual) favours!' Her audience, exemplified by the petite feminine woman with a wide-open mouth, finds the idea preposterous, representing the point of view of dominant culture. The caricature of the feminist's aged body, coarse facial features and bespectacled mannish gaze are a far cry from the kind of fashionable modern woman featured in posters.

Consider, for example, the artfully dressed consumer with a refined gaze, in the anonymous Belgian poster *Chaussures de Luxe* (*Luxury Shoes*) of ca. 1901 (Figure 7.4). Wearing an elaborately decorated Art Nouveau dress, the coiffed, hatted and bejewelled lady personifies good taste and discernment. Deftly holding a gold-rimmed magnifying glass to her eyes, her gilded gaze is a modern-day attribute that defines her as an elite consumer and connoisseur of handmade luxury goods. This is the kind of modern woman that Belle Epoque posters approvingly portray as exhibiting a measure of independence, deriving status as consumer and enjoying the pleasures of metropolitan life. In contrast, some posters feature blatantly sexualised images of women, as in Leonetto Cappiello's *Corset Le Furet* of 1901. At first glance this poster advertising corsets appears to do nothing more than present a titillating woman

Figure 7.4 Anonymous. *Chaussures de Luxe P. D. C.*, ca. 1901. J. L. Goffart, Bruxelles, 31.8 × 59 cm. Courtesy of the Poster Photo Archives, Posters Please.

for a desiring masculine gaze. However, given that the poster aimed to attract female consumers to whom it attempted to sell a feminine product, we must ask how it functioned for intended female gazes. The poster addresses the 'civilised' French female consumer by suggesting that she can acquire alluring powers of seduction by buying a corset that, as the poster claims, 'combines oriental suppleness with French grace'. Moreover, the redhead flaunts her body's curves seductively like a proto-Madonna. With a tilted head and coy smile, she displays her exhibitionist pleasure at advertising the 'hygienic, elegant, flexible' corset that 'holds tight but does not constrict'. It was during this period that feminists advocated getting rid of corsets altogether on medical grounds and to free women's bodies from handicapping constraints. The poster cleverly aligns itself with modern women's desires for bodily freedom rather than with the actual physical constraint of corsets. Women apparently found the message appealing since the success of the poster exceeded the expectations of the company that printed it.

A less conventional image of a young New Woman who is not wearing a corset is portrayed in Lucien Faure's ca. 1901 poster advertising Colette's novels *Claudine à l'école/Claudine à Paris* (still erroneously attributed here to her husband Willy) (Figure 7.5). It depicts the actress Polaire, who played Claudine on the stage and who, like Claudine in the novel, sported a cropped hairdo.[9] Clad in a loose dress with a relatively short hem (whose style reminds us that she is a schoolgirl), her face conveys the maturity of a young woman and her straightforward gaze meets the spectator's head on. Though still a teenager, the fact that she is not bound in a corset is significant, since usually images of the period portray girls as younger mirror reflections of their corseted bourgeois mothers and advertising in catalogues of late nineteenth-century department stores promoted corsets for teenage girls.

Figure 7.5 Lucien Faure. *Claudine à l'école/Claudine à Paris*, 1901. Charles Verneau, Paris, 100.5 × 140 cm. Courtesy of the Poster Photo Archives, Posters Please.

Leisure, Travel and Bicycle Posters

Another genre of posters that appealed to women advertised resorts, sports, train rides and bicycles. For example, Abel Faivre's *Chamonix* of ca. 1905 (Figure 7.6) promotes winter sports at Chamonix along with the Paris-Lyon-Mediterranean railway by featuring a woman skiing downhill in perfect lady-like composure, her bourgeois outfit and smart feathered hat firmly in place. The reassuring message is that she can handle the speedy snow slope as easily as the Boulevard's asphalt. The 1905 *Cycles Brillant* Parisian poster by Marondon (Figure 7.7) portrays two athletic women waiting by their bicycles in the countryside, wearing comfortable casual sports gear and showing that they are speedier cyclists than their three male companions seen trailing far behind. The poster depicts the two women in an authoritative, commanding position on the hill. Their gazes fortified by large field glasses, they spot their friends in the distance. The poster suggests that their achievement is due not just to the gleaming Brillant bicycle, which is

Figure 7.6 Abel Faivre, *Chamonix*, ca. 1905. J. Barreau, Paris, 105 × 75 cm. Courtesy of the Poster Photo Archives, Posters Please.

Figure 7.7 Marondon, *Cycles Brillant*, 1905. Paul Dupont, Paris, 140 × 106 cm. Courtesy of the Poster Photo Archives, Posters Please.

prominently placed in the foreground, but also to their own fitness and athletic capabilities. While the aim of such posters, of course, was to sell bicycles rather than liberate women, some of them adopted counter-hegemonic points of view that were likely to appeal to their targeted female consumers – modern women who craved new freedoms. The bicycle was associated with the New Woman not only in France but also in Britain and the United States. It attracted women who sought mobility and exercise, as advocated by M. E. Ward's 1896 manual, *Cycling for Ladies: The Common Sense of Bicycling*: 'Riding the wheel, you have conquered a new world [...] you become alert, active, quick-sighted, and keenly alive' (quoted in Garvey 1996: 113);[10] it also attracted middle-class women searching for relief from 'the narrowness of woman's sphere' and its 'disorder of the soul', as Marguerite Merington wrote in the June 1895 issue of *Scribner's* (ibid.: 113). In France, the president of the 1896 feminist congress, Maria Pognon, stated that the 'egalitarian, levelling bicycle' would liberate women (Weber 1986: 203). If the number of women buying bicycles did not equal that of men, the image of the modern woman on a bicycle, nonetheless, had a major presence in fin-de-siècle and Belle Epoque posters and caught the public imagination as a symbol for the New Woman. This was recognised by the author Georges Montorgueil who, in 1897 noted that the far-reaching influence of the bicycle was 'more violent than any revolution'.[11]

Posters that promoted public transportation also appealed to women's desires for mobility and travel. Ochoa y Madrazo's *Nord Express* of 1896, advertising the Grand European Express with sleeping wagons (serving major European capitals from Paris to St. Petersburg), appealed to middle- and upper-class women's patronage by featuring a fashionable cosmopolitan woman traveller. Many of these posters portray a New Woman who enjoys being in the public sphere and occupies it with confidence. For example, the 1905 French poster *La Framboisette* (Figure 7.8) by Portuguese-born Francisco Tamango, who worked in Paris, pictures a flamboyant woman of uncer-

Figure 7.8 Francisco Tamango, *La Framboisette*, ca. 1905. Robin, Paris, 111.5 × 156.8 cm. Courtesy of the Poster Photo Archives, Posters Please.

tain class and moral character flirtatiously sipping the sweet liqueur, La Framboisette. Seated alone in a train-station restaurant, next to a sign warning that this is a three-minute stop, she takes refuge from relentless schedules in the momentary euphoria of a drink. The train is about to depart, the conductor is ringing the bell to no avail, the porter is gesturing wildly, and the engine driver is ready to take off. Oblivious to them all, and to the pressures of set schedules, this traveller sipping her Framboisette continues to savour her pleasure while her provocative presence both amuses and disrupts public space. On the one hand, the poster stereotypes women as leisurely consumers in contrast to men as productive workers. On the other hand, it promotes a woman who transgresses feminine gender conventions by occupying public space with extravagant self-assurance. Her pose suggests the abandon of slight intoxication, appealing to potential female and masculine consumers differently. Women, who were known to be the primary consumers of sweet liqueur, are urged to drink it by identifying with her, in the hopes of gaining her allure; men are encouraged to fantasise drinking in her flirtatious company. Who is she and what is her class status? Her leisured manner and fashionable appearance suggest that her financial means are much greater than those of a working-class woman. Yet her carefree behaviour in public far exceeds what would have been considered appropriate for either middle- or upper-class women. Her social transgression, blatant sexual address and flamboyant fashionability all suggest that she is a demi-mondaine, which explains her unfettered freedom.

Though this sexualised image operates by seducing, it also endows the woman with an active stance and portrays her as insisting on her pleasure. Implicitly, it promotes new freedoms for women beyond the obvious one of having a drink. These include the pleasures of travel, independence and sociability, while channelling women's desires for freedom into acts of consumption. Because the sweet liqueur was a product known to attract primarily a female consumer base, we must entertain the possibility that the poster image of La Framboisette played to feminine fantasies and liberatory aspirations. If this is the case, she functions in a similar way to the film heroine of *Flashdance* (1983) who, as Angela McRobbie has shown, elicited identification among young women for the liberatory potential of her independence and achievement and for her rejection of normative expectations, rather than for the way she conformed to the stereotype of a sexy young woman (McRobbie 1991).[12]

Women and Work in Posters

While numerous late nineteenth- and early twentieth-century posters depicted bourgeois, upper-class women and demi-mondaines in public spaces, such women are usually not seen performing domestic duties. However, some Belle Epoque posters do feature the domestic worker attending to the private sphere in her professional role and costume to promote a variety of household goods. The domestic worker prefigures the twentieth-century prototype of the happy housewife who appears in subsequent advertising, promoting new products by implying that a housewife's life is perpetually improving with them. Francisco Tamango's 1903 poster *Aluminite* (Figure 7.9) features an aproned cook promoting flame-resistant cookware. Deftly cooking with her right hand, her other hand points to the words that praise the cookware as ideal ('Batterie de Cuisine Idéale'), anticipating advertising testimonials of the twentieth century. The poster invests her with professional authority and shows her as utterly composed while the flames engulf the cookware, demonstrating its great resistance to flames.

Figure 7.9 Francisco Tamango, *Aluminite*, 1903. B. Silvern, Toulouse, Paris, 96.5 × 132.1 cm. Courtesy of the Poster Photo Archives, Posters Please.

In addition to featuring women in traditional salaried positions in the bourgeois household, posters also featured women
working in newer types of professions outside the home.
Female office workers were popularised in posters promoting
typewriters and other office paraphernalia. Though hardly
considered at the pinnacle of female professions today, in the
late nineteenth- and early twentieth-century, women who
practised the professions of office clerk and typist represented
a new type of working woman who ventured into modern
opportunities. The 1892 *Yost, La Meilleure Machine à Écrire* (*Yost,
The Best Typewriter*) by Lucien Lefebre (Figure 7.10) promotes
the new Yost typewriter by featuring an attractive young office
worker typing with the grace of a pianist. Her corseted shapely
body reminds one of a Cheret nymphet, but her innocent-
looking profile and serious expression – eyes downcast as she
concentrates on typing – convey her industrious nature. Lean-

Figure 7.10 Lucien Lefebre, *Yost, La Meilleure Machine à Écrire*,
1892. Chaix, Paris, 80 × 60 cm. Courtesy of the Poster Photo
Archives, Posters Please.

ing forward towards the gleaming industrial machine, she types out the points of purchase of the new typewriter (no ribbon and irreproachable alignment), which are readable on the page next to her and on the one she is typing. Similarly, Pal's ca. 1898 poster *Imprimez vous-même* (*Make your own copies*) (Figure 7.11) uses a young feminine woman to advertise a mimeograph machine, Eyquem, which claims to reproduce copies automatically and quickly, as evidenced by the pile of copies and the sign announcing '3000 copies'. Dressed in her work outfit, her left hand raised victoriously, the young woman is a poster girl for the modern female office worker. These types of poster images, which sold the product, could appeal simultaneously to desiring masculine gazes and to the gazes of modern women, who wanted to enter a promising profession still identified with male clerks but did not wish to be stereotyped as masculine.

Figure 7.11 Pal (Jean Paléologue). *Imprimez vous-même*, ca. 1898. Gaby & Chardin, Paris, 139 × 101 cm. Courtesy of the Poster Photo Archives, Posters Please.

The 1919 poster *Labor: La Grève des dactylos,* by Swiss poster artist Jules Courvoisier, makes this point more explicitly (Figure 7.12). Dated several years after the end of the Belle Epoque, this poster does not portray a Belle Epoque woman. Rather, it depicts what appears to be a demonstration for women's rights. It ties modern women's demands for labour with demands for a typewriter whose brand name is 'Labor'. The poster thus links aspirations for salaried work outside the home with the visual image of a political demonstration. Depicting a throng of modern women marching on the street and announcing their strike, the poster also differs from Belle Epoque posters by introducing the image of New Women as a collectivity. The predominantly female group (which includes the occasional man and son supportive of their cause) lends the position of leader to the central female figure in a red dress with a raised arm whose foot, slightly ahead of the rest, transgresses the frame. The poster not only conflates demand for the product with the demand for labour, but also depicts a struggle to obtain broader emancipation. While *Labor* is not necessarily typical of posters of the post-Belle Epoque era, it helps clarify the argument that Belle

Figure 7.12 Jules Courvoisier, *Labor: Grève des dactylos!*, 1919. Affiches Sonor, S.A., Geneva, 128 × 95 cm. Courtesy of the Bibliothèque Forney, Paris.

Epoque posters assimilated New Women into consumer culture by popularising their images rather than making overt political statements for emancipation, or condemning the New Woman with the negative stereotypes of caricatures.

In conclusion, by appropriating aspirations associated with the New Woman, some Belle Epoque posters coined attractive images that became acceptable to the social consensus. These images embraced women's desires for new roles, behaviours and freedoms, and often portrayed the kind of active woman whom they aimed to win over as consumer. Furthermore, they courted female consumers' gazes not only when advertising corsets or shoes, but also when promoting bicycles, public transportation, sports or typewriters. Though mass culture in general and advertising in particular are often denigrated because of their exploitative roles, they can also offer permissible spaces for registering and affirming identities beyond previous social constraints. Some Belle Epoque posters that disseminated new identities of modern women must thus be credited with participating in shaping them. Though advertising posters did not promote modern women's broader agendas, which included legal and political rights such as the vote, they nonetheless encouraged women not only to patronise shops but also to gain a new mobility and presence in a wide range of social spaces, from the metropolis to the resort and the office. While merciless caricatures stigmatised the New Woman, advertising posters legitimised and popularised her.

I have proposed that certain types of Belle Epoque posters are important as images that simultaneously shaped, reflected, affirmed and curtailed the aspirations of New Women. If Baudelaire was right in judging press illustrations to have influenced nineteenth-century men and women who strove to look like the types portrayed in the print media of his time, surely advertising posters of the Belle Epoque, which were designed to influence their targeted audiences, had a great deal of impact on the New Women they portrayed. It is, however, equally important to realise that the New Women who came to constitute an important segment of the modern market, in turn influenced advertisers to strive to attract and please their gazes.

My thanks to Carrie Tarr for her helpful criticism and insights as well as editing. I am grateful to Joseph Bristoe, Cristina Cuevas-Wolf, Richard Ericson, Peter H. Reill, Serge Guilbaut, Maureen Ryan, Debora L. Silverman, Kerri Steinberg and Cecile Whiting for their encouragement of, and criticism on, my work on posters.

Notes

1. The most important critical study of advertising remains Williamson (1978), which however, does not address fin-de-siècle and Belle Epoque posters.
2. This is discussed in my article on 'The Pan-European Flâneuse' (Iskin 2003).
3. Baudelaire considered the illustrator Gavarni a painter of manners who, along with Daumier, created 'complements to [Balzac's] *Comédie Humaine*' (Baudelaire 1965 [1863]: 4). On the probable dates of Baudelaire's essay, see J. Mayne's introduction (Mayne 1965: xix).
4. (Italic in original.) Baudelaire contrasts the *lorette* to the 'kept woman' of the Second Empire by highlighting her independence: 'The Lorette is a free agent. She comes and she goes. She keeps open house. She is no one's mistress; she consorts with the artists and the journalists' (Baudelaire 1965 [1863]: 183). Translated by J. Mayne.
5. Published in English as *The Ladies Paradise* (Zola 1992). 'C'était la femme que les magasins se disputaient par la concurrence' (Zola 1970 [1883]: 92).
6. This was a growth of roughly 3 percent from 1872 (see Hellerstein et al. 1981: 273).
7. A majority of the research has been conducted in collections and archives in Paris (such as the Bibliothèque National, the Musée de la Publicité, the Musée Carnavalet and the Bibliothèque Forney).
8. This may be considered a counter-discourse. Terdiman (1985) discusses the notion of counter-discourse in the nineteenth-century press and in political caricatures by Daumier and others, though without attention to the fact that caricatures of feminists express a dominant discourse, rather than a counter-discourse.
9. Algerian-born Polaire, who was well known for not wearing corsets, appeared in major Parisian café-concerts during the 1890s. See Schimmel and Cate (1983: 146), which includes an 1898 photograph of Polaire with a cropped hairdo.
10. Garvey's study of American magazines (1996) discusses the 1890s phenomenon of women associating their quest for freedom with the bicycle.
11. For a discussion of posters that portray the modern woman bicycling and walking in the city, see Iskin (forthcoming, 2006).
12. *Flashdance* (Adrian Lyne, 1983) portrays a heroine who succeeds in pursuing her dream of becoming a dancer, overcoming numerous obstacles.

CHAPTER 8

AN AMERICAN IN PARIS: LOÏE FULLER, DANCE AND TECHNOLOGY

Naoko Morita

Loïe Fuller (1862–1928) is a dynamic, multivalent and contradictory figure in French dance of the Belle Epoque.[1] An American by birth, Fuller arrived in Paris in 1892 and appeared at the Folies-Bergère; her performances attracted the attention of artists such as Stéphane Mallarmé, Henri de Toulouse-Lautrec, Jules Chéret and Auguste Rodin. Though she possessed no formal training as a dancer or choreographer, she achieved international fame for her invention of the 'serpentine dance' as well as for her innovations in stage lighting. An inveterate entertainer, she was enthusiastic about the possibilities of advertising and was the only female performer with her own theatre at the Paris Exposition of 1900. This chapter aims to assess the originality of her place among women artists of the Belle Epoque and her contribution to music-hall culture and technology.

Fuller's Career as a Dancer

When Fuller established her prestige as an artist on the Parisian stage, her figure as a dancer was often described as ghostly or immaterial. In reality her physique was far from that of a typical dancer. Born the daughter of a boarding-house owner, Fuller began her career as a burlesque actress in Chicago and became a dancer only in her late twenties. She lacked the training and proportions to become a ballet dancer, and the style of dance she chose did not belong to any tradition; indeed, it was soon incorporated into modern dance, which allowed its practitioners freedom to experiment. Once she settled in Paris, she led the modern dance scene for about ten years (from 1892 to 1902), before the arrival of Isadora Duncan and Ruth St. Denis. After 1908, the year in which she wrote her autobiography (Fuller 1908), she ceased performing herself, but founded a dance school, and continued to stage her works till her death in 1928. Her career was, however, marked by a long struggle with the hierarchy and moral standards of the theatre world. In her private life, after a failed marriage in the United States, she chose to live with a Frenchwoman, Gab Sorère, later her assistant, who became her lifelong companion. Fuller was also responsible for her widowed mother, who shared all her adventures till 1908. Her unorthodox lifestyle was only possible because of her financial independence and moral freedom as an artist.

In her early years on the stage, Fuller played principally in melodramas, farces and burlesques. Short and stout, she specialised in the roles of an innocent young girl or a little boy, and never appeared in 'girlie' revues. In 1885, at the age of twenty-three, she was hired by Murray and Murphy's Company to play a leading role, including singing and dancing, in *Our Irish Visitors* in New York and Boston; but she still remained a modest burlesque actress. It was during her visit to London in 1890–91 that she got the idea of the 'skirt dance', the inspiration for the serpentine dance. She observed dancers at the Gaiety Theatre manipulating their long gowns as they followed a pattern of steps. Returning to New York, she took the lead role in *Quack, M.D.*, by Fred Marsden, playing a young widow whom a quack doctor tries to hypnotise. As an entr'acte, she performed a little 'skirt dance', which consisted in floating around the stage waving a filmy robe while vari-coloured lights were projected on to it. Surrounded by darkness, Fuller first appeared in a white light, clad in a white silk robe with a long train that she raised over her shoulders, making graceful rotational movements, vanishing and emerging from the darkness. Later in the dance, her rhythmic movements were tinted blue, purple and crimson (Lista 1994: 50–80; Current and Current 1997: 14–22, 30–36).

The dance, christened the 'serpentine dance', became her new routine and enabled her to break through from B-grade actress to a performer of a certain fame. In 1892, at the age of thirty, she was invited to perform in Berlin. She expected to perform at the Opera House but to her disappointment she had to perform at the Wintergarten, a music hall. Then, in Cologne, she had to dance in a circus between an educated donkey and an elephant that played the organ, and she felt extremely humiliated. Having written to the director of the Paris Opera, she arrived in Paris with very little money, her mother, and an English-speaking agent, Marten Stein; but the Opera did not engage her. Instead, thanks to Stein, she was engaged at the Folies-Bergère, under the management of Edouard Marchand (Lista 1994: 107–9, 112–3; Current and Current 1997: 46–50).

Inaugurated in 1869 as one of the first café-concerts in Paris, the Folies-Bergère had known several changes in management. In 1886, the theatre became the property of Mr and Mrs Allemand, whose son-in-law, Marchand, had a real talent for music-hall management and was to reign there until 1902. Under his management, the Folies developed into the greatest music hall in Paris, with sensational attractions involving acrobats or illusionists, and 'girlie' revues with the most popular singers and dancers. When Fuller arrived at the Folies, she had to compete with beautiful, sexy dancers like Emilienne d'Alençon and the Belle Otero. According to Roger Marx, there was a striking contrast between Fuller and the other dancers, who wore as little as they could and often emphasised a heaving of the breasts, a swaying of the hips or a rotation of the pelvis (Marx 1893: 107).[2] In fact Marx, an art critic, bureaucrat and general inspector of provincial museums for the French government, contributed much to establishing the artistic value of Fuller's dance (Figure 8.1). In his article in *La Revue encyclopédique*, he emphasised the fantastic nature of her dance style and lighting by means of various metaphors: 'In polychromatic waves of light, the exquisite phantom runs back and forth, skims the floor like a dragonfly, skips along like a bird, flaps her wings like a bat ...'[3]

Fuller was conscious of the importance of the ethereal nature of her performance, and was careful not to disillusion her fans. When interviewed, she always gave the impression that she was ten years younger than she was, and she even faked her age in her autobiography.[4] She enthralled not only the usual clientèle but also those who had seldom been inside a music hall, like intellectuals or the aristocracy. She gave a new respectability to the Folies-Bergère and, taking part in

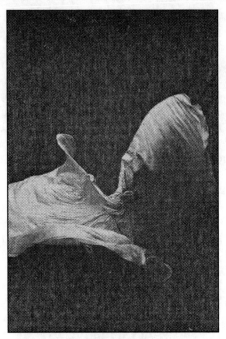

Figure 8.1 Loïe Fuller, ca. 1900. Photograph by Isaiah West Taber.

family matinées, won applause from mothers and children as well. Her challenge to social and artistic hierarchies resulted in a mix of high and low culture, characteristic of twentieth-century art. However, she always aspired to a more 'respectable' place to perform, and left the Folies-Bergère in 1894. But she continued to perform energetically, touring on both sides of the Atlantic, and in Paris she performed usually in prestigious theatres such as the Théâtre des Champs-Elysées and the Châtelet. She finally attained the Paris Opera in 1920 (Lista 1994: 619–32).

Loïe Fuller incarnated a new type of female dancer, conscious of the commercial value of her talent and the need for business acumen. However, her efforts were not always successful. She tried hard to patent her dance techniques and stage sets, but she could not completely protect herself from her numerous imitators. Sometimes her projects – for example the first representation of *La Tragédie de Salomé* (*Salome's Tragedy*) in 1895 – ended in failure, and she found herself out of pocket. As she got older and stouter, she could no longer cope with the vigorous movements of her repertoire. Because of her experiments in lighting, she ran the risk of blindness. And sometimes her projects extended into fields with which she was unfamiliar: when she conceived the idea of exhibiting Rodin's works in the United States, for example, she momentarily came into conflict with the sculptor because of her pushy manner. Whether or not she was successful, however, she incarnated a new type of artist-performer with a head for business.

Loïe Fuller and Women in Art

Fuller's artistic pursuits were favourably received when she arrived in France, in part because it was the time of the symbolist movement. In New York, when she had first danced the serpentine dance, critics had criticised it as a little too daring because of the transparent effect of the drapery which revealed her form when the stage was illuminated from the back (Current and Current 1997: 35). However in Paris the reputation of her dance was independent of its daringness. Instead, it came to be associated with the immateriality of the image or the sense of the ideal. According to Rastignac, a journalist writing in *L'Illustration*, Fuller was not as pretty as other famous dancers, but she was superior to the living, an unreal apparition as in paintings by Mantegna, not a woman of flesh and blood (Rastignac 1893: 26). He thought that the dancer lacked personality, but looked like a phantom symbolising 'ideal visions of eternity'.[5] Describing her dance as 'like a direct instrument of thought',[6] Mallarmé went so far as to compare it to hieroglyphics. There is a clear discontinuity in the style of poets' admiration for dancers before and after Fuller. Whereas Baudelaire and Gautier emphasised their palpable humanity, in the age of Mallarmé and Yeats what mattered was that the dancer was 'not a woman' (Kermode 1961: 71).[7]

However, the timing of Fuller's arrival in Europe proved to be good for another reason. Her debut in Paris in 1892 also coincided with the emergence of Art Nouveau, the subjects of which were drawn from nature, their lines flowing and sinuous, with an abundance of motifs inspired by a women's face, body or dress. Through her unique combination of light and motion, Fuller was Art Nouveau personified. Her dance, inspired by natural elements like fire, lilies, butterflies or clouds, effectively represented its spirit. A number of contemporary artists represented her in the form of paintings, sculptures, glass, ceramics, porcelain, jewellery and medallions. Clearly not every item featuring a butterfly-woman or a woman-flower was a representation of Fuller herself, but the motif of the woman with a supple body, ample robe and massive hair was 'the major obsession of the art of 1900' (Quiguer 1979: 26). As can be seen in Chéret's posters for merchandise or performances, the figure of the woman, be it as a consumer or as an object of admiration, was particularly popular in advertisements.

According to Claude Quiguer, the proliferation of such figures can be interpreted as the expression of men's desire to rediscover their attachment to the primitive and the organic. They do not reflect women's empowerment, but rather evoke the perpetual tension between women and society (ibid.: 28). However, Fuller herself was not passive in the midst of this flood of female iconography. Sometimes she commissioned artists herself and paid for their representations of her. She was also very aware of their use as advertising. The most famous items are the posters of her by Chéret, the sculptures by Pierre Roche and the bronze table lamps by François-Raoul Larche. Furthermore, after her success at the Folies-Bergère, her performances also inspired contemporary fashions (like Loïe Fuller skirts, Loïe Fuller hats and so on), which further contributed to her fame as a form of unintentional advertising.

It is interesting to note that while her image was to be found on a personal level in merchandise throughout the city, it was also transformed into a general, impersonal artistic motif at the Paris Exposition of 1900. A statue of Fuller was built on the pediment of the Palais de la Danse, one of the pavilions of the Exposition. In addition, Fuller was the only one of all the famous female entertainers at the Exposition to have her own theatre in the Exposition venue. A strange little building put up in six weeks, its façade was entirely covered with undulant plaster drapes and on the top was a life-sized statue of Fuller (Lista 1994: 331–51; Current and Current 1997: 134–37). She had definitively risen beyond the music hall and become recognised as a first class artist.

On the occasion of the Exposition, Fuller exerted her talent as an impresario. Wanting something fresh and provocative, she contacted a troupe of Japanese actors, Kawakami Otojiro and his company, who had been a success in New York and London (Chiba 1992; Lista 1994: 361–68; Current and Current 1997: 141–43; *Kawakami Otojiro* 2000). Kawakami's company featured the actress Sada Yacco, his wife, who was subsequently compared to Sarah Bernhardt. In Fuller's theatre, the troupe performed a one-act playlet, *The Geisha and the Knight*, a mixture of two well-known ancient Japanese tales, with a special emphasis on the death scene. The audience generally liked the contrast between the Japanese play and the American dance style, finding that the juxtaposition of two extremes – Japanese realism and American idealism – intensified the overall dramatic effect (Mauclair 1900: 283).

Although Fuller apparently never advocated female suffrage or other women's rights, her struggle and determination promoted the place of women in the theatre world, or at least such was the opinion of some contemporary journalists. For example, Judith Gautier, in an article in *Femina* (Gautier 1901: 324), emphasised the fact that, even though Japanese theatre (by which she meant kabuki) was originally created by women, women had not been allowed on stage in Japan for a long time and Sada Yacco was the first to defy the tradition.[8] Arguably, then, Fuller helped to advance the cause of Japanese actresses' rights, since Sada Yacco's brilliant success in New York, London and, above all, Paris enhanced the status of the actress in Japan. Even if Fuller herself did not consider her work in terms of women's liberation, Jules Clarétie, writing about *La Tragédie de Salomé*, described the performance as 'a vision of the theatre of the future, something like a feminist theatre' (Clarétie 1907).

Fuller and the 'Electricity Fairy' ('la Fée électricité')

During the nineteenth century, there were a number of developments in stage lighting, and when Fuller began to perform, different kinds of lighting were still used in parallel. Lighting with coal gas, introduced at the beginning of the century, and widespread by 1850, had the advantage of being brighter than oil lamps and centrally controllable, though it was polluting and dangerous. Limelight, with a beam which could focus on a single area on stage, became common in the 1850s. It competed with the arc lamp, the earliest form of electric illumination, which was more mobile and powerful than limelight. The incandescent lamp invented by Thomas Edison was adopted in European and American theatres during the 1880s and 1890s, but gaslights, arc lights and limelights continued to be used for certain effects. In France, spectacular effects were mostly developed in *féeries* and romantic ballets. Fuller herself was very aware of how she revolutionised the staging of dance by means of electric lighting.

Fuller had some knowledge of spectacular lighting effects from her experiences as an actress in the 1880s. She did not invent anything new in terms of technical equipment, but she developed new applications that she usually kept secret (Current and Current 1997: 94–96). Instead of using footlights or borderlights, she relied mainly on spotlights and magic lanterns. Her spotlights were common ones using a rotating disk with coloured gelatine circles around the edge; but she had secret ways of tinting the gelatine, to blend and dissolve the colours projected. She also made the slides of plain or frosted glass for her magic-lantern projectors herself. On them, she printed for example the photographs of the moon that she used for the 'cloud dance'.[9] In addition to these items, she invented a pedestal with a glass top upon which dancers, when lit from below, seemed suspended in air, and made an arrangement of mirrors to create multiple images. Her techniques of dyeing and painting silk also contributed to her lighting effects. She even became interested in radium when she learned that the substance was luminous, and wrote to Pierre and Marie Curie, who let her know that it was too dangerous to use for her performances. Their advice did not discourage her from trying out other chemicals to get a similar effect, and in 1898 she built a little laboratory in her backyard to experiment with phosphorescent salts (Lista 1994: 324–25; Current and Current 1997: 153–56). The study of lighting remained an obsession throughout her career and, as Mallarmé pointed out, no one else managed to link 'industrial achievement' with 'an intoxication with art' by substituting coloured lighting effects for all other stage sets.[10]

Fuller's familiarity with electricity made her the perfect representation of the spirit of the Exposition of 1900. Electricity had been introduced to a large extent in the Exposition of 1881, but it was used in a much more conspicuous way in 1900. The elevator of the Eiffel Tour had been electrified, electric trains and moving sidewalks circulated in the Exposition venue, and the Paris metro opened in July 1900. Part of the Machine Palace of 1889 was converted into the Electricity Palace in 1900. Its iron and glass structure was retained, but its surface was extravagantly decorated and the statue of an 'electricity fairy' built on the top. In front of it, a rococo-style water tower with a grotto and a fountain was constructed, both of which were illuminated at night on Sundays and holidays. In 1900, then, the energy and magic of electricity acquired an aesthetic status, representing the instability and fluidity of the world. The Palace poured forth the magical fluid that gave light and life to the entire show. And electricity, dubbed 'the Electricity Fairy', was often associated with women because of its role in the home and its fluidity. As Paul Morand put it, 'Women are flowers with light bulbs. Flowers with light bulbs are women'.[11] The fluid energy of electricity seemed synonymous with the flowing dynamics of Fuller's dance style (Silverman 1989: 298–300; Current and Current 1997: 138). Fuller thus personified the convergence of this fluid energy with the woman motif of Art Nouveau.

The 'Other Worldly' Aspect of Fuller's Dance

Fuller's dance style also coincided with a fascination for the spirit world. The end of the nineteenth century was a period of great scientific progress, but occultism and spiritualism still attracted much interest. In the 1890s, the human unconscious was being discovered through research into hypnotism, mediums and hysteria by Jean-Martin Charcot and Hippolyte Bernheim, and hypnotism became a very popular subject. When Fuller first performed her serpentine dance in New York, she played a widow whom a quack doctor tries to hypnotise. For this fantasy scene she dressed in a white silk robe and danced in a greenish light to soft, monotonous music. Her dance was a great success.

Fuller's first performance at the Folies-Bergère in 1892 was composed of four dances: 'the serpentine dance', 'the violet', 'the butterfly' and 'XXXX' also called the 'ghost dance'. As the title suggests, the last dance represented the evocation of spirits. Her style of dance, which caused the materiality of the body to vanish, was appropriate for expressing the spirit world. She also achieved other ghostly effects by using the magic lantern for lighting. Traditionally, magic lantern shows in fairs featured strange figures such as devils and ghosts, appearing out of the darkness. In the rational age of electricity it was more and more difficult to treat devils and ghosts seriously, but Fuller continued to exploit the possibilities of the magic lantern, creating works of fantasy out of this paradox.[12] In the 1920s, she used the shadowgraph and the magic lantern to express the suffering, destruction and death brought about by the Great War. *Les Ombres gigantesques* (1922), a fantasy ballet full of threatening shadows, is one of her works from this period.

Fuller's interest in the spirit world was also cultivated through her friendship with Camille Flammarion (1842–1925), a popular French astronomer of the time. Flammarion initiated her, not only to the relationship between colours and life, but also to the notion of the 'other world'. He published works on spiritualism and was a devoted collaborator of *La Revue Spirite*.

The term 'fairy' applied to electricity was not simply rhetorical, because in 1900 the natural and the occult sciences were not completely separated, even in the most advanced scientific circles. The development of research in psychology was closely related to the effects of rapid industrialisation, and the interest in organic, craft products and interior decoration that informed Art Nouveau can be considered a reaction against urbanisation. In an article about Fuller's performance in 1893, Rastignac declared, 'We always need dreams. When we cannot find them in poetry, we look for them in the delights of a café-concert. A dancer incarnates in her performance all the rêveries which can no longer be found in our terrible, hard modern life today'.[13]

In conclusion, what were Loïe Fuller's achievements? She arrived in Paris in 1892 as a thirty-year-old American dancer, without an official training in either dance or electric lighting, and innovated the dance scene. Although she contributed little in terms of the technique or language of dance, her achievements are to be found in every aspect surrounding dancing itself: stage set design (including lighting and costume), business sense, and the acquisition of respectability. In the midst of symbolism and Art Nouveau, she provided the motif of the dancer's ethereal body and was praised as a personification of these movements. However, her greatest quality was arguably her independent, original approach to work. Her stage works mark a fascinating intersection of magic and science, physics and metaphysics, professionalism and amateurism. Loïe Fuller was thus undoubtedly one of the main contributors to the multidimensional culture of the Belle Epoque.

Notes

1. For biographical information on Loïe Fuller, see Lista (1994) and Current and Current (1997).
2. According to Koritz, 'when middle-class women began to earn their livings as dancers, they rejected the role of erotic display in their performances, thus bringing with them to dance an ideology of woman's nature

and woman's place that conflicted with the dominant view of women on stage' (Koritz 1995: 6–7).

3. 'L'exquis fantôme accourt, s'enfuit, revient, se promène dans les ondes polychromes des effluves électriques. Il rase le sol avec la légèreté de la libellule, – sautille, se pose à peine comme un oiseau, s'avance, porté, croirait-on, sur la roue de la Fortune, – glisse en secouant ses ailes tremblantes, à la façon d'une chauve-souris' (Marx 1893: 107–8, approximate translation in Current and Current 1997: 57).

4. She wrote that she had just passed her twentieth birthday at the time of the first serpentine dance in 1891. She was actually going on thirty (Fuller 1908: 31).

5. 'l'idéal des visions de l'infini' (Rastignac 1893: 26).

6. 'comme un instrument direct d'idée' (Mallarmé 1945c [ca. 1896]: 312).

7. 'A savoir que la danseuse *n'est pas une femme qui danse*, pour ces motifs juxtaposés qu'elle *n'est pas une femme*...' (Mallarmé 1945a [1893]: 304).

8. In Japan, after a decree banning women from the stage in 1629, female roles were traditionally played by male actors. (This remains true today in kabuki.) Women were readmitted on stage only in 1891.

9. Magic lanterns and shadow plays acquired special importance in her works in the 1920s.

10. 'un accomplissement industriel'; 'une ivresse d'art' (Mallarmé 1945b [1886]: 307).

11. 'Les femmes sont des fleurs à ampoules. Les fleurs à ampoule sont des femmes' (Morand 1981 [1930]: 351)

12. Her phantasmagoria have something in common with the work of Georges Méliès (Ezra 2000: 109–15). Fuller herself became interested in cinematography after 1920 and made three films, *Le Lys de la vie* (1920–21), *Visions de rêve* (1924–25) and *Les Incertitudes de Coppelius* (1927), in collaboration with Gab Sorère. According to Lista (1994: 80), the latter two remained incomplete.

13. 'Tant qu'il est vrai qu'on a toujours besoin de rêve. Quand on ne le trouve pas dans les vers des poètes, on va le chercher dans les divertissements d'un café-concert. Une danseuse qui passe incarne toutes les songeries que ne donne plus la terrible vie actuelle, la dure vie moderne' (Rastignac 1893: 26).

CHAPTER 9

BECOMING WOMEN: CINEMA, GENDER AND TECHNOLOGY

Elizabeth Ezra

In 1898, the Parisian surgeon Eugène-Louis Doyen had himself filmed while performing a hysterectomy. His intention, at least initially, was to use this film, one of a group of six thought to be the first surgical films ever made, for training purposes. However, by 1907, this film was making the rounds of travelling fairground film exhibitors, where it was shown in a tent made up to look like an operating theatre, replete with wax anatomical figures, into which viewers were ushered by actors dressed as nurses and hospital interns (Meusy 1995: 123–24).

Doyen's films raise several issues concerning the often imbricated roles of gender and technology in film history. The connection between the birth of cinema and medical science is not limited to the shared billing between cinema and the new technology of X-rays as fairground attractions at the turn of the twentieth century. Auguste Lumière devoted much of his life to medical research, and it was this research, rather than the invention of cinema, that he apparently considered his crowning achievement (Cartwright 1995: 1). It is well known that the Lumière brothers refused to sell the patent to their innovative camera-projector to the likes of Georges Méliès at the historic first paying public film screening in December 1895, precisely because they felt that the new medium's greatest potential lay in its scientific applications rather than in entertainment. But what happens when science becomes a form of entertainment? Is it an accident that this convergence so often exploits sexual difference, indeed relies upon sexual difference for its entertainment value? At the turn of the century, Dr Doyen wrote in his magisterial *Surgical Therapeutics and Operative Technique* that '[s]urgery should ever remain an Art: all Surgeons should be true Artists' (Doyen 1917: 17). This paper seeks to ask to what extent this art and other forms of bodily manipulation have specific implications for women.

As film history has shown, despite this initial setback, Méliès would go on to make some five hundred films, including several that depicted the construction from ordinary objects of artificial women, who were then brought to life Pygmalion-like. These Pygmalion films, and films that show the dissection of women, are products of the same gendered discourse in which women are transformed into the objects of technological manipulation, or made and unmade. Such a discourse merges anatomical scrutiny and erotic spectacle, and, as we shall see, its strong presence in films made during the Belle Epoque would serve as a model for films made throughout the twentieth century.

Cut/Splice

In *Sexual Visions*, Ludmilla Jordanova contends that the practice of medicine is 'allied with privacy' while images of women are associated with public culture (Jordanova 1989: 134–36). I would add that it is precisely when medical science represents the female body that this private discipline is often turned into public spectacle. For example, Lisa Cartwright has pointed out that, although the inventor of the X-ray, Wilhelm Roentgen, X-rayed his own hand, it was the X-ray image of his wife's hand, taken in 1896, that was widely circulated in at first the medical, and then the popular press: 'Among the many physicians who immediately repeated Roentgen's experiments, a woman's hand, sometimes captioned as "a lady's hand"... became a popular test object' (Cartwright 1995: 115). Beth Gordon has observed that 'the public of 1895 was fascinated by the body and all of its phenomenal pathologies' (Gordon 2001: 188). We might ask to what extent this interest in pathologies real and imagined existed within a gendered framework. Méliès' *Escamotage d'une dame chez Robert-Houdin* (*The Vanishing Lady*, 1896), perhaps the best-known 'trick' film of all time, relies for its entertainment value on both the gender of the disappearing subject, played by Jehanne d'Alcy (Figure 9.1), and her reappearance as a skeleton, which gives the magician a fright. This hide-and-seek anatomy lesson perfectly emblematised the popular combination of masculine scrutiny (masquerading as 'X-ray vision') and sensationalised eroticism. From the often-discussed example of Charcot's visual studies of hysteria at the Salpêtrière to the *gommeuses*, or epileptic-like female dancers that populated Toulouse-Lautrec's work, to Bertha Roentgen's X-rayed hand: all these Belle Epoque representations of the body, whether explicitly or implicitly medicalised, are specifically gendered.

The early operation film can be situated in the context of the nineteenth-century passion for dissecting women. Elza Adamowicz (2001: 22) describes a turn-of-the-century fairground exhibit displaying 'the waxwork of a cataract operation where the disembodied hand of an assistant holds open the eye of an apparently compliant woman that the director's scalpel prepares to pierce'. Images of similarly 'compliant' women being fragmented and scrutinised were also prevalent in the more elite arts of painting and literature. Elaine Showalter has noted that men 'gain control over an elusive and threatening

Figure 9.1 *Escamotage d'une dame chez Robert-Houdin* (Georges Méliès 1896). Courtesy of the British Film Institute.

femininity by turning the woman into a "case" to be opened or shut. The criminal slashes with his knife. The scientist and doctor open the woman up with the scalpel or pierce her with the stake. The artist or writer penetrates the female case with sharp-honed imagery and the phallic pen' (Showalter 1991: 134). To this list, it is no great leap to add the filmmaker, whose tendency to divide the female body into part-objects has been widely commented upon. Richard Abel has pointed out that, when Dr Doyen took his camera operator to court for selling the operation films as his own, 'the court ruled that, because he had "first arranged his subject and planned the setting", Doyen was the principal author of these films, which were indeed worthy of legal protection. Within the framework provided by education, surgeon and filmmaker became analogous, not only as teachers, but as artists' (Abel 1990: 87). It is not necessary to rehearse the rather obvious parallels between filmic cutting and splicing on the one hand, and dissecting and manipulating (in particular, women's) body parts on the other, in order to appreciate the relevance of these operations for film studies, even from the very beginning. The first known example of a cut from one shot to another occurred in *The Execution of Mary Queen of Scots* (Alfred Clark, 1895), at the precise moment of decapitation (Salt 1996: 171).

One difficulty posed by these films is analogous to that experienced by literary scholars who wish to do a Freudian analysis of Sophocles' *Oedipus Rex*: the almost unavoidable risk of descending into tautology. What does it mean to say that these images are 'about penetrating the female body' when they are so *obviously* about penetrating the female body? One approach might be to read the operation scenes as a projection of the castration fantasy onto women's bodies. If women have no phallus, the story goes, then it must have been cut off; and images of women being cut open are the closest thing to performing this fantasmatic operation while remaining within the bounds of suspended disbelief. In this sense (when it relies upon sexual difference for its entertainment value), it is not inappropriate to regard the operation film as a kind of slasher film, and surgery as the new pornography. Carol Clover has pointed out that in the late twentieth-century slasher film, the victim 'is at her most effective in a state of undress, borne down upon by a blatantly phallic murderer ...' (Clover 1987: 206).

The tradition within French cinema of films that show women being cut (almost always by men) has continued throughout the twentieth century. One of the most notable examples of the genre is Franju's *Les Yeux sans visage* (1959), in which a surgeon kidnaps young women and removes their faces so he can graft them onto his daughter, who has been disfigured in an accident. In Godard's *Alphaville* (1965), Lemmy Caution shoots holes through the breasts of a naked woman in a pinup picture, illustrating the penetrating gaze of the shooting gun/camera and of the man who eyes the woman holding the picture. Later in the film, a group of male scientists file past a larger-than-life-sized photo of a naked woman in a display case. Finally, women's status as a conglomeration of part-objects is illustrated in the film when a woman stands on a conference table, only her legs visible in the frame, as she is stared at matter-of-factly by a group of lab-coated scientists. Roger Vadim's *Barbarella* (1968) literalises the concept of cutting, in the famous scene in which little doll-creatures hurl hundreds of tiny blades into the flesh of the eponymous heroine.

In a more recent film, cutting is overtly represented as a form of popular entertainment that harks back to the Belle Epoque. Patrice Leconte's *La Fille sur le pont* (1999) is about a romance between a knife-thrower and his assistant who, although she escapes serious injury, almost always gets nicked, in scenes that are invariably followed by a tender ritual of bandaging the wound. Another woman, a bride in full wedding regalia, is not so lucky (or perhaps, the film suggests, she is even luckier): she gets stabbed in the thigh while spinning on a wheel, blood seeping through her formerly virginal white gown in a none-too-subtle image of deflowering. This film is only making explicit, indeed playing on, a long tradition of eroticised cutting of women in French film history. Certainly a great many science fiction films, including relatively recent English-language films made by French directors, such as *Alien Resurrection* (1997) directed by Jean-Pierre Jeunet and *The Fifth Element* (1997) directed by Luc Besson, depict female characters splayed out on operating tables. These two films represent both strands of the tendency to make and unmake women on screen: in Jeunet's film, the 'perfect' creature Leelou is created by a team of scientists out of a fragment of DNA, and in the Besson film, Ripley is subjected to a Caesarian-like operation in order to remove an alien creature from her abdomen.

The late twentieth-century films described above have their antecedents in the Belle Epoque, particularly in the work of Méliès. Rae Beth Gordon suggests that Méliès may have been

'consciously drawing on medical science for his images of dismemberment, multiplication of the self, and convulsive movement' (Gordon 2001: 176–77), and that the filmmaker 'was not
unaware that these cinematic images might well remind spectators of [hysteria and epilepsy]' (ibid: 177). However, there is a
crucial distinction between portrayals of dismembered men
and dismembered women in Méliès' films. The magician figure
himself is shown losing his head on several occasions (in, for
example, *L'Homme de têtes* [1898], *L'Homme à la tête de
caoutchouc* [1902] and *Mélomane* [1903]). However, the magician always removes his own head, thus demonstrating that he
is in control, whereas women's heads are removed and/or
attached by the magician (as in *Fantasia Florida/Bouquet d'illusions* [1901] and *Les Illusions funambulesques/Extraordinary Illusions* [1903]). Similarly, women do not dress and undress
themselves, but are often shown having clothes thrown on
them or taken off them magically by the magician, in another
figure of making and unmaking. Méliès 'makes women' of
them, for example, when, in *Les Quat'cents farces du diable/The
Merry Frolics of Satan* (1906), the wizard Alcofribas removes the
outer garments of his seven, apparently male, wizardly assistants – the Seven Deadly Sins – thus revealing them to be
women. It can also be argued that Méliès was 'creating'
women from the (perhaps apocryphal) moment his camera
jammed in the Place de l'Opéra, with the subsequent jump cut
showing men appearing to change sex. The 'construction' of
women is at the heart of the castration fantasy: women are not
simply born as women, but instead fashioned into women
through dismemberment. (According to this fantasy, anatomi-
cally correct women do not exist prior to their dismemberment:
it is castration that makes women of them.) The castration
fable is actually a replay of the Adam and Eve story, in which
woman is a fabrication. The castrating gesture, imagined by
men, is then projected onto women in the male fantasy that a
woman is the perpetrator of the dismemberment.

The 'making and unmaking' of machine-like women in
films from the Belle Epoque to the present confers a kind of
power to men that can be undermined by the presence of
actual women. Women in Méliès' films are largely divided
between those who pose a threat – witches, evil fairies, nefari-
ous goddesses inclined to gobble up men – and those who are
entirely in thrall to a man: magician's assistants (conjured out
of thin air, made to levitate, or brought to life from an inanimate state); Blue Beard's wives dangling from ropes; benevo-

lent sea goddesses; and celestial creatures bearing aloft stars and planets. Both types of woman feature in one of the last films Méliès ever made, *A la Conquête du Pôle* (1912), which proposes two starkly dichotomised alternatives for women: as celestial helpmeets ushering the male explorers' space ships along, or as intrusive feminists who want to muscle in on the action. The latter are masculine, trouser-clad caricatures, suggesting that adventure and initiative are the antithesis of femininity, which is allied with ethereal affability and the desire to be of assistance to men (see Ezra 2000: 89–115).

In 'The Work of Art in the Age of Mechanical Reproduction', Walter Benjamin compared the filmmaker to a surgeon who 'penetrates deeply' into his subject, which 'consists of multiple fragments which are reassembled under a new law' (1978: 233–34). This impulse to dissect is intimately connected to the fantasy of (re)assembly. Some of the Méliès films that show the construction of a woman from spare parts also show her exploding into a shower of feathers or scraps of paper. For example, in *Les Illusions funambulesques* (1903), a conjurer assembles a woman from inanimate body parts before bringing her to life; after several more transformations in which she apparently eludes the magician's control, she disintegrates into a swirl of paper fragments before reforming. She then turns into a male chef, whom the magician rips to pieces. Her transformation into a male may diminish the violent impact of the image, but the ultimate impression is nonetheless one of a woman (originally constructed by the Méliès character, but who momentarily escapes his control) being torn to bits.

The same impulse that leads to depictions of anatomical scrutiny and the dismemberment of women in these films is also behind the images of constructed women in films of the Pygmalion or Frankenstein's monster variety. Linda Williams has drawn a parallel between Méliès' interest in automata (in his purchase and maintenance of several robots sold with the Robert-Houdin theatre) and his recreation of the Lumières' *cinématographe* when he failed to purchase the machine from its inventors at the Grand Café in 1895: '… Méliès seems to have been fated to repeat the invention/construction of machines capable of ever more perfect and lifelike simulations of the human body …' (Williams 1986: 525). The filmmaker would go on to explore this interest in creating and recreating bodies – particularly female bodies – in the films themselves. *La Statue animée*, for example, combines the Pygmalion story with detailed examination of a woman's body. In this 1903 film, a magician figure assembles the statue of a woman from a spinning ball, a handkerchief and a coat. When a drawing instructor enters with a group of students who proceed to inspect and draw the 'statue', it comes to life and mischievously steals the instructor's hat, before disappearing. The statue, created by the trickster magician, is clearly carrying out his wishes by foiling his rival. In *La Photographie électrique à distance/Long Distance Wireless Photography* (1908), Méliès plays an inventor who creates a magical camera that reproduces a life-size image of three women in a Three Graces pose from a small photograph, and that can also replicate the movements of a live model, as if televised. The 'televised' image, however, is clearly an idealised version of the all-too-human, and less obliging, human original. According to Linda Williams: 'The apparatus which makes possible "long distance wireless photography" packages the real-life bodies of women into safely proffered cheesecake tableaux. Individual female bodies become the simple stereotypes of femaleness which uniformly differ from the male' (Williams 1986: 529). For Williams, the machine that this film (and others like it) highlights is one that reproduces images of women's bodies; that is certainly true, but it is also important to recognise that these constructed women are also machines in themselves, which do exactly what they are programmed to do, and whose behaviour differs noticeably from that of real women. As Lucy Fischer puts it, in Méliès' films, 'woman (as woman) is gone, with only the male-fabricated image remaining' (Fischer 1996: 39).

Making Women Up

The 'male-fabricated image' discussed by Fischer is precisely the objective of dismemberment in many of the films described above. Even when the desire to manipulate women's bodies is not expressed literally in images of female mannequins being assembled by men, it is expressed metaphorically, through references to makeup. Such expressions evoke women's role in the debates about artifice and nature, and the nature of artifice, which have raged throughout first literary, and then cinematic, history. Baudelaire's notorious essay, 'Eloge du maquillage', follows in the tradition of Ovid's *Ars Amatoria* by singing the praises of women's cosmetics, though Baudelaire goes farther than Ovid in suggesting that, without the aid of a considerable amount of artifice, women are too horrible to contemplate. For Baudelaire, 'Woman must borrow from all the arts the means of elevating herself above nature, the better to capture hearts and make an impression on the mind. It matters little whether the ruse and the artifice are known to all, if they lead to certain success and an irresistible effect' (Baudelaire 1885: 102).[1] Conversely, in *Les Belles Poupées*, Théodore de Banville laments the erasure of 'natural' hierarchies effected by the use of makeup and other accoutrements of fashion: 'These days, all women look alike: the good, the bad, the gorgeous, the mediocre, and the horrible. They are painted, tinted, coiffed, tattooed and coloured by the same disgusting artifice' (Banville 1888: 340).[2]

In the French filmic tradition, women who are man-made (or remade, as in the case of the *Pygmalion/My-Fair-Lady*-inspired *Nikita* [Besson, 1990], whose heroine's personality is reshaped by a man) invariably receive a cosmetic makeover as part of the package. When the priest's assistant in *The Fifth Element* brings Leeloo a selection of women's clothing that the priest just happens to have lying around the house, he hands her, in addition, an instant makeup applicator. In between learning English and memorising crucial events in world history, Leeloo takes a moment to press the contraption to her face, which instantly becomes fully made up. This scene probably parodies, and in any case certainly recalls, scenes in other films in which the heroine's 'civilising process' includes a cosmetic makeover. In *Nikita*, for example, a central moment of the female protagonist's transformation (from rebellious criminal to docile, state-sponsored criminal) occurs when Jeanne Moreau, in a cameo role, instructs Nikita in the fine art – and, this being a French film, the philosophical lessons – of applying lipstick. As Moreau tells Nikita upon meeting her for the first time, 'Don't worry; we'll end up giving you a human form, which is an intermediate but nonetheless necessary stage before becoming the essential thing for man: a woman'.[3] In this exchange, paradoxically, artifice is humanising, in much the same way that it appears to be for Baudelaire. But in order to become fully human, artifice alone does not suffice. Humanity, for women, requires vulnerability. Moments after showing Nikita how to apply lipstick, Moreau adds, 'Let yourself succumb to that small fragility that will embellish your face: a smile ...'[4]

The application of makeup always proves to be merely an external sign of a less tangible transformation within. In the Belle Epoque and beyond, one of the most important steps in a constructed woman's evolution is that of becoming fragile or vulnerable. For example, in *The Fifth Element*, we see a medium close-up of the bewildered priest confiding to a bartender that he finds Leeloo, though 'the perfect being', oddly vulnerable and (he searches for the right word) '... human'. When he asks the bartender if he knows what he means, the camera swivels to reveal the bartender, a robot, who shakes his head. Besson's film here parodies science fiction's conventional interrogation of what it means to be human, but it also points up the nature of the gender roles inherent in the genre. Although Leeloo is the most 'perfect' creature in the universe, with more genes per square inch than any human (according to the film's 'scientific' logic, more is better when it comes to genes), her gender makes it imperative for her to evolve into a less perfect, more vulnerable and thus, the implication is, more feminine, creature in the course of the film. Belle Epoque precedents for such displays of feminine vulnerability abound. Trick films in particular, in which a male magician conjures women out of thin air, invariably convey the impression that the magician is 'taming' the woman, making her comply to his vision of what a woman should be. In *Bulles de savon animées/Soap Bubbles* (1906), Méliès makes women appear in a column of smoke, and then makes women's heads appear in soap bubbles that float up to pedestals, where they grow both bodies and wings. The illusionist then transforms them into butterfly kites, which he waves before flicking them away. The women are not seen again.

So, men may create women who are, in a sense, automatic, but they must not be autonomous. In these films, a woman's accession to humanity is achieved by her acquisition or assumption of stereotypically 'feminine' traits such as vulnerability, emotiveness and subservience. In Belle Epoque films this subservience, or at the very least pliability, is usually accompanied by sexual availability, either implicitly or explicitly, as in *Les Illusions funambulesques* (1903), when a life-sized doll comes to life the moment she is kissed by the magician. In later films, this vulnerability usually culminates in the woman's confession of love to the man, a speech-act that serves to make the woman less machine-like and more obtainable. We see this, for example, in Cocteau's *La Belle et la Bête* (1946), where Belle's words 'Je t'aime' bring the Beast back to life but at the same time demonstrate that she has yielded to him. A variation of this linguistic phenomenon occurs at the end of *Alphaville*, when Lemmy turns to Natasha as they are speeding away from the city in his Ford Galaxy and says, 'Think of the word "love"'. Once Natasha is able to conceptualise the magic word, she relinquishes both her apparent automatism and her autonomy; her transformation from unfeeling automaton to vulnerable woman in thrall to a man is complete. At the end of *The Fifth Element*, although it is Korben who must tell Leeloo he loves her, the survival of the world still depends on her acceptance of his declaration, which hinges on her succumbing to his charms. Such scenes of seduction are often accompanied by scenes in which the woman is shown learning to cry, which is emblematic of her acquired vulnerability. We see just such a teary apprenticeship in *The Fifth Element*, and in Kieslowski's *Bleu* (1993), in which a bereaved Juliette Binoche finally sheds a tear as she succumbs romantically to her dead husband's colleague.

Women begin these films as machine-like creatures either literally, in that they are cobbled together by a scientist or magician, or figuratively, in that they display an antisocial coldness. Both in the Belle Epoque films and in these later films, women are artificial creatures created by men, who can then breathe life into them, or 'humanise' them. It seems to matter little whether the women start out subservient or autonomous, that is, whether they serve another or themselves: they all ultimately end up serving the same master. Misogyny in these films is linked to a fear of technology and dehumanisation, which transforms autonomous women into automatic women. In *The Culture of the Copy*, Hillel Schwarz defines the main attributes of automata: 'Not physiognomy but responsiveness, sociability, sincerity have been at issue ... The more agile we become at replicating animate beings, the more we look to qualities social or immaterial (loyalty, love, despair, boredom, competitiveness, confusion) to tell ourselves from our creations ...' (Schwarz 1996: 360). In 'becoming women', the creatures in these films are made to relinquish their hyperbolic rationality and assume their traditional role in the conventionally gendered division of the Cartesian mind/body split. Women and technology, or the super-rational, have an analogous function, and are therefore conflated in these films: they are both desirable and threatening, potential sources of dismemberment (according to the castration fantasy) and destruction. Women are more reassuringly rendered as pure corporeal dummies, like the female mannequin named Francine that René Descartes took travelling with him on voyages (see Frude 1983: 121).

A 1997 film dramatising Marie Curie's discovery of radium, Claude Pinoteau's *Les Palmes de M. Schutz,* addresses the theme of gender and science in a chronological loop from the turn of the twentieth century to the turn of the twenty-first. One memorable scene depicts the meeting (which probably took place in 1901) of Curie and Loïe Fuller who dances, covered in electric light bulbs, after announcing that she wants to 'be phosphorescent'. Here, a woman wears the fruits of technological advancement on her body, like the Electricity Fairy that adorned the 1900 Paris Exposition. Technology thus merges with the woman's body – as the body of Marie Curie, woman of science, will, by the time of her death in 1934, practically glow from its prolonged exposure to radium. The electric light bulbs attached to Loïe Fuller may evoke the *lumières,* or enlightenment, not traditionally associated with women in the gendered Cartesian split, but here they are used as decoration, like so many spangles or sequins. Similarly, the women whose bodies were held up for inspection in science and in cinema were not themselves admitted to the exclusive fraternity of scientists and filmmakers. Their literal inclusion in the frame or under the microscope obscured their widespread social exclusion from the professional process of creation, thus making the achievements of Belle Epoque women such as Marie Curie (and, indeed, Madeleine Pelletier) all the more remarkable.

Notes

1. '[La femme] doit donc emprunter à tous les arts les moyens de s'élever au-dessus de la nature pour mieux subjuguer les coeurs et frapper les esprits. Il importe fort peu que la ruse et l'artifice soient connus de tous, si le succès en est certain et l'effet toujours irrésistible' (Baudelaire 1885: 102).
2. 'A présent, toutes les femmes se ressemblent, la bonne, la mauvause, la sublime, la médiocre et la pire. Elles sont peintes, teintes, coiffées, tatouées et coloriées par les mêmes ignobles artifices...' (Banville 1988: 340).
3. '... nous finirons sûrement par vous donner une forme humaine, étape intermédiaire et néanmoins nécessaire avant de devenir l'essentiel de l'homme: une femme.'
4. 'Laissez-vous envahir par cette petite fragilité qui va embellir votre visage, un sourire ...'

PART III

WOMEN AND SPECTACLE

CHAPTER 10

SPECTACLES OF THEMSELVES: WOMEN WRITING FOR THE STAGE IN BELLE EPOQUE FRANCE

Kimberly van Noort

Exoticised, desired, feared, vilified or celebrated, the Belle Epoque was obsessed by the figure of woman-as-spectacle. While women in the public sphere constituted the most visible objects of society's gaze – whether on stage, in the café, on the street or behind the feminist pulpit – the explosion of women's magazines and the advertisements they contained increasingly invaded the private domain, offered prying eyes the spectacle of women accomplishing the tasks of bourgeois femininity. As Martine Antle comments, the Belle Epoque 'rests principally on the staging and the exploitation of the feminine body' (Antle 1997: 9).[1] Whether decoratively arranged in her salon, carefully deployed on the promenade or strategically displayed on the stage, women and their bodies provided the background and the fuel for what Antle calls the 'Belle Epoque mythology of woman', namely the image of the ideal woman, freely consenting to her specularisation (ibid.: 9).[2] One of the most insidious and detrimental effects of this fetishisation of woman as object of the gaze was the obliteration of the concrete realities of women in general. This chapter will explore the specularisation of women by turning to the work of those women who were arguably the most 'looked-at': women in the theatre.[3]

While cinema in its infancy was already showing signs of fascination with women's bodies, theatre still remained the most important and influential form of popular entertainment at the time of the Belle Epoque. And stage actresses were the most visible, most identifiable of women. Indeed, much has been written on actresses, their social positions and the roles in which they were cast.[4] Little attention, however, has been given to women playwrights and their representations of the way women see and are seen, nor to the activism displayed by those working for the promotion of plays written by women. Yet arguably, the increased visibility of women playwrights after the First World War, and certainly after the Second, was prepared by Belle Epoque dramatists who managed theatres, organised dramatic societies and actively supported their colleagues. Rachilde, Jane Catulle Mendès, Marguerite Durand, Renée Vivien and Lucie Delarue-Mardrus were among those active in the theatre of the Belle Epoque. Feminist activists such as Nelly Roussel, Caroline Rémy (writing as Séverine) and Vera Starkoff wrote and staged plays. Sarah Bernhardt owned and managed several theatres, including the Théâtre de la Renaissance (1893–98) and the Théâtre Sarah Bernhardt, where she was at the helm from 1899 to 1921; and Gabrielle Réju (Réjane) established the Théâtre Réjane in 1906. Many of these women, particularly Rachilde, Durand and Bernhardt, also worked for the promotion of women playwrights, and many were involved in independent theatre productions and societies. This study examines, first the situation of the Paris stage at the end of the nineteenth century, then the plays written by the great actress, Sarah Bernhardt, then the activities of the group of women playwrights, the Association de Femmes Auteurs Dramatiques, known as La Halte.

The Paris Stage

Theatre has historically been the genre most resistant to female authors, and taking up the dramatist's pen at the time of the Belle Epoque already constituted a rebellious gesture. Despite the earlier successes of a handful of women playwrights such as George Sand and Delphine de Girardin, the stage remained virtually closed to women writers. In addition, theatre itself in France generally remained a closed shop. While increasing numbers of young authors wrote plays, their

chances of gaining access to both principal and minor theatres was next to impossible (Carlson 1972: 177). As a result,
numerous independent theatrical societies sprang up, institut-
ing the practice of matinee presentations showcasing new talent. From these societies sprang the main avant-garde
movements of the fin de siècle: Antoine's Théâtre Libre and
Lugné-Poe's Théâtre de l'Oeuvre.[5] However these venues
remained marginal and the Parisian stage was dominated by
the traditional programming of the Comédie-Française and
the stock melodramas of the other major theatres.[6]

At the same time, theatre was undergoing changes which
had an impact on both the nature of the theatre experience
and the role of the actress/female role as specular object. Most
importantly, in the mid-1880s theatres began dimming the
house lights. Public and critical outcry was swift and loud,
pointing to the still dominant view of theatre as a primarily
social rather than artistic experience. Even the actresses and
actors protested, objecting that their (specular) interactions
with the audience had been eliminated, thus diminishing
their art (Hemmings 1993: 32–45). Arguably, however, the
gradual dimming of the house lights, by focusing the gaze of
the spectator, contributed to an increased specularisation and
objectification of those on stage.

Women's roles on stage, meanwhile, were principally limited to the stock repertoire of seventeenth-century tragedy,
Romantic drama and comedy, and melodrama. As Bernhardt
herself lamented, actresses were presented with little choice
outside the roles of punished adulteress, suffering wife or pure
but victimised virgin (Bernhardt 1993: 140). These roles
elicited and conditioned the spectator's gaze, be it one of
desire, adulation, pity or disgust. Nevertheless actresses
retained a certain freedom and agency in their interpretation
of these roles, and Bernhardt's writings on the theatre focus in
large part upon the actress' ability to determine, at least in
part, the audience's reaction. In addition, theatres of the
period sometimes literally survived due to the drawing power
of their major actresses. Plays were written specifically to
showcase certain actresses, and audiences flocking to see their
favourite star may have been less attentive or attracted to the
role she was playing.

Lenard Berlanstein argues that, during the Belle Epoque,
attitudes towards women in the theatre underwent significant
change, in a move he terms a 're-gendering of the theatrical
experience' (Berlanstein 2001: 168). Increased numbers of

female spectators accompanied a shift in opinion regarding the social status of the actress, who gained new respectability due to her increased visibility off stage. Photographs of actresses proliferated, as did the demand for their endorsements of mainly beauty products in the rapidly growing advertising industry. Women went to the theatre to see the latest in fashion or to judge the benefits of products advertised (ibid: 168). At the same time, the growing cult of celebrity prompted the media to portray the private lives of actresses, often in scenes of bourgeois respectability which corresponded to the powerful discourse of domestication levied toward all women at the time. The result was the rehabilitation of the actress/courtesan model into one that the most respectable of female spectators could admit to admiring (ibid: 167). Thus, theatrical space was effectively de-sexualised and, theoretically, could offer more subjective agency to both the female spectator and the actress.

However, as John Stokes points out, the attempt to understand and reconstruct codes of 'looking' different from those of our own time is fraught with difficulties (Stokes et al. 1988: 4). An examination of acting techniques may help determine both what the actress sought to convey and what audience reactions were intended. Many contemporary commentators and theatre historians have remarked upon the 'statuesque' quality of many actresses' techniques (Horville 1977: 43–44). The popularity of the meaningful pose, the sudden adoption and maintenance of an often artificial stance at critical moments, is evident both from the surviving still images of plays and from contemporary comments (Stokes et al. 1988: 8). Both the technique of playing a statue and its valorisation by the press, including in photographic images, points to the continued offering up of the body of the actress to the gaze as an object to be either coveted or copied. This is the case, even when the body of the actress is cast in a male rather than a female role. Cross-dress roles ('en travesti') whereby an actress played an opposite sex role (to be differentiated from cross-dressing, which might have been more shocking), while not frequently seen on the stage were certainly not uncommon in Paris during the Belle Epoque and indeed expected for certain roles (Agate 1945: 158).[7] Réjane, Agar and most famously Bernhardt all played male roles, but, as Bernhardt remarks, they were invariably those of young, effeminate men like Hamlet and Lorenzaccio (Bernhardt 1993: 139–40). The male role may have actually contributed to the specularisation of the actress' body by distancing it from the woman herself, presenting a woman/actress, already staged, on stage in the role (but not the body) of a man.

Several of the leading actresses of the day who also wrote for the stage – Mlle Combier, Régine Martial, Henriette Dangeville (pseudonym Jean Séry), Marie Doumayrou (Renée Sigall) and, most important for this study, Sarah Bernhardt – wrote plays which focus on how women are seen by society. They often feature a female protagonist who is an actress, thus in a sense triply thematising the specular: a woman (already a spectacle), literally put on stage, and playing the role of an actress. By recognising and emphasising the larger role they had themselves been called upon to play, these actresses/playwrights offer valuable insight into the way women are constrained by being constructed as objects of the gaze, but can also draw on their specularisation for their own purposes. This is particularly evident in the work of Sarah Bernhardt, the very embodiment of the spectacle.

Sarah Bernhardt: Playwright

Bernhardt not only wrote several reasonably successful plays, she was the most 'visible' and looked at of actresses (perhaps of Belle Epoque women in general) and she displayed an acute consciousness of her role as a specular object, from which she profited both materially and ideologically (Figure 10.1). All Bernhardt's commentators, biographers and critics, admirers and detractors alike, dwell upon her seeming obsession with her own image.[8] Her reputation as a woman who staged herself and directed the staging of her public image is notorious. She emerges as the 'total' actress, both on and off the stage. But few have explored her self-obsession in relation to the opening up of the possibilities (albeit limited) of self-determination or at least self-conception to women during the Belle Epoque.

Berlanstein notes that Bernhardt began her career at a very crucial moment in the history of celebrity: 'She began to attract attention at the moment that early mass culture was born' (Berlanstein 2001: 219). From the eighteenth century actresses had enjoyed celebrity status, increasingly becoming what Berlanstein terms 'intimate strangers' by virtue of the biographical information circulated by the theatrical press. By the late nineteenth century, the proliferation of photographic images fuelled the growing cult-status of many actresses,

Figure 10.1 Postcard of Sarah Bernhardt in performance. Courtesy of the Bibliothèque Marguerite Durand.

including Bernhardt, Bartet, Réjane and Agar, and Bernhardt realised that power, for a woman, lay in the management of her own image as object of curiosity and desire. 'The central feature of this culture (early mass culture) was the representation of everyday life as the basis for commercial entertainment. Bernhardt offered up her eventful life for public consumption ... Her slender figure became a symbol of the nervousness of modern life' (Berlanstein 2001: 219). A pioneer of the self-fashioned woman using her public image to further her career, Bernhardt was immediately and vociferously attacked for having done so. Theatre critics were outraged at a woman who decided and orchestrated the terms of her own specularity and then profited from it. If Bernhardt was indeed as self-serving and egocentric as most of her critics suggest, the fact remains that she was hyper-conscious of the fact that the female body, and most acutely the actress' body, was a truly specular object, whose image reflected the needs and desires of the spectator and was reified or fetishised according to the structure of those desires. This lucidity is apparent in both her plays and her writings about the theatre, and provides a useful point of departure for a discussion of her work as a dramatist.

Several notable leitmotivs recur in all of Bernhardt's plays: the status of the actress, the strictures of marriage, women's sexual desires and the fetishisation of woman. Her first play, *L'Aveu* (*The Avowal*) (1888), a one-act piece first produced at the Odéon in 1888, deals with the punishment of a woman who, frustrated in her marriage, finds sexual satisfaction with another and has an illegitimate child.[9] At the opening of the play the child lies dangerously ill, and the heroine is shown agonising over the decision to tell her husband the truth in a desperate attempt to cleanse her soul and save the child. After her 'avowal', the husband reveals that he already knows her secret and has in fact given the child a lethal poison as punishment to her. Despite the highly melodramatic tone of the play, Bernhardt transmits a gritty portrait of the severe restraints placed upon women in marriage and of their dilemma when faced with sexual frustration. At the same time, the punishment, the death of the child, condemns the heroine to remain visible as the image of transgression, the spectacle of her grief embodying her deserved loss.

In *Adrienne Lecouvreur* (1907), Bernhardt revisits the thematics of women's desire, but from a different perspective, that of the refusal of a woman, here an actress, to bow to convention and her insistence (again fatal) on creating her own code of practice with regard to love and sexuality. *Adrienne Lecouvreur*, based upon the life of the eponymous eighteenth-century actress, rewrites and reworks the 1847 play of the same title by Scribe and Legouvé in which Bernhardt had starred many times (and which had originally been written for the great Rachel). Bernhardt thus re-envisions not only the story of her predecessor but her own previous role as the object of the gaze. Scribe's version focuses more on political intrigue and the comedy of manners, with the male lead dominating the stage; indeed, Adrienne herself does not appear until the second act. Bernhardt centres the action firmly on the concerns and experiences of the actress.

The play has a rather lengthy, complex plot, but the primary intrigue centres on Adrienne's long and very 'open' love affair with Maurice de Saxe. A highly successful actress, Adrienne is faced with hostility and rivalry on all fronts, despite her purity and innate generosity. Refusing to be baited into renouncing her love by the Duchesse de Bouillon, her rival for the affections of Maurice, she becomes the victim of an elaborate murder scheme. Bernhardt's Adrienne shares more than a few of the legendary attributes of her creator: acting represents

a total experience and the 'fragile' actress devotes so much
energy to her performances that her health is often compromised; surrounded by powerful men, including her patron
Voltaire, Adrienne nevertheless maintains an iron grip on her
artistic freedom.[10] She also displays a vivid understanding of
her position as an object of desire, a position created by the
gaze of others:

> [...] thanks to my career I am at the mercy of the public's love
> that I provoke by my play-acting of love; I attract the unstable
> and the mad. And my destiny chose that I love a hero, the man
> most seen and heard of in all Europe, and thus my love is
> turned over to public curiosity, to feminine jealousy, to the fick-
> leness of the pamphleteers.[11]

Equally compelling are Adrienne's progressive views on love
and male-female relations. While Scribe's Adrienne was a
stereotypical, dependent victim, Bernhardt's protagonist
rejects a conventional relationship with her wealthy lover:

> Duchesse: I do not know, Mademoiselle, who to envy more: the
> one who inspires such a passion or the one who feels it.
> Adrienne: She who feels it, Madame. My life resembles no
> other: I walk, eyes open, in an eternal dream. I hear only
> him, see only him, suffer only by and because of him.[12]

Adrienne reverses the paradigm and adopts the position of the
active, desiring lover, placing Maurice in that of the passion-
inspiring object. She refuses that her life be described along
conventional lines, according to a pre-established model. She
is not jealous of Maurice's many lovers, nor does she accept
that her image on stage be confused with her private self:

> Adrienne: O Madame, my rivals are all younger and more
> beautiful than I, but they are all great ladies, condemned to
> a thousand duties and always on their guard, belonging to a
> husband and a caste and required to bow before the wills of
> the king and of public opinion. Me, I am just an actress. I
> give myself to the public on stage, but at home I am entirely
> given to the being I love, without lies, hypocrisy or fear of
> blame; for I belong only to myself and I give myself wholly,
> body and spirit.[13]

By differentiating herself from her rivals she claims a desiring
position which, even as it entails a *chosen* submission to her
lover, allows her to determine the extent of her dependence on
him for happiness.

Two years after *Adrienne Lecouvreur*, Bernhardt's 1909 play, *Un coeur d'homme* (*A Man's Heart*), debuted at the Théâtre des Arts (Bernhardt 1911). In this play, Bernhardt again puts forth the themes of love, marriage, the autonomy of a strong, desiring woman and the objectification and specularisation of women. While the title seemingly promises a focus on the male hero, Paul, the play instead revolves around Jeanne, his wife's godmother and best friend, whom he passionately loves. The title functions as the first of the play's many substitutions and mirror images in which one thing or person stands in for another.

The play presents Jeanne's struggle both to resist Paul's overtures and to overcome her own desire for him. Ensconced in a stable if non-traditional marriage, she pinpoints Paul's tendency to reify and fetishise women, to make them into something they are not, and then to fall in love with that image: 'What you love in me is not myself, Jeanne de Valréal, but something else that I represent'.[14] Paul, a playwright, is clearly casting others in roles of his creation, envisioning her goddaughter Sabine as the suffocating, tyrannical wife and Jeanne herself as the older, more sensual, independent woman. Interestingly, though, Jeanne is indeed both herself and something else. After being rejected by Jeanne, Paul leaves Sabine and takes up with the beautiful socialite Ninon, an ornamental, narcissistic specular object played by the same actress as Jeanne (Blanche Dufrêne in the 1909 production). Paul confesses that a large part of his attraction to Ninon is based upon their resemblance and, in a key scene with Jeanne, dramatises Ninon's body in terms of Jeanne's:

> She has your eyes: but yours are more mysterious! Like you she has a rebel mane; she has the languor of your stride ... And when I have her in my arms, I clench my teeth, almost grimacing, in order not to murmur your name! And little by little it becomes you that I have before me; it is your breath that I breathe and I collapse in my drunken evocation.[15]

But the drama does not end there. Jeanne travels in disguise to Ninon's home in the hopes of persuading Paul to return to his wife and, unable to resist her passions, spends one night with him after seeing him in the arms of Ninon. It is as if the vision of her specularity, embodied by the woman who is her mirror image, unchains her desire. Self-objectification, a trait which, as John Berger argues, has been socialised as feminine, is recognised here as a source of pleasure, albeit ultimately dangerous and humiliating (Berger 1972: 22).

In the final act, Jeanne is happy to have brought Paul and Sabine back together, although she suffers from Paul's too-prompt substitution of his wife as love object. She has sacrificed her passion not from a belief in its immorality, but rather from a sense of solidarity with Sabine. Not only does she wish to ensure her goddaughter's happiness, she also wants to share with her an understanding of the facile duplicity of a man's heart. However, when Sabine learns that her husband's 'mystery' lover was none other than Jeanne, she rejects her, spitting in her face and calling her a 'bitch' ('sale femme'). Jeanne then throws herself out the window and falls to her death, destined to be unable to rid herself of the images of her created by others.

Bernhardt's plays, while neither financial nor critical successes, reveal that her consciousness of the position of women was more progressive than her critics would admit. By offering audiences images of women who refused the roles written for them by society and who seized the opportunity to become active, desiring subjects, Bernhardt contributed to the growing volume of writings about women's changing roles. Her plays also reveal, as Antle suggests (1997: 9), that the 'belle mythologie' of woman during the Belle Epoque, anchored in the specular image of women, was indeed just that, a mythology which blinded both contemporary and later spectators to the realities of women's lives.

La Halte

Although Bernhardt was perhaps the most visible of women playwrights, other women of the Belle Epoque were successfully writing plays and working to create venues for women as well. Among the several societies seeking to increase the exposure of new playwrights, one was administrated by and devoted to plays written by women: the Association des Auteurs Dramatiques Féminins, known as La Halte.[16] Founded in 1910 by Berthe Dangennes, this group regularly presented theatrical programmes at the Théâtre Michel on the rue des Mathurins. Dangennes, a novelist, essayist and playwright, oversaw the administration and production of the matinee programmes, which presented a variety of works: one-act plays, prose and verse monologues, saynètes, dance performances and operettas. La Halte recruited performers from the major theatres of Paris, including the Théâtre des Arts, the Théâtre Sarah-Bernhardt, the Théâtre Réjane, Vaudeville and others, to interpret the pieces. Works by Rachilde, Dangennes, Jeanne Fürrer, Nadige Nastri, Jane de la Vaudère, Judith Gautier, Jane Myrsand and André Guess, among others, were featured. In addition to the dramatic presentations, lectures sometimes opened or closed the programmes. Offerings included: 'Le Théâtre féminin' presented by M. Eddy Lévis; a presentation by M. Camille le Senne (Honorary President of the Association of Critics) and a lecture by Jane Catulle Mendès on 'women's psychology as seen by men' (Le Vassor 1912).[17]

La Halte appears to have had a respectable number of members and first Judith Gautier then Sarah Bernhardt were Honorary Presidents, although it is unclear how much they actually worked with the society. In addition to the theatrical programmes which were presented from 1910 to 1912, La Halte also held regular meetings: the 'Five O'Clock de la Halte' at the home of Dangennes where, according to the play lists: 'On the 14th of every month, the Members and Supporters of La Halte have the right to present their work, or have it presented, to the "Five O'Clocks of La Halte", before a public as select as numerous.'[18] Members were solicited to present plays and other works for consideration by the selection committee for inclusion in the Théâtre Michel programmes, and the group held at least one competition for which a prize of 200 francs was to be awarded to the best two-act play with six characters or less.[19]

While very few of the plays produced by La Halte made it to larger theatres or found publishers, the group's brief existence testifies to the increasing tendency of women writers to turn to the stage. These women quite openly put themselves and their dramatic works before the public eye, offering themselves as spectacle. This 'spectacle', however, like the plays of Bernhardt, seemed destined to throw back at the audience a mirror image of its regard. While little is known about the plays themselves, the physical format of the printed programmes is highly revealing (Figure 10.2). On their cover a young woman adorned in long flowing robes, arms bared, sits pensively in a chair rather oddly positioned near a quintessentially French road lined by chestnut trees. While overtly positioned as an object of desire, the image of the woman also conveys another message. One hand is decoratively lifted to her mouth, but the other holds a pen, showing the woman in the act of writing on a large open notebook. A lyre and a rolled sheaf of papers leans against the chair, attesting to her literary work. The contradictions of this image of a woman presented both as an object of the desiring gaze and as a writing subject mirrors the paradox offered by

Bernhardt – a calculated self-presentation which reveals the dramatist's/author's consciousness of the process of specularisation. Reinforcing this effect, the photos of Gautier and Dangennes which grace the covers of the programmes, and those of the playwrights themselves found inside, emphasise the specular while at the same time presenting the faces of the women who were the authors and patrons of these plays. The members of La Halte, by the very presentation of their work, signalled both a consciousness of themselves as objects and an affirmation of their place as autonomous creators.

While women of the Belle Epoque seemed destined to remain constricted by the conventions of specularity of the time – as objects of both a masculine and a feminine gaze – women in the theatre strove to produce and promote roles both on stage and off which offered the power of self-determination and subjectivity. By making a spectacle of themselves, as they wrote, produced, patronised and starred in plays written by women, they played an active role in the history of the period and passed on valuable insight into the creativity and lucidity of women of their time.

Figure 10.2 La Halte programme of 1911. Courtesy of the Bibliothèque Nationale de France.

Notes

1. 'repose principalement sur la mise en scène et l'exploitation du corps féminin'
2. 'mythologie de la femme à la Belle Epoque'
3. In this paper, I will be addressing mainstream theatre, although many of the observations made are applicable to both music hall and lyric theatre.
4. For an overview see Berlanstein (2001) and Martin-Fugier (2001).
5. For an overview of dramatic societies and avant-garde theatre during the Belle Epoque see Henderson (1971).
6. For an account of the plays produced, see Henderson (1971).
7. For an analysis of cross-dress roles in modern France, see Berlanstein (1996).
8. The number of works on Bernhardt is far too great to present an exhaustive list here. Among the best see Hahn (1930), Pronier (1942), Verneuil (1942), Taranow (1972) and Richardson (1977).
9. This play was also published under the title *The Holocaust* (*L'Holocauste*).
10. For an interesting perspective on Bernhardt's grip on her art, see Lavendan (1938: 57–63).
11. 'Et je suis au contraire, grâce à ma carrière, vouée à l'amour public que je fais naître par mon jeu d'amour; j'attire à moi les déséquilibrés et les fous. Et mon destin a voulu que ce soit un héros que j'aime, et ce héros est l'homme le plus en vue, le plus bruyant de l'Europe et mon amour est livré à la curiosité publique, à la jalousie féminine, à l'humour des pamphlétaires' (Bernhardt 1907, *Adrienne Lecouvreur* II, i).
12. 'Duchesse: Je ne sais, mademoiselle, lequel il faut le plus envier: celui qui inspire une telle passion ou celui qui la ressent.
    Adrienne: Celle qui la ressent, madame, ma vie ne ressemble à celle de personne: je marche les yeux ouverts dans un éternel rêve. Je n'entends que lui, je ne vois que lui, je ne souffre que par et pour lui' (ibid.: I, xi).
13. 'Adrienne: Oh madame, mes rivales sont toutes plus jeunes et plus belles que moi; mais ce sont des grandes dames soumises à mille devoirs et précautions, appartenant à un mari, à une caste, devant tenir compte de la volonté du roi, de l'opinion publique; moi, je suis une simple comédienne. Je me dois au public sur scène, mais, rentrée chez moi, je suis tout à l'être que j'aime sans mensonges, sans hypocrisies, sans crainte d'une blâme; car je ne suis qu'à moi, et je me donne toute, corps et âme' (ibid.: I, xi).
14. 'Ce que vous aimez en moi, ce n'est pas moi, Jeanne de Valréal, c'est l'autre chose que je vous représente' (Bernhardt 1911, *Un coeur d'homme* I, ii).
15. 'Elle a vos yeux: mais les vôtres sont plus mystérieux! Elle a, comme vous, une crinière rebelle; elle a la langueur de votre marche ... Et quand je l'ai sous mon étreinte, je serre mes dents jusqu'au grincement pour ne pas murmurer ton nom! Et, peu à peu, c'est vous que j'ai là sous mes yeux; c'est votre haleine que je respire et je m'effondre dans mon ivresse évocatrice!' (ibid.: III, x).
16. Should anyone know of other such societies, I would greatly appreciate receiving any information.
17. 'La psychologie des femmes vue par des hommes'.
18. 'Tous les 14 de chaque mois, les Membres et Adhérents de "La Halte" ont le droit de représenter ou faire représenter leurs oeuvres aux "Five O'clock de la Halte" devant un public aussi nombreux que sélect.'

19. Information about La Halte and its presentations was gleaned from programmes conserved at the Bibliothèque de l'Arsenal in Paris. Unfortunately, only programmes from about half of the known performances of
La Halte are conserved there and most of the plays were never published.
Other bits of information have been found in drama reviews of the
period. My thanks to the librarians of the Arsenal for helping in this
research.

CHAPTER 11

BEING A DANCER IN 1900: SIGN OF ALIENATION OR QUEST FOR AUTONOMY?

Hélène Laplace-Claverie

A number of dancers – both real and fictional – haunt the imaginary of the fin de siècle, in France and throughout Europe (Ducrey 1996). However, this almost exclusively masculine imaginary includes figures who are, to say the least, contradictory. Deified and disdained, idolised and stigmatised, the ballet dancer is an object of both fascination and repulsion. She may be the archetype of the femme fatale (evident in the incredible vogue for the role of Salomé in various artistic domains); but she also incarnates the darker side of a period which condemned her to be just 'a little woman who dances' (Colette 1913: 970), a proletarian of the *entrechat* destined to be both worker and courtesan.

Subject to the sexual pleasures of gentlemen in morning coats, trainee ballerinas at the Opera and music-hall artists alike got their revenge by proclaiming their freedom as independent women. Although they had to give up words in the exercise of their profession, they had plenty to say, as is evident in the testimonies some of them left behind, whether as memoirs or as fictionalised autobiographies. Whilst they may not have achieved the quality of Colette's texts devoted to music-hall entertainers – like *La Vagabonde* (1984 [1910]) or

L'Envers du music-hall (1913) – their books express, however clumsily, a female point of view on the tensions and ambiguities of the Belle Epoque (even though some of them were written and published much later).

For the purposes of this study, I will draw principally on *Le Ballet de ma vie* (1955) by Cléo de Mérode, *Mes cahiers bleus* by Liane de Pougy (published posthumously in 1977) and *My Life* (1927) by Isadora Duncan (translated into French in 1932).[1] Cléopâtre-Diane de Mérode (1875–1966) left the *corps de ballet* of the Paris Opera in 1898 in order to pursue an independent career in Europe. Considered the most beautiful woman of the period, her image was reproduced in thousands of copies in posters and postcards (Figure 11.1). Her love affairs gave rise to endless rumours which she tried in vain to refute in *Le Ballet de ma vie*. In contrast, Liane de Pougy (1869–1950) assumed her role as a celebrated demimondaine with panache (Figure 11.2). Born Anne-Marie Chassaigne, later Princess Ghika in 1910, then sister Anne-Marie-Madeleine de la Pénitence in 1945, Pougy clearly had an unusual career (Chalon 1994: passim), the first part of which was characterised both by her theatrical performances and her amorous intrigues. As for American dancer Isadora Duncan (1877–1927), she was indisputably the best known of the three. An expatriate in Europe from 1900 onwards, she invented a new form of dance, free from the canons of classical ballet, by returning to the roots of ancient Greek culture. But as her different writings show, she also proposed a reflection on the position of women in modern society.

At the time of the Belle Epoque, dancers were torn between licence and liberty,[2] and often made to pay dearly for their desire for independence. Unable to earn a proper living in such a risky profession, many of them found themselves back under the yoke of male power, escaping the authority of a husband to become the prey of a rich patron. Despite being muzzled, however, many of them wanted to write about their experiences, even if they had to wait years before doing so. For although the dancer, whose eloquence lies in her body, is by definition someone who does not write, and despite the stereotype of the illiterate beauty or 'illiterate ballerina' (Mallarmé 1945b [1893]: 307), the desire to write is not rare among the disciples of Terpsichore, muse of the dance. A need for intellectual and artistic recognition? A form of compensation? A desire for self-justification? After examining first Mérode, Pougy and Duncan's desire to write, then the contradictions of their lives, I hope to show that, far from being typical of the period, these dancers

Figure 11.1 Postcard of Cléo de Mérode, based on a photograph by Reutlinger. Courtesy of the Bibliothèque Marguerite Durand.

Figure 11.2 Postcard of Liane de Pougy, based on a photograph by Reutlinger. Courtesy of the Bibliothèque Marguerite Durand.

were out of step with the norm, which explains both their role
as precursors in terms of morality and the distrust they aroused
on the part of their (female) contemporaries.

The Desire to Write

Declaring oneself a writer when one is (or has been) a dancer
is a form of provocation. What artist could be further from the
world of words than the enchantress whose aesthetic skills are
accompanied by absolute silence? Yet Mérode, Pougy and Duncan proved that dancers can also be cultivated women, capable of wide reading and likely to frequent great writers (Marcel
Proust in the case of Mérode, Jean Lorrain and Max Jacob as
regards Pougy, Edward Gordon Craig and Serge Essenine in the
case of Duncan). Their love of literature sometimes translated
itself into the desire to write, giving rise to collections of memoirs or, more rarely, works of fiction, or even poetry.[3]
    In the preface to her autobiography, Duncan shows that
she is aware of the presumptuous nature of such an enterprise,
considering herself unworthy of such a noble art:

> I confess that when it was first proposed to me I had a terror of
> writing this book. [...] It has taken me years of struggle, hard
> work and research to learn to make one simple gesture, and I
> know enough about the Art of writing to realise that it would
> take me again just so many years of concentrated effort to write
> one simple, beautiful sentence (Duncan 1927: 1).[4]

The dancer's humility is not feigned. Drawing a parallel
between the language of literature and choreography, Duncan
suggests, like Stéphane Mallarmé, that these are each
demanding disciplines, the mastery of which requires hard
work, patience and application.
    Pougy's attitude to writing is quite different in that she does
not seem to question her literary competence. Thus, after setting
out to become a popular novelist in the late 1890s, she published a series of mediocre works without a qualm. First *L'Insaisissable* (1898), then *Myrrhille* (1899) and *Idylle saphique* (1901),
followed by *Ecce homo* (1903), *Les Sensations de Mademoiselle de
La Bringue* (1904), and finally *Yvée Lester* (1906) and *Yvée Jourdan*
(1908). What these texts have in common is their basis in autobiography, which is both their weakness and their strength. The
author draws her inspiration from the circles she frequented,

which allows her to provide thumbnail sketches of Parisian high society. The pseudonyms she uses scarcely attempt to fool the reader and the novels belong to the purest tradition of the *roman à clefs*, with all its pettiness, voyeurism, barely disguised settling of scores and complacent self-aggrandisement. Placed under the microscope of one of its own, the microcosm of Paris is just a pathetic theatre of shadows. But in *Mes cahiers bleus*, Pougy shows she was also capable of writing a moving tribute to postwar women, so different from the Belle Epoque coquettes:

> The thin little women of today, pale and sickly, a little blue around the eyes and nostrils, their chests sunk, their shoulders hunched, showing their tiny little legs and their frail bare arms, give the faint impression of mauve, trembling lilac.[5]

So the woman who is generally considered to be one of the models for Odette de Crécy in Proust's *A la recherche du temps perdu* (1954) had the nerve to act like a writer, even if it meant attracting gibes. For it was not the done thing for a woman to be a blue-stocking, especially if, like Pougy, she claimed a threefold right to freedom: the right to perform on stage, the right to lead a life which defied the moral standards of the day, and the right to make her voice heard by writing. Of the three forms of freedom exemplified by the artist, the courtesan and the woman of letters, the last was the most unacceptable in that it encroached on an intellectual universe usually reserved for men. Women could get away with being actresses or dancers, since these were inferior arts depending on interpretation and not creative powers. But claiming to be a writer was truly scandalous.

Mérode's *Le Ballet de ma vie* deserves a special status, since it was written for specific reasons. Almost eighty when it was published in 1955, the former dancer used her autobiography to dissipate a certain number of misunderstandings, correct errors and take stock of what many would call a steamy past. A member of the Belgian aristocracy,[6] young Cléo had become the talk of the town around 1896, following her supposed liaison with King Leopold II. The second chapter of her book goes back over this episode in order to demystify it. Comparing the rumour to a tunic of Nessus, she evokes the calumnies she was subjected to in the press and the ineffectiveness of her denials, with a mix of irritation, fatalism and pain. She found herself in a similarly humiliating situation on the occasion of other more or less sensational scandals, like the Falguière affair, named after the sculptor who in 1896 exhibited a statue of her completely naked. Though she protested that she had only posed for the head, malicious gossip went wild.[7] This type of controversy, the inevitable price of fame, was already the prerogative of Belle Epoque women who were admired and envied (the precursors of what the cinema industry would call 'stars'). Mérode's autobiography, then, offers the image of an old lady seeking to restore her integrity, and looking back on an extraordinary life in order to try and justify it in the eyes of polite society which, in 1900, had a certain idea of what a woman should be.

Between Licence and Liberty

The different female figures evoked here shared a desire for freedom which led to a refusal of women's position in society at the time of the Belle Epoque. Becoming a dancer meant choosing to perform on stage to earn a living. It was thus a rejection of the institution of marriage and its corollaries, principally motherhood.

This rejection is clear from the outset in Mérode's autobiography. Writing both on her destiny as a woman artist and on various social issues, she reveals that marriage for her was incompatible with a life dedicated to the theatre. Choosing one meant refusing the other, and in her case there seems to have been little hesitation, 'I loved liberty too much to tolerate the idea of becoming dependent on others one day'.[8] As a member of the corps de ballet of the Paris Opera, Mérode realised that financial independence was the sine qua non of freedom. Once she became a 'star', she decided to leave the Palais Garnier and perform in certain Parisian music-halls – notably the Folies-Bergère – where the financial rewards were greater. For financial reasons, too, she undertook numerous tours abroad (Germany, the United States, etc.), which implied sacrifices with regard to her private life. But such efforts were necessary for dancers wanting to enjoy real material independence; otherwise, they generally had no other choice but to turn to prostitution in one form or another. Mérode knew this was the price to pay to escape such a fate and she accepted it. She gave up marriage and maternity, and accepted solitude and a nomadic existence, the 'downside of fame'.[9] But in the bittersweet conclusion of *Le Ballet de ma vie*, the dominant impression is definitely one of accomplishment.

Duncan is even more virulent than Mérode on the topic of marriage, no doubt partly because of her parents' early divorce. However, personal trauma is not in itself enough to explain her objections to the yoke of matrimony. Even if it meant incurring the wrath of puritanical America, Duncan worked from an early age for the 'emancipation' of women, with the energy of an woman with a mission:

> [...] I decided, then and there, that I would live to fight against marriage and for the emancipation of women and for the right of every woman to have a child or children as it pleased her, and to uphold her right and her virtue. These may seem strange ideas for a little girl of twelve years old to reason out, but the circumstances of my life had made me very precocious (Duncan 1927: 17).[10]

She underlines her visionary lucidity on this matter:

> At the present time I believe my ideas are more or less those of every free-spirited woman, but twenty years ago my refusal to marry and my example in my own person of the right of the woman to bear children without marriage, created a considerable misunderstanding' (ibid: 18).[11]

This cult of personal freedom needs to be connected with the way Duncan translated it into her art. By inventing 'free dance', she got rid of the constraints imposed on women's bodies both in society (through the wearing of corsets) and in classic dance (with its anti-natural positions, codified gestures, shoes for dancing on points, etc.). Indeed, her influence in this domain has been crucial (Allard 1997).

Pougy's *Mes cahiers bleus* is a diary kept from 1919 onwards (though not published until 1977) which intersperses her self-portrait with memories of the past. Her attitude to marriage is coloured by the fact that, as her biographer Jean Chalon has shown, she experienced her own marriage as a young woman as an irreversible trauma. Her wedding night, paradoxically the night when lovemaking is legal, was experienced as a rape, incarnating for ever, in her eyes, the loss of innocence. In a previously unpublished phrase quoted by Chalon, she declared, 'Married at seventeen, innocent and ignorant, I must have received a nervous shock at too young an age and my subconscious remembers it and bemoans it'.[12] In contrast, she presents her ostentatious career as a dancer-courtesan as a form of liberation, or rather as a way of assuming her intellectual, social and sexual freedom as a woman.

The disillusionment with marriage was even more dramatic when it led to a second, even more painful ordeal, that of pregnancy and childbirth. Like Duncan, Pougy perceived this double event as a long nightmare. The two women formulated their disgust and revolt at women's sacrosanct reproductive mission with the same violence. Refusing biology as destiny, they denounced the unbearable nature of such bodily violence as an act of aggression, a sacrifice imposed from without, a renunciation of personal fulfilment in order to *give* birth. The expression 'give birth' ('*donner la vie*' in French) is revealing in that giving birth means putting one's own life at risk, metaphorically if not literally. It means risking being dispossessed, no longer existing except by proxy through one's progeny.

Nevertheless, there are two important differences between Pougy and Duncan. While Pougy admits to having no maternal instinct whatsoever, to the extent that she abandoned husband and child without a shadow of remorse,[13] Duncan experienced motherhood as a revelation. After dying a thousand deaths in childbirth, which she describes as the most appalling torture, worthy of the Spanish Inquisition, she forgot it all once the child appeared. And far from feeling imprisoned and alienated, she was convinced that she was accomplishing her destiny as a woman.[14] In addition, unlike Pougy, Duncan used her experiences to make a universal claim for women's rights, as illustrated by her statements about childbirth:

> It is unheard-of, uncivilised barbarism, that any woman should be forced to bear such monstruous torture. It should be remedied. It should be stopped. It is simply absurd that with our modern science painless childbirth does not exist as a matter of course. [...] What unholy patience, or lack of intelligence, have women in general that they should for one moment endure this outrageous massacre of themselves? (Duncan 1927: 195).[15]

Condemning male hypocrisy, Duncan sets herself up as a spokesperson for the cause of women (even if she denies being a *feminist*, a word with too many connotations for her in the American context). To do this, she does not hesitate to transgress certain religious taboos – like the (in)famous biblical judgement, 'in sorrow thou shalt bring forth children' – whilst remaining aware of the risks involved in such a declaration of independence. The problem of being an unmarried mother in a rigid patriarchal society is one which many women artists had to resolve during the Belle Epoque. And for want of alternative solutions, many had to resign themselves to living off their charms. They had chosen to be artists in order to escape male authority, but they found themselves, in an ironic twist of fate, obliged to seduce a rich patron to meet their needs.

This situation with regard to actresses is well known and has been analysed recently by Anne Martin-Fugier (2001). The lot of dancers was just as bad, since their pay was as low – particularly at the Opera – and their careers as vulnerable. Hence the need to procure other sources of income and accept all sorts of compromises. Even Mérode, who gives an idealised vision of her trajectory, frequently intimates how sordid life on the other side of the stage could be (as when she evokes her peers in the corps de ballet of the Paris Opera).

The Exception, Not the Rule

How unusual were the lives of women dancers in the context of the Belle Epoque? One answer might be found in the text Colette devotes to Isadora Duncan in her posthumous collection *Paysages et portraits* (2002 [1958]: 173–77). Colette insists first of all on the solitude of the rebellious dancer, condemned to launch herself on to the stage against the backdrop of 'oppressive, greenish-grey curtains with no way out and which open just to let her pass through, so little and so alone ...'.[16] But this impression of vulnerability is immediately cancelled out by the wild energy she deploys. Comparing her 'aggressive, stubborn' knee to a 'ram's head', Colette likens her performance as a whole to a 'bacchanalian orgy'.[17]

However, the main interest of the text lies elsewhere, in Colette's look at the women in the auditorium. Turning away from the dancer on stage, Colette sets out to depict the reactions of the women in the audience:

> Watching all these women applauding Isadora Duncan makes me think how strange women are. Half-risen to better shout out their enthusiasm, they lean over, bound, helmeted, collared and unrecognisable, towards the little creature naked beneath her veils, firmly upright on her irreproachable light feet, her smooth hair loose ...
>
> Make no mistake about it! They are cheering her, but they do not envy her. They acknowledge her from afar, and watch her with admiration, but as an escapee, not a liberator.[18]

In this extract, Colette distinguishes two types of women through their contrasting styles of dress. While Duncan is 'naked beneath her veils', the women watching remain imprisoned in their corsets and 'helmets'. The military metaphor suggests, in addition to strict discipline, the tyranny of pseudo-finery as a form of transvestism. 'Unrecognisable', the hostages of social codes determined by men, these women seem dispossessed of their own image. Furthermore, they are seated or 'half-risen', whereas Isidora stays firmly upright, her head free, her hair loose. Their bearing and posture reveal the extent to which each is alienated.

The second paragraph confirms the dichotomy between two opposing female worlds. If one perpetuates the tradition of an outmoded past, the other looks forward to the period following the Great War, synonymous for women with social and professional progress. Another, geographical, antithesis is also in play, given that Isadora, the wild American, has come to shake up the overly restrained Parisians. As Chalon (1954) notes, the archetypal figure of the 'Parisienne', emblem of the Belle Epoque, is truly ambiguous. It symbolises 'the accomplishment of their highest hopes for women conscious of having a destiny',[19] but it transforms those women into the 'pure products' of a consumerist epoch. Pougy was often told, 'You're a work of art',[20] and treated like an object for export, representing France's image abroad like a perfume or a haute couture dress (Laplace-Claverie 2001).

This theme can be further illustrated with reference to the famous Russian Ballets, which delighted Paris from 1909 onwards. Roland Huesca (2001) demonstrates the ambivalent role reserved for women within the audiences of these Ballets. Openly exhibited as icons, they were both overvalued and exploited to various ends: 'Deprived of power, but cultivating aestheticism, women made their mark on these evenings. Their acquired, well-ordered beauty incarnated a somatic culture where the play of power and money could be read'.[21] His argument echoes certain pages of Zola's *Nana* (1880), which shows the ravages caused by prostitution in Parisian high society. Female beauty within the theatre setting had become a marketable investment, a sort of 'woman-share' in the stock-market sense of the word.

It is worth recalling that Gabriel Astruc, promoter of the first season of the Russian Ballets, had equipped the Théâtre du Châtelet with a 'corbeille', or dress circle, for the event. The term 'corbeille' (which also means 'basket') designates the trading-floor of the Palais Brongniart, headquarters of the Paris stock exchange. In its new context it designated part of the auditorium situated just below the circle, where Astruc assembled a throng of pretty girls to flatter the gaze of male spectators. The *Figaro* reviewed it thus:

> A delicious innovation to the circle caresses the eye as soon as one enters, obviously due to the inventive mind of the prestigious Master of our springtime Revels, Gabriel Astruc: a 'corbeille', a real 'corbeille' without a single black coat, bald head or beard; exquisite shoulders, dresses in an adorable harmony of colours, a cascade of precious stones shimmering on creamy flesh: the prettiest women in Paris.[22]

Unashamedly using the female body for promotional purposes, the 'corbeille' at the Théâtre du Châtelet marked the apotheosis of woman as object, her individuality denied, as Astruc's own account of his tactics confirms:

> I had exhibited the fifty-two prettiest actresses in Paris in the front row, alternating blonde and dark manes of hair, which brought applause from the orchestra stalls even before the curtain went up! On the upper level a second 'corbeille' was lit up by little ballet dancers from the Opera, invited as a body [...][23]

Thus the 'fruit' laid out in Astruc's 'corbeille' ('basket') were young trainee actresses and dancers, reduced to the status of animals (as in the use of the word 'manes' to describe their hair) and treated as an indistinguishable mass (as in the allusion to a 'body' of ballet dancers). The situation was all the more humiliating in that these young women, condemned to be extras in the auditorium of the Châtelet, all aspired to be applauded for their performance on stage, as artists.

To conclude, the status of women writer-dancers at the Belle Epoque was founded on three paradoxes. First, as silent dancers they tried to make themselves heard by becoming writers, even years after the end of their careers; second, as women they tried to conquer their freedom by going on the stage, but often sunk into a more demeaning state of dependence than in marriage; and third, their incarnations of the idealised image of the Artist was completely out of synch with the realities of women's lives. These three paradoxes are fundamental to the modern age, and the twentieth century would try, with more or less success, to address them.

Translated by Carrie Tarr

Notes

1. It would be interesting to draw on the testimonies of other dancers such as Caroline Otero (1926) and Loïe Fuller (1913), and to compare female points of view with those of writers such as Jean Lorrain, Maurice Barrès, Jean de Tinan, Joris-Karl Huysmans or Pierre Louÿs, all of whom represent the fascination exercised by dancers in the period 1880–1914; but this is outside the scope of the present study.

2. An allusion to an expression used by Jean Chalon in his biography of Liane de Pougy, 'Licence excludes all forms of liberty' ('La licence exclut toute liberté') (Chalon 1994: 42).

3. In *Mes cahiers bleus*, Pougy draws attention to a 'sensitive, well-written book of verse' ('un livre de vers, sensibles et bien faits') published by one of her rivals, Emilienne d'Alençon (Pougy 1977: 54).

4. J'avoue que j'éprouvai, quand on me proposa d'écrire ce livre, une véritable terreur. [...]
   Il m'a fallu des années de lutte, de travail acharné et de recherches pour apprendre à faire un seul et simple geste, et je sais assez ce que c'est que l'art d'écrire pour me rendre compte qu'il me faudrait encore autant d'années d'effort tenace pour écrire une seule phrase, simple et belle (Duncan 1932: 7).

5. Les petites femmes d'aujourd'hui, étroites, malingres et blanches, un peu bleuies sous les yeux et aux ailes du nez, la poitrine rentrée, les épaules légèrement voûtées, montrant leurs petites jambes menues, la nudité de leurs bras frêles, donnent l'impression fragile du lilas mauve et tremblant (Pougy 1977: 104).

6. Cléo de Mérode is thus her real patronymic and not a 'nom de guerre' with a particule, as was the case for Liane de Pougy and Emilienne d'Alençon.

7. This episode gave rise to a very interesting exchange of letters between Mallarmé and Georges Rodenbach (Mallarmé 1949: 144–48).

8. 'J'aimais trop la liberté pour supporter l'idée d'avoir un jour à dépendre d'autrui' (Mérode 1955: 274).

9. 'revers de la célébrité' (ibid.: 353).

10. [...] je décidai une fois pour toutes que je consacrerais ma vie à combattre le mariage, à lutter pour l'émancipation des femmes, pour le droit de toutes les femmes à avoir un ou plusieurs enfants quand elles le voudraient, et à conserver leur droit et leur honneur. Ce sont des idées qui peuvent paraître étranges chez une petite fille de douze ans, mais les circonstances de la vie m'avaient rendu précoce (Duncan 1932: 24).

11. J'imagine qu'aujourd'hui mes idées sont plus ou moins celles de toutes les femmes affranchies, mais, il y a vingt ans, mon refus de me marier et l'exemple que je donnais par moi-même pour une femme d'avoir des enfants sans être mariée, suscitèrent une indignation générale (ibid.: 25).

12. 'Mariée à dix-sept ans, innocente, ignorante, j'ai dû recevoir un choc nerveux trop tôt et mon subconscient qui se souvient se lamente' (Chalon 1994: 29).

13. Remorse was to come later, when her son, aviator Marc Poupe, was killed on the field of battle during the Great War.

14. On this point, and on the unspeakable wrench felt by the dancer on the death of her two children, see Maurice Lever (1987).

15. 'C'est une barbarie inouïe, une barbarie de sauvages que les femmes soient encore forcées de supporter des tortures aussi monstrueuses. Il

faudrait remédier à cela. Il faut que cela cesse. Il est tout simplement absurde qu'avec notre science moderne l'enfantement sans douleur ne soit pas la règle. [...] Il faut vraiment que les femmes aient une patience ridicule ou un manque complet d'intelligence pour accepter un instant cet effroyable massacre d'elles-mêmes!' (Duncan 1932: 197).

16. 'de rideaux gris verdâtre, d'accablants rideaux sans issue qui s'entrouvrent seulement pour la laisser passer, si petite et si seule...' (Colette 2002 [1958]: 149).

17. 'agressif et têtu'; 'front de bélier'; 'bacchanale' (ibid.: 150).

18. 'Je songe à la bizarrerie féminine, en regardant toutes ces femmes qui applaudissent Isadora Duncan. Levées à demi pour mieux crier leur enthousiasme, elles se penchent ligotées, casquées, colletées, méconnaissables, vers la petite créature nue dans ses voiles, debout sur ses pieds intacts et légers, et dont les cheveux lisses se dénouent...

    Qu'on ne s'y trompe pas! Elles l'acclament, mais ne l'envient point. Elles la saluent de loin et la contemplent, mais comme une évadée, non comme une libératrice' (ibid.: 153–54).

19. 'l'accomplissement du suprême espoir de toute femme consciente d'avoir un destin' (Chalon 1994: 37).

20. 'Vous êtes un objet d'art' (ibid.: 41).

21. 'Privée de pouvoir, mais cultivant l'esthétisme, la femme marque de son empreinte ces soirées. Accumulée et ordonnée, sa beauté incarne une culture somatique où se lisent les jeux du pouvoir et de l'argent' (Huesca 2001: 14–15).

22. Au balcon, une innovation caresse délicieusement l'œil dès l'entrée. On y reconnaît l'esprit inventif du prestigieux intendant de nos Menus Plaisirs printaniers, j'ai nommé Gabriel Astruc: une corbeille, une vraie corbeille, sans un seul habit noir, sans un seul crâne, sans une seule barbe; des épaules exquises, des robes d'une harmonie de ton adorable, un ruissellement de pierreries qui miroitent sur les chairs laiteuses: les plus jolies femmes de Paris (Brévannes 1909).

23. J'avais 'exposé', au premier rang, les cinquante-deux plus jolies comédiennes de Paris et organisé l'alternance des toisons blondes et des chevelures brunes, ce qui fit éclater les applaudissements de l'orchestre dès avant le lever de rideau! A l'étage supérieur s'épanouissait une seconde 'corbeille' formée par les petites ballerines de l'Opéra, invitées en corps [...] (Astruc 1931).

≈ CHAPTER *12* ≈

VISIONS OF RECIPROCITY IN THE WORK OF CAMILLE CLAUDEL

Angela Ryan

Writing in 2002, Odile Ayral-Clause sums up as follows some aspects of Camille Claudel's unique contribution to women's creative representation and to nineteenth and twentieth-century sculpture:

> Defiance was probably the most visible characteristic of Camille Claudel. She defied the prejudiced society in which she lived in almost every step she took: her choice of a career in sculpture; her entrance into a previously all-male atelier and a liaison with the master of this atelier; her determination to sculpt the nude with as much freedom as her male counterparts; her persistence in soliciting state commissions for works that were sure to offend the warped notion of propriety favored by male officials. Each of these choices challenged the prejudices of Claudel's time (Ayral-Clause 2002: 256–57).

Claudel's artistic heritage is even today a challenge to received ideas about the taste and sensibility of the Belle Epoque. Her work is as far from the iconography of Art Nouveau as from the poster-art or cinematic representations of the human body, particularly the female body. Her chosen mode was sculpture and, even more unusually for a woman, she worked within its full range: this is one measure of her genius, and explains why her work cannot be located too closely in the period's aesthetic

models. Sculpture is by its nature more drawn to the intempo-
ral, especially in the case of large or monumental pieces. This
is not to say that Claudel did not innovate, but that she
insisted on working in the mainstream rather than being confined to the category of 'woman artist'. One would not expect
to find reflected in her sculpture of stone, marble or precious
materials the ephemeral aspects of Belle Epoque fashions, or
trends found in genres whose medium is less enduring. Typical
Belle Epoque women are not to be found there. What is radical and transformative in her work is her modelling of the
intimate space in which people communicate, her passionate
and spiritual treatment of the body, of human flesh, and her
representation of loving interaction; and her achievement is
due in part to her representation both of the female body and
of the male-female couple in a de-commodified mode,
through the construction of intimacy or eroticism freed of
stereotypical 'male gaze' voyeurism.

This chapter will look at two sculptures, *Sakountala* and *Les
Causeuses*, masterpieces of Camille Claudel's 'Belle Epoque' of
personal and artistic freedom (before her sequestration in
1913), with particular regard as to how they represent the
female as both narrative subject and subject of the dramatic
situation, and in so doing offer a new vision of human relations. It will further look at two aspects of Claudel's particular
constraints as a female creator. First, the question of the men-
toring of the woman artist, since Claudel's reputation and success suffered so much from her close association with another,
male, sculptor (Auguste Rodin), and secondly, the question of
the reception and autonomy of the radical female artist since,
after her relations with Rodin became hostile, she was excluded
from social contact by her family's exploitation of the laws of
that time concerning psychiatric institutionalisation.

Sakountala (Figure 12.1), shown at the 1888 Salon, consists of
a pair of larger than life-size figures, and derives its title from the
heroine of the fifth-century Hindu drama of a Brahmin girl, Sakountala, loved by the king Duchmanta. When a curse wiped out
Duchmanta's memory, Sakountala, not recognised as his wife,
was forced to hide in the forest and bear her child there; only the
ring Duchmanta had given her could restore his memory, but it
had been lost in the lake. It was found years later by a fisherman
and the lovers were reunited. The sculpture depicts this moment
of union. It was very well received, winning an honourable mention at a period when women faced enormous barriers in such a
male-dominated area.[1] *Les Causeuses* (Figure 12.2), a small-size

Figure 12.1 *Sakountala*, Camille Claudel. Photography by Bruno Jarret. Courtesy of the ADAGP and DACS.

Figure 12.2 *Les Causeuses*, Camille Claudel. Photography by Bruno Jarret. Courtesy of the ADAGP and DACS.

sculpture representing a group of women in conversation, sheltered by a screen, was created in 1895, carved in marble in 1896 and in onyx in 1898. It was also well received, according to Monique Laurent (1988: 77), for its originality and for the artist's technical brilliance.

These two works are characteristic examples of Claudel's unique treatment: the representation of erotic (but non-phallocentric) passion between man and woman in the first case, and the interaction of women in the other. In addition, they show her ranging between the large-scale *Sakountala* and the exquisite small-scale carving in onyx of *Les Causeuses*. This is also evidence of the difficulties she faced as a woman artist at that period:

> The critics who condemned her for not being able to create a new style, as Maillol and Brancusi did, failed to understand that her battle was focused in a different direction. As a woman of the nineteenth century, she came up against the social and artistic limits imposed upon her. She struggled endlessly to be accepted as a sculptor in her own right, without any gender qualifications and restrictions. This is probably why she returned to large works even though she had created small-scale masterpieces with *Les Causeuses* and *La Vague*. Knowing that only large works were viewed as worthy of a great sculptor and that miniature sculpture was often branded as decorative or 'feminine', she abandoned a genre in which she showed real innovation. As it is, Claudel left behind sculptures that were frequently as daring as any of Rodin's yet endowed with their own distinctive spirituality (Ayral-Clause 2002: 257).

Sakountala

The sculpture *Sakountala* was greeted with enthusiasm in 1888 by critics such as André Michel and Paul Leroi, as well as by Claudel's brother, the poet Paul Claudel. It represents the two bodies of Duchmanta and Sakountala united by passion and tenderness, the reciprocity of their emotion refusing any polarised signification of gender, age, power or nature. Both bodies are represented with softness; the right-hand male has something of Pan, with the goat-like modelling around the genitals, and this is further suggested by the way the left-hand female figure has a hand brushing against the tail-like technical element. They are configured as enlaced together in a common space-volume (a three-dimensional area shaped like an irregular ovoid taking in all the most projecting points of the body as represented), the dynamism of which is reciprocal from all points of view. The regard, touch and response of each to each is shared, not given by one and endured or yielded by the other. One of them is higher placed, bending over the other, but with no apparent signification of hierarchy. This rare union of force and delicacy in the exchange of emotion reminds one of Browning's:

> And a voice less loud, through its joys and fears
> Then the two hearts beating, each to each!
>
> (Browning 1991: 358)

A contrast may be made for illustration with Rodin's *L'Eternelle idole* (Figure 12.3), also a pair of figures in close erotic contact. Here, however, the woman as subject is absent. The female figure is very differently configured spatially in relation to the male: she leans back, hands holding her feet, as if enduring his attentions. He is positioned within her space-volume, while she does not move into his. The way she is represented – the doll-

Figure 12.3 *L'Eternelle idole*, August Rodin. Photography by Bruno Jarret. Courtesy of the ADAGP and DACS.

like gravity-defying breasts, the withdrawn expression and the lack of reciprocal regard – make her a sexual object, not subject.

A striking feature of *Sakountala* is its semiotics of reciprocity. Each figure is portrayed as received into the other's space-volume. Duchmanta's body from waist to brow is positioned within the curve formed by Sakountala's body from brow to knee. Sakountala's arms reach into the space-volume of Duchmanta's body: the sharing of bodily space-volume is such that she can at the same time cover her breast, and embrace him. His arms encircle her and his face reaches up to her in a pose that combines both abandon and clasp: she leans towards him and bows her head so that their faces touch, each of them equally abandoned to the other, with neither passivity or aggression on either side. The particularly beautiful modelling of muscle in Duchmanta's arms, shoulders, back and buttocks represents strength and also abandon, seizing her in, and at the same time yielding to, an embrace. His body is straining up to meet hers, whilst hers is flexed downwards to meet his, yet the most careful examination of the modelling of muscular action cannot see any overreaching on either part. He exerts muscular force to reach up against gravity and she, to bend down against gravity: each strains to reach, touch, embrace and mingle with the other, whilst at no point invading the other or appropriating the other's control of their own space-volume. This, although much of the body of the one is in fact inside the other's space-volume, but by invitation, by being drawn in.

The facing planes of the bodies and the different elements of their attitudes in relation to each other bear out this reciprocity of emotion (and contrast with Rodin's work). The line of her right shoulder parallels that of his left shoulder; her right forearm and his left upper arm are also in parallel. The pairing of the bodies forms a series of diamond shapes. First, his left and her right arms, the line of her neck and his face; second, that formed by the line of her back and thigh, and his back and a line through their jaw lines, repeated in the line of her bent left arm; third, that formed by her right calf and flexed foot, and his left buttock and thigh. This gives further emphasis to the flow of emotion in union, and displays Claudel's unique vision of perfect male-female unity. This vision of bodily union is her lasting contribution to women's creativity. Rather than representing women's changing social roles at the time of the Belle Epoque, her focus was the archetypal body itself.

There is in this sculpture little male-female disparity in bodily architecture, such as might otherwise have constrained and explained this reciprocity on a dominant-male / seductive-female model. It is remarkable that the bodily semiotics of gender are represented without being dichotomised. Both bodies are smooth and supple, both strong and muscular, both have beautiful flowing lines and also strong bones, articulations, feet, shoulders and faces. Femininity and masculinity are signified, but not as oppositions to each other, in competition or conflict. The muscular strength of Duchmanta's body is clearly marked, but at the same time, the bunching of the gluteal muscle, perfectly modelled and showing the urgency of his upward movement to reach Sakountala, is not discrepant with the modelling of her calf muscles. Their thighs are rather similarly modelled: her muscles and his are relatively at rest at this point. Her buttocks are not flexed as are his, the pose representing her at rest at this part of her anatomy. Her arms are 'supported' by his body, and their musculature reflects this, whilst his arms are flexed to reach up to her. We could imagine how their bodily architecture might be differently modelled if their positions were reversed, she straining up against gravity, with the weight 'above' her limbs, and he leaning down, part-supported by her, partly resting on a support: there might then be a marked differentiation of male and female bodily effort, though not necessarily, since both bodies are represented within a broadly similar cognitive archaeology of softness and strength. The pose, a semiotic choice and fully semantically 'charged', emphasises the tenderness of the two bodies, each represented as receiving the other in an embrace which does not demand but offers and receives.

To put it another way, the plasticity of this work depicts no hierarchy of beauty or type of beauty, no hierarchy of strength, still less aggression or domination, whether because there is no difference in strength, no dichotomy in perception of aesthetic form, or because each articulates him/herself in relation to the other so that any difference is not significant. This is remarkable and unusual in a sculpture of erotic passion between man and woman. It marks Claudel's achievement in terms both of her vision and her technical genius. It further constitutes, I suggest, a rare representation of woman, equal to and in harmony with man, not brave victim of events, but active subject of her narrative. The legendary narrative of Sakountala showed her female vulnerability: without Duchmanta's memory to give her identity in the view of oth-

ers, and with a child to increase her vulnerability, she suffered
and endured danger. Once Duchmanta is restored to consciousness, their temporary inequality of consciousness and of
suffering is resolved: as two individuals, their reciprocity is
complete and their communication is enabling for both. This
is what is represented in the sculpture. Claudel's vision of
mutual love is both timeless and, from our perspective,
anachronistically modern. Claudel's brother Paul wrote of this
sculpture as being both chaste and passionate (Ayral-Clause
2002: 90). In my view, it is erotic in the extreme. I suggest that
what Paul Claudel described as 'chaste' was its quality of reciprocal passion in which woman and man are sharers, not
hunter and prey. Paul Claudel's own ideas of female sexuality,[2] emanating from a period in which female sexuality is
polarised into legitimised chastity versus sinful eroticism, may
have led him to use the notion of chastity to express the otherwise unthinkable concept of legitimated female desire.

Les Causeuses

Apart from its beauty, the technical achievement of the carving of *Les Causeuses* is remarkable, more particularly in the
case of the onyx, since this is so challenging a medium. As the
illustration shows (Figure 12.2), the precious material and the
harmonious curves make it a thing of light and reflection. Students to whom I showed it (their first view of it, without background knowledge) saw intimacy, comfort, group strength and
exchange between equals. 'Women are listening to one of
them who is telling a secret,' said one; 'they are sheltered, no
one dominates, they are listening to the speaker and they all
feel safe'; 'one can see they are women, by their backs and
their waists and the way they are close to each other'.

There is a harmony of proportion between head and body,
distinct in each case, but on a common scale. The head of the
speaker is higher than the others, and she has a hand raised
as a kind of skeptron (or sceptre) designating the right to
speak, to use Pierre Bourdieu's term (Bourdieu 1982: 105). This
does not, however, organise the grouped bodies into a power
hierarchy, but rather a configuration of sharing: each will
speak in turn. The heads of the listeners in the middle in front
(M), on the left (L) and on the right (R) are intimately near
each other: M and R are close to touching each other. The
faces of L, M and R are on a parallel plane to the figure at the

back B. The napes of the necks of L, M and R are stretched forward and their backs are in alignment, as if to place the faces on a common 'listening plane'. This gives the attitudes of each body a dynamic determined, not by the individual relationship of each to its personal territory and then the interrelationship of these individuals centred in their territories, but rather in relation to a median territory, in common to all four, a shared space of reference. R's body is swayed, almost touching the head of M who is turned to the left: each of their bodies is organised spatially in function of the listening-space which unites them to B, as if they did not realise, or it did not signify, that each body is entering on the personal space of the other. This configuration of bodies is distinct from that, for example, of Rodin's *L'Eternelle idole*, in which the bodies of the couple each negotiate a confrontation of personal space, one figure impacting on the space of the other, whose body language portrays an unwilling endurance of this sexual predation (Figure 12.3).

One of the remarkable elements of Claudel's *Les Causeuses* arises from the union of carving and medium. The variegated transparency of the onyx shows to great effect in the arrangement of the hair, for example: it is formal and stylised, with references to classical tradition, whilst at the same time being lightened and illuminated by the play of varied transparency. The illustration (Figure 12.2) shows this particularly well in the hair arrangement of L, where the Grecian chignon and bandeaux are especially beautiful. These figures, grouped closely together and absorbed in a common interest, in an intimate space, are at the same time dignified, archaic and archetypal, hieratic. To use Luce Irigaray's term, they are represented in a mode which is absolutely non-specular (Irigaray 1974). These are not women *as opposed to* men, or women in competition with men, or each other, for the right to speak and be heard. There is no 'male gaze' or commodification of the female body. What is celebrated is human communication, interaction and understanding, represented, and this is the crucial point, in the non-polarised feminine, or the non-gendered space of women's talk. The paradox from which Claudel's art frees itself is that women can only, if at all, and then temporarily, be freed from the gendering of the space of communication when speaking amongst themselves. As with Cixous' *écriture féminine* (1975: 45), this mode of human communication, whose aim is to free itself from the distorting patriarchal economy, is represented as possible not only (albeit perhaps

more usually) for women, but for *humans*. Instead of representing the politically charged, gendered and power-distorted
public space in which the two sexes generally meet, Claudel
represents human communication, in potential at any rate, as
a plural polyloquy of persons.

This aspect of the cognitive architecture of *Les Causeuses*
contrasts with the normally unhelpful distortion of our view of
human relations. Why, in a species which was from the origin
double, both male and female, have we generated an apparent incapacity to conceive of plurality, or duality, or any *more-
than-one-ness*, other than in terms of hierarchy? Why is it
always material to know who was first of the two, or the
stronger, or the dominant, or the master over the other? Any
attempt to answer these questions takes us into areas of cognitive psychology which are much larger than the frame of
this study. However, the group dynamic of *Les Causeuses* is
unbounded by such conceptual limitations. Even if we have
not yet solved the problem of how women and men are to
speak to each other in a way consistent both with personal
and group fulfilment, we are still able to participate as spectators in Claudel's vision of communication unburdened by history. This gives point to her having sheltered this little world,
this parallel universe of chat, by a screen, an ironic *'causerie-
corner'*. As Randi Greenberg of the National Gallery of Women
in the Arts remarked to me,[3] the usual translation of *Les
Causeuses – The Gossips* – is distorting and diminishing with its
connotations of stigmatised female communication, and
undermines the sculpture's wider meaning. A better wording
might be *The Conversation* or *Women Talking*.[4]

Biographical Issues

Camille Claudel's artistic reputation, always high amongst a
core of admirers, has grown significantly in the general public
since the major exhibitions of 1984 in Paris curated by
Monique Laurent and Bruno Gaudichon, and the *catalogue
raisonné* by Bruno Gaudichon, Anne Rivière and Danielle
Ghanassia (1999). However, there is a certain dilemma to be
resolved by the critic. Claudel's biography has featured so
largely in accounts of her work as almost to overshadow the
interpretation of her art. In my reading of *Sakountala* and *Les
Causeuses*, as elsewhere in an analysis of *L'Age mûr*, I am concerned to avoid biographical overdetermination, and indeed

have proposed an alternative to the received interpretation of the latter work, based on a semiotic analysis of its plasticity (Ryan 2002: 13–28). At the same time, Claudel's lived experience as a woman artist is of importance in increasing understanding of the specificity of female creativeness and its reception. On the one hand, these two major works can be read *as sculptures* without assumptions as to their 'autobiographical' function: after all, the plastic artist is no more dependent than the writer on the confessional, even if the metalanguage of art is perhaps more inclined to forget this basic fact than that of literature, since the last century at any rate. On the other hand, there is the importance of Claudel's achievement in her time, particularly in the light of the extraordinary constraints of the period on the female sculptor in general, and on Claudel in particular.

This last point has to some extent been the more difficult to demonstrate with clarity, in that there is too much evidence. Some accounts of Claudel's difficulties tend to try to re-establish her credentials as an artist, which suffered so much from the time of her incarceration by her family, by a redistribution of artistic credit for work done between herself and her teacher Rodin. This area is so complex that even the latest (and excellent) biography by Odile Ayral-Clause (2002) does not attempt to be an exhaustive account, though it certainly maps the territory very well. Though the present study could not include a frame as wide, two incontrovertible facts may be recorded.

The first is that today's standards as to the teacher's obligations in the teacher-student relationship would not be met by that of Rodin in relation to Claudel. This is not to judge Rodin according to an anachronistic ethical frame, but to restate that the *reasons* why these standards have arisen, the potential abuses, misinterpretations and danger to talent and achievement from which they endeavour to protect, must have applied to the reality of Claudel's case. In other words, while the question of right or wrong behaviour cannot be judged out of context, such a barrier to women artists' achievement and recognition was nonetheless real, and had a negative impact on Claudel.

Secondly, both the treatment of mental illness and the rights of the mentally ill have changed profoundly, and Claudel's sequestration for the second half of her life, by her mother and brother, could not happen today. Again, while we should arguably not judge those responsible by today's standards, the *reasons* why it is not possible today mean that it was abusive then, and had a negative impact. It must be taken into account, in interpreting Claudel's status as an artist, that after some thirty years of artistic activity she spent twenty-nine years of captivity in mental asylums, prevented from seeing or writing to anyone without her family's permission – it was even given out that she was dead. Having become Rodin's pupil in 1883, at nineteen, when he was forty-three, she was taken against her will to the asylum of Ville-Evrard in 1913, at forty-nine, and died in that of Montdevergues in 1943 aged seventy-nine, largely of cold and hunger.[5]

This renders more difficult, but more significant, any attempt to situate her in the cultural history of the pleasure-driven Belle Epoque. Her period of freedom ended with it; we lack a later context from which to view her. I have addressed this by counter-implication in my readings of *Sakountala* and *Les Causeuses*. Her crucial achievement is the representation of the female body at a period in which a new liberation and at the same time new forms of constraint seemed to appear in fashion and other aesthetic paradigms. What has become the signature Belle Epoque representation of the popular aesthetic of feminine beauty, the Caroline Otero model of bodily presentation through corsetry, dress and the relationship between the body and social space, has little to do with Claudel's mode of expression. *Sakountala* represents a revolution in male-female mutual emotion expressed in the paired body, *Les Causeuses* a new vision of non-gendered social space. Just as Claudel's choice of career showed an exceptional artistic independence – sculpture was for various reasons a very difficult, costly, laborious and financially insecure profession for all sculptors, but with many additional limitations for women – her place in the history of plastic expression is highly individual.

In the end, while the facts of Claudel's life can only with difficulty be excavated from accounts filtered through contemporary received ideas, we are left with the reality of her works. The place of the woman artist of the Belle Epoque seems like one of Rodin's heads of Camille: beautiful, significant, but blinded from without, or half-buried in their marble matrix. Claudel's own works, on the other hand, are strong, luminous representations of men and women. Timeless, powerful and charged with emotion, they offer a revolutionary vision of the human condition, the unified mind-body subject, undistorted by gender stereotypes.

Notes

1. See Ayral-Clause (2002: 108): 'A women could not be expected to have genius: if she did, she was perceived as sexually ambiguous'.
2. One of Paul Claudel's letters refers to Camille Claudel's confinement in the asylum as punishment for her 'sin' of having terminated a pregnancy with Rodin (ibid.: 195).
3. My thanks are owed to Ms Randi Greenberg, Curator, National Museum of Women in the Arts, Washington, D.C.; to Tomás Tyner, photographer, UCC, who digitalised the images; Fiona Kearney, Arts Officer, UCC for technical help and advice; Fiona du Boucher-Ryan, Kinitlla du Boucher-Ryan and Deirdre Healy for their input; Dr Margot Miller and David Miller for their kind hospitality during part of this research. This article was written with generous support from the Irish Research Council for the Humanities and Social Sciences.
4. 'Causer' in French does not necessarily imply female speakers or disrespected speech, whereas 'gossip' carries more negative rhetorical colour.
5. For an account of conditions of the time, see Lemoine (1998); for examples of period eugenism, see Stewart (2001).

PART IV

WOMEN, WRITING AND RECEPTION

CHAPTER 13

FEMINIST DISCOURSE IN WOMEN'S NOVELS OF PROFESSIONAL DEVELOPMENT

Juliette M. Rogers

The Belle Epoque witnessed a great blossoming of new women writers, yet few can be called feminist in any late twentieth-century sense of the term. In fact, later generations have often dismissed women novelists from the Belle Epoque as anti-feminist, a famous example being Simone de Beauvoir who, in *Mémoires d'une jeune fille rangée* (*Memoirs of a Dutiful Daughter*, 1974 [1958]), singles out Colette Yver as one of those anti-feminist novelists whom her conservative father admired.[1] Clearly the women represented in women's novels are neither openly political activists nor radical revolutionaries compared to their feminist counterparts in the second half of the twentieth century. Yet a number of women writers portrayed women in active, intellectual roles, and therefore helped to create new images of women in their works, images that I would label 'feminist.' In this chapter, then, I will be looking at ways in which various forms of feminist discourse are embedded in novels of professional development written by women of the Belle Epoque, focusing in particular on Gabrielle Reval's *Sèvriennes* (*Women of Sèvres*, 1900), Colette Yver's *Les Cervelines* (*Brainy Women*, 1903), Marcelle Tinayre's *La Rebelle* (*The Rebel*, 1905) and Colette's *La Vagabonde* (*The Vagabond*, 1984 [1910]).

Novels of Professional Development

These four novels introduce one of the more popular types of
heroine of the time, namely the professional woman, torn
between her professional and personal aspirations rather than
between the traditional 'sexual versus maternal' stereotypes so
prevalent in nineteenth-century novels. *Sèvriennes* follows the
lives of a group of young women during their graduate training at the Ecole Normale for women in the Parisian suburb of
Sèvres. It begins with the entrance exams and initial impressions of the central character, Marguerite Triel, and ends with
her decision at graduation that she will choose not to pursue
a teaching career after all. *Les Cervelines* focuses on two
'brainy' women, Jeanne Boerk, a medical student, and Marceline Rhonans, a history professor and orientalist, each of
whom has to weigh the consequences that a potential
romance would have on her professional life. Jeanne rejects
the advances of her supervisor at the hospital, while Marceline
falls in love with a young doctor. However, she ends up rejecting his traditional requirements for their marriage and, as the
novel closes, plans to travel to the Middle East to pursue her
research. *La Rebelle* follows the story of Josanne, a journalist,
who writes for a women's magazine in Paris. After reviewing a
feminist work, *La Travailleuse* (*The Woman Worker*), she meets
and falls in love with its author, Noël Delysle. Torn between
her desire for independence and her love of Noël, she finally
decides to marry him. In *La Vagabonde*, the main protagonist
Renée Néré tells the story of her solitary life as a divorcee working as a mime in the music halls of Paris. She too falls in love,
with one of her music hall admirers, but decides in the end
that she should continue with her career as a writer and a
mime, rather than falling back into the traps that married life
holds for women.

Among the historical factors accounting for the representation of professional women such as these in Belle Epoque novels are the educational reforms for girls dating from the first
decades of the Third Republic, including the creation of public
secondary schools for girls in 1880 and obligatory primary
school for all French children in 1883. These reforms often had
a double-edged nature. While they promoted literacy and education for women of all social classes, they remained conservative about the long-term goals for women. Public education
was supposed to help women to become better mothers and
wives, not emancipated individuals in French society.[2] These

conflicting goals had a direct impact, both positive and negative, on the generation of writers such as Colette (born 1873),
Reval (born 1870), Tinayre (born 1877) and Yver (born 1874),
who experienced the Republic's educational ideology person-
ally.[3] Due to the large number of women attending schools,
the literacy rate among women climbed considerably and the
number of women writers of that particular generation was
considerable (Sauvy 1986: 243–45). The new education system
undoubtedly influenced the types of heroines they portrayed
and the ways that they tackled difficult feminist issues.

Reflecting the conflicting goals of the Third Republic
reforms, the protagonists of women's novels of professional
development often find themselves forging traditional paths
in innovative settings. That is, they may become lawyers, journalists, doctors or professors, but it is assumed that they will
maintain traditional bourgeois values while doing so. Many
of them excel in 'women's' or 'children's' fields, for example in
girls' education, children's medical care or divorce trials. Those
who work in 'neutral' or traditionally masculine domains,
such as laboratory research, archeology or the arts, often bring
in a 'feminising' discourse to their advantage.[4] And even
though they are intelligent and successful, almost all of them
give up their career goals in the last five or ten pages of the
text in order to devote themselves entirely to husband and
children. Thus, in line with the Republic's legal and pedagog-
ical reforms, they benefit from new opportunities for women,
but not too much and certainly not at the expense of femininity or maternity. This type of conclusion, where the romance
plot triumphs over the quest for professional fulfilment, may
leave us with an 'anti-feminist' view of both Third Republic
reforms and the Belle Epoque heroines they produced.

However, novels of professional development can also be
considered a subgenre of the *bildungsroman* in which, typically,
the process of evolution is much more important than the
(often negative) final outcome. As Jeffrey Sammons argues, the
bildungsroman cannot be expected to contain an individual's
reconciliation with society: 'It does not matter whether the
process of *Bildung* succeeds or fails, whether the protagonist
achieves an accommodation with life and society or not …
There must be a sense of evolutionary change within the self, a
teleology of individuality, even if the novel, as many do, comes
to doubt or deny the possibility of achieving a gratifying result'
(Sammons 1991: 41).[5] In Maurice Barrès' *Les Déracinés* (2004
[1897]), for example, most of the young students abandon

their professional and political aspirations due to their disgust
with the scandals and corruption that they encounter when
they move to Paris. In André Gide's *L'Immoraliste* (1972 [1902]),
the protagonist gives up his promising career as an orientalist
due to the rigidity of the academic institutions and in order to
discover his 'true' nature. Similarly, women professionals, dis-
illusioned by the inflexible rules in their professions, the unfair
treatment of women and the constant badgering by husbands
and colleagues, often renounce their dreams of changing the
world in which they work. In both male and the female versions of the novel of professional development, the protagonists struggle with their decision, trying to find ways to make
their personal aspirations synchronise with the demands of
their profession. It is this decision-making process that is the
crucial component of the text, not the final outcome. But critics' reactions to men and women quitting show a double standard: while men are seen to be freeing themselves from the
chains of a dogmatic social or professional institution, women
are admitting defeat, acting conservatively and retreating to a
life of ease and comfort.

Despite the 'renunciation plots' that repeatedly mark the
endings of women's texts of the Belle Epoque, the main body
of their novels displays a variety of portrayals of articulate,
independent and sometimes rebellious working women. It is
these depictions that allow for feminist readings and even
anticipate the developments of second wave French feminism
in later decades of the twentieth century.

Nelly Roussel and the Discourse of Bourgeois Feminism

Nelly Roussel's dynamic lecture, 'L'Eternelle Sacrifiée' ('She Who
Is Always Sacrificed'), delivered no less than fifty times in 1905
and 1906 alone (Albistur and Armogathe 1979: 24), provides a
primary source for the expression of bourgeois feminism at the
Belle Epoque and a touchstone for the feminist discourses
reflected in women's novels (Roussel 1979).[6] The lecture
addresses many of the basic issues of the day, such as women's
education, work, marriage rights and social equality. However,
in 1905 Roussel, like so many other feminist activists, did not
claim the suffrage movement in France as crucial for women's
liberation. It was not until early 1914 that she joined the new
Ligue National pour le Vote des Femmes (National League for

Women's Vote) and became an active spokeswoman for women's suffrage (Waelti-Walters and Hause 1994: 278). Her lecture, therefore, contains no traces of the suffrage argument.

One of the first elements that Roussel insists on is equality. She states very eloquently:

> To sum it up in a few words, 'feminism' is simply the doctrine of *natural equivalence* and *social equality* of the sexes. [...] our claims deal not only with *justice*, toward which their [men's] upright nature and generosity cannot remain indifferent, but also with an issue of *general interests;* for the liberation of woman, the flowering of the feminine soul, which has been proscribed, chained, and unappreciated for such a long time, will open up a new era of peace, love, and beauty for the whole of humanity (Roussel 1995: 20, author's emphasis).[7]

Roussel's simple definition gives a clear idea of what Belle Epoque feminists wanted: social equality and the recognition of the natural equivalences that exist between men and women. She believed that the implementation of these two basic rights would not only better the situation of women, but would improve all of French society.

In the area of marital status, Roussel also speaks out against the status quo, where women are restricted by social requirements and even by legal doctrine:

> For my part, I never attend a marriage, be it civil or religious, without experiencing a very painful feeling. At an epoch when it is maintained that slavery has been abolished, in a *republic* based on *liberty* and *equality*, how can this oath of *obedience* sworn in public by a human creature be permitted? (Roussel 1995: 26–27).[8]

She expands her remarks to address those who might claim that the oath is merely a formality, underlining the fact that most men would never agree to take an oath of obedience to another human being and to the state of slavery that they insist upon for their wives, even as a part of a ritual ceremony. Further, she reminds the audience that men are not always the most capable in a household and can even bring ruin upon a family because of the law that men should always rule over their wives and children (ibid.: 27).

As for education, Roussel believed that girls and boys are both harmed by the separate educational values that the French schools teach:

I find the difference between the two moralities and the two educations in everything: we are always reminded of duties, while you, Gentlemen, are insufficiently reminded of them. We are taught only sacrifice, the abdication of all pride, of all our natural rights, and of our most legitimate desires, while a man is told only about his freedom, his power, his greatness, and his virility; even in his games, his brutality, his egoism and his arrogance are flattered! (ibid.: 32).[9]

Although some of these educational disparities are the result of cultural prejudice (and continue in France even today), Roussel's assumption is that a coeducational environment would greatly reduce the different messages given to girls and boys and would diminish the stereotypes and ignorance that each sex has of the other. She points to the systems of coeducation in the United States, England and Holland at the time and praises their efforts toward creating equality and understanding between the sexes (ibid.: 32).

In the area of work, Roussel explains that women, being individuals, should not always be restricted to the single role of wife and mother:

In the name of which right, which principle, is each one of us refused the liberty to follow our vocation, obey our natural tendencies, choose ourselves the kind of occupation suitable for us? In the name of what right is the field of our activities restricted and a predetermined path, the same for everyone, imposed on us? (ibid.: 22).[10]

This passage demonstrates Roussel's rhetorical verve – her impassioned speeches were famous for rousing crowds to their feet – but the claims she makes are uncomplicated. Women should be allowed to choose their roles in life, not be assigned one profession only (wife and mother) simply because they are women. This one lecture gives an excellent overview of some of the major demands and visions of the feminist movement at the Belle Epoque.

Women's Novels and Feminist Discourse

When we look at the work of novelists writing during these pre-war years, we find characters articulating statements that are very similar to Roussel's feminist discourse.

In the area of social equality and natural equivalence, Tinayre's *La Rebelle* echoes Roussel's statements. In the opening passage, Josanne Valentin reads from a new book called *La Travailleuse* and finds herself reflected in its words:

> She (the poor woman) took pride in giving all her effort, employing all her energy, to develop her personality. And thus she noticed that she had merited more, that she could earn more, than her daily food, clothing and shelter: moral independence, the right to think, speak, act and love as she pleased, that right which men had always taken and always denied her.[11]

Josanne agrees that women should have the same rights as men and that, when they set themselves to work and 'develop their personality', they will arrive at the same conclusions as men: life should include more than the basic necessities of food, clothing and shelter. Although she never asserts that women are the same as men, she clearly believes that there is a natural equivalence between the two and that social equality is necessary.

In the area of marital status, Renée Néré in Colette's *La Vagabonde* echoes Roussel's discussion of the obedience clause in the marriage contract. Renée dwells on the problems of being an obedient wife in the marriage relationship when discussing her first husband's infidelities: 'After the first betrayals, the revolts and submissions of a youthful love determined to hope and to endure, I settled down to suffering with an unyielding pride and obstinacy, and to producing literature' (Colette 1955: 27).[12] She explains that her husband required that she be courteous to his mistresses, and even made her take one out for a walk while he was sleeping with a new one. When she objected to his orders, he beat her. And yet, when she divorced him, everyone blamed her: 'At the time of our divorce the world was almost ready to lay all the blame on me, in order to exculpate "that good-looking Taillandy", whose only fault was that he was attractive and faithless' (ibid.: 29).[13] Her first marital experience, where obedience was not only expected but required, has thus put her on her guard and given her a wary detachment from future lovers and husbands.

In the area of educational values, Marguerite Triel in Reval's *Sèvriennes* (1900) expresses her surprise when she discovers that the elite teacher training school for women, the Ecole Normale de Sèvres, gives the young women students both physical and intellectual freedom, liberties that were rarely found in girls' schools in late nineteenth-century France. Marguerite states: 'I am astounded by the English-style liberty here: people come and go in the school, and go out on Sundays, without saying where they are going ... They leave us responsible for our actions; the rules adopted here are those of confidence and liberty'.[14] The first-year advisor, Mlle Vormèse, also comments on the importance of independent thought at the Ecole Normale de Sèvres, rather than on the rote learning that is usually emphasised in high schools: 'At the end of the first month here, some students have reacted, noticing that their professors require more than the erudition of a dictionary, and that they show more appreciation for spontaneous traits and personal reflections than for the simplistic discoveries of bookish students'.[15] Here Reval offers a model for Belle Epoque women's education that does not insist on sacrifice, duty and submission, as Roussel had described it, but rather on independence, intelligence and creativity. Neither Marguerite nor Mlle Vormèse argues for coeducation, since both find that the bonding that occurs between women at the Ecole Normale is vital for their moral and psychological development. However, their belief is that women's education should focus on intellectual and moral independence, not on obedience and abnegation.

In the area of work, Yver's *Les Cervelines* (1903) offers a reflection of Roussel's feminist sentiments, despite the fact that, unlike Tinayre, Colette and Reval, who are usually categorised as moderate feminists, Yver was aligned with a very conservative agenda (and is still considered a conservative anti-feminist by many critics). Although some of her main feminist characters are portrayed in an unsympathetic light, there is a positive feminist element in *Les Cervelines*, which echoes Roussel's demand for women to be allowed to choose their careers, and not be restricted to the roles of wife and mother. When Doctor Jean Cécile asks Marceline to give up her career as a historian and professor in order to marry him, she is astounded and equates the request with the act of dying:

> When you asked me, 'Will you be my fiancée?' you know that I answered that I was. But to cut me off from everything! To take away my reason for living! To make of me a new being, give me another life, change me, put me to death in fact, because that [giving up my career] would be the same as dying![16]

Even though Jean believes that this request is not his own personal wish, but rather his conservative mother's desire that

Marceline 'give up her books', we see a conservative penchant in his own thoughts when the narrator states: 'But his mother was right. As an established doctor with a rich clientele, he couldn't have a *schoolteacher* as a wife. In society, there are a host of subtle or ridiculous laws that are inevitable, without one's knowing why exactly'.[17] While Jean at first claims that he will be able to change his mother's mind, he ends up siding with her and requests that Marceline sacrifice her career.

What is interesting here is that Marceline is seriously tempted by the marriage offer. But during a week of seclusion where she lets herself think things over, a brief visit from her intellectual friend, the medical student Jeanne Boerk, convinces her that she must remain 'married' to her books. Jeanne tells her: 'Let's not have false modesty; women like you and I have other things to do than start a family: we must be bright enough to render our services to our fellow creatures and to pay our debt to the human community'.[18] After she listens to Jeanne's reasoning, Marceline realises that she would be living in a terrible emptiness if she abandoned her research project and her teaching in order to live as wife and mother in the conservative bourgeois society of a small provincial city. Thus Yver's heroine endorses Roussel's statement that women should be allowed to follow the vocation that best suits them and not be pinned down to the single role of wife and mother.

Yver occasionally portrays the scientific genius of Jeanne Boerk as a hardhearted and unusual quality for a woman, yet Marceline is continually presented as a sympathetic character, whose struggle with her decision is reasonable and worthy. She is introduced as a 'creature of exception' with a 'prestigious mind' (Yver 1903: 71) and as 'nervous, sensitive and intuitive' (ibid.: 65). These adjectives denote a sensitive, sophisticated individual rather than a monstrous 'New Woman'.

Overall, these passages demonstrate that the protagonists of a number of Belle Epoque novels express opinions that match up with some of the feminist beliefs of their time. Although none of them are political activists, their thoughts and actions reveal an interest in and support of a woman's right to pursue a career and live on her own, if she so desires. Marriage and family are not their only 'career options', even though some do end up choosing that path. The authors endorse their characters' balancing act, where they give equal weight to their professional and their personal lives, by portraying them as conscientious and intelligent young women, not as flighty socialites or through other negative stereotypes associated with feminist activists. In *La Rebelle*, for example, Josanne is described as two different women:

> There existed in her two women: the 'higher' one, the proud, the valiant, the 'rebel', who wanted to liberate herself, to heal and live in her chaste solitude, – and the other, the inferior, the submissive, who still conserved, in her blood and in her nerves, the ancient poison, the need for tears and caresses, the morbid taste of love's suffering.[19]

This dual nature, with its conflicting needs, is not critiqued either by the narrator or by other characters in the text. Josanne's boss, Monsieur Foucart thinks of her as 'intelligent, courageous, exact and proud' (Tinayre 1905: 46). In contrast, Foucart's wife, the 'great feminist', is treated with a touch of irony: 'around her fortieth birthday, she threw herself into feminism as others throw themselves into religion'.[20]

Like Josanne, Marceline in *Les Cervelines* and Renée in *La Vagabonde* also suffer from competing inner desires and personalities. The reader can thus see that the social pressures and ideologies confronting the protagonists are complicated matters, and that one-dimensional 'feminists' are perhaps not as realistic as more conflicted female characters who show contradictions in their thoughts and behaviour while they weigh the pros and cons of marriage versus a career. The authors who created these characters are not 'anti-feminist', but prefer to portray the problematic conditions that existed for working women during the Belle Epoque. Even though they may not have written feminist tracts or gone on lecture tours like Nelly Roussel, they provide positive feminist sentiments for their readers that contrast with the more conservative lines of thought also prevalent during the Belle Epoque.[21]

In three of the four novels discussed in this chapter, the protagonists choose *not* to marry at the end of the novel and in two of them, they even decide to remain in their chosen professional careers. While these types of endings are rare for the Belle Epoque, clearly they do exist. And in each novel, the protagonists go through painstaking decision-making processes in which they deliberate the merits of pursuing their career or pursuing a private relationship. Their final choice, either to work or to marry, is thus not of primary importance. Rather, it is the development of their capacities for independent thinking and the process of critical evaluation of their individual situations that are significant. From this perspective, we can better appreciate how the novelists in question incorporated a feminist discourse while portraying the difficult choices and societal pressures experienced by professional women.

Notes

1. Beauvoir states: 'My father was no feminist; he admired the wisdom of the novels of Colette Yver in which the woman lawyer, or the woman doctor in the end sacrifice their careers in order to provide their children and husband with a happy home' (Beauvoir 1974 [1958]: 104). Yver's later texts became much more openly critical of the feminist movement. In *Dans le jardin du féminisme*, for example, the narrator reproaches the feminist movement because it does not work within existing social structures but, rather, works 'against men' and, like other revolutionary movements, is 'based on hatred' (Yver 1920: 8–9). However, I would argue that Yver's novels of the Belle Epoque, particularly between 1903 and 1912, offered readers a broad range of feminist values and goals that corresponded to the wide variety of feminist thought of the period.
2. Many Third Republic education reformers, including Camille Sée, Jules Ferry, Octave Gréard and Paul Rousselot, believed that women educated in state schools would be better able to instill Republican values in their children. Their main goal was to block the influence of the Catholic Church on future generations, not to emancipate women (see Margardant 1990).
3. Gabrielle Sidonie Colette (1873–1954) attended the public girls school in her native village of Saint-Sauveur-en-Puisaye until the age of fifteen when she received the brevet. Gabrielle Reval (1870–1938) graduated from the Ecole Normale de Sèvres in 1893, taught at the girls' high school in Niort until 1899, then married and began writing novels in 1900. Marcelle Tinayre (née Marguerite-Suzanne-Marcelle Chasteau, 1877–1948) earned the Baccalaureat degree before marrying. Colette Yver (Antoinette Huzard, née de Bergevin, 1874–1953) did not attend state school, but began by publishing a novel for children when she was seventeen, *Mademoiselle Devoir* (*Miss Duty*) (1892). *Les Cervelines* was her first work for adults. See Waelti-Walters 1990: 186–88, 190.
4. For more on the methods used by female characters to feminise the public sphere of work in Belle Epoque novels, see Rogers 1997, especially pp. 20–24.
5. In the original eighteenth-century German *bildungsroman*, the protagonist achieved some sort of reconciliation and reintegration with his community after a series of adventures and discoveries. However later versions of the *bildungsroman* in other countries did not continue with the same format. For a history of the origins and transformations of the genre, see James Hardin's introductory essay to the collection *Reflection and Action: Essays on the Bildungsroman* (Hardin 1991: i-xvii).
6. It is reproduced in English translation (Roussel 1995) in the anthology of feminist texts from the Belle Epoque edited by Jennifer Waelti-Walters and Stephen Hause, which provides a number of different views of feminism from the period (Waelti-Walters and Hause 1994).
7. 'Le "féminisme", pour le résumer en quelques mots, c'est tout simplement la doctrine de l'*équivalence naturelle* et de l'*égalité sociale* des sexes. [...] il y

a, dans nos revendications, non seulement une question de *justice*, à laquelle leur droiture [des hommes] et leur générosité ne peuvent rester indifférentes, mais encore une question d'*intérêt général*; car l'affranchissement de la femme, l'épanouissement de l'âme féminine, si longtemps méconnue, proscrite et enchaînée, ouvrira pour l'humanité tout entière, une ère nouvelle de paix, d'amour et de beauté!' (Roussel 1979: 41, author's emphasis).

8. 'Pour ma part, je n'assiste jamais à la célébration d'un mariage, civil ou religieux, sans éprouver une impression très pénible. A une époque où on prétend avoir aboli l'esclavage, dans une *république* basée sur la *liberté* et sur *l'égalité*, comment peut-on admettre ce serment *d'obéissance*, prêté en public par une créature humaine!' (ibid.: 67).

9. 'En toutes choses je retrouve la différence des deux morales, des deux éducations: à nous on ne parle que de devoirs, à vous, Messieurs, on n'en parle pas toujours assez. On ne nous enseigne que le sacrifice, que l'abdication de toute fierté, de nos droits les plus naturels, de nos désirs les plus légitimes, mais l'homme, on ne l'entretient que de sa liberté, de sa puissance, de sa grandeur, de sa virilité, on flatte jusque dans ses jeux sa brutalité, son égoïsme, son orgueil!' (ibid.: 88).

10. 'Au nom de quel droit, au nom de quel principe refuse-t-on à chacune de nous la liberté de suivre sa vocation, d'obéir à ses tendances naturelles, de choisir elle-même le genre d'occupation qui lui convient?... Au nom de quel droit prétend-on restreindre le champ de notre activité et nous imposer une voie déterminée, la même pour toutes?' (ibid.: 49).

11. 'Elle (la femme pauvre) a mis son orgueil à donner tout son effort, à employer toutes ses energies, à développer sa personnalité. Et elle s'est aperçue, alors, qu'elle avait mérité, qu'elle pouvait conquérir autre chose que le pain quotidien, les vêtements, le logis: l'indépendance morale, le droit de penser, de parler, d'agir, d'aimer à sa guise, ce droit que l'homme avait toujours pris, et qu'il lui avait refusé toujours' (Tinayre 1905: 13).

12. 'Après les premières trahisons, après les révoltes et les soumissions d'un jeune amour qui s'opiniâtrait à espérer et à vivre, je m'étais mise à souffrir avec un orgueil et un entêtement intraitables, et à faire de la littérature' (Colette 1984 [1910]: 1083–84).

13. 'Lors de notre divorce, on ne fut pas loin de me donner tous les torts, pour innocenter le "beau Taillandy," coupable seulement de plaire et de trahir' (ibid.: 1085).

14. 'Je suis ébahie d'une liberté aussi anglaise, on va on vient dans la maison, on sort le dimanche, sans dire où l'on ira ... On nous laisse responsables de nos actions; le régime adopté à l'école est celui de la confiance et de la liberté' (Reval 1900: 38).

15. 'Au bout d'un mois [ici], quelques-unes ont bronché, s'apercevant que leurs professeurs exigeaient autre chose qu'une érudition de dictionnaire, et qu'ils se montraient plus sensibles aux traits spontanés, aux réflexions personnelles, qu'aux découvertes trop faciles des bouquineuses' (ibid.: 75).

16. 'Quand vous m'avez dit: "Voulez-vous être ma fiancée," vous le savez, je vous ai répondu que je l'étais. Mais me sevrer de tout! me retirer ma raison d'être! faire de moi un être nouveau, me donner une autre vie, me changer, me faire mourir enfin, car mourir n'est que cela!' (Yver 1903: 280).

17. 'Mais la mère avait raison. Médecin établi et de clientèle riche, il ne pouvait avoir pour femme une *institutrice*. Il y a dans le monde une foule de

lois subtiles ou ridicules qui forment ainsi, sans qu'on sache au juste pourquoi, une fatalité' (ibid.: 269).

18. 'N'ayons pas de fausse modestie; des femmes comme vous et moi ont autre chose à faire que de fonder un ménage: nous devons être assez lumineuses pour rendre, en ce sens, service à nos semblables et payer notre dette à la communauté humaine' (ibid.: 294).

19. 'Il y avait en elle deux femmes: celle "d'en haut", la fière, la vaillante, la "rebelle", qui voulait se libérer, guérir et vivre dans sa chaste solitude, – et l'autre, l'inférieure, l'asservie, qui conservait encore, dans son sang et dans ses nerfs, le poison ancien, le besoin des larmes et des caresses, le goût morbide de la souffrance d'amour' (Tinayre 1905: 134).

20. 'vers la quarantaine, elle s'était jetée dans le féminisme comme d'autres se jettent dans la devotion' (ibid.: 44).

21. The complex issues found in these Belle Epoque novels were harbingers of the struggles encountered by second-wave feminism and the *Mouvement pour la Libération des Femmes* (MLF) almost sixty years after these texts were written. For example, it was not until 1965 that women were allowed to work outside the home without first receiving their husband's permission, an issue raised by the protagonist Laure Deborda in the 1903 novel *L'un vers l'autre* (*One Toward the Other*) by Louise-Marie Compain. Professional equality between men and women was not instituted until the Roudy Law of 1983, even though women's salaries still remained approximately thirty percent behind men's salaries. And it was not until 1970 that the law on parental authority was passed, including Article 371, which stated that parental authority was to be shared between mother and father. Thus the husband is no longer automatically the head of the household in France, an issue of central importance to the female protagonists of both *La Rebelle* and *L'un vers l'autre*.

CHAPTER 14

DANIEL LESUEUR AND THE FEMINIST ROMANCE

Diana Holmes

Writing as a Woman at the Belle Epoque

'What would you have me do?' asks Renée Néré, heroine of Colette's *La Vagabonde* (Colette 1984 [1910]), when her lover objects to her semi-naked performances on the music-hall stage, 'Sewing, or typing, or street-walking?'[1] (Colette 1986: 122). Ways of making an independent living were limited for women at the Belle Epoque. Renée, like Colette, chose the stage, but both the fictional heroine and her author found another means of survival: writing. Increased demand for publishable text and the expansion in female readership produced some limited openings for women in the literary profession. The Belle Epoque was a period of dramatic expansion of the printed word, thanks to advances in the technology of printing, improved communications, the 1881 law on freedom of the press – and an insatiable appetite for stories from a now almost entirely literate population. In Paris alone there were over fifty daily newspapers and most of them, from the bourgeois end of the market to the tabloids of the day, carried a *feuilleton* or serialised story which would subsequently be published in book form. According to Anne Marie Thiesse's survey in *Le Roman du quotidien* (Thiesse 1984: 20) the newspaper was a gender-divided space, with the *feuilleton* considered a largely female preserve.[2]

It was not only in the newspapers that women were coming
to be seen as the principal target audience for popular fiction.
According, for example, to Yves Olivier-Martin's *Histoire du
roman populaire en France* (1980), from about 1880 the popular
novel (*roman populaire*) became almost synonymous with the
romantic novel (*roman d'amour*) (Olivier-Martin 1980: 16). In
French the romantic novel is variously labelled 'roman
d'amour', 'roman sentimental' or sometimes 'roman à l'eau
de rose', literally 'rosewater novel', a metaphor which con-
notes both blandness and sentimentality. If all popular fiction
lacked *distinction* in Bourdieu's sense of the word, the romance
novel was the least culturally valued sub-genre within an
undistinguished field. But the brute commercial fact was that
romance novels elicited and met huge reader demand. Writing was a difficult career to break into for a woman (as all the
male pseudonyms attest), but an illegitimate genre – one
already condemned to critical disdain not least because it
catered for female readers – offered an easier point of entry.
Thiesse found that only two to three percent of authors over all
were female at the period, but women make up seventeen percent of her list of popular authors (Thiesse 1984: 183–84), and
most of these were writing within the genre I want to call
romance. Of the forty-nine authors of the 'roman sentimental
populaire' listed by Thiesse, ten are women. Thus men also
authored the romance, though Thiesse points out that the
social origins of this group of writers are distinctly more proletarian or *petit bourgeois* than for those producing any other
category of literature. Just as the low status of the genre made
it an easier point of entry for women writers disadvantaged by
their sex (and sometimes also by class), so aspiring male writers handicapped by an undistinguished class background
could find a way in to writing as a career through the popular
romance – though once associated with this most feminine,
hence unesteemed type of literature, they had little chance of
acceding to the higher spheres of the literary firmament. This
meant that most of the male writers of *romans sentimentaux*
depended on their literary earnings, hence on their capacity to
understand and respond to a female readership. Although by
no means uniquely authored by women, the popular romance
became a mainly female domain, and one that extended
across class boundaries. The genre became a space within
which women wrote and read, working out in fictional terms
the contradictions between desire and social necessity, living
vicariously the thrill of being loved and wanted, indulging

utopian dreams but also recognising the dangers incurred by breaking the rules that governed female behaviour.

Defining Romance

If romance is to be a useful term it requires definition. Love may be a staple ingredient of Western fiction, but not all narratives that include a love story can be classified as romances. Like all genres, the romance is historically variable and shifting, but certain narrative and thematic features remain constant, at least across the late nineteenth and the twentieth century. Three features relating to plot, narrative mode and the exploration of female identity and desire will serve here to define what constitutes the romance, both as a durable category of modern fiction and as a specific and immensely popular (in both senses) element of the female imaginary in Belle Epoque France.

Firstly, the romance plot is both driven and structured by passionate romantic love. The central question posed by a romance narrative is: 'Can this mutually desiring couple be together?' The answer to this question is then pleasurably delayed by the negotiation of a series of obstacles, which may conclude in either a happy or an unhappy dénouement.

Secondly, in terms of narrative mode, the romance occupies a variable place on a spectrum that runs between realism and melodrama. Romance is commonly associated with fantasy; but if we adopt Rita Felski's definition of realism as 'an attentiveness to the depiction of a social reality which is not relativized as the product of a subjective consciousness [but demonstrates] confidence in an external and knowable world' (Felski 1989: 81), then the consistent presence of realism within romance becomes apparent. Romantic fictions are rarely modernist texts that foreground their own textuality, nor are they concerned solely with the heroine's subjectivity. They may vary in the extent to which they are precisely located in time and space, but whether situated (for example) in 1890s Paris or in an undated, loosely defined present, they place their heroines in a world of social relations and material necessities that the reader can recognise as 'real'. At the same time romance shapes its plots and characters by deploying the devices of melodrama: coincidence, pathetic fallacy, bodily signifiers of moral traits, binary oppositions. This heightens the mythical dimension of the romance – the sense that we are dealing not just with a tale of contemporary life but with the symbolic representation of a collective emotional drama.

The third characteristic of the romance is at once thematic and structural. Romances are love stories, and within them love is represented as supremely life-affirming, intense and utopian. However, since romance also provides one of the few public spaces in which women can dramatise and thus reflect upon the dilemmas of their lives in a patriarchal society, the genre rarely makes the experience of heterosexual love the simple fulfilment of a woman's destiny. Rather, it tends to establish a socially produced conflict between conformity to the rules of feminine behaviour and personal fulfilment, then to work to resolve this (in which case the dénouement will be happy) or to explore the impossibility of its resolution. The romance poses the question of how to be a good woman – and what that might mean – whilst remaining true to some core of self that is denied by normative definitions of female virtue. At the time of the Belle Epoque, romance became particularly significant: though this was a repressively patriarchal society, its liberal and expanding literary industry nonetheless offered women readers and writers a dedicated arena in which to explore female identity and desire.

A celebrated example of the genre is *Le Maître de Forges* by the best-selling male author Georges Ohnet (1848–1918), published in 1882 and even by Ohnet's standards an exceptional commercial success. Ohnet was much derided by the critical establishment for his love-centred plots and melodramatic style, but no one denied that he knew how to please his readers (Todd 1994: 22). Love drives the plot: Philippe Derblay, the brilliant, handsome and thoroughly virtuous bourgeois hero loves Claire de Beaulieu, beautiful, wilful daughter of an aristocratic family. Claire is jilted by her fiancé, the shallow and debauched Gaston de Bligny, and on the rebound agrees to what on her side is a dishonest, because loveless, marriage with Philippe. The plot traces her sentimental education as she learns to love her husband, the true hero, and ends in perfect happiness. The melodrama of evil rivals, heartache that turns into near-fatal illness, a duel in which Claire saves her husband from the bullet of the man she once loved, is interwoven with the realist depiction of class antagonism in the early Third Republic, the waning fortunes of the aristocracy, Philippe's modernity as a Polytechnique-trained engineer. Love is presumed to be supremely important, and to find it Claire must weigh her passionate will to self-affirmation (she is a proud, intelligent young woman, 'resolute and decided, a little masculine in character'[3]) against a growing recognition that the path to happiness lies in submission to the will of the eminently lovable Philippe. Ohnet's dénouement firmly reinstates patriarchal values, but because Philippe provides an example of consistent, unwavering and passionate love, the romance offers the female reader the vicarious pleasure of being the adored object of masculine attention and finally of reconciling desire, social obligation and virtue.

Daniel Lesueur

Daniel Lesueur was the pen-name of Jeanne Loiseau (1860–1921), one of the most successful authors of *romans populaires* of the Belle Epoque. Her work extends across the class spectrum from romances that are also *romans d'idées,* and were serialised in the major 'serious' newspapers, to less cerebral, more action-packed romances that appeared in (for example) the popular daily *Le Petit Journal.* Almost entirely lost from history, she does not (unlike, for example, her contemporary and fellow romantic novelist Marcelle Tinayre) appear in Sartori and Zimmerman's very useful bibliography and biography of French women writers (Sartori and Zimmermann 1991), though Makward and Cottenet-Hage do include (and praise) her in their literary dictionary of women writing in French (Makward and Cottenet-Hage 1996). Born in 1860, she was the daughter of educated, middle-class parents who lost their fortune when she was still very young, so that she was obliged to earn a living as a teacher and governess both in France and England.[4] In 1882, as Jeanne Loiseau, she published a volume of poetry that was well received and indeed won the 1885 *grand prix de l'Académie française* for poetry. She rapidly extended her range to the novel, with her first, *L'Amant de Geneviève (Genevieve's Lover),* appearing in 1883. Those historians of popular literature who mention Lesueur seem to agree that she did not write from financial need because she was the wife of Henri Lapauze, the curator of the Palais des Beaux-Arts (Thiesse 1984: 190); but in fact her marriage to Lapauze took place only in 1904 when she was forty-four years old and already had a daughter.[5] It is more probable that Lesueur began her career with the intention of making writing, rather than teaching, her means of financial support, and that, by the time she married Lapauze, she was already a well-known and commercially successful writer.

Lesueur published a series of long novels between the 1880s and her death in 1921, most of them serialised in the press before they appeared in book form, and many of them also subsequently adapted for the stage by their author. She became the first woman to be elected to the *Société de gens de lettres* in 1900 and went on to become a member, then the vice-president, of the society's executive. She collaborated from 1897 with the feminist daily *La Fronde*, accepting lower prices for her stories from the start because '*La Fronde* interests me' with (as she put it in a later letter) 'its staying power, its influence and its fine humanitarian and feminist victories'.[6] Lesueur was a member of the first jury of the *Prix fémina vie heureuse*, a prize established by a group of women writers in 1904 when, to their shared indignation, Myriam Harry failed to win the Prix Goncourt for her novel *La Conquête de Jérusalem* (*The Conquest of Jerusalem*, 1904). This first jury brought together several of the major women writers of the Belle Epoque: Marcelle Tinayre, Gabrielle Reval, Anna de Noailles, Séverine, Lucie Delarue-Mardrus. I hope to demonstrate that although, like so many of that generation of *femmes de lettres*, Lesueur was cautious about being identified primarily as a feminist, and although she shared some of the less progressive attitudes of her era, particularly on class, race and colonialism,[7] she is an important figure in any mapping of women's cultural history at the Belle Epoque. Like popular women novelists of subsequent generations, Lesueur tackles feminist issues through pleasurable narratives. 'If she did not exactly create the popular feminist novel' writes Olivier-Martin, 'she did renew it and set her own stamp on it'.[8]

Lesueur's *oeuvre* ranges from *romans à idées*, addressed essentially to a middlebrow, reasonably well-educated readership, to swashbuckling *romans à sensation* that appeared in the mass circulation *Petit Journal*. The former are set mainly in contemporary Paris, and peopled by characters drawn from the cultured elite – writers, composers, intellectuals, industrial leaders, aristocrats – but they also contain lively plots and elements of melodrama. The more down-market novels play on a wider and more dramatically contrasted range of social classes, from rich, landed gentry to peasants and servants, and their plots, whilst centred in France, also take the reader to exotic locations as they employ suspense, dramas of concealed identity, radical shifts in fortune and violent confrontation to engineer a compulsive absorption in the fictional world. Yet both types of novel deal with moral dilemmas, explore the conflict between passionate love and the need for social acceptance, and question normative sexual morality. Lesueur's work assumes no sharp distinction between the reading pleasure of an educated, intellectually sophisticated public (of the sort we can assume read *La Fronde*, for example) and that of a literate but less leisured and cultivated 'popular' readership. My argument is broadly this: that Lesueur provided her many and varied readers with the pleasures of romance whilst addressing social and psycho-emotional issues from a moderate feminist perspective – that is, within a moral and political framework very close to the 'genteel feminism' of *La Fronde*.[9] The fictional mode, however, and the genre's privileging of a female perspective and female desire, also allowed for the inclusion of more radical elements. Lesueur's fictions (like those of Marcelle Tinayre) are woman-centred, contestatory of the narrow scope of female lives under patriarchy and of the sexual double standard that denies the legitimacy of female desire. Rather than seeing this as a subversion of a quintessentially feminine genre, I would argue that Lesueur simply exploited the potential of the romance to provide a critical commentary on gender relations, and – as her success demonstrates – that she did so in a way that strongly appealed to her contemporaries.

Novels of Adultery

The classic romance script is that of the fairy story: single girl meets single boy, they work their way through a series of problems or obstacles before reaching the ideal conclusion of marriage. Lesueur's love stories, though, are more often than not novels of adultery, a sub-genre in which the narrative is driven by conflict between the patriarchal family unit formed by marriage and the individual's desire.

In *Justice de femme* (*Woman's Justice*, 1893), Simone is the faithful, if mildly discontented wife of Roger Mervil, a composer twelve years her senior. Motivated by an ill-defined but troubling sense of curiosity and dissatisfaction, by anger at her husband's casual if episodic infidelity, and by the desire inspired by a handsome, seductive and attentive man, Jean, she begins an affair and discovers in sexual passion 'the joy, so extreme for any human creature, of satisfying the unquenched desire that lies secreted within each of us'.[10] But despite his answering passion, and the intensity of her love for him, Simone gives up Jean and ends the affair to devote herself to her husband, her daughter and soon to a second pregnancy. The cost of her brief indulgence of desire is high: she realises gradually that the second child is Jean's and, in a thoroughly melodramatic dénouement, both the love child and Simone herself die, as if she were doubly punished for her fall from grace. Focalised largely from Simone's perspective, however, the novel's punitive ending fails to erase its sympathetic treatment of her quest for a wider experience and for erotic and emotional fulfilment. The concluding episodes dramatise the risks incurred by a woman who flouts the sexual rules, risks not only to herself but also to her children. The reader has nonetheless been positioned with Simone in her dissatisfaction with marriage and her fulfilling experience of passionate desire.

In *Haine d'amour* (*Love's Hatred*, 1894), Vincent de Villenoise's very correct romance with the young and virginal Gilberte (which concludes, in classic romance fashion, in a happy marriage) is doubled by the more compelling narrative of his lengthy affair with Sabine, a divorced woman much closer to his own age. Their affair pre-dates Sabine's divorce, which was caused by her husband's discovery of the couple *in flagrante delicto*. Vincent feels beholden to this woman now condemned to social ostracism and relative poverty, but he no longer returns her passionate love. Though Sabine's passion is destructive and dangerous, so that she gradually assumes the role of the *femme fatale* in contrast to Gilberte's bland innocence, she remains the novel's most interesting character and the locus of its exploration of the will to self-affirmation and fulfilment. The framing love story between Vincent (a modern Prince Charming, rich, handsome and single) and the undercharacterised Gilberte remains somewhat insipid, whereas Sabine's desperate attempts to win back Vincent's love, to survive as an independent woman through her painting, and to deal with the difficulty of ageing in a culture that sets great store by women's youthful beauty constitute the major interest of the novel.

Nietzschéenne (*The Nietzschean Woman*, 1908) is the most 'feminist' of the three novels discussed here, for the eponymous 'Nietzschéenne', Jocelyne Forestier, is a more successful version of Sabine, who wins the hero's love through her independence, her strong-willed indifference to the prevailing codes of feminine behaviour, and her intellectual and practical competence. Jocelyne has lost her place in respectable society by deliberately, passionately losing her virginity – offering herself to the fiancé she loves when she discovers that their marriage is to be prevented by a jealous rival. She now lives alone, and if she refuses to become the mistress of the married Robert, this is not for reasons of morality but out of concern for his wife and children ('ah! If it weren't for them, how I would love to defy [the world's] hypocritical proprieties, to trample them underfoot'[11]) and because, having struggled to achieve an independent existence and a degree of social esteem, she will not put these at risk by an adulterous liaison.

In Lesueur's romances, the pleasure and fulfilment offered by passionate love are celebrated and explored, but they are also weighed against all that may be lost through the indulgence of passion: social recognition, security, and a sense of personal integrity. Her plots dramatise the heroine's ethical and existential quest to find a way of being that falls neither into the trap of self-abnegation or loss of self in conformity to the normative view of female virtue, nor that of uncontrolled emotion that can inflict damage on others and on the self. The heroines seek to fulfil womanly duties in as far as they support a decent world (motherhood, loyalty and, in the case of the 'Nietzschéenne' Jocelyne, social reformism) but not at the expense of a passionately felt desire for self-affirmation and exploration.

As perhaps in most romances of the period, Lesueur's women have limited scope for action, and passionate love is both a form of and a figurative representation of the will to self-fulfilment. Desire for the hero is not merely reactive, but comes from within: it is a yearning towards what is variously defined as 'the unknown' ('l'inconnu', Lesueur 1893: 174), 'unfulfilment' ('l'inassouvi', ibid.: 115), 'the unique, prodigious and inexpressible adventure of one's own life' ('l'aventure unique, prodigieuse, de sa propre vie, indicible', Lesueur 1908: 173). The dilemma – which I would argue is one that many women readers at the time would have identified with – is this. The path of female virtue (marital fidelity or celibacy as a single woman) produces material and social security, and a sense of socially confirmed identity. But to be a virtuous woman means the acceptance of a severely limited destiny: confinement to the domestic sphere and in many cases an arid or dully routine emotional life. Extra-conjugal passion is life-enhancing, it provides intense affirmation of the individual's identity and uniqueness and it opens up the world – but it is also severely threatening. In each of the novels discussed here, Lesueur shows that any flouting of the rules of women's sexual and emotional behaviour is harshly sanctioned and represents a severe threat to future well-being. Simone's adultery leads directly to her death and that of her child; Sabine, caught *in flagrante delicto* by her husband, is divorced and plunged into social limbo and poverty; Jocelyne's passionate and deliberate loss of virginity as a single girl blights her reputation and her whole life. The dénouements of all three novels tip into melodrama, killing off the heroine and thus preventing any lasting adulterous union. This could be read as a conservative narrative move – patriarchal order is restored – but it also figures the difficulty of reconciling female self-fulfilment with the social order. Love is absolutely central, but cannot – in this social context – produce a satisfactory conclusion.

The Other Woman

One of the classic devices to produce narrative tension and delay the dénouement of the romance narrative is the inclusion of rivals, especially female rivals, who also refine the work's definition of 'how to be a woman', normally by functioning as the heroine's foil or negative. Thus in Ohnet's *Le Maître des forges,* Athénaïs Moulinet is not only a vulgar arriviste consumed with jealousy for the noble-born heroine and hence determined to steal any man that she loves, she is also downright evil, 'the most evil creature one could imagine on this earth'.[12] In the Delly romances (the first published in 1907) the rival sins by excess, daring to openly express desire for the hero and to take active steps to have her (evil) way with him, her appearance and speech coded as lacking womanly discretion; but she is always punished by the plot.[13] Lesueur's romances also use the rival in this way: Gisèle in *Justice de Femme*, Sabine in *Haine d'Amour*, Huguette in *Nietzschéenne*, each claims the right to uncompromising self-fulfilment, scorning the attempts to reconcile duty and desire, the wish to combine concern for the other with concern for the self, that characterise romance heroines. '*I* cultivate my *ego* (to use an expression that men should not be allowed to have all to themselves)' declares Gisèle to Simone in *Justice de Femme*. 'You on the other hand cultivate a load of old prejudices [...] such as a code of marital behaviour invented by these gentlemen to our detriment, and their greatest possible advantage'.[14] Sabine, with her openly expressed 'unquenchable passion of body and heart',[15] claims the right to male prerogatives, to the extent that she shocks her lover by appearing in male clothing. These secondary female characters represent the danger of excess, of a lack of emotional control, of an incautious flouting of social proprieties. Their failure to display 'tact, moderation, modesty' and their 'lack of a sense of moral propriety'[16] are punished by loss of the desired lover and in two of these three cases by death.

The binary opposition heroine/rival and the excessive style of the 'other women' contribute to the pacy, high colour narrative that befits a popular serial designed for fast reading. But in Lesueur's texts this is not the whole picture. Although in purely diegetic terms the 'other women' suffer for their impropriety, Lesueur's narrative voice is a tolerant and non-judgemental one. Her narrative technique employs multiple focalisers, hence conflicting viewpoints, including that of the 'other woman'. These 'other women' also function to dramatise the limits on female behaviour and to articulate anger at double standards and oppression, particularly the double standard of sexual behaviour that condemns Gisèle and Sabine to social opprobrium and humiliating divorce proceedings while their male sexual partners find their social standing unchanged or enhanced. New Woman aspirations find an explicit voice in the novels through these characters.

Moreover, there is more than one sort of 'other woman' in these novels. The docile, dependent child-wife also acts as negative foil to the heroine, particularly in *Nietzschéenne* where the bird-brained, doll-like Lucienne, the hero's wife (Lesueur 1908: 211), is contrasted to the competent, independent Jocelyne. Other women can also be positive characters, and female friends are cherished with an emotional intensity that at times has erotic undertones ('Ah!' says Gisèle to Simone, 'if I were a man I know how I'd dry those lovely eyes!'[17]), suggesting an early example of Adrienne Rich's 'lesbian continuum'.[18] Daughters are portrayed with a Colettian sense of the *déchéance* or decline involved in the passage from girlhood to womanhood: Simone, watching her daughter Paulette, reflects that, 'this freshness of spirit, this plenitude of feeling, seemed to her both admirable and touching. She too had possessed these things, and had lost them'.[19]

Romances of Modernity

Lesueur's romances skilfully operate the genre's blending of melodrama and realism. The function of the texts' melodramatic techniques (the thematic over-determination of place, weather and appearance, the use of dramatic contrast and coincidence, closure through violent and unexpected deaths) is to produce rapid, varied reading pleasure, to give a sense of energy and exhilaration, as well as to identify love and desire with a utopian drive for happiness. But Lesueur's romances are also 'rooted in political, economic and social reality':[20] her fictional world is the world of modernity, where scientific inventions, workers' living conditions, industrial relations, the divorce laws as well as cultural fashions and social mores have important functions in the plot. And her modernity needs women, just as women need to be part of the exciting, changing public world. In *Nietzschéenne*, Robert learns how to manage his factory by taking the advice of the clear-sighted, visionary Josyane, who in turn relishes her engagement with the new world of technology, whereas in *Justice de femme* and *Haine d'Amour*, Sabine and Simone seek in love a means of escape from their confinement to a domestic, private world. Robert, a secondary character in *Haine d'Amour* but one who, as an engineer and inventor, represents the energy and excitement of the modern age, comments pityingly on that very gendered division of spheres that made the romance synonymous with the women's novel. Women suffer more from unhappiness in love, he says, for 'that's all they have to occupy them. It's quite natural that they should make it the centre of their existence'.[21] Love is central to Lesueur's novels, but its place at the heart of women's preoccupations is seen to be culturally determined rather than driven by nature.

Lesueur herself was a successful 'New Woman' who exploited the possibilities of a traditionally female genre within the new conditions provided by the Belle Epoque. Her novels provided readers with a dramatised but recognisable image of their own lives, as members of a sex still firmly maintained in a dependent and submissive role by the law, by political and economic power, and by a thoroughly androcentric culture, yet also as women potentially empowered by a modern world of changing technologies, state education, the legalisation of divorce, and the newly audible voice of feminism.

Notes

1. 'Que voulez-vous que je fasse? De la couture, de la dactylographie, ou le trottoir?' (Colette 1910 [1984]: 1172)
2. Although it is beyond the range of this study, there is scope for a close consideration of the relationship between the *feuilleton* with its multi-strand narratives, melodramatic plotlines and suitability for an interrupted,

intermittent style of consumption, and the equally female genre of the contemporary soap.

3. 'résolue et decidée, un peu masculine de caractère' (Ohnet 1882: 47).
4. Loss of a dowry as a result of the family's financial problems seems to have been a liberating factor for several women writers of the late nineteenth/early twentieth centuries. Colette's first marriage to Willy – hence her entry into a literary and bohemian milieu – resulted in part from her dowryless state, and Simone de Beauvoir was only allowed to pursue her education because her impoverished father recognised that she would be obliged to earn a living.
5. The Daniel Lesueur dossier in the Bibliothèque Marguerite Durand contains a letter dated 4 January 1904 from Lesueur to Durand, inviting the latter to a celebratory tea after the former's marriage to Lapauze. There are also letters written around 1914 to a grown-up daughter, Gaby, but I have not yet managed to discover the paternity of Gaby.
6. 'La Fronde m'intéresse (avec) sa durée, son influence et ses belles victoires humanitaires et féministes' (Letters to Marguerite Durand, 6 December 1897 and 9 December 1900). On Lesueur's work for *La Fronde*, see also above, Chapter 3.
7. In the double-volumed *Le Masque d'amour* (*The Mask of Love*, 1904), for example, class hierarchy is naturalised by the attribution of an innate nobility to the aristocratic hero and heroine, whilst the most evil character is the product of *métissage* or mixed blood. The Indians encountered when the colourful narrative shifts to South America are described as 'primitives' and 'like children' (Lesueur 1904: 182)
8. 'Si elle n'a pas créé le roman populaire féministe, elle l'a fait sien en le renouvelant.' (Olivier-Martin 1980: 228)
9. Máire Cross refers to *La Fronde*'s 'féminisme en dentelles' or 'genteel feminism': 'The image of feminism was to be one of genteel reasonable demands rather than one of any radical attempt to overthrow the system, either by the abolition of marriage, or taking over parliament or gaining immediate access to political power' (Cross 2000: 109). Also see Maggie Allison's analysis of *La Fronde*, Chapter 2 above.
10. 'la joie, si excessive pour toute créature humaine, de tromper l'inassouvi qui veille dans le secret de l'être' (Lesueur 1893: 115).
11. 'Sans cela, comme j'aurais plaisir à les piétiner, à les braver, leurs convenances hypocrites' (Lesueur 1908: 177).
12. 'tout ce qu'on pouvait rêver de plus mauvais sur la terre'(Ohnet 1882: 168).
13. Delly was the pen-name of a sister and brother writing team: Marie (1875–1947) and Frédéric (1876–1949) Petitjean de la Rosière. They published their first romance in 1907 and went on to write around a hundred romantic novels, all of them best-sellers. An extreme case of the other woman as sinister rival is *La Biche au bois* (date not established) in which the evil (and significantly foreign) Myrrha Nadopoulo tries all sorts of underhand tricks to win the rich and aristocratic hero, finally trying to murder the heroine only to die herself, savaged by the hero's loyal dog.
14. 'Moi je cultive mon *moi* (pour employer une expression dont les hommes n'auront pas seuls le privilège). Toi tu cultives un tas de vieux préjugés [...] le code conjugal tel que ces messieurs l'ont fait à notre usage et à leur plus grand profit (Lesueur 1893: 29–30).'
15. 'ardeur inapaisable de la chair et du coeur' (Lesueur 1894: 121).
16. 'tacte, mesure, pudeur', 'défaut de tenue morale' (Lesueur 1893: 235).

17. 'Ah! si j'étais un homme, je saurais comment m'y prendre pour sécher ces beaux yeux-là!' (ibid.: 142].
18. Adrienne Rich's influential 1980 article 'Compulsory Heterosexuality and Lesbian Existence' introduces the term 'lesbian continuum' to signify 'a range [...] of woman-identified experience; not simply the fact that a woman has had or consciously desired genital sexual experience with another woman' but 'many more forms of primary intensity between and among women' (Rich 1992: 178).
19. 'cette fraîcheur d'âme, cette plénitude de sensation, lui semblaient une chose admirable et touchante. Elle l'avait possédée, cette chose, et elle l'avait perdue.' (Lesueur 1893: 170).
20. '(une oeuvre) enracinée dans la réalité politique, économique et sociale' (Makward and Cottenet-Hage 1996: 379).
21. 'Les femmes n'ont que ça pour les occuper. C'est tout naturel qu'elles en fassent la grosse affaire de leur existence' (Lesueur 1894: 232).

CHAPTER 15

VIRGINAL PERVERSION/RADICAL SUBVERSION: RACHILDE AND DISCOURSES OF LEGITIMATION

Jeri English

As a stated misogynist, a female trespasser in the production of Decadent fiction and a creator of novels imbued with potentially sexually subversive feminist themes, Rachilde was a sometimes shocking and nearly always problematic author and public figure. Beginning her career in the late nineteenth century, when 'the many debates about women culminated in the idea of "the war of the sexes" and in a violent antifeminist and misogynist fury',[1] Rachilde remains today canonically marginal despite her initial literary successes.[2] In this chapter, I will examine polemically opposed discourses of legitimisation in prefaces to two works by Rachilde: Maurice Barrès' preface to the 1889 re-edition of *Monsieur Vénus* (Barrès 1977 [1889]); and Claude Dauphiné's 'Présentation' to the 1982 re-edition of *La Jongleuse* (*The Juggler*) (Dauphiné 1982). Barrès' preface to *Monsieur Vénus*, written shortly after the first appearance of the text and entitled 'Complications d'amour' falls into Gérard Genette's category of the 'préface ultérieure' (Genette 1987: 177), in which the author of the preface uses his or her institutional prestige to recommend the novel of a new, unknown or scandalous writer to a contemporary public. In contrast, Dauphiné's preface to *La Jongleuse*, written eighty years after the novel's first edition, conforms to Genette's cate-

gory of the 'préface tardive' (ibid.: 177) which seeks generally
to transform the literary canon and establish a place in it for
an overlooked, forgotten or misunderstood text. There is no
question that Rachilde was, over the course of the twentieth
century, effectively forgotten: even her most famous novel
Monsieur Vénus was insignificant at the moment of its more
recent re-edition by Flammarion in 1977. Possibly fearing the
repercussions of their decision to re-edit an author who suffered from 'total oblivion' (Ferlin 1995: 112),[3] Flammarion
chose not only to reproduce Barrès's preface but also his original letter to Rachilde offering his literary authority as a legitimising force for her novel, along with a copy of the stamped
envelope in which the letter was sent.

Written nearly one hundred years apart, the preface by Barrès and the preface by Dauphiné each use validating discourses specific to their particular cultural context. As this
analysis will show, Barrès sought to mitigate the scandal and
outrage that followed the publication of *Monsieur Vénus* by
emphasising Rachilde's femininity, youth and innocence, and
by minimising the revolutionary potential (and literary
longevity) of the novel. At the same time, his continual
emphasis on the very perversity of the novel's sexual themes is
a clear attempt to seduce potential readers with physical
images of the virginal author's sordid fantasy life. In contrast,
Dauphiné, appealing to a late twentieth-century feminist public, draws close parallels between the author and her sexually
subversive heroines. The revolutionary elements of *Monsieur
Vénus* that Barrès attenuates in his preface are precisely those
that Dauphiné highlights to convert a sceptical feminist public to a positive reading of Rachilde, downplaying the author's
stated misogyny by portraying both *La Jongleuse* and *Monsieur
Vénus* as inherently, if unconsciously, feminist. The shocking
sexual themes that Barrès emphasises to 'tantalise' his public
(Holmes 1996b: 27)[4] are precisely those that should, according
to Dauphiné, arm twentieth-century feminist readers in a fight
against the author's neglect. By reclaiming Rachilde's novels
from their initial public condemnation and the 'muddled and
sexist reactions of writers like Barrès' (Finch 2000: 208),
Dauphiné hopes her public will save the marginal writer from
the 'literary purgatory'[5] where she awaits canonical legitimisation. The figure of Rachilde thus becomes, in Dauphiné's
preface, the centrifugal force in a canonical debate.

The outrage, astonishment and admiration that erupted
with the publication of Rachilde's first major novel *Monsieur*

Vénus in 1884 were largely reactions to the 'calling into question of gender roles' (Rogers 1998: 241)[6] that dominate the text. The public's indignation was aroused by the novel's protagonist, Raoule de Vénérande, a powerful and androgynous aristocrat who assumes outward masculine gender trappings and refers to herself using masculine grammatical forms: '"You must bear in mind that I am a boy," she said, "an artist whom my aunt calls her nephew [...]"' (Rachilde 1992: 53).[7] Infatuated with the beauty of Jacques Silvert, a lower class, sensual and effeminate florist with feminine instincts (ibid.: 54), Raoule seduces him, subjugates him as her mistress and wife, and finally brings about his death. As Jennifer Waelti-Walters points out, fin-de-siècle readers would have read this destruction of a male by a female character as 'an unspeakable perversion' (Waelti-Walters 1990: 161). With the publication of *Monsieur Vénus*, Rachilde was initially rejected by French literary society: 'Certain salons would no longer receive her, and she was treated like a pornographer' (Ferlin 1995: 89).[8] Legally, Rachilde's work was immediately censured: according to her biographers, the novel was ordered to be seized in Brussels, and the author was sentenced to two years in prison and fined two thousand francs.[9] Melanie Hawthorne suggests that Rachilde may have actively sought this legal condemnation and published *Monsieur Vénus* 'as part of a larger publicity move' (Hawthorne 2001: 90), relying on the likely scandal of her work to advertise her name. It is undeniable that *Monsieur Vénus* made Rachilde an immediate scandalous star: by the time *La Jongleuse* appeared in 1900, 'Rachilde's reputation was at its zenith' (Hawthorne 1990: xviii) and the author was clearly established within the literary institution. Whether a product of skilful marketing or the unsuspecting object of institutional denunciation, *Monsieur Vénus* launched Rachilde's career and brought her first literary renown, while at the same time propelling her into a fray of resentment. The fury that surrounded *Monsieur Vénus* led Rachilde to occupy a social and literary position located somewhere 'between perversity and refinement'.[10]

Barrès' Preface, 1889

From the first sentence of his preface, Barrès establishes a decisive discursive distance between himself and *Monsieur Vénus*, as well as from its naïve, childlike author: 'This book is somewhat abhorrent, but I cannot say that it shocks me' (Barrès 1992: 1).[11] In his immediate use of the first-person singular, Barrès signifies the degree to which he is imbued with discursive authority by the literary institution. He immediately aligns himself with the 'few of the serious-minded'(ibid.: 1)[12] who are cultured enough to appreciate this 'wonderful masterpiece' (ibid.: 1),[13] despite its lack of literary professionalism and its painful vulgarity. Interestingly, while carefully constructing his own distance from the text, Barrès emphasises the novel's close relationship to its historical context. To prove to his public that *Monsieur Vénus* is unlikely to inspire a new generation of novelists bent on revolutionising the sexual status quo (and can thus be read simply as a harmless diversion), Barrès links the creation of *Monsieur Vénus* to the *'mal du siècle'* (ibid.: 6).[14] Rachilde's virginal perversions become in this reading 'a very significant symptom' (ibid.: 7)[15] of the literary and social climate of the late nineteenth century, and as such will have no lasting effect on the literary institution. To further reassure his readers, Barrès suggests that that *Monsieur Vénus* is only a 'little masterpiece' (ibid.: 3),[16] a minor and non-threatening textual amusement.

The thematic basis of Barrès's prefatory recommendation can be summed up in a single sentence: although *Monsieur Vénus* is shocking (and excitingly perverse), it could never be a truly dangerous novel since it is *only* the frivolous product of an instinctive, naïve, young girl.[17] He fosters this perception of Rachilde by using a highly restrained and specific vocabulary throughout the ten pages of his text. The word 'singularité' and its derivations, as well as the word 'vierge' appear four times throughout the preface; 'instincts' appears six times and 'curiosité' five times; and, perhaps most importantly, variants on the expression 'jeune fille'[18] (including 'jeune femme', 'petite fille' and 'enfant') appear nineteen times in ten pages. Barrès' preface becomes, then, an apology for the figure of Rachilde, who belongs, by virtue of her youth and inexperience, to a category of 'sly, self-centred and passionate little beasts' (Barrès 1992: 3).[19] Barrès asks his potential public to read Rachilde with little critical judgement since her age, gender and virginity obviously limit not only her experience but also her aesthetic and literary skills.[20] He appeals in his preface to physical manifestations of Rachilde's girlish defencelessness, assuring his readers that despite her outrageous text, the author conforms to society's cultural standards of femininity. Rachilde, he asserts, is not a monster, but rather 'a schoolgirl of sober and reserved demeanour, very pale, it's true, but her paleness was that of a studious schoolgirl, a girl in all the senses, somewhat slender, somewhat frail, with tiny restless hands [...] (ibid.: 1–2).[21] Barrès' portrait of a tiny, pale and disquietingly delicate writer conforms to the discursive tendencies unveiled in Rachel Sauvé's (2000) analysis of prefaces to women's texts in the nineteenth century. According to Sauvé, the general practice in these prefaces was to reduce the female-authored novel to its supposed universal 'sign of femininity'.[22] The preface writer emphasised the 'frivolity, changeability, instinct and irritability'[23] of the author, validating the existence of the female-authored text while minimising its importance.

If readers find Rachilde's unsophisticated novel to be filled with 'childishness' (Barrès 1992: 3),[24] this is, in the paradigm of the late nineteenth century, because its protagonist is born of 'virginal ignorance – a virgin who was I believe quite out of her depth' (ibid.: 4).[25] In fact, what is essential for Barrès is that his potential readers never envision Raoule de Vénérande, the worldly androgyne who appropriates the masculine gender trappings of dress, hair, language, sport and décor,[26] as the textual representation of her creator. Rachilde, Barrès asserts, is in fact so pure and virginal, so utterly ignorant of the sadistic world of Raoule de Vénérande that she wrote her novel almost by accident:

> Truly, the little girl who wrote this wonderful *Monsieur Vénus* was not privy to this aesthetic [...] It was merely that she had certain base impulses [...] When she took up her pen to describe those extraordinary maidenly excitements of hers it was out of instinct (Barrès 1992: 2).[27]

Barrès goes so far as to posit the creation of Raoule de Vénérande by Rachilde as utterly incomprehensible to him and, presumably, to his like-minded public. 'I have never known anything more mysterious than this knowing depravity that erupts in the dreams of a virgin [...]' (ibid.: 1).[28] Barrès' desire to create a strict binary opposition between Rachilde and her powerfully androgynous character is again rooted in the gender stereotypes of the period, where it was generally presumed that 'when women write, it isn't art or they aren't women'.[29] Women authors were often accused of masculinity (Sauvé 2000: 61) or of belonging to a third, unnameable gender, writing as 'part women, part men, neither women nor men, monsters, *hybrid* beings'.[30] Male critics in this fin-de-siècle society were wary of the female author who wrote under a masculine pseudonym, seeing in this practice 'the hint of a tendency towards virility that would have explained abnormal intellectual ability in a woman, the renunciation of disappointed femininity'.[31]

With her androgynous name and her novels' subversive themes, Rachilde came dangerously close to fulfilling the expectations of this fin-de-siècle society, which generally assumed that all writing by women was autobiographical and could result in nothing more than 'the direct transposition of a love affair'.[32] Furthermore, since Rachilde herself often dressed as a man, cut her hair short and had business cards engraved with 'Rachilde, homme de lettres', the reading public was quick to assimilate Rachilde with Raoule, seeking in the author 'the signs of the depravation of her heroine'.[33] Interestingly, despite Barrès' efforts to deny any relation between Rachilde, 'a child most gentle and retiring' (Barrès 1992: 1)[34] and 'the very specific actions of an arrogant young woman' (ibid.: 4),[35] the name 'Rachilde' remains, years after the publication of *Monsieur Vénus*, synonymous with 'Raoule de Vénérande.' *Monsieur Vénus* is to this day 'the novel which conclusively determines the image we have made of Rachilde' (Dauphiné 1991: 54),[36] not only because her public and critics accuse her of rewriting the same text throughout her life (ibid.: 9), but because even today's readers understand Raoule as a textual representation of Rachilde. According to Marilyne Lukacher, 'Monsieur Vénus is a composite of Rachilde's search for sexual and intellectual identity' (Lukacher 1994: 119); Marc Angenot (1986) proposes that 'Rachilde identifies with her heroine, and believes herself to be depraved, perverted, nervous, hysterical, dissolute'.[37]

Dauphiné's Preface, 1982

In marked contrast to the late nineteenth century, where women intruded into the domain of literary creation at the price of their sexuality, the tendency at the end of the twentieth century has been not only a privileging of women's writing but also a questioning of the process of literary canonisation.[38] To be included in the category of texts worthy of study, dissemination and preservation,[39] a work was historically expected to correspond to 'universal' criteria of stylistic and thematic merit. In the eyes of the literary institution, texts were evaluated objectively and their aesthetic value (or lack thereof) was intrinsic; furthermore, works considered 'literary' formed a natural and harmonious unity. Since 1970, however, postmodern, postcolonial and feminist critics have begun to dismantle this notion of universality and to re-examine the institutional strategies that have traditionally valued certain works while excluding others.[40] Generally, critics who would destabilise the literary canon believe that the institution masks its processes of selection so that the criteria for inclusion in the canon appear to be politically neutral aesthetic values. According to Karen Lawrence, 'literary tradition and canon formation have always involved cultural narratives disguised as aesthetic principles but constructed upon assumptions about class, gender, language and race' (Lawrence 1992: 4). A growing number of contemporary literary critics now see canon construction as inextricably linked to historically variable sociocultural practices.

It is in this cultural and literary climate that Dauphiné published her seventeen-page 'Présentation' of *La Jongleuse* in 1982 at Les Editions des femmes. Dauphiné centres her recommendation of Rachilde precisely on the very practice of gender subversion that Barrès downplayed in his preface, underlining the similarities between Rachilde and Raoule de Vénérande in a four-page recommendation of *Monsieur Vénus*. She asserts the need for feminists to rediscover Rachilde from the first page of her preface, where she declares that 'a feminist reading of this book [*Monsieur Vénus*], as for the following books, is imperative in our view'.[41] Dauphiné's use of the first-person plural (in contrast to Barrès's use of the first-person singular) speaks to a reading collective, a feminist public who will undertake the revolutionary act of reading Rachilde. In fact, it seems that for Dauphiné the reception and study of *La Jongleuse* as an individual novel are secondary to the presentation of Rachilde as a feminist model and the call to arms of feminist readers to rediscover her corpus. Dauphiné blurs this inclusive call to intellectual arms with a pseudo-objective discourse, suggesting her mandate would be a collective truth:

> It should at last be time [Il serait temps] for Rachilde, so unfairly excluded from the Parnassus because she was disruptive, to obtain her rightful position in our literary history.[42]

Here, her use of the impersonal form 'il serait temps' serves to postulate her belief in the necessity of re-evaluating Rachilde's work as universal. She insists, still in the impersonal form, that

'*It is necessary* to reread Rachilde: this is not a reverent vow, it's a demand. We can no longer scorn or ignore her' (my emphasis).[43] Dauphiné exhorts us ('we' as a global group) to re-examine Rachilde's corpus precisely *because* of the author's 'vision of the world, of love and of women'.[44] Only in re-valorising her sexually subversive fiction can we join Rachilde in 'the fight against the triumphant patriarchy of the era',[45] against the dominant patriarchal ideology that excludes her works from the literary canon.

By the time *La Jongleuse* was published in 1900, Rachilde had already published several similarly outrageous novels, including *La Marquise de Sade* (1887) and *Madame Adonis* (1888). By 1897, Rachilde had become 'the great lady of Parisian literature'.[46] Significantly, she had also radically altered her social status through marriage, becoming in 1889 the wife of Alfred Vallette, future head of the publishing house Mercure de France. According to Dauphiné, the newly married Rachilde quickly gave up her masculine accoutrements (Dauphiné 1991: 81). Perhaps significantly, then, the protagonist of *La Jongleuse* is a wealthy and beautiful thirty-five-year-old widow, resolutely feminine in dress and in speech. Whereas Raoule's love-mistress Jacques in *Monsieur Vénus* is weak, effeminate and silly, Eliante Donalger's suitor in *La Jongleuse* is a headstrong, twenty-two-year-old medical student seemingly brimming with masculinity. For this reason, Eliante Donalger's sexual domination of Léon Reille in *La Jongleuse* is arguably more subversive than Raoule de Vénérande's subjugation of Jacques Silvert in *Monsieur Vénus*. Solitary and independent, with no desire to remarry or engage in heterosexual relations, Eliante reduces Léon in one striking scene to the position of passive spectator to her orgasm with/within a sexualised vase.

In both *Monsieur Vénus* and *La Jongleuse*, as with much of Rachilde's fiction, the female protagonist casts aside traditionally 'feminine' sexuality to achieve an enormous, and for a nineteenth-century public, worrying power over her male lover. Since it is now common practice to read textual representations of sexual transgressions as subversive of phallocentric ideology, it should not be surprising that the rhetoric of legitimisation of Rachilde's writing has undergone such a profound modification from Barrès' preface in 1889 to Dauphiné's in 1982. The two preface writers do, however, share a common sentiment: for Dauphiné, as for Barrès, the importance of Rachilde's work is only secondarily literary. But whereas Barrès seeks to defend Rachilde against accusations of perversion and androgyny by portraying her as innocent, virginal and girlish, Dauphiné argues that Rachilde should be re-read precisely because 'she affirms against the spirit of the age that one can live differently, that a woman has the possibility, the right in any case, to conceive of the couple in a different way, to control the game of love'.[47] We have to reread Rachilde, proposes Dauphiné, precisely *because* she is perverse, dissident and outrageous. In sharp contrast to Barrès, who fought throughout his preface to distance Rachilde from Raoule de Vénérande, Dauphiné poses Eliante Donalger, and more importantly Raoule, as direct textual representations of the author. In an interesting fallback to the nineteenth-century practice of reducing women's fiction to autobiography (and more precisely to the telling of personal love stories), Dauphiné suggests that Rachilde invented Raoule de Vénérande to settle the score with 'recent and painful events in her personal life',[48] her unreciprocated love for Catulle Mendès.

Far from seeking then, like Barrès, to establish a moral distance between author and character, Dauphiné proposes that 'Mademoiselle de Vénérande, whose name significantly evokes the fierce huntress, the cruel Diana, the Amazonian dispenser of subtle poisons, refusing all sexual submission, seems to be *closely related* to her creator' (my emphasis).[49] Dauphiné argues that the close relationship between Raoule and Rachilde is not only psychological, but also physical and aesthetic:

> Firstly, she resembles her physically with her haughty appearance and her strange eyes; secondly, she has the same audacity, the will to not depend on anyone, and certainly not on Men; thirdly, she shares her longings for the ideal, her dream of a passion freed from meaning .[50]

This mapping of character onto author is a far cry from Barrès' insistence on Rachilde's virginal innocence in his preface. Evidently, while a fin-de-siècle public could not tolerate a close relation between Rachilde and Raoule, Dauphiné believes that a potential feminist public in the 1980s needs to see in Rachilde the same sexual subversion as in her transgressive character.

As I have suggested above, textual analyses of the representation of Raoule de Vénérande in *Monsieur Vénus* and Eliante Donalger in *La Jongleuse* certainly seem to hold sexually revolutionary potential for the contemporary feminist critic. Nonetheless, it is undeniable that, as Holmes points out, 'the subversive power of such narratives is attenuated [...] by

Rachilde's determination to observe the codes of Decadence
and by that refusal of feminism later articulated in a lengthy
polemical essay entitled "Pourquoi je ne suis pas féministe"'
(Holmes 1996b: 39). Notwithstanding her efforts to establish
literary posterity for this long-marginalised woman writer,
Dauphiné also acknowledges Rachilde's misogyny, allowing
that the author had 'little respect for women in general, and
literary women in particular'.[51] Indeed, Rachilde's general
view of women as 'unreliable creatures' (Lukacher 1994: 111)
and her manifest antifeminism undermine attempts to interpret her gender deconstruction as a subversive feminist position. Marilyne Lukacher sums up the dilemma of the
twentieth-century feminist critic's engagement with Rachilde
in the following way: 'While Rachilde's writing can be read as
an act of protest against women's plight in fin-de-siècle
France, her thinking can by no means be readily assimilated
to a feminist perspective' (ibid.: 109).

Conclusion

To justify the study of Rachilde to a late-twentieth-century
public, Dauphiné therefore attempts to downplay the author's
antifeminist stance. For Dauphiné, Rachilde is a valuable
object of study because of her innate espousal of feminist
themes and *despite* her personal rejection of feminism:
'Although she was mistrustful of feminism, the author could-
n't have been clearer: a woman's freedom begins with the possibility of refusing to give a man what he expects'.[52] With this
legitimising discourse, Dauphiné positions herself in direct
opposition to Barrès who, a century earlier, portrayed Rachilde
as infantile and feminine, denied all similarities between the
author and her powerful character, and minimised the role of
gender in her novel, all to assure his readers of the author's
lack of revolutionary force. To fulfil his prefatory function as
Rachilde's literary patron in a society at once titillated and
disgusted by the author's sexual ambiguity, Barrès portrayed
Monsieur Vénus as unique and inimitable, rejecting any view of
the novel as a possible instigator of a disturbing literary trend.
Conversely, in order to find a place inside the newly desta-
bilised literary canon for a problematic and forgotten writer,
Dauphiné portrays Rachilde as an inherently feminist figure
and posits her androgynous fictional characters as tools for
important late-twentieth-century feminist scholarship.

Notes

1. '[L]a multiplication des débats sur les femmes culmine donc dans l'idée de "guerre de sexes" et dans un violent déchaînement antiféministe et misogyne' (Planté 1989: 17).
2. Although Rachilde's literary career spanned over sixty years, she fell into near total obscurity during the later part of her life, and her death in 1953 'passa pratiquement inaperçue' (Ferlin 1995: 111).
3. 'Méritait-elle l'oubli total, celle qui a compté pendant plus d'un demi-siècle dans la vie littéraire, au double-titre de romancière et de critique?' (ibid.: 112).
4. Marc Angenot characterises Barrès' preface as 'émoustillée' – titillating or tantalising (Angenot 1986: 137).
5. 'purgatoire des lettres' (Dauphiné 1991: 365).
6. 'Le scandale central est donc manifestement celui de la remise en question des rôles sexuels' (Rogers 1998: 241).
7. '"Mais souvenez-vous donc que je suis un garçon moi," disait-elle, "un artiste que ma tante appelle son neveu [...]"' (Rachilde 1977 [1884]: 53).
8. 'Certains salons ne veulent plus la recevoir, on la traite de pornographe' (Ferlin 1995: 89).
9. See David (1924: 21–22), Angenot (1986: 152), Hawthorne (1990: xi), Ferlin (1995: 89–90), Rogers (1998: 239) and Hawthorne (2001: 88–100).
10. 'entre perversité et raffinement' (Ducrey 1999: 613).
11. 'Ce livre-ci est assez abominable, pourtant je ne puis dire qu'il me choque' (Barrès 1977: 5).
12. 'quelques esprits très réfléchis' (ibid.: 6).
13. 'merveilleux chef-d'oeuvre' (ibid.: 6).
14. 'La maladie du siècle, qu'il faut toujours citer et dont *Monsieur Vénus* signale chez la femme une des formes les plus intéressantes, est faite en effet d'une fatigue nerveuse, excessive et d'un orgueil inconnu jusqu'alors' (ibid.: 19).
15. 'un symptôme très significatif' (ibid.: 20).
16. 'petit chef-d'oeuvre' (ibid.: 14).
17. Diana Holmes highlights the tension Barrès creates in his preface between author and product: 'Barrès's device for encouraging sales of his protégée's work was to play on the public's fascination with the paradoxical conjunction of virginal innocence and erotic fantasy. The implied oxymoron of chaste perversity underlay the appeal of both author and text' (Holmes 1996b: 27).
18. At the end of the nineteenth century, the official definition of 'jeune fille' was the following: 'Personne du sexe féminin, non-mariée, nubile et jeune encore' (Larousse 1865: 369). This etiquette also had a connotation ironically expressed by Flaubert: 'Jeune Fille: Articuler ce mot timidement. Toutes les jeunes filles sont "pâles" et "frêles." Toujours "pures." Eviter pour elles toute espèce de livre, les visites dans les musées, les théâtres [...]' (Flaubert 1965: 175).
19. 'petits animaux sournois, égoïsts et ardents' (Barrès 1977: 14).
20. 'Ni moraliste, encore qu'elle esquisse une théorie de l'amour, ni psychologue, bien qu'elle analyse parfois, ni artiste, malgré ses scintillements [...] Elle écrit des pages sincères, uniquement pour exciter et aviver ses frissons' (ibid.: 16–17).

21. 'une pensionnaire d'allures sobres et reservées, très pâle, il est vrai, mais d'une pâleur de pensionnaire studieuse, une vraie jeune fille, un peu mince, un peu frêle, aux mains inquiétantes de petitesse [...]' (ibid.: 6).

22. '[L]a marque du féminin [...] est essentielle à la recevabilité des textes' (Sauvé 2000: 95).

23. '[F]rivolité, versatilité, instinct, irritabilité, ces prédicatifs du discours médical se transforment, dans les préfaces, en éloge d'une sensibilité' (ibid.: 92).

24. 'enfantillages' (Barrès 1977: 14).

25. 'l'ignorance d'une vierge, d'une vierge qui se mêlait, je crois, de ce qu'elle n'avait pas regardé' (ibid.: 16).

26. According to Barbara Havercroft, the signs of Raoule's masculinity include her Turkish cigarettes, her boyish haircut, her androgynous bedroom, as well as her military accoutrements. Raoule de Vénérande 'adopte, avec enthousiasme, le rôle actif souvent réservé aux hommes [...] s'approprie une tenue vestimentaire masculine' ('adopts, with enthusiasm, the active role reserved for men [...] and wears male clothing') (Havercroft 1992: 50), and often uses masculine grammatical forms.

27. 'Certes, la petite fille qui rédigeait ce merveilleux *Monsieur Vénus* n'avait pas toute cette esthétique dans la tête [...] Simplement, elle avait de mauvais instincts [...] C'est d'instinct qu'elle se prit à décrire ses frissons de vierge singulière' (Barrès 1977: 13).

28. 'Ce vice savant éclatant dans le rêve d'une vierge, c'est un des problèmes les plus mystérieux que je sache [...]' (ibid.: 6).

29. '[Q]uand les femmes écrivent, ce n'est pas de l'art, ou ce ne sont pas des femmes' (Planté 1989: 214).

30. 'mi-femmes, mi-hommes, ni femmes ni hommes, des monstres, des êtres *hybrides*' (ibid.: 269).

31. 'Les critiques masculins voulurent le plus souvent y voir l'indice d'une tendance à la virilité qui aurait expliqué une puissance intellectuelle anormale chez une femme, le reniement d'une féminité déçue' (ibid.: 34).

32. 'la transposition directe d'une expérience amoureuse' (ibid.: 90).

33. 'les signes de la dépravation de son heroïne' (Ferlin 1995: 91).

34. 'l'enfant la plus douce et la plus retirée' (Barrès 1977: 6).

35. 'les actes très particuliers d'une jeune femme orgueilleuse' (ibid.: 16).

36. 'le roman décisif pour l'image qu'on se fabriqu[e] de Rachilde' (Dauphiné 1991: 54).

37. 'Rachilde s'identifie à son héroïne et se croit comme dépravée, pervertie, nerveuse, hystérique, vicieuse' (Angenot 1986: 20).

38. Although the expression 'literary canon' is more current in English and North American criticism, the French literary institution certainly upholds the hierarchy of 'classic' literature. In her analysis of the authors studied in French lycées between 1880 and 1925, Martine Jey finds that 'dès 1803 le [premier] canon d'auteurs français est constitué' ('the canon of French authors was established as early as 1803') (Jey 1998: 20). Alain Viala prefers the term 'classique' to describe the texts that hold 'le haut du pavé dans l'institution littéraire et scolaire' ('take pride of place in the literary and educational establishments') in France (Viala 1993: 13).

39. According to Viala, the link between the French literary canon and the academic institution is circular but easily defined: 'Si un auteur est bon, il mérite d'être enseigné; et réciproquement, si un auteur est enseigné, on peut supposer qu'il est bon (important)' ('If an author is good, he deserves

to be taught; and conversely, if an author is taught, he is presumed to be good [important]' (Viala 1993: 14).

40. Lillian S. Robinson, for example, suggests that 'it is probably quite accurate to think of the canon as an entirely gentlemanly artefact, considering how few works by non-members of that class and sex make it into the informal agglomeration of course syllabi, anthologies and widely-commented on "standard" authors' (Robinson 1997: 3).

41. 'Une lecture féministe pour ce livre [*Monsieur Vénus*], comme pour les suivants, s'impose à nos esprits' (Dauphiné 1982: 7).

42. 'Il serait temps enfin que Rachilde, si injustement exclue du Parnasse, parce qu'elle dérangeait, obtienne la place qui lui convient dans notre histoire littéraire [...]' (ibid.: 22).

43. 'Il faut relire Rachilde... ce n'est pas un vœu pieux, c'est une exigence. On ne peut plus la mépriser ni l'ignorer' (ibid.: 23).

44. 'vision du monde, de l'amour et de la femme' (ibid.: 22–23).

45. 'la lutte contre la phallocratie triomphante de l'époque' (ibid.: 10).

46. 'En 1897, Rachilde apparaissait comme la grande dame des lettres parisiens' (Ducrey 1999: 613).

47. 'elle affirme contre l'esprit du temps qu'on peut vivre autrement, qu'une femme a la possibilité, le droit en tout cas, de concevoir différemment le couple, de diriger le jeu de l'amour' (Dauphiné 1982: 21).

48. 'de récents et pénibles événements de sa propre vie' (ibid.: 8).

49. 'Mademoiselle de Vénérande, au nom significatif évoquant la chasseresse farouche, la Diane cruelle, l'amazone dispensatrice de poisons subtils, refusant tout assouvissement sexuel, semble entretenir des *rapports étroits* avec sa créatrice' (ibid.: 8).

50. 'Premièrement, elle lui ressemble physiquement avec son allure altière et ses yeux étranges; deuxièmement, elle en a l'audace, la volonté de ne dépendre de personne, surtout pas de l'Homme; troisièmement elle partage ses aspirations à l'idéal, son rêve d'une passion dégagée de sens (ibid.: 8).

51. 'elle ne tenait guère en estime les femmes en général et les femmes de lettres en particulier' (ibid.: 168).

52. 'Bien que se défiant du féminisme, l'écrivain ne pouvait être plus clair: la liberté de la femme commence par la possibilité de refuser à l'homme ce qu'il attend [...]' (ibid.: 19).

Figure 16.1 Portrait of Renée Vivien, after the original pastel drawing by Belgian symbolist artist Lucien Lévy-Dhurmer. Originally printed as a frontispiece to *Poèmes de Renée Vivien, Vol. II* (1975 [1923–24]).

CHAPTER 16

DECADENCE AND THE WOMAN WRITER: RENÉE VIVIEN'S *UNE FEMME M'APPARUT*

Tama Lea Engelking

Vivien and the Literature of Decadence

When Renée Vivien's autobiographical novel, *Une femme m'apparut* (A Woman Appeared to Me) was first published in 1904, it shocked and revolted the critics who had admired the finely crafted verse of the five books of poetry she had previously published. Her only novel, *Une femme m'apparut* tells the story of her lesbian relationship with Natalie Clifford Barney, using a heavy-handed decadent aesthetic that even the decadent novelist Rachilde criticised as outmoded and 'already horribly decayed', not least in its use of the androgyne figure (Goujon 1986: 275). This much-misunderstood novel, variously defined as a symbolist novel, an allegorical prose poem, a confession, and a psychodrama, still has the power to shock and unsettle its readers. Its originality, however, has often been overlooked by readers who view Vivien's decadence as merely derivative or who focus on how it relates to the poet's love life and the dark side of her psyche. My reading here will concentrate instead on how Vivien was able to adopt decadence as part of a conscious feminist strategy to redefine the relationship between creativity and sexual identity. Although decadence is usually associated with misogyny, Vivien uses its emphasis on artifice and the dual nature of 'the feminine' to frame her ideas about the woman writer and highlight the woman-centred poetics that is central to her creative vision.

An Anglo-American poet whose real name was Pauline Tarn (Figure 16.1), Vivien had a short but prolific literary career. Born in London in 1877, between 1901 and her death in 1909 she produced more than a dozen volumes of poetry, several collections of prose poems, a book of short stories, two translations from the Greek, and a biography, all written in French, in addition to her novel which she published in two different versions. *Une femme m'apparut* is situated midway in Vivien's publication history, essentially at the height of her career during the especially productive period of 1903–1904 when she was writing three to four books per year and immersed in creating French translations of poems by Sappho and other ancient Greek women writers. Vivien was a conscientious craftswoman whose poetry was admired for its formal purity although its Sapphic content was considered quite controversial. Critics of her day referred to her as 'Baudelaire's Daughter' and 'Sappho 1900', highlighting her strategy of absorbing various literary influences and consciously placing her works within known literary traditions. Vivien's choice of title for her novel, taken from a line in Dante's *Divine Comedy* where he is reunited with Beatrice, places her in a tradition of male writers who celebrate their female muses.

While Vivien connects her work with previous conventions, she does so in order to inscribe her difference into otherwise recognisable forms.[1] Although Vivien's only novel seems to stand out as an anomaly, its appropriation of female characters actually corresponds to the writing strategies she pursues in her other works. Her translations and expansions of Sappho's love poems, for example, fall into a long line of Sapphic imitators who have most often usurped Sappho's voice to tell a heterosexual love story. Vivien, however, uses the voice of a female persona to address the female beloved, and is thus able to recuperate Sappho as a lesbian by restoring the first person female speaker to her original status.[2] She pursues a similar feminist strategy in *Une femme m'apparut* which features a *femme fatale*, and an androgynous character, both of whom she recasts as lesbians. Her treatment of these stock characters is not a simple recycling of the decadent repertory as critics such as Mario Praz suggest (Praz 1956: 374). She experiments with this misogynistic genre for reasons related to her own feminist and artistic agenda.

Vivien's primary identification was as a poet, but she may have deviated into prose forms due to the different way that the poetry of the period and decadent prose tended to represent women. Decadence is usually seen as a prose movement whereas poetry is more often associated with symbolism. In addition, as Jeanette Foster points out in her survey of sexual variance in French literature (Foster 1985), decadent prose writers tended to show little sympathy for lesbian behaviours. Their work portrays lesbians as crazy, violent and destructive, and link murder, suicide and ruin to lesbian sexuality. Foster also indicates that in many decadent prose narratives, lesbian characters end up 'converting' to heterosexuality when they discover that they prefer men to women after all (ibid.: 114). Poets, on the other hand, portray lesbians in a much more sympathetic light, representing the lesbian as 'synonymous with a mysterious world of feminine pleasure', according to Elaine Marks (1979: 361). By writing a decadent novel, then, Vivien was placing her own vision of lesbianism into a convention whose ideas she wanted to challenge directly.

As one of the first women writers of the twentieth century to write openly about women loving women, Vivien extended her challenge to the very notions of sexual identity and 'the feminine' that underlie much decadent fiction. The fin de siècle was a period of 'sexual anarchy', to use Elaine Showalter's term (Showalter 1992), which coincided with the first systematic investigations into sexual psychopathology. A wide variety of deviant sexual behaviours such as lesbianism, cross-dressing and homosexuality found their way into decadent fiction, which highlighted the flexibility and permeability of conventional gender boundaries. The fluidity of gender lines is reflected in the parade of characters featuring the traits of both sexes that appeared in decadent fiction – the aggressive *femme fatale*, the Androgyne, the mannish lesbian and the effeminate Dandy.

For a lesbian writer like Vivien, decadence provided a handy tool since, as Bridget Elliott and Jo-Ann Wallace point out, the woman writer can adapt 'literary and visual conventions that are already coded "homosexual"' (Elliott and Wallace 1994: 39).[3] On the other hand, decadence casts female sexuality in a particularly negative light because it is steeped in a misogynist ideology that goes back to Baudelaire and his preference for the artificial (art) over the natural (woman) whom he described as 'abominable'.[4] According to this dichotomy, women are tied to their natural functions and bodies, whereas men can rise above nature to become artists. When not portrayed as reproductive slaves or voracious *femmes fatales*, women become artificial art objects created by male artists through the use of make-up, fashion, jewellery, art and literature, with the goal of distancing their creations as far as possible from nature. Imagination, creativity and culture are the prerogative of the active male artist. As Jennifer Birkett explains, 'Woman's place for the artists and writers of the decadence was inside the work of art, as an image to fix the male imagination' (Birkett 1986: 159). By taking up the active role of artist herself, and placing lesbian desire and a woman-identified androgynous writer at the centre of her decadent novel, Renée Vivien used familiar decadent conventions to reveal and challenge the underlying gender biases of the genre.

Vivien was not the only woman writer of her generation to adopt decadence to fit her particular needs. The French novelist Rachilde, for example, embraced decadence partially motivated by the desire to shock the public in order to build her readership. This was not a concern that Vivien shared since she was wealthy enough to publish her books at her own expense. Decadence also attracted the poet H.D.[5] who found it a rich source of images that she could shape into what Cassandra Laity calls 'a modernist poetics of female desire' (Laity 1996: 33). But Laity also warns of the dangers, and refers to feminist revisions of decadence as a double-edged sword for women writers who can easily internalise the negative imagery they are seeking to escape. This, she concludes, is the case with Vivien who allowed the '"dark" side of Decadence to rule her imagination' (Laity 1990: 235). Other critics who focus on the failures of Vivien's personal life, especially her fascination with death and the anorexia and alcoholism that destroyed her health and led to her death at age thirty-two, come to the same conclusion. Lillian Faderman, for example, compares Vivien's death to the suicide of Swinburne's decadent heroine, Lesbian Brandon, the result of internalising decadence (Faderman 1981: 361–2). Susan Gubar also points to the consequences Vivien suffered in her life for internalising sadistic images of the lesbian *femme fatale* (Gubar 1984: 49).

Biographical Readings/Literary Readings

Colette helped perpetuate this negative image of Vivien in *Le Pur et l'impur* (1932) where she portrays Vivien as an artificial creature with unhealthy habits, whose Parisian apartment, with its dimly lit interior, exotic furnishings and funeral perfumes, Colette found nauseating. Yet Colette admits that her friendship with Vivien was not literary, and that it was only when she was able to forget that Vivien was a poet that she began to feel a real interest in her (Colette 1991 [1932]: 602). Those who read *Une femme m'apparut* as a purely autobiographical account fall into the same trap as Colette who found Vivien the woman more interesting than Vivien the writer. Indeed, the novel is typically read as a *roman à clef* that draws its cast of characters from Vivien's real life address book, as Gayle Rubin makes clear in her introduction to the book. But the physical appearance of the book, as it was originally published, draws attention away from real life and towards a consideration of decadence as an aesthetic choice.[6] Vivien designed her novel to resemble a decadent art object, essentially enclosing her love story in a highly stylised and artificial packaging. She commissioned the Belgian symbolist painter Lucien Lévy-Dhurmer to create a cover illustration for the 1904 edition, which also included a reproduction of de Vinci's androgynous *Saint Giovanni* and an El-Greco-like portrait of *Notre Dame des Fièvres*. Although Vivien posed for many portraits, some of them in costume, she chose not to include her own image among the illustrations. Using a synesthetic technique reminiscent of Huysmans' des Esseintes (Huysmans 1977 [1884]), she set the mood by prefacing each chapter with fragments of music.

Just as the physical appearance of *Une femme m'apparut* exudes decadence, so does its content. The novel is set in a series of decadent dream-like décors filled with moonlight, exotic flowers, heavy perfumes, fog and slithering snakes; the language is highly stylised and the tone generally dark and melancholic. As with most decadent novels, plot is subordinate to description. The first person narrator, who seems to be a version of the author herself, tells the story of her love affair with Vally, whose halo of blond hair, ermine cape and ice-blue eyes easily identify her as Natalie Clifford Barney. Vally is described as the narrator's destiny, 'the incarnation of eternal feminine temptation', and from the beginning the narrator can see that the cold yet seductive and sensuous Vally will never be faithful or love her in return with the same intensity of emotion. The following lines, in which the narrator refers to the first two weeks spent in Vally's company, capture the tone of the narrative. She describes herself as living 'in the stupor of an acolyte drunk with the fumes of sacred incense ... . When I was suffering under her silent refusal of herself, she brought me black iris and Persian arums, dark lilies blooming under the eye of perverse archangels. In rapturous agony I gazed at her Florentine smile, her eyes of fatal blue, but I loved even more the moonlight of her misty hair' (Vivien [1904] 1982: 3).[7] Eventually, the desperately unhappy narrator consoles herself with Eva, a composite character who seems modelled after both Eva Palmer (one of Barney's friends and lovers) and Hélène von Zuylen, the woman who replaced Barney in Vivien's affections. The narrator is caught between choosing Eva and Vally, and the novel ends ambiguously, without revealing the narrator's ultimate decision.

While Vivien's need to tell her side of her relationship with Natalie Clifford Barney may have initially inspired her to write and then rewrite her novel after their brief reconciliation the following year, that included a trip to the island of Lesbos, there is much more to *Une femme m'apparut* than a simple love story.[8] It provides the backdrop, a sort of Art Nouveau theatre set, against which characters engage in impassioned discussions of all sorts of literary issues, from Sappho's sexual orientation to the nature of publishing. In fact, the bulk of the narrative is devoted to such questions, which also lead the main characters to express the most overtly feminist statements found in Vivien's work. Vivien lends her voice to two separate characters in order to separate the story of her relationship with Barney/Vally from a discussion of women's writing, thus steering her readers toward a literary and not literal reading of the text. The first person narrator, who is desperately in love with the cold-hearted Vally, is obviously Vivien herself, but we can also identify her with San Giovanni, an androgynous woman writer who represents a composite alter ego of the narrator, as Gayle Rubin suggests. She describes San Giovanni as 'Renée's better half, her common sense, the courageous poet of Lesbos: in short, the core of Vivien's identity which remained intact from the devastation of her unhappy passion' (Rubin 1982: xiii).

Vivien's division into two separate characters not only provides the narrative framework for the novel, but also illustrates a major theme of the book, one that hints at the temperamental differences that led to the failure of the Barney-Vivien relationship in the first place. Barney spells out these differences in her unpublished memoir when she complains that Vivien was more responsive to her verses and speeches than to her kisses and caresses.[9] Barney, who considered her life as her greatest literary work, was at odds with Vivien whom she accused of stealing beauty from life to put into her verses. Barney's complaint highlights another reason that drew Vivien toward decadence, namely the subordination of life to art. By separating the character of the writer from the love-sick narrator, Vivien diverts attention away from the biological woman being driven by her physical needs and emotions, and toward the creative artist. Despite Barney's best efforts to engage Vivien in life, Vivien's novel is essentially about literature, and reflects a feminist ideology deeply rooted in her poetics, not in the actions or inactions of her short existence.

Une femme m'apparut provided Vivien with a forum to reiterate the woman-centred poetics she was creating around Sappho, mainly through the character of San Giovanni. Major sections of the narrative are given over to this character who expounds her theories, recites her poems and stories, and even reads excerpts from her fan mail and critical reviews of her work. Described as looking like 'Leonardo's equivocal Saint John, that Androgyne whose Italian smile glows so strangely in the Louvre' (Vivien 1982: 5), with the slim hips and small breasts of an adolescent, San Giovanni is referred to throughout the novel with the feminine pronoun 'elle'. Like Vivien, San Giovanni is a Greek scholar who identifies so closely with Sappho that she is certain she was a disciple of the poet from Lesbos in a previous life. San Giovanni is a published poet with a small but faithful following of readers; however, she presents a negative view of writing in the context of a mixed society. That is, much of the novel takes place in Paris, where male readers, critics, scholars and even husbands and potential husbands interact with the female characters, much to the dismay of both the jealous narrator and San Giovanni. In one of the longest chapters in the novel, San Giovanni complains extensively to her friends about the difficulty of being a *femme de lettres* in this environment.

The closed urban/interior settings preferred by decadent writers also dominate *Une femme m'apparut*, and contrast sharply with the more open and natural settings of Vivien's Mytilène poems where she imagines Sappho's island as a separatist utopian refuge for women. According to Elyse Blankley, Mytilène represents 'a symbolic space in the female imagination that frees the poet from culture's gender judgments' (Blankley 1984: 57). Although the Paris of 1900 seemed relatively tolerant of deviant sexuality, Vivien's novel illustrates some of the problems that stood in the way of creative lesbian women whose perceptions of women loving women clashed with the perverse literary and visual images of lesbians usually associated with fin-de-siècle France. The unhappy role of the woman writer that weighs so heavily on San Giovanni in the novel is far removed from the joy, harmony and serenity that characterise the women in Vivien's positive Sapphic poems such as 'Psappha revit', although they all share an ideology that rejects men and celebrates women.[10]

Instead of finding pleasure in writing, San Giovanni calls it a bad habit, 'a hideous disease' that she compares to drug addiction. She finds commercial publication particularly disturbing. The published author is compared to a prostitute who has sold her soul instead of her body, and San Giovanni roundly condemns the curiosity of her readers who want to invade her private life, what Vally calls 'that public spying organized around the life of a writer' (Vivien 1982: 37). The poet is revolted, for example, by the request of one male admirer for a portrait, and deeply offended by another who tries to convince her that men are not as disgusting as she thinks. She rebels against 'this so-called admiration which is addressed more to the woman than to the artist', and reiterates the decadent doctrine that the true end of Art is to distance itself as far as possible from Nature (ibid.: 37). True stories are of no interest to San Giovanni. The implication is that readers should value Vivien's novel more for its creativity than for its resemblance to her life.

For Women Only: Vivien's Sapphic Reappropriations

Besides railing against male readers, San Giovanni is eager to defend the idea that Sappho was a lesbian, something that the readers of 1900 did not take for granted. For centuries classical scholars had championed various theories about Sappho's life that depicted her as heterosexual. Among them we find arguments 'proving' that she had a daughter, was married, killed herself out of unrequited love for a younger man, or was a courtesan. In her poetry, the introduction to her translations of Sappho, and again in *Une femme m'apparut*, Vivien refutes Sappho's supposed heterosexuality, calling her 'the greatest of the misunderstood and slandered' (Vivien 1982: 6). She adopts a more academic tone to make this same point in the biography of Sappho that prefaces her 1903 translation: 'Faced with the unfathomable night that envelopes this mysterious beauty, we can only glimpse her, divine her, through the stanzas and verses of hers that are left to us, and there we find not the least tender shiver of her being towards a man' (my translation).[11]

This is essentially the position that San Giovanni defends in *Une femme m'apparut*, but she takes it a step further. Not only does she believe that Sappho has never loved a man, but she finds the idea of the heterosexual sex act in general so repulsive that, in her words, 'Sadism and the rape of children seem more normal to me' (Vivien 1982: 38). San Giovanni's overtly anti-male position, which turn-of-the-century critics found to be the most appalling aspect of the novel, is reinforced by conversations with Vally and the narrator who agree that 'men are the Unesthetic par excellence' (ibid.: 34). Vally even elaborates a theory that blames the paucity of women poets on men:

> If there are only a few women writers and poets, it is because women are too often forced by convention to write about men. That is enough to paralyse any effort toward Beauty. Thus the only woman poet whose immortality equals that of statues is Psappha, who didn't deign to notice masculine existence. She celebrated the sweet speech and the adorable smile of Atthis, and not the muscled torso of the imaginary Phaon (ibid.: 34).[12]

Vivien's novel also contains feminist diatribes against marriage and maternity that are reminiscent of positions taken by the 'New Woman'. San Giovanni, for example, describes pregnancy as hideous and animal-like, a notion supported by the narrator who is tormented by the thought of a recently married friend being barbarously violated on her wedding night, and by the possibility that 'hideous maternity would deform that slim sexless body' (ibid.: 54). It is against this idea of heterosexuality that San Giovanni pits her notion of love between women, which she describes as pure, chaste, and harmonious, utterly void of the animal-like lust she attributes to man. Although she herself has loved women, the Androgyne explains that she has experienced no sensuous yearnings. Anna Livia (1995) calls this sort of cold sexless desire, which is also found in Vivien's poetry, a 'sexual white-out'. It is essentially a poeticised version of lesbian love, more literary than physical. It is also a version of women loving women that is far removed from the titillating scenes of lesbian lovemaking that male decadent writers concocted for the voyeuristic pleasure of male readers, a point reinforced by San Giovanni who explains:

> Men see in the love of woman for woman only a spice that sharpens the flatness of their regular performance. But when they realize that this cult of grace and delicacy will permit no sharing, no ambiguity, they revolt against the purity of a pas-

sion which excludes and scorns them.' As to myself,' she added, almost solemnly in the strength of her sincerity, 'I have raised the love of noble harmonies and of feminine beauty to a faith. Any belief which inspires ecstasy and sacrifice is a real religion (Vivien 1982: 36–7).

By writing men out of the scene, Vivien is able to claim lesbianism for women's eyes only. By writing out woman's 'natural' functions as heterosexual mate and mother, she also succeeds in separating the female from the feminine, which then becomes highly stylised and artificial, as we can see in the many descriptions of the perfumed, bejewelled and made-up Vally who dons a variety of different costumes in the novel, and whose lips are even described as 'sculptured meticulously by a most skilled hand' (ibid.: 9). That hand, however, may be her own as Vally is an active participant in her role-playing, sometimes choosing costumes as a Venetian page or Greek shepherd that emphasise her androgynous charms. In other words, the starring *femme fatale* of Vivien's novel is a dandified lesbian with androgynous characteristics! The narrator highlights Vally's mutability by referring to her as 'another Androgyne, vigorous as an ephebe, graceful as a woman' (ibid.: 9). Vivien later qualifies this standard of androgynous beauty when Vally explains 'Adolescent boys are beautiful only because they resemble women … they are still inferior to women whom they do not equal either in grace of movement or harmony of form' (ibid.: 7). This stance is entirely consistent with the disdain for men and the masculine that runs throughout the novel.

Vivien is clearly writing against the grain of decadent thought that promoted the ephebe as the true ideal of esthetic beauty. From the Greek word for 'early manhood', the ephebe was a feminised male (not a boyish woman) who combined physical beauty with a moral purity the decadents believed was not shared by the more easily corruptible and morally and intellectually inferior woman. According to Bram Dijkstra, this type of androgynous male beauty was especially prevalent around 1900 when it was promoted by intellectuals such as Oscar Wilde whose homosexuality was rooted in a platonic idealism shared by a large group of poets and artists (Dijkstra 1986: 199–200). As with the Romantic male poets who appropriated feminine qualities to merge them into an androgynous *male* poet, the decadent androgyne also tipped the gender balance in favour of the male.[13] Within this gender dynamic the virile woman becomes the most monstrous of creatures.

Joséphin Péladan even invented a new term for her in his four-teen-volume *La Décadence latine* – the Gynander (Péladan 1979 [1891–2]). Péladan's intent was to separate the true Androgyne, whom he saw as the 'artistic sex par excellence', from those pitiful women who ape men, among them lesbians and blue-stockings. This is also the case in Catulle Mendès' famous les-bian novel *Méphistophéla* (Mendès 1890). That novel, according to Barbara Spackman, 'confirms the feminist suspicion that fin-de-siècle androgyny is a one-way street, an appropriation of the feminine by the masculine rather than a pacific reconcili-ation of opposites' (Spackman 1998: 819).

Vivien reverses this strategy in *Une femme m'apparut* when she appropriates decadent icons such as the lesbian, *femme fatale* and Androgyne, and uses them to illustrate the sepa-ratist woman-centred vision that she translates into her poet-ics. The nature of that vision is clearly articulated by the narrator of *Une femme m'apparut* who, early in the novel, describes her theory of the hermaphroditic nature of the uni-verse where everything is divided into male and female prin-ciples: 'Everything that is ugly, unjust, fierce, base, emanates from the Male Principle. Everything unbearably lovely and desirable emanates from the Female Principle' (Vivien 1982: 6). She sees these opposing forces as equally powerful, but antagonistic, with one ultimately triumphing over the other. The narrator, of course, is rooting for a feminine victory: 'We hope in silence for the decisive triumph of the Female Princi-ple, the Good and the Beautiful, over the Male, that is, over Bestial Force and Cruelty' (ibid.: 6).[14]

Vivien's theory, summed up briefly in the novel, is found in a more fleshed out version in 'La Genèse profane' ('The Profane Genesis') published in her 1902 collection of prose poems. This prose poem is a retelling of the creation story that explicitly links creation with poetry. Vivien describes the world as the product of two eternal and opposing forces represented by Jeho-vah and Satan. Jehovah, corresponding to 'the Male Principle', is associated with violence, animals, springtime, light, sky, the poet Homer and epic poetry. Satan's work, which corresponds to 'the Female Principle', is highlighted by his creation of the mys-tery of night, clouds, autumn, flowers, flesh, woman, Sappho and lyric poetry; in short, the essence of the decadent poetic imagery Vivien develops in her lesbian poems and the basis of the woman-centred poetics she created around Sappho.

Conclusion

What is significant in *Une femme m'apparut* and 'The Profane Genesis' is both the impossibility of any compromise or merging of the two opposing sides, and the literary nature of their struggle which she specifically links to poetry. Vivien's confrontation with decadence as an either/or proposition, raises her reader's awareness of just how profoundly her poetry-centred vision of the universe deviates from the binary system underlying decadence where the feminine term is subordinate to the masculine. The androgynous poet of *Une femme m'apparut* and the separatist vision she represents illustrate Vivien's creative literary strategies as she works within a familiar male-authored convention, to reclaim it for women. It is easy to lose sight of just how subversive Vivien's woman-centred version of decadence is, if, like many readers, we focus on the failures of the author's tragic personal life. Instead, we should follow the advice that San Giovanni offers her readers in *Une femme m'apparut*, and consider Vivien as a writer first. By focusing on the woman writer's creativity, we can appreciate how Vivien was able to manoeuvre around the usual system of opposites, unveiling androgyny as a sexist myth and appropriating decadent figures to serve her own feminist ends.

Notes

1. A good example of this is Vivien's 'Sonnet féminin' from her 1902 volume *Cendres et Poussières*. She takes advantage of rules governing feminine rhyme and grammatical gender to feminise her poem. See Engelking 1993.
2. Joan DeJean traces Sappho's influence on the French literary tradition, and especially the way her voice has been co-opted by male authors (DeJean 1989).
3. Elliott and Wallace's discussion focuses on *The One Who is Legion, Or A.D.'s After Life*, the decadent novel that Natalie Clifford Barney wrote in 1930 loosely based on her relationship with Renée Vivien, with illustrations by Romaine Brooks. See also above, Chapter 5.
4. For Baudelaire's influential views on women as merely 'natural' see also above, Chapter 9, page xxx.
5. H.D. was the pen name of Hilda Doolittle (1886–1961), American poet, novelist, translator and essayist who spent most of her adult life in London and Switzerland. See Benstock 1986.
6. This is not the case with the two modern editions of this work. Both the 1982 English translation and the 1977 French edition of *Une femme m'apparut* include prefaces that closely link Vivien's life to events in the novel.

7. 'la stupeur d'un acolyte ivre de parfums sacrés ... Elle m'apportait, lorsque je souffrais de ses refus silencieux, les iris noirs et les arums de Palestine, lys de l'ombre éclose sous le regard des archanges pervers. Je contemplais, dans une angoisse heureuse, sa bouche au sourire florentin et ses yeux d'un bleu mortel, mais je préférais encore le clair de lune de ses vagues cheveux' (Vivien 1977 [1904]: 31). All subsequent references to *Une femme m'apparut* in the text will be to the 1982 English translation by Jeannette Foster, with the original French in a note quoted from the 1977 edition.

8. Although Barney admired certain passages in Vivien's novel, she is generally critical of *Une femme m'apparut* which she describes as absurd, and influenced by the 'bad taste' of the Belle Epoque. Her own version of their relationship appears in *Souvenirs indiscrets* (1960), also collected in Livia's English translation (1992: 2–59). Vivien published a revised version of *Une femme m'apparut* in 1905 where Barney appears in a more positive light as Lorély.

9. Barney's unpublished autobiography is part of the huge bequest she left to the Bibliothèque littéraire Jacques Doucet in Paris which also contains over 40,000 letters written to her. For a catalogue of the Barney bequest, see Chapon (1976).

10. For a discussion of Vivien's Mytilène poems see Blankley (1984: 45–67) and Holmes (1996a: 83–103).

11. 'En face de l'insondable nuit qui enveloppe cette mystérieuse beauté, nous ne pouvons que l'entrevoir, la deviner à travers les strophes et les vers qui nous restent d'elle et nous n'y trouvons point le moindre frisson tendre de son être vers un homme' (Vivien 1903: x).

12. 'S'il n'y a qu'un petit nombre de femmes écrivains et poètes, c'est que les femmes sont trop souvent condamnées par les convenances à célébrer l'homme. Cela a suffi pour paralyser en elles tout effort vers la Beauté. Aussi, le seul poète-femme, dont l'immortalité est pareille à l'immortalité des statues, est Psappha, qui n'a point daigné s'apercevoir de l'existence masculine. Son œuvre n'en porte ni la trace ni la souillure. Car elle a célébré *le doux langage et le sourire désirable* d'Atthis, et non le torse musclé de l'imaginaire Phaon' (ibid.: 99–100). Emphasis in the original.

13. See, for example, Diane Long Hoeveler's analysis of five English Romantic poets who, she argues, use androgyny as 'a poetic technique designed to merge the fictional masculine and feminine in one new and redeemed being – the androgynous male poet' (Hoeveler 1990: xiv).

14. 'Tout ce qui est laid, injuste, féroce et lâche, émane du Principe Mâle. Tout ce qui est douloureusement beau et désirable émane du Principe Femelle' [...] 'Nous espérons en silence le triomphe définitif du Principe Femelle, c'est-à-dire du Bien et du Beau, sur le Principe Mâle, c'est-à-dire sur la Force Bestiale et la Cruauté' (Vivien 1977: 6, 7).

Figure 17.1 Anna, Comtesse de Noailles, 'One of the greatest contemporary poets'. Photograph by Henri Manuel. Courtesy of the Bibliothèque Marguerite Durand.

CHAPTER 17

SENSUAL DEVIATIONS AND
VERBAL ABUSE: ANNA DE NOAILLES
IN THE CRITIC'S EYE

Catherine Perry

From the time of her earliest publications Anna de Noailles (Figure 17.1) became the most popular, the most celebrated, and also the most denigrated female poet in early twentieth-century France.[1] Admired by writers, thinkers, and artists throughout Europe, this literary 'star' of the Belle Epoque was the only woman writer of her times in France to receive the highest public recognition, despite nationalist critics who distrusted her Greco-Rumanian origins and could not bring themselves to consider her a legitimate French poet. Noailles' first book of poetry, *Le Coeur innombrable* (*The Innumerable Heart*), published in 1901, was an immediate best seller, not only for the quality of its verse but also for its openness to sensuality from a woman's perspective, which harmonized with a tendency at the Belle Epoque to cultivate pleasure. Noailles' popularity even surpassed that of Colette for many years. In 1921 the Académie française bestowed upon her its prestigious 'grand prix de littérature'. The following year she became the first female member of the newly instituted Belgian *Académie royale de langue et de littérature françaises*; and in 1931 she was the first woman ever to receive the rank of 'Commandeur' in the Légion d'Honneur. Her reputation even extended to the

United States where she was nominated, alongside Marcel Proust, for *Vanity Fair*'s 1923 'Hall of Fame' (Amory and Bradlee 1960: 80). This official recognition would be Noailles' swansong. Her popularity decreased by the end of the First World War, when Modernism disrupted the apparent confidence of the Belle Epoque and gained ground with poets such as Guillaume Apollinaire and Paul Valéry, and her readership declined dramatically after her death in 1933.

The present essay proposes to show how some of the views formulated on Noailles during her lifetime were passed down virtually unexamined to critics in the later twentieth century, thus reducing her impact on French literature and, if we may take her to be a case study, reducing the importance of other women writers as well. On the one hand, a study of Noailles' critical reception exposes a variety of ideologies governing 'correct' poetic practice in the early twentieth century, when poetry was still widely read. On the other, Noailles' own conceptions of poetry and her responses to critics provide insights into the battles that she had to wage in order to be accepted as a French writer.

Starting with *Le Coeur innombrable*, Anna de Noailles published nine volumes of lyric poetry, three novels, a book combining novellas with a series of meditations on gender issues, a collection of prose poems, and, at the end of her life, an autobiography spanning her childhood and adolescence. She also wrote countless essays and book prefaces. Reflecting her position at the cusp of the antithetical world views of nineteenth-century Romanticism and twentieth-century Modernism, a discrepancy between form and content characterizes her poetry, in which dynamic concepts and images strive to dissolve a largely classical structure. By actively engaging with her French literary heritage while finding inspiration in Greek paganism and in the thought of Friedrich Nietzsche, Noailles constructed an original poetic world, one that often emerges as modern in spite of its Romantic trappings. Her work is best described as Dionysian – ecstatic, sensual, erotic, playful, sometimes violent, and always marked by a tragic undercurrent that becomes magnified in her later poetry.

Despite the extensiveness and diversity of her writings, and despite the recognition she received earlier in the century, it seems to have been the critical consensus from the 1930s until recently that Noailles was little more than a second-rate poet who owed her success to meta-literary factors, the most significant being her 'exotic' type of beauty, her power of seduction, her ebullient wit, her assertive and unconventional personality, the salons and publishing houses to which she had access, the snobbism of Parisian high society, and the most ephemeral bestower of value, fashion. Such an assessment has originated in a general misperception of her life, personality and thought. Since the late 1980s, however, new biographies have helped establish little-known circumstances that surrounded the poet's lifelong commitment to artistic creation and have evidently sparked new interest in her work. One small example may illustrate this change of outlook: a recent article in the *Magazine littéraire* quotes Noailles in the first paragraph, clearly identifying her as part of the French literary heritage.[2]

Gender and Reception

Even a cursory glance at the numerous essays written on Noailles during her lifetime uncovers a striking disparity among her contemporaries regarding the literary value of her work. Although critics may not have tackled its hybrid nature in explicit terms, their equivocal responses suggest that they confronted the difficulty of determining what place it should occupy in the world of French letters. Noailles was often reproved for her disorderly mind, her excessive concentration on the senses, her amoralism, and her faults in poetic technique, all of which were perceived as characteristically 'feminine'. Yet, when discussing the 'faults' in her poetic style, the socialist critic Léon Blum, one of her more perceptive readers, wrote in 1908 that the 'bizarre nature' of Noailles' taste may well have reflected 'a voluntary rebellion against the ordinary rules of good taste'.[3] In his effort to understand the significance of her work, Blum concluded that, in all likelihood, such 'faults' were the price readers had to pay when confronting an original voice: 'It appears unquestionable to me', he wrote, 'that, for the first time since Baudelaire and Verlaine, Madame de Noailles has introduced new feelings and expressions into the common patrimony of poets' (Blum 1962: 423–24).

Among critics who were favourable to Anna de Noailles, we find that she was repeatedly designated a 'genius', an inspired poet in the Romantic vein. To measure the significance of this term when applied to a woman, we only have to consider how Mme Alphonse Daudet wrote, in 1898, regarding the sisters of great male writers, that they were blessed with nothing more than 'a scrap of genius astray in women's nature' (Planté

1989: 1). The word 'genius' under the pen of some critics is, of course, not as laudatory as it may seem, if talent is missing from the picture. Yet Noailles was often perceived as an accomplished artist. In 1913, the British critic and poet Mary Duclaux declared her to be 'the greatest [poet] that the Twentieth Century ha[d] as yet produced in France, perhaps in Europe' (Duclaux 1920: 185). In the same year, Jean Schlumberger applauded her artistry: 'against all odds, [she] possesses that respect for the sacred character of the work of art, that proud creative humility that is seldom bestowed upon women'. Several writers believed that Noailles presented fresh versions of feminine sensibility in artistic form. For the German poet Rilke, she belonged to a privileged group of women lovers who had the rare gift of converting an excess of emotion into poetry (Rilke 1944: 77–84). Among her contemporaries perhaps no one captured the character of Noailles' work with greater sympathy and insight than Marcel Proust. Through the figure of the Vicomtesse de Réveillon, his unfinished novel *Jean Santeuil* explains her social personae as so many veils designed to shield an intimate poetic vocation, when poetry was still a favoured genre but the notion of inspiration was increasingly targeted as naive and deluded, if not presumptuous: 'this intimate essence of things, which she did not mention, [was] in reality the only one that was truly important to her ... her poetry always returned to it'.[4] Proust took further care to distinguish the poet from the historical woman. In a 1907 article on Noailles' poetry, he insisted that her self-representations did not belong to her 'social, contingent self', but rather, that they expressed 'the deep self that individualizes works and makes them last'[5] Because her poetry conveys the illusion of an unmediated sensory experience, Proust compared it to Impressionist painting. Instead of representing the natural world directly, as in a realist aesthetics, Noailles' poetry demonstrates the idealist awareness that 'the Universe represents itself within the mind'.[6]

As a woman, Anna de Noailles inevitably drew the attention of male writers, artists and critics. In their view she was disclosing, if not 'betraying', secrets of the female psyche that had long been withheld from them. In a tribute to Noailles written shortly after her death, the poet Fernand Gregh reflected on her power to modify and 'expand the notion of woman' (Gregh 1933: 17). But if she was successful from the time of her earliest publications, it was also due to several factors in the contemporary horizon of expectations. As François Mauriac reflected shortly after Noailles' death, her early work conveyed the 'tormented' spirit of French youth at the turn of the century (Mauriac 1933: 1). The energy that appeared to flow through her texts corresponded to vitalist currents of thought, exemplified in the philosophy of Henri Bergson. A diffuse movement, broadly defined by the label 'Naturisme', was then in vogue. As a literary analogue of Impressionism, it advocated a sensory approach to reality as the primary means of knowledge and as the basis of aesthetics. According to Roger Charbonnel, the cult of sensuality was then part of an aesthetics grounded in the body, understood 'as the original fount of all our joys and even as the initial condition of all aesthetics, harmoniously combining experienced sensations rather than lifeless ideas'.[7] Noailles' work also appealed to a readership that had lost its ties with institutionalized religion and with conventional morality. Here was a female poet who dared exemplify the words of Nietzsche in *Ecce Homo*: 'Morality is not attacked, it is merely no longer in the picture' (Nietzsche 1967: 291). Here, then, was a female poet who praised desire, the body, and the senses, without a trace of shame or guilt.

Such an orientation could only displease a number of critics, who objected to Noailles' emphasis on sensuality and to what they regarded as her excessive emotionalism and lack of measure. Although she wrote poems with a Hellenistic bent from the beginning of her career, and in her later work elegies displaying a stoic vision, Noailles was perceived as yielding unrestrainedly to her inspiration. Even critics such as Nicolas Ségur, who admired her work to the point of placing her among an exclusively male cohort of European 'geniuses', did not hesitate to assert her 'feminine' lack of reflection: 'Dominated by the fatal divinities of her sex – love, sensuality, and fear – she is hardly capable of speaking anything else but the language of emotions and instinct' (Ségur 1926: 146). In 1904, the Spanish philosopher and critic Ortega y Gasset hailed Noailles' work for its vitality and unaffected qualities as contrasted with the 'decadent', 'obscure', and 'devitalised' art of the French Symbolists (Ortega y Gasset 1963a [1904]: 33–36). But twenty years later, espousing a biological view of literary creation, he concluded that Noailles' poetry reflected the 'soul of a plant-like body'. Ortega's essay ends with an attack against women poets, perceived as going against Nature, hence against their own nature, which is private rather than universal, and which belongs to the intimacy of the boudoir rather than the public forum (Ortega y Gasset 1963b [1923]: 429–35).

In his 1909 study of women's literature, Jules Bertaut characterized Noailles' poetry as a 'monstrous' intensification of sensations, directed paradoxically toward the most paltry natural settings: 'It seems that the power of every one of this woman's senses is magnified tenfold, to the point of monstrosity, ... ardour, fever, enthusiasm allow [her] to commune with nature, not in front of one of those grandiose scenes capable of uplifting the most mediocre and unimaginative soul, but at the mean sight of a parish priest's country garden or a suburban vegetable plot!' In this light Noailles lacks objectivity as well as all sense of measure: 'great poets were men and ... even the most romantic amongst them knew how to keep a sense of measure and retained their lucidity in their most daring exaltations ... / Madame de Noailles, on the other hand, is a woman. As such, she is a being lacking equilibrium, or at least who tends at every moment to lack equilibrium' (Bertaut 1909: 139, 144). Bertaut's study prompted articles by other critics, such as the nationalist Pierre Lasserre, who subscribed wholeheartedly to his argument (see Lasserre 1909; also Fresnois 1909).

At the turn of the century, a female poet who adopted Nature as a dominant trope in her poetry could still confront a dismissal like the one Charles Baudelaire elegantly disguised in his 1861 essay on Marceline Desbordes-Valmore. Though praising the poet for her qualities of heart and her spontaneous inspiration, Baudelaire excludes, in fact, her work from the domain of authentic poetry: 'If the clamour, if the natural sigh of an elite soul, if the heart's desperate ambition, if sudden, unthinking talents, if all that is gratuitous and comes from God, suffice to make a great poet, then Marceline Valmore is and always will be a great poet' (Baudelaire 1976: 146). Despite the positive way in which he uses the word 'Nature' and its derivations in the essay, he locates them in terms that make Nature antithetical to high art. Ironic distance, which differentiates the author from the lyric voice, is a necessary premise in Baudelaire's definition of the poet. In contrast to female poets who, like Desbordes-Valmore, employ a 'fervent and thoughtless style' (ibid: 147), those who challenge men on their own territory must be excluded from the realm of poetry. Baudelaire harshly declares that their works are 'sullied by those masculine foibles that become monstrosities in women' (ibid: 146) because, in trying to imitate the intellect, with which they are not endowed, they are attempting to go against Nature, that is, against female nature, hence against the nature of things. Desbordes-Valmore earns Baude-laire's admiration precisely because she knows how to remain in her 'natural' place, whereas those other women he casti-gates can only be impious imitators, inscribing 'sacrilegious pastiches of the masculine mind' (ibid: 147, 146). Henceforth, women who aspired to write poetry would find themselves caught in a double bind: either they remained 'natural' and were ultimately cast into irrelevance as poets, or they were perceived to imitate men, and thereby became 'blasphemers'.

It is not surprising, then, that many critics failed to delin-eate the intellectual currents in Noailles' work; and when they did observe such currents, it was frequently in the framework of polemics directed against the philosophies inspiring her aesthetics. Around 1900, a few years after her discovery of Schopenhauer, Noailles was reading Nietzsche, whose thought corresponded to her own ethics of energy and heroism, com-bined with a tragic sense of the human condition. If Jules de Gaultier, one of the thinkers who introduced Nietzsche's phi-losophy in France, perceived that her poetry gave artistic form to the metaphysics of a generation influenced by nineteenth-century German philosophy (de Gaultier 1924: 217), others saw a typically feminine narcissism in her verse, not under-standing her idealism, as expressed in the following verse: 'A being seeks nothing but itself ... O Desire, sumptuous voyage toward our fascinating image'.[8] Neither would some critics accept her rejection of traditional metaphysics. A few months after Noailles' death, Yves-Gérard Le Dantec wrote a long arti-cle denouncing the imitative nature of her poetry. It soon becomes apparent, however, that his criticism is largely guided by moral and religious considerations. Quoting from a poem addressed to dead interlocutors, 'I affirm, seeking your vast and empty nights, that naught survives the warmth of veins!',[9] Le Dantec rebukes Noailles for her disbelief: 'I find no grace in such gratuitous affirmations, especially coming from a woman, and even if they are proffered with such rhythmic firmness' (Le Dantec 1933: 296). Precisely on account of her talent and her popularity, Noailles was perceived as a threat to religious order, and consequently, to social order: 'O Siren, one would have to be born deaf or turn a deaf ear not to enjoy your clever music. But what do you bring us that is not a lie, as well as harmony?' (Mondadon 1930: 713).

One cannot disregard the challenges posed to female writers of the Belle Epoque. Despite the country's growing liberalism, French critics, most of them male, were still predominantly

conservative and often dismissive of, if not downright hostile
to, women who competed with men in the domain of art,
unless their expression reassuringly conveyed traditional values. In the context of French poetry, a genre that remained
largely masculine at the turn of the century, Noailles faced the
challenge of establishing her legitimacy as a universal poet,
unrestricted by gender. Contesting the tendency of critics who
dubbed her 'une poétesse', for instance, she would maintain
that she was 'un poète'; and the poet, in her definition, is a
quasi mythical being, the 'freest' of all, one whose spirit moves
in 'infinite space' (Noailles 1921a: 2). Her texts reflect an
awareness that women do not enjoy entire freedom of access to
artistic language, or more generally to the Word – insofar as it
belongs to the 'spirit' – and that to grasp at such freedom constitutes a form of transgression.

Nationalism and Reception

Not only did Noailles' gender present an obstacle in the literary scene, but her ethnic background also provoked resistance
to her recognition as a French writer. In the historical context
of the growth of right-wing nationalism which in French politics followed closely upon the Dreyfus Affair, she stood out as
an alien, all the more so because she defiantly took the side of
the 'other' that Dreyfus soon came to represent, just as she
upheld Socialist values against the aristocratic values of her
in-laws. Evidence of her difficult position in this regard may be
found in a personal notebook of Maurice Barrès, suggesting
how some Parisian circles spurned Noailles around 1899 on
account of her foreign origins: 'Madame de Noailles and
Madame de Chimay [her sister] [...] were playing the role of
Dreyfus supporters at the reception of Madame de Montebello,
who said: 'French, you two? ... Where do you get that right? ...
Come now, you are nothing but street urchins from Byzan-
tium! ...'.[10] The prefatory poem to Noailles' 1901 *Le Coeur*
innombrable alludes to these textual and political issues. In the
very first verse the poet takes hold of France through the pos-
sessive adjective 'my', while simultaneously reaching for a
universal, non-gendered voice through the impersonal pronoun 'one': 'My France, when one has nourished a Latin heart
with the milk of your Gaul'.[11] Not only does the speaker have
a Latin heart that both extends beyond France's boundaries
and incorporates them, but he or she also addresses France

through its maternal origins, as Gaul, the Latin name given to France by the Romans. Noailles thereby asserts her right to a place among French poets for she partakes of the same cultural origins, in the cradle of Western civilisation. Inferring, through the image of the nourishing milk, that Gaul is her own mother as well, she further stresses her affective lineage with the French. She then declares that she has settled on the banks of the Seine, there to construct her home, which can be read as a metaphor for her work. Through this poem Noailles implies that her will to write in French proceeds from her cultural birthright and also from a deliberate choice that stresses her freedom. Noailles' poetic appropriation of France did not escape the attention of the nationalist Charles Maurras, who reflected on this 'capture' by 'a gluttonous little soul' in the first paragraph of his May 1903 essay on 'Feminine Romanticism' (Maurras 1927 [1903]: 196). When interviewed for *L'Echo de Paris* one month earlier, Noailles had already responded to Maurras, as it were, by insisting that she was not a foreigner (Noailles 1903). Many years later, in her autobiography, she reaffirmed her intimate attachment to the French soil, personified as a mother: 'This *our place*, even when we criticise it, is still that part of the world where we live, where we work, where we wish to amplify our destiny and to die: it is an instinctive kiss on a mother's cheek'.[12]

This denigration of Noailles on ethnic grounds, which was very much part of the nationalist discourse during the Belle Epoque, continued into the early 1920s. Upon her reception of the French Academy's literary award in 1921, she sustained what can only be characterised as verbal abuse from a nationalist historian, Frédéric Masson, 'Perpetual Secretary' of the Academy and thus its spokesman, who presented the prizes of the year. His speech was made public in the daily *Le Temps* on 2 December 1921. First, Masson applauds other poets for the normative French qualities of their verse – 'regular', 'harmonious', 'conforming to classical models'. When he turns to Noailles, without naming her, he gives erroneous information on her family as well as her birth which he places outside of France. He then identifies her in disparaging terms with the Orient and with conventional feminine traits that necessarily tarnish her poetry, thus implying that she does not belong to the French soil or to its poetry:

> [S]he sings, somewhat like those delightful poetesses who, in the *Arabian Nights*, bring to the tales of Scheherazade a joie de vivre

as well as the terror of death. It is as if Saint-Aubin had engraved,
two centuries beforehand, her portrait in his *Odalisque*, one of the
most charming evocations of a delightful and perfumed Orient,
saturated with bonbons and fragrances ... That is where she
should be taken, in her country on the shores of the Bosporus – a
Bosporus that she has created and where no one's throat is slit ...
In verse that she sometimes abandons, unfinished, like a wreath
of flowers that a young girl does not care to tie and drops on the
meadow, she delights in all that surrounds, adorns, suits her visage; she delights in all of nature, and in its flowers, fruits, and
vegetables; for she discards nothing that pleases her gaze, sings
to her ears, stirs in her heart. She has discovered and she
expresses a form of Pantheistic poetry that has adapted to
France, introducing forms, sensations, and expressions that are
novel here. As we consider these poems, some of which are close
to being masterpieces, is it permissible to think that it might have
been worthy of the author to conform entirely to the rules of
prosody in the country she adopted? (Masson 1921)

Displayed in Masson's speech is a typical French tendency
toward the correct, or 'pure' use of the language, according to
the standards set by the French Academy itself in the seventeenth century. Since a proper linguistic usage indicates the
cultural and national stature of the speaker or writer, it is
understandable that Masson would cast Noailles as a foreigner in order to dismiss her as a French poet. Moreover, the
gendered nature of his lack of respect transpires in the images
and terms, such as 'Odalisque', 'bonbons', and especially the
verb 'taken', with which he belittles Noailles and reminds her
of woman's traditional passivity.

Anna de Noailles had no choice but to react. The following
day, on 3 December 1921, the newspaper *Le Temps* printed her
response, addressed to the paper's director under the guise of
correcting Masson's biographical errors. Though couched in
gracious terms, Noailles' corrections serve in fact as the pretext
for a stronger critique. Ironically, a French Academician, who
should take pride in his respect for precision, proves himself to
be far less precise than his Belgian counterparts:

Please allow me to rectify a few errors in my biography that
slipped, and this is quite natural, into Mr Frédéric Masson's
charming academic speech, reprinted yesterday in *Le Temps*. I
wish to avoid too many contrasts between the details that will
appear shortly at the Belgian Academy of French Language,
where I am to be inducted, and Mr Masson's shimmering narrative (Noailles 1921a).[13]

Noailles' wit appears in three words – 'natural', 'charming', and 'shimmering' – that would normally be applied to women, but it is the male critic who is now given a taste of his own medicine. Turning to the Academician's memories of her childhood, Noailles highlights his contradictions and reverses his subtle accusations: 'convinced that I was born on the shores of the Bosporus, Mr. Masson seizes this pretence to paint gracious oriental visions'.[14] Thus, it is not she who portrays the Orient in fictive terms, but Masson himself who is given to 'poetic' embellishments. He now emerges as the one who displays the very faults he believed to have denounced in her. With a reference to literary forefathers such as Montaigne, Ronsard, Racine and Hugo, Noailles then emphasizes her legitimacy as a French poet. Finally, she corrects the derogatory qualification of 'poétesse' that Masson bestowed upon her by describing herself as 'une poète de France' [sic]. In making the masculine 'poète' a feminine word, she reclaims poetry for women. A few years after this incident, Noailles even reclaimed the 'impurity' of her own poetry by humorously defending her neologism of 'nopure poetry' ('poésie papure'), in contrast with the notion of 'pure poetry' upheld by Henri Bremond (Noailles 1926: 31).

Conclusion

Such examples illustrate how Anna de Noailles resisted her incorporation into the French literary establishment as a merely 'feminine' poet. While she clearly wanted to be recognized, she aimed to be so on her own terms, often refusing to abide by the conventions of poetic practice and of gender definitions. But literary history has ignored until recently the more forceful aspects of her venture, retaining of her the earlier views of leading critics. Among them André Gide was foremost in excluding her from the canon in his anthology of French poetry (Gide 1949: 42–45), while the opinion of those like Proust was branded as nothing more than flattery (Gide 1997: 296–97). Few women writers of the Belle Epoque who attempted to present more audacious perspectives on female experience escaped severe criticism. In his last work, *La Comtesse de Noailles oui et non*, Jean Cocteau pertinently remarked that, if the poet was going through purgatory, the very definition of the word implies that she would emerge from it in due course (Cocteau 1963: 95). If Cocteau is right,

Noailles' literary return in the early twenty-first century might well signal the advent of a new 'Belle Epoque'.

Notes

1. I gratefully acknowledge Bucknell University Press and the Associated University Presses for permission to use portions of analyses from my book *Persephone Unbound: Dionysian Aesthetics in the Works of Anna de Noailles* (Perry 2003).

2. The article cites her characterisation of a poem by Francis Jammes as 'un de ses poèmes où il trempait encore sa plume dans la rosée, avant de la tremper dans l'eau bénite, pour reprendre la délicieuse expression d'Anna de Noailles' ('one of the poems where he was still dipping his pen in the morning dew, before he began to dip it in holy water, to adopt Anna de Noailles' delightful expression') (Delvaille 2001: 85).

3. All translations are my own. As my argument requires fairly extensive translation, I have given the original French only where this may be of particular use or interest to the reader.

4. '[C]ette essence intime des choses dont elle ne parlait pas [était] en réalité la seule qui fût vraiment importante pour elle … ses vers s'y rapportaient toujours' (Proust 1952: 305).

5. 'Tout ce qui peut constituer le moi social, contingent, de Mme de Noailles, … il n'en est pas parlé une seule fois au cours de ces quatre cents pages [*Les Éblouissements*] … [I]l n'y a pas de livre où le moi tienne autant de place, et aussi peu; où en tienne autant … le moi profond qui individualise les oeuvres et les fait durer, si peu le moi qu'on a défini d'un seul mot en disant qu'il était haïssable' (Proust 1994: 232–33).

6. 'Maintenant – et c'est cette étape vers un idéalisme plus profond que marquent *les Eblouissements* – … [e]lle sait que la pensée n'est pas perdue dans l'univers; mais que l'univers se représente au sein de la pensée' (ibid: 236).

7. '[L]a source première de toutes nos joies et même … la condition initiale de toute esthétique combinant avec harmonie des sensations vécues et non de froides idées' (Charbonnel 1909: 32).

8. 'L'être ne recherche que soi / … / Désir, somptueux voyage / Vers notre fascinante image' (Noailles 1920: 379).

9. 'J'affirme, en recherchant vos nuits vastes et vaines, / Qu'il n'est rien qui survive à la chaleur des veines!' (Noailles 1927: 19).

10. 'Mme de Noailles et Mme de Chimay (les deux petites Brancovan) font les Dreyfusistes chez Mme [Jean] de Montebello qui leur dit: "Vous des Françaises! … De quel droit? … Allons donc, vous êtes des gavroches de Byzance! …"' (Barrès 1930: 108).

11. 'Ma France, quand on a nourri son coeur latin / Du lait de votre Gaule' (Noailles 1901: 3).

12. 'Ce *chez nous*, même quand on le gourmande, c'est bien l'endroit du monde où l'on vit, où l'on travaille, où l'on souhaite amplifier son destin et mourir: c'est un instinctif baiser appuyé sur la joue maternelle' (Noailles 1926: 77).

13. 'Voulez-vous me permettre de rectifier quelques détails biographiques erronés, me concernant, qui se trouvaient – cela est bien naturel – dans le charmant discours académique de M. Frédéric Masson, que le *Temps* a

reproduit hier. Je voudrais qu'il n'y eût pas trop de contrastes entre les précisions qui s'établiront prochainement à l'Académie belge de langue française où je dois être reçue et le chatoyant récit de M. Frédéric Masson' (Noailles 1921b).

14. 'Néanmoins, convaincu que j'ai vu le jour sur les bords du Bosphore, M. Masson en prend prétexte pour nous dépeindre de gracieuses visions orientales' (ibid.).

Figure 18.1 Marguerite Audoux, 'The seamstress of letters', ca. 1910. Courtesy of the Bibliothèque Marguerite Durand.

CHAPTER 18

PROLETARIAN WOMEN, PROLETARIAN WRITING: THE CASE OF MARGUERITE AUDOUX

Angela Kershaw

Marguerite Audoux (1863–1937) came to the attention of the French reading public in 1910 when her autobiographical first novel, *Marie-Claire*, was awarded the Prix Fémina (Audoux 1958 [1910]) (Figure 18.1). The contemporary press was fascinated by the story of the abandoned little girl turned shepherdess, then dressmaker, and then novelist. Interest in Audoux and in *Marie-Claire* has never been exclusively textual, but has focused on the relationship between the author's situation and her aesthetic output; necessarily perhaps, since the socio-political context of literary production is the defining aspect of proletarian writing.[1] Critics have continued to interpret Audoux within this dual framework of aesthetic quality and socio-biography, and have consecrated Audoux as a pioneer.[2] While she was not the first member of the *classes illettrées* ever to take up a pen, she is seen as the first to have created an aesthetic object worthy of critical attention out of her authentic working-class experience. My own interest in Audoux is precisely in the interplay between texts and contexts, and thus my analysis seeks to be at once literary, political and historical. I offer a reading of Audoux that is both class- and gender-conscious and, in accordance with the theme of the present volume, seek to situate Audoux's work in relation to the two decades of French history that have become known as the Belle Epoque.

Audoux wrote four novels and several short stories, but is chiefly remembered for the *Marie-Claire* stories. The first of these was a Belle Epoque publishing sensation; its sequel takes Belle Epoque Paris as its subject matter. Whilst *Marie-Claire* enjoyed tremendous popularity and critical attention,[3] *L'Atelier de Marie-Claire* (*Marie-Claire's Workshop*) (Audoux 1987 [1920]), was much less widely read.[4] Both novels are highly autobiographical first-person narratives. *Marie-Claire* recounts the narrator's childhood and adolescence in the 1860s and 1870s. Orphaned at the age of five, Marie-Claire is brought up in a convent in Bourges, and at the age of thirteen, is sent to work on a farm. In *L'Atelier de Marie-Claire*, the reader discovers Marie-Claire in Paris, employed in the fashion industry, perhaps the most emblematic industry of the Belle Epoque. The novel provides valuable documentary evidence about the working and living conditions of the female urban proletariat in Belle Epoque Paris. The following analysis, then, offers a picture of the Belle Epoque from the perspective of a working-class woman. It also considers why *Marie-Claire* was so acceptable to the Belle Epoque reader, as well as possible reasons for the relative failure of the later novel. If, as the 1987 preface to *L'Atelier de Marie-Claire* suggests, by 1920 'times had changed',[5] how can the changes that affected the reception of Audoux's work be defined?

Audoux and Proletarian Writing

I have suggested that the sine qua non of proletarian writing is its socio-political context. Michèle Touret has noted that, according to Henry Poulaille's understanding of the term, the criteria for the definition of proletarian writing are extra-literary: 'There are no innate literary qualities; knowledge of the subject, personal experience and existential interest are the only bases for (proletarian) literature [...] Internal criteria of good style are replaced by criteria relating to the non-literary'.[6] Jean-Pierre Morel has suggested that within the proletarian genre, 'fiction' is no longer defined as the opposite of 'fact', but rather, as the relationship between the world and the writer:

> Henceforth, fiction is no longer the opposite of what is verifiable and controllable, as positivism understood it to be, but is rather the element of invention and creation – or 'production', to

adopt one of the words that was very much in vogue at the time
[ie in the inter-war period] – that is necessary precisely in order
that that movement can be achieved truthfully.[7]

The theoretical and political debate over proletarian writing in
France began in earnest in the inter-war period, stimulated by
attempts in the Soviet Union to define the social and political
role of Soviet writing (Morel 1985, Chapman 1992: 10–92).
The French debate came to a head in the early 1930s in the
context of *Monde's* survey on proletarian literature (1928–29)
and the Kharkov congress of revolutionary writers of November 1930. The debate can be divided into (at least) four camps.
For Poulaille, proletarian literature was by definition produced
only by members of the working class, and did not express any
specific political allegiance. For the communist Henri Barbusse,
director of *Monde*, any writer sympathetic to the proletarian
cause could produce proletarian literature, whatever their class
of origin. However Barbusse was opposed to the sectarian views
of the Soviet RAPP (Russian Association of Proletarian Writers)
for whom proletarian literature was synonymous with dogmatic party literature. The French *Association des écrivains et
artistes révolutionnaires* (AEAR) initially shared the views of the
RAPP; however, communism's more flexible approach to literature from late 1932 permitted a rapprochement between Barbusse, the AEAR and the Party. The populist school of Léon
Lemonnier and André Thérive saw the working class as an
important topic for literature, but was criticised by more politically engaged theorists for advocating an external depiction of
the proletariat by bourgeois writers. To analyse Audoux's work
in the context of this debate is only partly anachronistic: by
1920, the foundation stones of the polemics had already been
laid.[8] Bogdanov's Proletkult had been in existence in the USSR
since 1917, with the aim of supporting the proletariat in their
march towards socialism via cultural action (Struve 1972:
27–28).[9] In France, Barbusse had founded the review *Clarté*,
subtitled *Bulletin français de l'Internationale de la pensée*, in 1919.
Whilst Morel convincingly demonstrates that the Soviet debate
on proletarian literature only began to filter through to France
in the late 1920s (Morel 1985), Ragon shows that discussions
about the social function of literature were nonetheless a feature of French literary life directly after the Great War (Ragon
1986, Béroud and Régin 2002: 73). Poulaille situated Audoux
within the debate on proletarian literature by including her in
his *Nouvel âge littéraire* of 1930.

Critics have tended to interpret Audoux's *Marie-Claire* novels according to the extra-literary criteria cited by Touret, as works of authentic *témoignage*. Her novels exemplify proletarian writing as Poulaille understood it. Touret notes that proletarian writing often tells stories of childhood, since 'the child is the most proletarian of proletarians, the most suppressed of the suppressed'.[10] Audoux's narrator encounters oppression on three levels: because she is a child, because she is working-class, and because she is a woman. According to Touret's analysis, childhood is represented by proletarian writers dichotomously as unhappy and as idyllic (*malheur/idylle*); Audoux's writing bears out this hypothesis. The material circumstances of Marie-Claire's childhood seem to promise nothing but *malheur*. The novel's opening pages represent childhood in terms of abandonment (the death of the mother and unexplained departure of the father), fear (of her sister's taunts) and shame (at being seen naked by a group of passing chimney sweeps). In the convent, childhood becomes associated with illness and deformity, as many of the abandoned children are also victims of some physical disorder: Ismérie is a dwarf, Colette's legs are paralysed, Marie-Claire herself suffers with her eyes. Garreau suggests that abandoned children are represented as 'damned creatures',[11] fated to experience misery; this opinion is expressed by various secondary characters: 'One morning, la mère Colas gave us a real scolding, and told us we were children of misfortune'; '"Oh yes", she said, "your mother was tubercular, and Sister Gabrielle says that you're going to die soon"'.[12] However, *Marie-Claire* does not endorse this discourse of fatalism, but represents it as another source of oppression for the working-class child. Marie-Claire's triumph is precisely her ability to feel joy despite her circumstances, and this is the source of what Octave Mirbeau's preface described as the 'gentle, melodious light which rises from the novel, like the sun which rises on a beautiful summer morning'.[13] Indeed, the overall impression of childhood the reader takes away from the text is one of *idylle*. This is largely achieved through the representation of Marie-Claire's affective relationships which are, for the most part, naïve, simple and pleasant, and through the representation of nature. The positive construction of rural childhood is reiterated in *L'Atelier de Marie-Claire*, where the childhood reminiscences of the urban *ouvrières* (women workers) evoke a rural idyll which contrasts sharply with their urban existence and to which they dream of returning. In both texts the material circumstances of childhood appear as a source of misery, but the working-class child also experiences childhood both immediately and retrospectively, as an adult, as an ideal state of existence.

Audoux's representation of work is also typical of the thematic interests of proletarian literature, and can be said to be governed by Touret's *malheur/idylle* dichotomy. Whilst the Mother Superior presented farm work to Marie-Claire as *malheur*, Marie-Claire experiences it as *idylle*:

> I could not help thinking of the Mother Superior when she had said to me with such scorn, 'You will milk the cows and you will look after the pigs'. When she said it, she seemed to be inflicting a punishment on me, and yet looking after the animals brought me nothing but contentment. I would lean my head against the cow's flank so that I had more strength, and my bucket soon filled up. A froth formed on the top of the milk which took on many different hues, and it seemed so marvellous in the bursts of sunlight that I never tired of looking at it.[14]

The environment of the *atelier* is also presented in idealistic terms, again via the motif of sunshine:

> The sun seemed to be laughing with us too. It beamed through the window pane and its rays played on the basket of threads and on the sewing machine. It was still very warm and Bergeounette opened the window wide to let the sunshine come right inside.[15]

In Marie-Claire's experience, it is the social organisation of work, rather than work per se, that produces misery. When she is working for the ideal boss, work can be a pleasure, and employers and fellow workers function as a surrogate family. When the boss creates an exploitative relationship between employer and employee, work becomes a source of *malheur*. However, Audoux provides a counter-example. Factory work is in itself a source of misery because it has an immediate effect on the body of the worker, as Marie-Claire discovers when the seasonal unemployment that is the lot of the female workers in the workshop forces her into this environment. In the fur factory, the fibres enter the lungs and cause nosebleeds; in the leather factory, the hard physical labour causes the workers to become hunchbacked (Audoux 1987: 49–50), and factory work ruins the seamstresses hands so that they can no longer do fine needlework (ibid.: 60). *L'Atelier de Marie-Claire* is a less 'sunny' book than *Marie-Claire*, but it is not a tale of unabated misery; the tone of optimism it shares with the first novel is due in no small measure to the narrator's sense that she is better off in her workshop than many other workers in Paris.

Class and Gender at the Belle Epoque

The *malheur/idylle* framework which governs the texts' thematic content announces a relationship to the stereotype of the Belle Epoque that cannot be accounted for in terms of simplistic binarism. For Audoux's texts are both characteristic of, and stand in opposition to, that stereotype. As Mirbeau's characterisation of *Marie-Claire* suggests, there is a sunny, joyous ebullience to these novels which both conveys the pleasure of the narrator and is pleasurable to the reader, and thus corresponds to the notion of the Belle Epoque precisely as an era of pleasure. Audoux's comments on the writing process testify to her concern for the pleasure of the reader, insofar as beauty of style emerges as paramount:

> I then work on my sentences for a long time. I cross things through. I scribble things out. Sometimes I throw a whole chapter away because I don't like it any more. Never satisfied, I start over and over again, tirelessly.[16]

Nonetheless, what emerges incontrovertibly from the *Marie-Claire* texts is that the experience of the female urban proletariat at the turn of the century contrasts strongly with the dominant image of Belle Epoque Paris, embodied, for example, in the famous statue of *La Parisienne* which topped the monumental entrance to the *Exposition universelle*. *L'Atelier de Marie-Claire* represents two separate, but related, spheres of female experience: that of the *grande bourgeoise*, and that of the *ouvrière* who toils to create the luxury products which define the identity of the former. A great army of badly-paid, under-nourished seamstresses living in tiny, squalid rooms who, because of the rhythm of the bourgeois social season, are either hopelessly over-worked or unemployed, are required in order to create the sorts of dresses in which *La Parisienne* was clothed. This opposition is encapsulated in the episode concerning Mme Linella. It is the season of the races at Longchamps and the seamstresses have been working day and night to satisfy the demanding clients:

> There were nights that were so hard that tiredness eventually got the better of us and the *patron* would find us asleep with our heads on the table. We were quite stiff with cold, and our cheeks stayed creased for a long time where we had been resting them on our arms.[17]

Not content with the embroidered dress that has been made, Mme Linella demands a replacement. Her imperious tone perfectly conveys the individualism at the heart of bourgeois exploitation of the working classes:

> And she took a breath before adding drily, 'And you will deliver it to me on Sunday morning before ten o'clock.' Not looking at her, Madame Dalignac replied, 'You are asking for the impossible. We have not got time'. The client's eyes grew hard as if she were going to lose her temper. 'Honestly!' she said. But she softened: 'I cannot go to Longchamps without this dress'. And she carried on insisting how much she needed a dress with no embroidery for this special day.[18]

The exploitation of one woman by another is summed up in Mme Linella's final – and successful – attempt to persuade the seamstresses to do the job: 'So Madame Linella tried cajolery. "It's alright, you will just have to work a bit later, that's all"'.[19] Having witnessed the terrible conditions under which the seamstresses have been working for weeks, the reader responds to Mme Linella's persuasiveness with revulsion. The seamstresses are exploited solely because of upper-class caprice: Mme Linella does not even wear the dress that has cost so much effort.

L'Atelier de Marie-Claire thus provides a corrective to the image of Belle Epoque Paris as populated exclusively by creatures of luxury and pleasure. As they stitch, one of the seamstresses sings the refrain 'Paris, Paris, paradis de la femme' (Audoux 1987: 226): the full irony of this incantation only emerges when these lines are repeated as Mme Dalignac dies after years of overwork. The seamstresses' experience of being a woman in Belle Epoque Paris is far from paradisiacal. Their stories are of tales of physical, emotional and economic misery inflicted upon them because of their class and because of their sex. Sandrine dies of tuberculosis because she has neither the time nor the money to look after herself. Bergeounette is regularly beaten by her abusive husband. Gabielle, falling pregnant as a result of her own naïvety, suffers tremendous self-loathing because she has internalised the shame her society imposes on the unmarried mother. *L'Atelier de Marie-Claire* is a work of *témoignage* and its interest, as Poulaille would doubtless have agreed, is largely documentary: Audoux uses the fictional form to commit her life experiences to paper in order to bear witness to the real lives of working-class women in Belle Epoque Paris.

The question remains as to the potential political import of Audoux's novels. It is clear from Poulaille's *Nouvel âge littéraire* (1930) that Audoux did not see herself as a political novelist. Poulaille, revealing here of course his own views on the nature of proletarian writing, cites an interview with Audoux on the subject of her novel *De la ville au Moulin* (*From Town to Mill*, 1932):

> 'Does this book have a … social message, or a humanitarian one?'
>
> 'Neither social, nor socialist, nor humanitarian – just human. Oh, I know them all too well, those theorists and their theories … And in any case I don't get involved with all that, I am a poet. I look, I admire, I love, I remember. Life and Nature are enough to inspire me …' [20]

Poulaille is not guilty of casting Audoux in his own image: Audoux's novels indeed do not convey any specific ideological allegiance. It will however be clear from the preceding analysis that they do offer social commentary, but without recourse to narratorial intervention. As Nina Hellerstein notes in her study of narrative technique in *Marie-Claire*, Audoux tends to 'present information indirectly and obliquely' (Hellerstein 1995: 248); the impressionistic play between the perspectives of the child protagonist and her mature narrative self are a far cry from the didactic style of socialist realism. Indeed, the stylistic qualities of the text have been noted by many critics – words such as 'beauty' and 'lyricism' recur frequently, and commentators often praise the simplicity and effectiveness of Audoux's imaginative descriptive passages. Audoux's novels are not characterised by the often documentary and analytical style of the socialist realist text. Whilst her novels are certainly not *romans à thèse*, the relationship between the world and the writer, which for Jean-Pierre Morel constitutes the space for fictional creativity, is a space in which Audoux can show that the ways in which certain individuals are inserted into their social context are unacceptable. This is more true of *L'Atelier de Marie-Claire* than of *Marie-Claire*. In the first novel, the dilemmas encountered by the protagonists are presented exclusively from a personal perspective. The eviction of the

Sylvain family from the farm is a result of a particular organisation of rural work and the distribution of land amongst different categories of individuals; Marie-Claire's desertion by the man she loves is a result of the difference in their social status. However, although the reader is aware of the broader, structural contexts of these and other episodes, the characters do not interpret their experiences in terms of the collective, and no narrative voice provides such an analysis. Ultimately *Marie-Claire* remains a charming story in which characters face adversity with a combination of personal resignation and optimism that leaves the social structures that are at the root of their difficulties unchallenged. As François Talva pointed out in 1938, Audoux's characters 'do not know the meaning of anger' (Talva 1982: 54). Instead of giving voice to her oppression, Audoux seeks to escape it via the imagination: 'In her serene notion of happiness, she forgets the wrong that has been done to her' (ibid.: 58). And if, as Talva suggests, 'for Marguerite Audoux's characters, the imagination is as much their downfall as their salvation', this is perhaps because their imagined happiness precludes the transformative action that might improve the real conditions of their misery.[21]

The possibility of transformative action is raised in *L'Atelier de Marie-Claire* when Audoux makes use of irony to expose social injustice. One of the seamstresses, Bouledogue, is able to place some analytical distance between her experiences of work and the factors which render it oppressive. She points out that 'since we work more at busy times, we deserve to earn more', and when Bergeounette teases her, suggesting that she might like to start a revolution, Bouledogue replies: 'work should never be a hardship'.[22] Bouledogue also has an answer to clients like Mme Linella: 'If no one was prepared to work late, then the clients would just have to manage'.[23] But in response, Marie-Claire expresses one thorn in the side of Marxism: the workers are too oppressed to contemplate revolution: 'In the depths of my being I knew that she was right, but I could not see how we could do anything else, and I was annoyed with her for adding her reproaches to our tiredness'.[24] Bouledogue's remarks do not constitute a sustained political commentary, and the text does not encourage worker's revolt; on the contrary, it presents capitalism as an insoluble dilemma. Mme Dalignac is the perfect *patronne* whose priority is to pay a fair wage to her workers. However, the result of her putting people before profit is the collapse of her business, which threatens her workers with unemployment. Mme Doublé, her sister-in-law, is her antithesis: this hard-headed businesswoman is condemned by the text for putting profit before everything, however it is conceded that her brand of capitalism is required to rescue the *atelier* from ruin. The text offers no synthesis of the opposition between Dalignac and Doublé: in both novels, the ideal *patron(ne)s* meet misery and financial ruin, whilst the exploitative *patron(ne)s* succeed. It is difficult then to interpret Mme Dalignac's downfall. Even if we read Mme Dalignac as a victim of an inherently unjust system, the text has no standpoint from which to oppose that system, nor to suggest that it should, or could, be changed. Whilst the documentary evidence Audoux provides might be used by others for militant purposes, the text does not seek to convey a militant discourse of its own.

The Context of Reception

What hypotheses regarding the different reception of these two novels can be put forward on the basis of the preceding analyses? To discuss the acceptability of a text to an audience, it is necessary to know who read that text. Yet whilst statistics concerning print runs are available (according to Martin and Chartier's *Histoire de l'édition française* [1986], 75,000 copies of *Marie-Claire* were printed within a few weeks of the award of the Prix Fémina), data regarding actual readership are difficult to obtain. What is clear is that the reading public is not the same as the buying public, and, as Victor Serge pointed out in 1932, it is exclusively the latter who create literary successes:

> It is the tastes of the buying public which create what today might be called the literary climate, to use a fashionable term. The writer whom this public ignores will never reach the reading public from the poorer classes, or at least, will only do so with great difficulty. In any case, the poorer classes have absolutely no influence over the press and the reviews.[25]

That *Marie-Claire* was a commercial success and *L'Atelier de Marie-Claire* was not indicates that the bourgeoisie read the first text in massive numbers, but did not read the second. How can we account for this difference? A class-focused reading reveals significant differences between the two texts. Whilst Marie-Claire exposes her disadvantaged situation as an abandoned working-class child, she does not rail against it, and does not demand change. The Marie-Claire of the first novel is content to serve others obediently provided that they treat her with kindness, and preaches resignation in the face of adversity. This, combined with the idyllic mode via which Audoux transposes her personal experience, the novelty value of the text, and Mirbeau's patronage, was calculated to find an appreciative audience amongst a Belle Epoque bourgeois readership seeking to have its opinions confirmed rather than challenged. Thanks in part to its stylistic qualities, *Marie-Claire* is simply a pleasure to read. Aesthetic pleasure can present a problem for proletarian literature: Touret suggests that Poulaille was both fascinated and worried by the notion of aesthetic pleasure in novels (Touret 1989: 98), and Morel points out that proletarian literature is open to the charge of providing a pornography of misery (Morel 1977: 21). But there is nothing perverse in taking pleasure in a text such as Marie-Claire, 'which exudes radiant goodness'.[26]

However *L'Atelier de Marie-Claire* is more problematic since it represents an aestheticisation of proletarian misery that is uncomfortable to read. In its representation of class difference, the text reveals social realities of which a conservative readership might prefer not to be reminded. It depicts 'working conditions which only interest a few scarce syndicalists and some journalists'.[27] As Serge remarked: 'For God's sake, the buying public does not pay to be shown things that are pretty unpleasant to hear about if you enjoy the good life!'.[28] Furthermore, the second novel emerged into a problematic literary context. Whilst both *Marie-Claire* and *L'Atelier de Marie-Claire* correspond to Poulaille's ideal of non-partisan *témoignage*, they do not, as we have seen, seek to incite transformative action. Audoux's refusal of any politically engaged perspective means that her texts would have found few enthusiasts amongst the interwar advocates of a partisan revolutionary literature. Indeed, in his discussion of the political debate over proletarian literature, Morel does not cite Audoux as a point of reference for contemporary critics (Morel 1985). *L'Atelier de Marie-Claire* probably fell between two camps: unacceptably apolitical and too conservative in its message for the proponents of revolutionary literature, and too realistic in its account of working-class experience for a mainstream conservative public, it is hard to see where it could have found a readership. Garreau's conclusion is pertinent: 'anyone at all, from whatever background, will be able to recognise themselves in [*Marie-Claire*]', whereas *L'Atelier de Marie-Claire* 'is rather less like a mirror onto which one can project oneself'.[29]

The case of Audoux suggests then that it is justifiable to speak, with René Garguilo, of a Belle Epoque for proletarian literature:

> The period which preceded the 1914 war was particularly favourable as regards proletarian literature. Its boundaries were extended and its technique improved.[30]

Left-wing critics of Audoux's own period, such as Serge (1890–1947), were in agreement. For Serge, the reason was that the pre-war bourgeoisie had felt secure in its domination, and 'intelligent tyrants allow the poets to sing songs of liberty at their tables'.[31] The Belle Epoque offered a less contentious landscape for the proletarian writer than the postwar period. It would perhaps be more accurate to cite the Russian revolution as the significant point of rupture. After 1917, 'proletarian' no longer meant simply the oppressed masses, an unfortunate by-product of industrialisation, but an organised, politicised group whose interests had been championed across an entire nation, and whose ideology was seeking to penetrate the industrialised West. In 1910, a successful proletarian writer did not represent a threat to the bourgeois world view; one as politically neutral as Audoux could in fact confirm it. However in 1920, the designation 'proletarian' had an entirely different resonance. And furthermore, politically motivated debates over the proletarian genre were beginning to occupy the literary territory. If we agree with the writer of the preface to the 1920 text that *L'Atelier de Marie-Claire* is not aesthetically inferior to *Marie-Claire*, we must conclude that extra-literary criteria were more favourable to Audoux's success in 1910 than in 1920. It was Audoux's Belle Epoque readers that gave her literary success and consequently an income that exceeded that of the average seamstress.

Gendered Readings

The (anonymous) 1987 preface to *L'Atelier de Marie-Claire* offers an explanation of the failure of the novel that is based on gender: postwar readers apparently preferred to devour the rather racier tale of Victor Margueritte's *Garçonne* (Audoux 1987: 8). Such an argument would be difficult to prove: for example, Jennifer Milligan's work on the interwar popular romance suggests that texts expressing highly conservative gender messages sold in large numbers between the wars (Milligan 1996:

159–69). However it is certainly the case that both *Marie-Claire* novels present a view of gender that is conservative rather than radical in the context of their time. Marie-Claire's ambitions never extend beyond the domestic sphere; she corresponds to a mid-nineteenth-century stereotyped ideal of femininity based on 'sobriety, patience, love of work, resignation, moderation in desires, simplicity in tastes' (McMillan 2000: 98).[32] She is the reverse of the New Woman, who, in James McMillan's words, 'was ready to turn her back on the traditional domestic ideal in favour of a career and the pursuit of individual self-fulfilment', and whose advent tormented traditionalists in the years between 1880 and 1914 (ibid.: 141).[33] In *L'Atelier de Marie-Claire*, the conventional gender identity of the *ouvrières* is reinforced by their work in a conventionally 'feminine' profession (ibid.: 164). Whilst Audoux's novels problematise traditional family relationships and women's roles within family structures, her conservative representation of femininity – in particular her domesticisation and feminisation of the workplace – neutralises the potentially radical import of the documentary evidence the novels present. Milligan is right to point to 'a fundamental rejection of the way in which motherhood is promulgated in a patriarchal society' in *L'Atelier de Marie-Claire* (Milligan 1996: 131). However it is noteworthy that Milligan can suggest only that Audoux 'seems to argue' for legislative reform (ibid.: 128): Audoux in fact offers no strategies for progress in the novel, but contents herself with presenting the raw data on the basis of which *others* might perhaps argue for reform. For Garreau, the most that can be said is that Audoux is 'perhaps a little bit feminist'![34] Ultimately, neither novel troubles the understanding of gender which, according to McMillan, had become current in French society by 1914 and which, according to Mary Louise Roberts, still obtained after the war:

In this essentially conservative society, which nonetheless remained haunted by the nightmare of France's revolutionary past and fearful of the consequences of further political turmoil, the maintenance of a gender order based on sexual difference was widely regarded as fundamental to the preservation of social stability (McMillan 2000: 218).

In the decade after the war, legislators, novelists, social reformers, journalists, and feminists of all political stripes invoked the importance of a domestic and maternal role for women. They demonstrated a strong urge to return to a pre-war era of security [...] (Roberts 1994: 10).

Gender was of course a contentious theme in Belle Epoque France, since those who sought to maintain traditional gender roles inevitably came into conflict with those who sought to disrupt them. Audoux must, in my view, be located within the former group: both *Marie-Claire* novels offer conservative messages about gender which threatened neither the pre- nor the postwar 'gender order'.

Notes

1. Garreau (1997) represents a sustained attempt to analyse Audoux's output rhetorically, but not without reference to her biography and to the context of her novels. Garreau has recently produced a considerable body of work on Audoux. See also his 1991 biography and his two-volume study *La Famille de Marguerite Audoux* (1998). Prior to the publication of Garreau's work, two biographies of Audoux were available: Georges Reyer's *Un Cœur pur: Marguerite Audoux* (1942) and Louis Lanoizelée's *Marguerite Audoux* (1954).
2. 'Marie-Claire is not like any other novel; in terms of genre, it is not modelled on any other literary work ...' (*Marie-Claire* ne ressemble à aucun autre roman; il n'a pas de modèle générique dans la littérature ...) (Garreau 1991: 159). All translations are my own.
3. On the reception of *Marie-Claire*, see Roe 1983: 48 and Garreau 1991: 170ff. I should like to thank David Roe for his generosity in making available to me material on Audoux both from the *Bulletin des Amis de Charles-Louis Philippe* and from other sources.
4. 'This second novel was only moderately successful' ('Ce second roman n'est qu'un demi-succès') (Garreau 1991: 212).
5. 'les temps ont changé' (Audoux 1987: 8).
6. 'Il n'y a pas de qualités littéraires innées; la connaissance du sujet, l'expérience personnelle, l'intérêt existentiel peuvent seuls fonder une littérature [...]'; 'Les critères internes du bien-dire sont remplacés par des critères de rapport à du non-littéraire' (Touret 1989: 81–82).
7. 'Des lors, la fiction n'est plus, comme pour le positivisme, l'opposé du vérifiable et du contrôlable, mais la part d'invention et de fabrication – de "production", pour reprendre l'un des mots les plus en faveur à l'epoque – indispensable justement pour que ce mouvement puisse s'accomplir dans sa vérité' (Morel 1977: 22).
8. See Chapman 1992, 12–13: discussions of proletarian literature were taking place in France before the First World War, for example in articles by Jean-Richard Bloch and Marcel Martinet. See also Martinet 1976: 18.
9. The term 'Proletkult' is an abbreviation of 'Proletarian Culture'.
10. 'l'enfant est le plus prolétaire de tous les prolétaires, le plus soumis des soumis' (Touret 1989: 92).
11. 'des êtres maudits' (Garreau 1997: 50).
12. 'Il arriva un matin que la mère Colas nous accabla de reproches, disant que nous étions des enfants de malheur'; "Ah! oui, reprit-elle; ta maman était poitrinaire, et sœur Gabrielle dit que tu mourrais bientôt'" (Audoux 1958: 18, 22).

13. 'lumière douce et chantante qui se lève sur le livre, comme le soleil sur un beau matin d'été' (Mirbeau in Audoux 1958: 9).

14. 'Je ne pouvais m'empêcher de penser à la supérieure, quand elle m'avait dit d'un ton méprisant: "Vous trairez les vaches, et vous soignerez les porcs!" Elle avait l'air de m'infliger une punition en disant cela, et voilà que je n'éprouvais que du contentement à m'occuper des bêtes. Pour me donner de la force, j'appuyais mon front contre le flanc de la vache, et bientôt mon seau s'emplissait. Il se formait au-dessus du lait une écume qui prenait des teintes changeantes, et, quand le soleil passait dessus, elle devenait si merveilleuse que je ne me lassais pas de la regarder' (Audoux 1958: 136).

15. 'Le soleil paraissait rire avec nous aussi. Il rayonnait à travers la vitre et cherchait à se poser sur la corbeille à fil et sur la machine à coudre. Sa chaleur était encore très douce et Bergeounette ouvrit toute grande la fenêtre pour qu'il pût entrer à son aise' (Audoux 1987: 14–15).

16. 'Je travaille ensuite longuement mes phrases. Je rature. Je biffe. Parfois, je mets au panier tout un chapitre qui ne me plaît plus. Jamais satisfaite, je recommence inlassablement' (Garreau 1991: 91).

17. 'Il y avait des nuits si dures que le sommeil finissait par nous vaincre et que le patron nous retrouvait endormies, la tête sur la table. Nous étions toutes raidies par le froid, et la joue que nous avions appuyée sur le bras restait longtemps fripée' (Audoux 1987: 92).

18. 'Et elle reprit haleine pour ajouter d'un ton sec:
– Et vous me la livrez dimanche matin avant dix heures.
Mme Dalignac répondit sans la regarder:
– Vous demandez une chose impossible, nous n'avons plus le temps.
Les yeux de la cliente se durcirent comme si elle allit se fâcher:
– Par exemple! fit-elle.
Elle se radoucit pourtant:
– Sans cette robe je ne pourrais pas aller à Longchamps.
Et elle continua d'insister sur l'extrême besoin qu'elle avait d'une robe non brodée pour ce jour spécial' (ibid.: 97).

19. 'Alors Mme Linella se fit câline: – Allons! Vous veillerez un petit peu. Voilà tout!' (ibid.: 97).

20. 'Est-ce un livre de tendances … sociales, humanitaires?
– Ni sociales, ni socialistes, ni humanitaires, humaines. Oh! je les connais trop les théories et les théoriciens.
… et puis moi je ne me mêle pas de tout ça, je suis un poète. Je regarde, j'admire, j'aime, je me souviens. La Vie et la Nature cela suffit à m'inspirer …' (Poulaille 1986 [1930]: 257–58).

21. 'ignorant la colère'; 'Dans la conception sereine de son bonheur, elle oublie le mal qu'on lui a fait'; 'l'imagination des personnages de Marguerite Audoux […] les perd […] autant qu'elle les sauve' (Talva 1982: 54, 58, 57).

22. 'Puisque nous travaillons davantage dans les moments pressés, nous méritons de gagner davantage'; 'Le travail ne devrait jamais être une peine'(Audoux 1987: 46).

23. 'Si personne ne voulait veiller, les clientes seraient bien forcées de s'en arranger' (ibid.: 77).

24. 'Tout au fond de moi-même je lui donnais raison; mais je ne voyais pas comment on eût pu faire autrement, et je lui en voulais d'ajouter ses reproches à notre fatigue' (ibid).

25. 'Ce sont les préférences du public acheteur qui font aujourd'hui ce qu'on peut appeler, d'un mot en vogue, le climat littéraire. L'écrivain dédaigné par ce public n'arrivera pas, ou n'arrivera qu'avec une extrême difficulté, à toucher le public liseur des classes pauvres qui du reste n'exerce aucune influence sur la presse et les revues' (Serge 1976: 8–9).
26. 'gonflé de bonté rayonnante' (Poulaille 1937: 5).
27. '[c]onditions de travail qui n'intéressent [...] que quelques rares syndical-istes, quelques journalistes' (Zylberberg-Hocquard and Liszek 2002 : 45).
28. 'Le public acheteur ne paie pas, que diable!, pour qu'on lui montre des choses plutôt déplaisants à connaître quand on a la vie douce !' (Serge 1976: 12).
29. 'tout un chacun, de quelque bord qu'il soit, va pouvoir s'y reconnaître'; 'est beaucoup moins un miroir dans lequel on puisse se projeter' (Garreau 1992: 16,19).
30. 'La période qui précéda la guerre de 1914 fut particulièrement faste pour la littérature proletarienne. Son domaine s'étendit et sa technique s'améliora' (Garguilo 1989: 13).
31. 'Les tyrans intelligents permettent aux poètes de chanter, à leur table, la liberté' (Serge 1976 [1932]: 15).
32. McMillan is quoting Lucille Sauvan's *Directions*, a nineteenth-century education manual.
33. See Chapter 1 above.
34. 'peut-être un peu féministe' (Garreau 1991: 215).

PART V

COLONISED
AND OTHER WOMEN

Figure 19.1 Hubertine Auclert. Courtesy of the Bibliothèque Marguerite Durand.

CHAPTER 19

COLONISER AND COLONISED IN HUBERTINE AUCLERT'S WRITINGS ON ALGERIA

Edith Taïeb

Hubertine Auclert's *Les Femmes arabes en Algérie* (*Arab Women in Algeria*) was published in 1900. It consists of a collection of articles previously published in *La Citoyenne* when Auclert was still living in Algeria, a country which she left on the death of her husband in 1892. This chapter aims to demonstrate the originality and subversiveness of Auclert's feminist discourse on the French presence in Algeria in these (and other) articles, particularly in comparison with the orientalist discourses of other writers of the period.[1]

When Hubertine Auclert (1848–1914) (Figure 19.1) departed for Algeria in 1888 to join her husband, who had been appointed a justice of the peace in Frenda, she was already recognised in France as the champion of political rights for women. In fact, having arrived in Paris in 1873 to join feminist activists Léon Richer and Maria Deraismes,[2] she had soon distanced herself from them because they were only claiming civil rights for women (basically, the right to divorce, to sue for paternity and to receive equal pay for equal work). Situating herself in the tradition of women activists of 1789 and 1848, Auclert affirmed the need to 'subordinate women's civil emancipation to their political emancipation'[3] and claimed the double right for women to vote and to be eligible for election. Calling for a Republic which would recognise the rights of both women and the underprivileged, she managed to get herself elected as a delegate to the *Congrès ouvrier socialiste* in Marseilles in October 1879, in the hope of concluding 'a defensive and offensive pact against our common oppressors'.[4] But even if she succeeded in getting the principle of social and political equality for women written into the programme of the *Parti ouvrier*, she soon realised that the proletariat was not ready to admit that the specific oppression of women (the institutionalisation of the husband's appropriation of the body, possessions and labour of the married woman, due to the Napoleonic Code) prevented women's struggle from being fully encompassed by the class struggle. For Auclert, men needed to realise that they could not simply use women with impunity, and thus in 1881 she refused to pay her taxes, after trying in vain to get herself on the electoral roll. In her view it was not acceptable that women should pay taxes they were not authorised to vote for, nor contribute through their taxes to the upkeep of a government which voted laws against them. That same year, she founded the newspaper *La Citoyenne* (1881–1891), to win over public opinion to her idea that the advent of a 'true Republic' was necessarily linked to the emancipation of women (Auclert 1882a: 1). Clearly in her eyes, the Third Republic did not merit such a fine name. In fact, she based her demands for women's political rights on the failure of what she called the '*Res hominum*' (Auclert 1882b: 1), as opposed to what she aspired for, a 'democratic republic' (Auclert 1891: 1). She argued that the demonstrable incapacity of men in power to assure the happiness of the men and women they governed testified to the urgent need for the massive intervention of women, at men's side, in every political assembly and every aspect of the civil service.

The Hypocrisy of the French Republic

It is important to take into account the arguments developed by Hubertine Auclert, particularly in *La Citoyenne*, during the years preceding her departure for Algeria. Auclert's feminist commitment is in part indebted to 'her acute sensitivity [which] made her feel the suffering of others',[5] as recalled by Marie Chaumont in her introduction to her elder sister's posthumous work (Auclert 1923: 2). Her demands were motivated by the psychological and physical sufferings of women in France, as well as in Algeria. Thus, despite Joan W. Scott's assertion to the contrary (Scott 1996: 116), Auclert did not wait to go to Algeria to denounce the physical violence endured by women, as confirmed by various articles she wrote, including the evocatively titled 'The vivisectioned woman' (Auclert 1883: 1), which I have analysed elsewhere (Taïeb 2001). The multiplication of animal metaphors assimilating men to predators and women to prey in order to denounce the predatory society established by men in power signifies that, for Auclert, the 'sublime words' of the Republican motto mask the brutal reality of social relations, which were every bit as violent as in periods prior to the declaration of the Republic and in those societies which France prided itself on 'civilising' (Auclert 1879: 149). As her biographer Stephen Hause points out, Auclert, always on the lookout for arguments to back her thesis on the necessity of women's rights, had already made the telling observation that men's inability to govern had become even more evident in the colonies than in France (Auclert 1889: 1; Hause 1987: 135). In other words, Auclert's critical observations regarding the behaviour of the French authorities in Algeria echo the analysis she had previously developed regarding the system of male domination over women in France, which she referred to as 'masculinism' (Auclert 1890: 1–2).

In *Les Femmes arabes en Algérie*, Auclert first denounces the fact that it was impossible for the Arabs to express their point of view on matters concerning their country even though they, more than anyone else, had interests to defend there; and naturally she attributes this state of affairs to the fact that they had no representatives in the Chamber of Deputies. She establishes a direct link between the political exclusion of the Arabs and their economic destitution; thus, in her view, the reason why the Arabs did not have enough to eat was because they did not vote, their work being 'not rewarded at its true value because of their disparaged, abject condition'.[6] And she declared that in order to exist both individually and collectively, in order to be able to defend themselves and their possessions, it was indispensable that 'the natives in Algeria should be armed with the ballot paper'.[7] It is notable that Auclert frequently uses the term 'armed', right from the first issues of *La Citoyenne*, to highlight the merciless nature of the latent war waged by men against women through the law (Auclert 1881b: 1). The parallel that she establishes between women in France and indigenous Algerians is based on the premise that, 'For the government, those who do not vote are necessarily scapegoats'.[8] To the extent that, on the one hand Algeria was considered a French territory, and on the other 'in a true Republic, the government of all should be for all',[9] Auclert uses the political exclusion of the Arabs to denounce yet again the hypocrisy of the French Republic. And just as she had affirmed to the workers present at the *Congrès ouvrier socialiste* in Marseilles in 1879 that a 'Republic which maintained women in a state of inferiority could not create men equal',[10] so she argued that the soft attitude of the French authorities towards Arab laws and customs authorising the rape of children, polygamy and the repudiation of women, would fatally compromise the future of the French presence in Algeria by making assimilation impossible (Auclert 1889: 1).

The Need for Women's Involvement

If the 'woman question' is, for Auclert, the 'Gordian knot which, once severed, would allow the social question to be resolved',[11] it is because in Algeria, as in France, men in power pandered to the desires of the majority of men against women and against the general good, in order to serve their own immediate interests. To men who claim their superiority over women, she retorts that their heads are 'too high in the clouds'[12] to respond to the aspirations of the people they are cut off from, and that they would do better to let women manage the affairs of state as they managed their own households. She juxtaposes the lack of foresight of men in power with the common sense of women whose upbringing forces them to attend to the most pressing needs of their immediate family circle. For her, the exclusion of women from the political domain in France had detrimental effects on France's administration of its colonies. Thus she protests at the fact that representatives carrying out a government inquiry in Algeria to 'approach the natives about the possibility of assimilation'[13] only questioned their leaders. As she points out, the interests of the Arab people and their leaders were diametrically opposed, since the latter – who to a certain extent served as intermediaries for the French administration and had the right to ten percent of the taxes they were responsible for levying from the population – could not be in favour of assimilation which would threaten their privileges. She maintains that the conflict of interests between the people, who had 'everything to gain from becoming French',[14] and their leaders, who would have lost both their privileges and their best source of income, would certainly not have escaped women (Auclert 1900: 23). She concludes that only women were really capable of carrying out such an inquiry in Algeria, not just because of the inability of male officials 'to hear with their ears, see with their eyes, and take account of the *desiderata* of non-voters who for them do not count'[15] but because, being themselves outside the law, they would feel empathy with the Arab people and would think to get the opinion of 'those who are the most oppressed, the most deprived of liberty among conquered peoples: Arab women'.[16] Besides, given that only women would have been allowed to approach Muslim women, the colonisers were committing a strategic error in depriving themselves of female officials who alone could 'morally' conquer Algeria by bringing 'Frenchification' into the home (Auclert 1900: 26). For Auclert, the French were wrong to neglect the opinion of Arab women, who had helped their husbands defend the soil of their homeland, and wrong not to recruit women investigators 'so as to really know the opinion of the Arab world on the administration to give Algeria'.[17] Furthermore, women investigators with a smattering of Arabic would not have aroused distrust or wounded Muslim sensibilities, and so would have been able to familiarise Arab women with French ways of life and thought (Auclert 1900: 26).

In *La Citoyenne*, Auclert regularly pointed out how, through their stubborn refusal to share their rights with women, Frenchmen doomed their enterprises to failure, and how, by liberating themselves, French women would contribute to the liberation of humanity in general. In the case of Algeria, she suggests that Muslim women would be the first to desire assimilation, that is, the same law for both French and Arabs, a law which would enable them to escape from the constraints they suffered under Islamic customary law. She was appalled by the respect French courts accorded to Arab 'anomalies' (ibid.: 47), including allowing fathers to sell their pre-pubescent daughters to the highest, often the oldest bidder, which she considered tantamount to authorising 'child rape' (ibid.: 42). She denounces the cowardice of French magistrates who, by applying Islamic customary law which was 'so formally in contradiction with our French law',[18] annulled freely consented marriages and delivered women to the men who had bought them when they were just little girls, sometimes even before they were born. To stop these 'marital rapes', Auclert argued that the law which forbade girls to be contracted in marriage

before the age of fifteen should be applied to all French territories (ibid.: 49). The question was, how this could be achieved
within a system of justice controlled exclusively by men.
Auclert, who had long denounced the 'sexual solidarity'
between men which benefited 'murdering husbands' (Auclert
1881d: 1), could only repeat her credo: if women in France
had their share of power, they would not tolerate a law allowing the rape of children on territory administered by France,
and if men tolerated this 'crime', it was because of their solidarity with those who profited from it (Auclert 1900: 49).

Auclert applies the same reasoning to the question of
polygamy, arguing that if French women were able to vote
and pass laws, they would long since have delivered their
'African sisters' from 'offensive polygamy and intolerable
promiscuity with their co-wives'.[19] She refuses the pretext of an
ontological difference put forward by men to justify on one
side of the Mediterranean what they condemned on the other.
She points out that polygamy was once widely practised, even
by the Franks, but she argues that civilisation has driven it
out, since it was 'both against nature and contrary to human
dignity',[20] thus allowing an ironic reflection on France's so-
called civilising mission in the conquest of Algeria. Furthermore, she insists on the fact that Arab women were against
polygamy, offering as proof the insults with which young
women nearly always responded to the first compliments of a
man 'already equipped with several wives',[21] expressing their
horror and disgust for what they called the 'conjugal kennel'.[22]
Auclert habitually sought out the illogicalities of those who,
through their laws had, for example, supported the idea that
women lacked judgement by putting them in the same category as the mentally ill in order to deprive them of a certain
number of rights, including the right to bear witness in a civil
court, whilst at the same time recognising their criminal lia-
bility. These illogicalities clearly revealed the dishonesty of
those who, far from caring about the general good, had in
mind the preservation of the interests of the male minority to
which they belonged. If the 'French conqueror' said to the
Muslim, 'I despise your race, but I concede my law in favour of
yours; I give the Koran precedence over the Code',[23] it was simply because he hoped to divert the Arabs' attention and stifle
any political awareness which might have led them to rebel
against the subaltern position imposed on them by the French
Republic. In fact, Auclert argues, 'by focusing the Arabs' cerebral activity on their bestial instincts, [polygamy] annihilated

their intelligence and atrophied their brain'.[24] Drawing on her own inquiry into the matter, having questioned a number of Arabs, she declares that they all confessed that 'there was a permanent state of war in the households of men with several wives'.[25] Furthermore, she insists on the fact that in the end it was the children who suffered the most from the sufferings inflicted on women by men (an argument she had often used in relation to the condition of women in France).

Auclert had already warned French legislators about the broader demographic consequences of the separation of the public and the private spheres in France, since it often resulted in the destitution of French women, particularly mothers. She thus set herself up against those who pretended to defend the interest of the family by confining women to the domestic sphere. For Auclert, men's contempt for women resulted literally in death, in Algeria as in France. If she invoked the agony endured by unmarried mothers in France in order to demand less severity in cases of infanticide, she argues that in households of four or eight, as there were in Algeria, the 'fierce jealousy' between co-wives would inevitably lead to crime. She cites a recent case of a young woman who had slit the throat of her rival's baby 'like a kid goat', claiming that 'for babies in a polygamous family, all the father's wives are wicked stepmothers'.[26] Polygamy did not even help to populate the vast terrain of Algeria, since the reproduction of the species was restricted by 'the bestial excesses of the polygamous male and the woman's sterility, due to the abuse and atrophy she suffered in childhood'.[27] Since polygamy did not have women's consent and could not be defended from the point of view of the collectivity, for Auclert it was essential that it be abolished.

The Republic's Complicity in the Oppression of Algerian Women

As was her custom, Auclert petitioned deputies and senators to draw attention to the situation of Arab women, 'whose barbarous treatment was tolerated by France'.[28] In the process she underlined the fact that the Republic could not encourage polygamy and the marriage of pre-pubescent children on one side of the Mediterranean and condemn them on the other 'without being in contradiction with its own principles'.[29] No doubt she did not really expect support from those she had so often accused of being more concerned with keeping up appearances than with respect for human dignity and the principles of freedom and equality inscribed on the front of Republican buildings. Rather she hoped to provoke a response from the French authorities which would allow her to pursue her line of attack. And in fact the decision of the Interior Minister to whom her petition had been forwarded, as communicated to her by the President of the Chamber of Deputies, made it clear that the refusal to modify the situation of Arab women was motivated by the fear of provoking 'agitation amongst the native population, already preoccupied with projects for reforms, which it would be better to avoid'.[30] Reading such a response from an elected representative of the Republic, Auclert may well have called to mind what she had claimed in other circumstances, that those who presented themselves as the heirs of the Revolution were 'singularly degenerate sons' (Auclert 1887: 1). She does not hesitate to express publicly the indignation that such hypocrisy provoked in her:

> What? Ideas are in the air, progress is driving men forward, and only those vanquished by the French Republic are to languish in their old ways? Muslim Algeria is to maintain the status quo, while everything around is moving forward? [...] Under the cover of its civilising mission, France has dispossessed the Arabs of the land of Algeria, and now it is claiming respect for the barbarianism of the vanquished in order to leave them outside the civilisation in the name of which it vanquished them? It's unimaginable![31]

Declaring that the Interior Minister, objecting to a 'fanciful danger', was 'more Muslim than Mahomet himself', she points out that a 'good' Muslim, Kassim-anim Bey, counsellor at the court of appeal in Cairo, was calling for a law against polygamy and repudiation, and in favour of education for women, and of allowing women to live independently and free to choose their own husbands (Auclert 1900: 73). But in any case, Auclert considered that it was pointless to try and avoid unrest, which would inevitably take place at the time of assimilation; she thought such unrest would be passing, and that it would 'rekindle the noble past of the Muslim race and set it on the path to progress'.[32] There was thus no need to invoke it as a reason for denying Arab women their rights.

One of the most important of women's rights was the right to education, and for Auclert, girls' education represented a major factor in the struggle for a form of assimilation which would put an end to the tyranny Arabs were subjected to. She accuses the French authorities of playing into the hands of those who were opposed to mixing between the Arabs and the French by allowing the *Conseil Général d'Alger*, in 1861, to abolish the allocation to schools for girls, on the grounds that education was not relevant to women in an Islamic community where they lived sequestrated lives. She argues that it was precisely the sequestration of women which maintained the Arabs under the coloniser's yoke and made them an easy prey. French men should admit that they had an interest in authorising Muslim tyranny, since 'the ignorance of native women assured them of the exploitation of the entire race'.[33] She is suggesting here that as long as the 'colonised' indulged in 'sexual excesses', they would not think to defend their freedom or possessions; but she also denounces the financial benefits claimed by the French under the pretext of respecting Islamic rights of succession. When a Muslim woman, who was allowed to inherit one third of her father's estate, had no co-heirs, the French state effectively seized the other two thirds. Auclert demanded the cessation of this 'pillage', which revealed the 'tacit convention between brigands' whereby the French seemed to say to Muslim men, 'we will let you rob women on the condition that, when you are not there, we will rob them ourselves'.[34]

The Need for Women's Rights

Refusing to accept the inevitability of a fate that condemned the majority of the population to misery, Auclert frequently points out how those in power confuse the causes and effects of their domination. How could the colonisers seriously complain that Arabs remained untouched by French civilisation and yet refuse to initiate them into it by providing them with an education in whatever they were reproached for not knowing? Prolonging this line of questioning, Auclert wonders, 'what would be the excuse for the conquest [of Algeria] if the Arab who has been conquered in order to be civilised (sic) continues to live in a state of nature'?[35] Taking literally dominant discourses on France's civilising mission, she challenges the government of the Third Republic to act in accordance with the principles they claim to stand for. But in the meantime, she accuses it of having openly doomed to failure the encounter between coloniser and colonised which could have been a source of happiness for two peoples united by common interests. And she dates this failure back to the moment when the *Conseil Général d'Alger* gave way to Arab men's desire to have the girls' schools closed. For Auclert, this decision had sounded the death knell of assimilation: 'For women who had been swiftly won over to our civilisation, as they are, would have been of great help in conciliating the Arabs and forging inside contacts in the Muslim world'.[36]

The only measure which would have satisfied Auclert, and which would have allowed the Arabs to become 'children of the Republic' (Auclert 1900: 69), would have been to assign male and female Arabic-speaking teachers to the French primary schools in Algeria and so allow native girls and boys to gain access to them. Just as in France she had recommended that boys' schools should be open to girls in the hope that 'children of both sexes sitting on the same school benches might enter life as comrades, hand in hand, valuing and respecting each other, and not as enemies as they do today',[37] so she maintains that mixing in Arab-French schools, through the 'games, competitiveness and efforts of the children'[38] would allow 'ridiculous racial prejudice, which makes us take the superiority of our education for a natural superiority, to be nipped in the bud'.[39]

Hubertine Auclert's writings on Algeria, and in particular on Algerian women, were not only extraordinarily incisive for their time, challenging both the hypocrisy of Republican discourses on women and on France's 'civilising mission' and the orientalism and exoticism of other metropolitan contemporary writers, they are still of relevance today. They put us on guard against the temptation to confine the 'other' to a totally alien form of humanity under the guise of respecting the 'other's' difference. By drawing on experiences common to women on both sides of the Mediterranean, linking their suffering to the ways in which their bodies and labour are appropriated by men, Auclert demonstrates that the oppression of women is not the fact of any one particular culture but of a worldwide culture, which she calls 'international masculinism' (Auclert 1890: 1). For Auclert, the shared experience of oppression suggests that women would be better than men at recognising what they – and mankind in general – have in common, despite their differences, and thus better able and willing to work together to build a more just, harmonious and democratic world.

Translated by Carrie Tarr

Notes

1. See, for example, Yee (2000 and Chapter 20 of this book).
2. For more on Léon Richer, Maria Deraismes and Hubertine Auclert, see Albistur and Armogathe (1977 and 1978), Sowerwine (1978), Krakovitch (1980), Bidelman (1982) and Klejman and Rochefort (1989).
3. 'subordonner l'affranchissement civil de la femme à son affranchissement politique' (Auclert 1881a: 1).
4. 'un pacte d'alliance défensive et offensive contre nos communs oppresseurs' (Auclert 1879: 149).
5. 'sa sensibilité extrême [qui] lui faisait ressentir la souffrance des autres' (Auclert 1923: 2).
6. 'en raison de leur condition abjecte, déprécié, non rétribué à sa valeur' (Auclert 1900: 16).
7. 'les indigènes d'Algérie soient armés du bulletin de vote' (ibid.: 16).
8. 'Pour des élus, les non-votants sont nécessairement des boucs émissaires' (ibid.: 21).
9. 'dans une vraie République, le gouvernement qui procède de tous doit être à tous' (Auclert 1882a: 1).
10. 'République qui maintiendra[it] les femmes dans une condition d'infériorité, ne pourra[it] faire les hommes égaux' (Auclert 1879: 149).
11. 'nœud gordien qui, une fois tranché, permettra[it] de résoudre la question sociale' (Auclert 1885: 1).
12. 'ils planaient trop haut' (Auclert 1886: 1).
13. 'pressentir les indigènes relativement à l'assimilation' (Auclert 1900: 23).
14. 'tout à gagner à devenir français' (ibid.: 23).
15. 'd'entendre par leurs oreilles, de regarder par leurs yeux et de tenir compte des *desiderata* des non-votants qui pour eux ne comptent pas' (ibid.: 23).
16. '[d]es êtres qui chez les conquis sont les plus opprimés, les plus privés de liberté: les femmes arabes' (ibid.: 24)
17. 'pour connaître véritablement l'avis du monde arabe sur l'administration à donner à l'Algérie' (ibid.: 26).
18. 'si formellement en contradiction avec notre droit français' (ibid.: 47).
19. 'de l'outrangeante polygamie et de l'intolérable promiscuité avec leurs co-épouses' (ibid.: 63).
20. 'aussi anti-naturelle que contraire à la dignité humaine' (ibid.: 63).
21. 'déjà muni de plusieurs femmes' (ibid.: 66).
22. '*chenil conjugal*' (ibid.: 66).
23. 'Je méprise ta race, mais j'abaisse ma loi devant la tienne; je donne au Koran le pas sur le Code' (ibid.: 64).
24. 'concentrant toute l'activité cérébrale des arabes sur l'instinct bestial, [la polygamie] annihil[ait] leur intelligence et atrophi[ait] leur cerveau' (ibid.: 65).
25. 'la guerre était en permanence dans la maison de l'homme qui avait plusieurs épouses' (ibid.: 65).
26. 'chaque bébé d'une famille polygame a[vait] pour marâtre toutes les femmes de son père' (ibid.: 67).
27. 'l'excès de bestialité de l'homme polygame et la stérilité de la femme due aux abus et à l'atrophiement dont elle a[vait] été victime dans son enfance' (ibid.: 68).
28. 'qui [étaient], avec la tolérance de la France, si barbarement traitées' (ibid.: 69).

29. 'à moins d'être en contradiction avec son principe même' (ibid.: 70).
30. 'dans la population indigène, déjà préoccupée de projets de réformes, une agitation qu'il conv[enait] d'éviter' (ibid.: 73).
31. 'Eh quoi! les idées volent, le progrès pousse les hommes et les conquis de la République Française seuls croupiraient en leurs vieux errements? L'Algérie mahométane devrait rester dans le *statu quo*, pendant que tout marche autour d'elle? [...] La France a, sous le couvert de la civilisation, dépossédé l'arabe du territoire de l'Algérie et maintenant, elle arguerait de son respect pour la barbarie du vaincu, pour le laisser en dehors de la civilisation au nom de laquelle elle l'a conquis? Cela est inimaginable! (ibid.: 74–75).
32. 'ressusciter[ait] à son noble passé et [qu'elle] mettra[it] en marche vers le progrès la race musulmane' (ibid.: 76).
33. 'l'ignorance de la femme leur assur[ait] l'exploitation de toute la race indigène' (ibid.: 140).
34. 'nous vous laissons détrousser les femmes, à condition que quand vous ne serez pas là, ce sera nous qui les détrousserons' (ibid.: 141).
35. 'où serait l'excuse de la conquête [de l'Algérie] si l'arabe que l'on a assujetti pour le civiliser (sic) continuait à vivre à l'état de nature?' (ibid.: 143).
36. 'Car les femmes gagnées promptement, comme elles le sont, à notre civilisation, nous auraient puissamment aidés à nous concilier les Arabes, à nous ménager des intelligences dans le monde musulman' (ibid.: 143–44).
37. 'les enfants des deux sexes assis sur les mêmes bancs d'école [arrivent] dans la vie camarades, la main dans la main, s'estimant, se respectant et non plus comme deux ennemis qu'ils sont aujourd'hui ' (Auclert 1881c: 1).
38. 'fusionn[ant] avec les jeux, l'émulation et les efforts des enfants' (Auclert 1900: 142).
39. 'tuer dans l'œuf le ridicule préjugé de race qui nous fait prendre notre supériorité d'éducation pour une supériorité native' (ibid.: 142).

CHAPTER 20

THE CHIVALROUS COLONISER: COLONIAL FEMINISM AND THE *ROMAN À THÈSE* IN THE BELLE EPOQUE

Jennifer Yee

In the years around 1900, no doubt in part as a reaction against the previous literary generation's pursuit of 'art for art's sake' ('l'art pour l'art'), an increasing number of French novelists produced works which corresponded to the idea that writers had an important social and moral function to fulfil. As Pierre Citti puts it, 'around 1900 most novelists wanted, or accepted, or allowed it to be said that their work [...] dealt with or asked a moral or social question' (1987: 240). While such a belief in the social role of the writer was of course not entirely new, it produced a widespread tendency to write novels with what could be called an 'educational purpose', so that the Belle Epoque in France saw the rise of the *roman à thèse*, defined by Susan Suleiman as 'a novel written in the realistic mode, which signals itself to the reader as primarily didactic in intent, seeking to demonstrate the validity of a political, philosophical, or religious doctrine' (1983: 7). It is in fact a rhetorical genre that aims to persuade, and as such is in many ways resolutely anti-modern. Some of these novels nevertheless merit study today, firstly because they deal with the great issues of their time and secondly – perhaps primarily – because they often fail to fulfil the agenda they set themselves, revealing fissures in the ideological fabric of their time. This chapter looks at two examples of the *roman à thèse* from the Belle Epoque that are situated at the intersection of colonialist and feminist discourse, Pierre Loti's *Les Désenchantées* (1906) and Charles Géniaux' *Les Musulmanes* (1909).[1] It focuses on internal conflicts within the two narratives, in order to reveal the inherent contradiction in French attitudes towards the Oriental woman and the harem, which in turn points to an unresolved tension in French ideas of the Orient.

The Story of *Les Désenchantées*

Published in book form in 1906, *Les Désenchantées* was one of Loti's biggest print runs, with 419 editions during the author's life (Buisine 1988: 243). The critics, with the exception of Rachilde, were also very positive: Jules Bois in *Les Annales* even read in it the 'evangelism of pity and justice', nothing short of a modern crusade (Lefêvre 1939: 96–98). Set in Istanbul, this novel tells the story of three young women brought up within Islam who revolt against the social codes in force in the early years of the twentieth century. The details of the plot itself are in many ways less intriguing than the extraordinary circumstances in which the novel was written, detailed accounts of which can be found elsewhere (for example Lefêvre 1939, Quella-Villéger 1986: 243–51, Buisine 1988: 217–44, Szyliowicz 1988: 94–116).

   Les Désenchantées was written when Pierre Loti was already a famous, middle-aged author renowned for his novels on exotic themes, among them his first novel set in Turkey that recounted a tragic love affair with the Turkish Aziyadé. In an exact parallel, the novel tells the story of André Lhéry, a famous, middle-aged novelist renowned for his writing on exotic themes and particularly for a novel set in Turkey about his tragic love affair with the Turkish Nedjibé. Lhéry, the fictitious character, returns to Istanbul, the scene of his youthful romance and of his first novel. He receives a letter from three Turkish women who present themselves under pseudonyms and ask him for a meeting. At the meeting, as at most of their subsequent meetings, the three women remain veiled. Over time Lhéry learns that their 'real' names (still in the novel) are Djénane, Mélek and Zeyneb and that they are young Turkish women of aristocratic families who have been brought up by French governesses, but are trapped by the traditional constraints on women in Turkey. The three women persuade Lhéry, rather against his will, to write a novel that will plead against the predicament of the modern Turkish woman by telling their story. The novel will be called

'Les Désenchantées', and will incorporate some of the letters written by the women themselves. However, a romantic attachment, that is not made explicit until it is too late, forms between the ageing novelist and the young Djénane. She is too proud to ask his help to escape her doom and, forced to return to the husband she has rejected, she takes poison and dies while writing a final letter to Lhéry ...

So much for the story within the novel. In reality Loti's story was indeed based on an encounter with three veiled women, but unbeknownst to him the woman who presented herself as the mysterious and tragic Leyla (Djénane in the novel), was Maria Lera, a Frenchwoman strongly influenced by Swedish feminism who worked as a professional journalist under the pseudonym Marc Hélys.[2] She and her two friends had initially sought to meet Loti in disguise simply as an amusement, because of his fame and partly also 'to teach him a lesson' (Hélys 1924: 18), but they rapidly formed the project of manipulating him into writing a 'feminist' novel. This literary hoax was first unmasked in an anonymous article in 1908, and more importantly in an article by Marcelle Tinayre (1909),[3] but these attacks do not seem to have had much of an impact until after Loti's death in 1922, when Marc Hélys published *L'envers d'un roman: le secret des 'Désenchantées' révélé par celle qui fut Djénane* in 1924. The other two women, the daughters of a French aristocrat settled in Istanbul with his Circassian wife, did in fact flee Istanbul after publication of the novel (Figure 20.1).

Figure 20.1 'Leyla Zeyneb Neyr', the names used by Marc Hélys (pseudonym of Maria Lera), Zennour and Nouryé with Pierre Loti, who called them respectively Djénane, Zeyneb and Mélek in *Les Désenchantées* (1906). Originally printed in Hélys (1924).

In the novel, the three Turkish women approach the fictitious novelist Lhéry in order to ask him to write a novel 'on behalf of the Turkish woman of today',[4] in the hope that they will be of use to hundreds of their sisters. These are, then, three characters in search of an author, but also a *thèse* in search of a *roman*. Now in exemplary tales interpretation is guided by what Suleiman calls 'interpretative utterances' within the fiction (1977: 478), and *Les Désenchantées* is no exception. In the form of letters that were included with only slight changes in the novel, the three veiled women frequently provide direct verbal indications of how their stories should be used by the text. The characters are thus writers and readers of their own story, offering interpretations of it that may or may not correspond with those of the narrator or of Lhéry, the fictitious author. Indeed, in many ways these characters have chosen a particularly unlikely author, as Lhéry himself points out: 'A book aiming to prove something – you who appear to have read my work and know it well, do you think that is my style?'[5] He even warns them that he is tempted to plead *against* their cause, since he sees himself as 'an old-fashioned man', who might declare war on the modern education of Turkish women and insist on a 'return to the contented peace of your grandmothers'.[6]

Curiously enough, after the novel was published Loti does appear to have taken its cause to heart, despite his own otherwise traditionalist attitude. He pleaded the cause of Turkish women to feminist meetings in France, which rather moved Marc Hélys who was present at one of these occasions.

Les Musulmanes

Les Musulmanes deliberately sets out to rewrite Loti's story, transferring it from Turkey to Tunisia, which had been effectively under French control since 1881. Charles Géniaux was far from being a naïve admirer of *Les Désenchantées* and was one of the first to suggest that it did not represent an authentic account of Turkish women's claims (even alluding to the possibility of a hoax). *Les Musulmanes* sets out to give a realistic portrait of Tunisian women, whereas Loti was accused of portraying Turkish women as if they could suffer from the sophisticated melancholy of Parisians.

Set in Tunis, *Les Musulmanes* depicts life among Tunisian women, based on Charles Géniaux's own notes and the observations of his wife, Claire.[7] Géniaux thus uses his wife to take the male Western gaze into the closed spaces of the women's quarters, producing not so much a novel as a work of 'observation', which 'aims ... to contribute to the emancipation of Muslim women' (Géniaux 1909: x). *Les Musulmanes* is a classic *roman à thése* which identifies each individual character with an idea or a particular problem. This is highlighted by the fact that the characters' names are translated from the Arabic. The two heroines are Nijma and Nefissa or 'Etoile' ('Star') and 'Précieuse' ('Precious'): Etoile leads the way for the ideal young Muslim woman of the future, while her sister Précieuse, compared to an exquisite jewel, is obviously too fine to survive. Some of the names are ironic: a relative of the girls, 'Madame Crown-of-the-Kingdom', far from being treasured by her husband has been repudiated not once but several times. Letifa, a frail young friend, is married to Monsieur Pure, a venerated *cadi* (a Muslim magistrate) who has already killed two thirteen-year-old wives through exhaustion and who is 'in charge of the supervision of religion and morality'.[8]

The two sisters symbolise different paths out of the harem. Etoile is betrothed to a Tunisian man who has studied in France and holds progressive views on the place of women. At the end of the novel this young couple initiates a new life, in the French quarter of Tunis, rejecting the veil and the closed doors of the harem, despite the curses of Etoile's father and the insults of the Arab populace. Meanwhile Précieuse, who is in love with René, a French officer, is forced to marry the man her father has chosen for her; she attempts to run away with René but falls from the rooftops to her death. While Etoile is clearly set up as showing the way forward for young Muslim women, tragic Précieuse presents the main romantic interest. This story of the doomed love of an exotic woman for a French man was not new; it had been popularised by Pierre Loti's novels, particularly *Aziyadé*, in which the young Turkish heroine dies after her lover's departure. *Aziyadé* was however published in 1879, at a time when the late Romantic model of exoticism still dominated. A generation later, Précieuse's death does not simply follow the stereotype of impossible love between East and West; rather, it is part of a sustained demonstration of the condemnable nature of arranged marriages in Islamic society and a plea for French colonial intervention to alleviate the condition of women within North-African Islamic society.

It is of course not surprising to encounter a feminist thesis concerning Islamic society in the early years of the twentieth century, which were marked by the beginning of various movements, increasingly linked to nationalist anti-colonialism within Islamic society, that sought to reform the condition of women in Muslim states. In Egypt these campaigns were to become a truly coordinated feminist movement with the creation of the Egyptian Feminist Union in 1923. In Turkey, the revolution of 1908 was to lead to widespread reforms; the codes governing family law and the rights of women were fundamentally revised from 1917 onwards (Bakalti 1996: 34, 37). In *Les Musulmanes*, one can recognise in the Westernised Tunisian man who marries Etoile a figure of the 'Jeunes Tunisiens', modelled on the 'Young Turks' who were already active around the turn of the century. But *Les Musulmanes*, like *Les Désenchantées*, was written by a Frenchman with the help of a Frenchwoman, and for a mainly French public. The world it reflects is at least as much one of European fantasy as of Tunisian fact. Naturally, the fact that Frenchwomen were far from having won their own battles is never mentioned.[9] Mervat Hatem, speaking of early Egyptian feminism, points out that 'By thinking of themselves as all powerful and free vis-à-vis Egyptian women, Western women could avoid confronting their own powerlessness and gender oppression at home' (Hatem 1992: 37). The subterfuge is even more striking in the case of these two 'feminist' imperialist novels, which were written by men who apparently felt feminism was less desirable in France.

In many ways the French Republic's colonial ideology of the 'civilising mission' ('mission civilisatrice') is at the heart of *Les Musulmanes*: it effectively required Islamic femininity to act as a signifier of the need for cultural change. The unhappy Précieuse functions as a plea for intervention by the French officer who, left ill-defined, acts as a cipher for French masculinity in general, and of course for French imperialism. The French, according to one contemporary novelist, are unique in being 'chivalrous colonisers' ('colonisateurs chevaleresques', Mathey 1902: 72). And the narrative structures called on by traditional French romantic gallantry are very similar to those used in support of the 'civilising mission'. In a 1902 novel set in Algeria, the French hero proposes to the young Kabyl girl he loves in these terms: 'Miassa, I have come to you as a supplicant and also as a liberator. Along with my soul I offer you the keys that will open the doors of the unknown for you, and the fresh air of freedom of which you are deprived. Do you accept me as your guide?'[10] The French imperial hero presents himself as liberator, and the Muslim woman is the discursive key to conquest as her sufferings call for and justify colonial intervention.

The Two Novels: Similar Patterns

Both *Les Désenchantées* and *Les Musulmanes* set out to criticise the traditional position of women within Islam and seek social alternatives that are clearly first and foremost narrative solutions. The failure of the 'mixed marriage' as a solution necessitates the death of the romantic Oriental heroine who has fallen in love with the 'roumi' (the French character), Lieutenant René in *Les Musulmanes* and the novelist Lhéry in *Les Désenchantées*. A more positive solution is put forward directly by Géniaux in *Les Musulmanes* – the modern marriage of a Westernised Muslim couple – and theoretically in *Les Désenchantées*, through the letters of the three women pleading for moderate reforms that would tend towards a similar conclusion. Nevertheless, in both novels the main narrative energy and dramatic tension lie with the mixed couple whose romance must necessarily end in tragedy. Thus the *real* fantasy of the young Muslim women, the reader understands, is true love which, by definition, means the love of a Western man. As one of the Turkish women in *Les Désenchantées* tells us explicitly, a novel or poem about an 'Oriental woman' always has the same subject: 'Love, more or less complete, ending in death...' and in today's world, she continues: 'I am speaking, of course, of love with a foreigner, the only sort of which the modern, cultivated Orientale, who has become self-aware, is capable'.[11] Guilty and impossible, the inner desire of the Turkish/Tunisian woman – the love of a Westerner – must be frustrated.

The harem theme in these novels is thus the nexus of some curiously contradictory issues. Most obviously, the Muslim woman is presented as the victim of an oppressive society that deprives her of her most basic rights, which demonstrates the need for a modernisation of Islamic society. Indeed, it is the 'victimisation of women, more than their erection as a sexual symbol of permissiveness' (Juilliard Beaudan 1994–95: 39) that is the great leitmotiv of Orientalist writing during the Belle Epoque. These novels are structured in such a way that it is not the attempt to find an internal solution, but the hidden love of the Muslim woman for a Western man, which stands for progress. They can therefore be seen as truly imperialist novels, since they set up a narrative situation which represents a desirable and desired colonisation, configuring imperialism metonymically as the penetration and possession of a people by its longed-for masters. And yet at the same time this desired imperialism is impossible and doomed from the start.

These novels are therefore to some extent subversive of their own progressive, imperialist thesis.

Two Types of Novel in Conflict

According to Suleiman's definition, the *roman à thèse* can only operate effectively if it sets up a system of unambiguous values (1977: 487). The ambiguity or paradox that we have just observed in these two novels is thus a serious problem. In fact these contradictions can best be understood by reading each of them as containing two types of novel, of which only one is a *roman à these*, a reading which is particularly pertinent in the case of *Les Désenchantées*, with its two authors.

Other readings have also pointed out its double nature, beginning with Raymonde Lefêvre's *Les Désenchantées de Pierre Loti* (1939), which represents the first critical reaction to the affair. Her main concern is to judge the three women responsible for the hoax, which she condemns for its lack of 'délicatesse', suggesting that what Maria Lera really wanted was to inspire one of Loti's novels and become one of his heroines, motivated by her own experience of disappointed love (Lefêvre 1939: 8). Loti himself, she claims, hoped to use the basic, banal love story given him by Lera in order to 'improve the condition of women cloistered in harems' (ibid.: 18, 19). Lefêvre thus initially suggests the coexistence of two narrative modes within the novel: Maria Lera cum Marc Hélys' second-rate love story and Loti's highbrow *roman à thèse*. Yet she goes on to suggest that Loti only expressed feminist opinions against his better instincts, and that the *thèse* of the book was fed to him, 'they made him put it forward ... they prompted him to write it, and almost imposed it on him' (ibid.: 109). She thus contradicts her earlier argument, saying that the *thèse* belongs to Marc Hélys, not to Loti. And setting aside the *roman à thèse* altogether, Lefêvre also sees the novel as containing two modes of writing: an admirable descriptive element that is 'pure Loti' alongside a melodramatic, exaggerated narrative element, belonging to facile sentimental literature, that she sees as the invention of a mere 'femme de lettres' (ibid.: 85). In other words, in this two-handed writing, with a man and a woman holding the pen alternately or one holding the pen for the other, the gold is the man's and the dross the woman's. In this reading the *roman à thèse* does not seem to belong to *either* author.[12] In fact, the double nature of the writing of *Les Désen-*

chantées dates back to before the novel itself was begun. Marc Hélys, recounting her version of the hoax in 1924, claimed that it began as a game and became serious almost *by itself*, as she wrote Loti the first letter as 'Djénane': 'I had begun this letter by chance, without premeditation, but *something powerful, that was not my own will, guided my hand*. All the pity that these young Muslim women inspired in me rose from my heart to speak in their name' (Hélys 1924: 36–38, my italics). In other words she herself, the author behind the author, was writing at two levels and as if with a divided identity.

It is indeed a profoundly divided novel, in which each of the two 'authors' thought he/she was writing quite a different novel from the one that we read today. Loti was writing a novel for his hidden, secret sources (the veiled women), in memory and in honour of his dead heroine/mistress Aziyadé, and perhaps inspired, towards the end, by the romantic potential of the mysterious Djénane. Lera-Hélys was subversively rewriting *Aziyadé* as the vengeance of three women against Loti's repeated 'landing, loving, leaving' story, and also setting forth her (very moderate) feminist views concerning the condition of Turkish women. And what the reader of the time read was a *roman à thèse* doubled with a tragic romance. To a lesser extent this is true of *Les Musulmanes* also since, as we have seen, the two sisters' very different fates indicate not only different ways forward for women within Islam, but also two ways of writing about the figure of the 'Orientale': the *roman à thèse* concludes with the marriage of the young Tunisian couple and their adoption of a modern Westernised lifestyle, while Précieuse's tragic death and doomed love for René come straight from the tradition of Romantic exotic literature. This double destiny can best be understood if we read the novels as drawing generic inspiration from two separate types of orientalist literature, the colonial *roman à thèse* and the Romantic exotic novel.

Increasingly from the 1880s onwards, the French 'exotic' novel had been transformed into the 'colonial' novel, which saw itself, among other traits, as having a mission to inform the metropolitan readership of the reality of life in the colonies. This seriousness of purpose often slipped from the purely educational towards the programmatic, addressing the great questions of colonialism. Perhaps the most prominent of the theses put forward by the *roman colonial* was the need for colonial intervention to bring the supposedly universal values of French civilisation to what we now speak of as 'the developing world'. In the case of Muslim countries, this point was often illustrated through a portrayal of the condition of women in Islamic society (very much in line with certain media discourses' appropriation of pseudo-feminist motives in our own era). Rather than simply indulging the reader's fantasies of Oriental women locked up in their harems, the new novel about the Oriental woman at the turn of the century gives 'a more thoroughly researched description of her condition, and calls for her liberation' (Mendelson 1989: 297). This concern for precise documentation and an accompanying call for action are implicit in both *Les Désenchantées* and *Les Musulmanes*.

Nevertheless, both novels reflect the coexistence of an older, Romantic-exotic form that is far removed from the realism of the *roman à thèse*. Both novels, while they develop a thesis in favour of social reform, also tell a tragic love story that acts out the impossibility of the relationship between the colonising power and the dominated people. In *Les Musulmanes* this double plot reflects a certain generic instability derived from what Suleiman sees as the split between the *roman* and the *thèse* in the *roman à thèse* (Suleiman 1983: 22). The inclusion of Précieuse's tragic plot-strand is a case of what Suleiman terms 'overflow': elements that do not contribute directly to the novel's thesis and even distract from it (ibid.: 202–16). In *Les Désenchantées* the need for progress is argued explicitly in Djénane's letters; but the 'overflow' theme of the impossible love between Djénane and Lhery is more crucial to the melancholy tone of the novel in general, itself closely related to the dominant theme of Romantic nostalgia and the loss of the exotic to the encroaching modern world. This 'belated exoticism' has been analysed in Chris Bongie's book *Exotic Memories* (1991), and Loti himself, that great master of the exotic, was conscious of the conflict between his own love of the 'old' Turkey and what he saw before him. The fictitious novelist Lhéry, arriving in Stamboul after many years' absence, 'was afraid of being *disenchanted* by the new Turkey'.[13] The 'disenchanted' of the title thus refers also to the Western novelist caught between two incompatible visions of the Orient, just as the novel itself is torn between nostalgia for the disappearing old Orient and desire for modernisation.

Whatever the intentions of its author/s, *Les Désenchantées* is a novel in conflict, and the conflict is situated between two opposed visions of the Other: the late-Romantic, Orientalist nostalgic vision and the imperialist, 'progressive', modernising vision. In the former, the Other is a fading echo of what the West has lost; in the latter the Other is a project, an imperfect or unfinished object that must be reformed. While Marc Hélys wrote almost entirely from the progressive vision, with its aim to reform Islamic womanhood, Loti belongs to the tradition of belated Romantic nostalgia. Both meet in the theme of the helpless female captive in her harem. And the Hélys/Loti split is clearly indicative of a deeper split between two coexisting and incompatible attitudes towards the 'Orientale', a conflict of narrative interests that surfaces to some extent even in the more univocal *Les Musulmanes*. The 'Orientale', that classic synecdoche of the Orient itself, is constructed both as a creature of the irretrievable past that can only be loved and lost, and as a subject to be reformed.

This schizophrenic text, at war with itself, parallels our own contradictory reactions, as post-colonial feminists, to the problems raised by what has been called 'third-world feminism'. We may reject the idea of 'le colonisateur chevaleresque' while still wishing to reform the condition of women around the world, yet we are necessarily aligned with the dominant powers of neo-imperialism.

Notes

1. Charles Hippolyte Jean Géniaux (1870–1931) published many novels about Brittany or North Africa.
2. Born Hortense-Marie Héliard in 1864, she became Mme Carlos Lera (sometimes spelt Léra in French texts) through her marriage to a Mexican diplomat in 1886; they separated around 1893 and she became a professional journalist, generally using the pseudonym Marc Hélys; she died around 1956/1958.
3. For further details on Marcelle Tinayre's debunking of *Les Désenchantées'* claim to represent authentic Turkish women's desire for emancipation, see the following chapter. (Many thanks to Margot Irvine for her cooperation in maintaining our chapters on a parallel course.)
4. 'en faveur de la femme turque d'aujourd'hui' (Loti 1906: 126). All translations from the French are my own. The original French is given in the endnotes only when quotations are from the novels themselves.
5. 'Un livre voulant prouver quelque chose, vous qui paraissez m'avoir bien lu et me connaître, vous trouvez que ça me ressemble?' (ibid.: 173).
6. 'Un homme du passé' ; un 'retour à la paix heureuse des aïeules' (ibid.: 174–75).
7. Claire Géniaux's name appears as joint author alongside her husband's in 1918 for *Le Cyprès*; she was later to publish novels in her own right. Claire's contribution to the research for *Les Musulmanes* is acknowledged initially, but it is hard to know how much of a role she played in the actual writing.
8. 'chargé de veiller sur la religion et les bonnes mœurs' (Géniaux 1909: 42–43).

9. On the legal front, progress was of course being made in France, but slowly: for example, 1884 saw the reintroduction of divorce, while only in 1907 were working women legally entitled to dispose freely of their own wages (McMillan 1981: 26–28). Both rights had long been available to women in many Islamic societies.

10. 'Miassa, je suis venu vers vous en suppliant et aussi en libérateur. Je vous offre avec mon âme les clefs ouvrant sur l'inconnu et sur le grand air libre dont vous êtes sevrée. Voulez-vous de moi pour vous guider sur la route?' (Marival 1902: 176).

11. 'L'amour plus ou moins complet, et, au bout, la mort ...'; 'Je parle, bien entendu, de l'amour avec un étranger, le seul dont soit capable l'Orientale cultivée, celle d'aujourd'hui qui a pris conscience d'elle-même' (Loti 1906: 292).

12. Irene Szyliowicz, writing more recently on the Oriental woman in Loti's work, has also been disapproving of this double structure within *Les Désenchantées*, and particularly of the love theme that links Djénane and the novelist Lhéry: '... the reader is confused by a double message – is she committing suicide as a political statement against the oppression of Turkish women, or is she taking her life in a romantic gesture of Weltschmerz because she can never hope to marry the European with whom she has inexplicably fallen in love?' (1988: 108).

13. '... avait peur d'être *désenchanté* par la Turquie nouvelle' (Loti 1906: 93, my italics).

CHAPTER 21

MARCELLE TINAYRE'S NOTES D'UNE VOYAGEUSE EN TURQUIE: CREATING SOLIDARITY AMONG WOMEN

Margot Irvine

One of the most popular women writers of the Belle Epoque, Marcelle Tinayre (1871–1948) is chiefly known for her best-selling novels, particularly *La Maison du péché* (*The House of Sin*, 1902) and *La Rebelle* (*The Rebel*, 1906), which led to her nomination for the Legion of Honour.[1] Tinayre became associated with other women writers of the period when she joined the staff of the feminist newspaper *La Fronde* in 1898. Her ties to the women's literary community were further strengthened in 1904 when she was named to the all-female jury of the *Prix de La Vie heureuse*, the ancestor of the prestigious literary prize, the *Prix Fémina*, which exists to this day. In her novels, Tinayre is most concerned with questions of love and women's right to physical pleasure. She advocates women's right to education and believes that it is by giving women the right to work that they will be able to choose their destiny. Nevertheless, Tinayre's engagement with feminism in her novels does not effectively challenge widely held beliefs about the subordinate role of women in society.[2] As Diana Holmes points out, Tinayre's novels 'address a number of the real conditions and problems of her female readers' lives, and solve them, pleasurably, at the level of fantasy and without implying any serious challenge to existing institutions and ideologies' (Holmes 1996: 57).

Despite the timid feminism of her novels, Tinayre's travel book, *Notes d'une voyageuse en Turquie* (*Notes of a Woman Traveller in Turkey*, 1910), does contain a feminist message. Through the descriptions of the women she encountered during her travels in Turkey, Tinayre offers a critique of dominant representations of Oriental women in France during the Belle Epoque. Tinayre travelled very little beyond France and made only three trips outside Europe, of which her journey to Turkey was the first.[3] She undertook this journey for at least two reasons: first, her brother-in-law, André Tinayre, had been named French vice-counsel to Turkey in 1906, and the trip gave her the opportunity to visit him and his wife, Marguerite, as well as her friends Paul Belon and Adrien Billiotti in Constantinople (Quella-Villéger 2000: 290). Second, her biographer Alain Quella-Villéger writes that Tinayre had been interested in Turkey for some time as an admirer of descriptions of the country by Pierre Loti, Claude Farrère and Renée Vivien (ibid.: 281). Despite the fact that she arrived in Turkey at a critical moment in the country's history,[4] Tinayre seems less interested in describing the political situation than she is in providing French readers with a description of the lives of Turkish women. Her *Notes d'une voyageuse en Turquie* takes the form of a diary with loosely dated entries. It is divided into four sections, first *Jours de bataille et de révolution* (*Days of Battle and Revolution*), *Choses et gens de province* (*Provincial People and Things*), *Premiers jours d'un nouveau règne* (*First Days of a New Reign*), and finally *La vie au harem* (*Life in a Harem*). This travel diary appeared in *La Revue des Deux Mondes* from July to November 1909, before being published by Calmann-Lévy in 1910. Quella-Villéger writes that its subject, a woman travelling in Turkey and describing the condition of women there, attracted a great deal of interest and that the book was generally well received (ibid.: 294).[5]

Competing Visions of Turkey

Nineteenth-century European women travellers invariably set out to describe the women they meet in the countries that they visited (Monicat 1996: 29). What distinguishes *Notes d'une voyageuse en Turquie* from earlier works is Tinayre's desire to downplay any differences between French and Oriental women. She writes that it is her conviction that all women from every country end up understanding each other and she seems

determined to encourage such understanding in her book
(Tinayre 1910: 187). She diminishes the alterity of the Turkish
women in her depictions of them, furnishing her readers with
portraits considerably different from those they may have read
in such popular books of the Belle Epoque as Pierre Loti's *Les
Désenchantés* (1906). Tinayre writes, for example, that:

> [p]eople here [in France] still believe in the legendary harem
> and I observe, once more, the fascination that the Oriental
> woman exerts on the European, the prestige of the veil ... Every
> hidden figure, forbidden, is for that reason believed to be beau-
> tiful. [...] Everywhere they see Djénane and Aziyadé ... When I
> try to rectify this too literary image of Turkish women, they are
> disappointed. And yet if this dream, this ideal creation has its
> beauty, the reality is so much more moving![6]

Tinayre's aim, then, is to give her readers something different.
Notes d'une voyageuse en Turquie has a feminist objective: to
erase the differences between Turkish women and their European sisters and create solidarity among them. This chapter
examines Tinayre's project and contrasts her travel book with
competing visions of Turkish women, most notably those of
Pierre Loti, to whom Tinayre herself refers repeatedly. His
name first appears at the beginning of *Notes d'une voyageuse
en Turquie* when she describes her confusion upon arriving in
Constantinople:

> So complicated a city! The Bosphorous, Marmora, the Golden
> Horn, the European shore and the Asian shore, Pera, Galata,
> Stamboul, Scutari, all this is Constantinople, and in my imagi-
> nation it is chaos. I have read the right authors, the specialists on
> the Orient, Gautier, Loti, Farrère, and my memory is full of sump-
> tuous images and phrases ... Oh mosques! Oh minarets! Oh
> caiques! Cypresses of Eyup, tomb of Aziyadé, small yali of Beïcos,
> I can see you well ... But the topography, the material arrange-
> ment of all these seas, of all these cities, and of all these conti-
> nents that enter one into the other, I have not yet grasped them.[7]

Although at this early point in her narrative she defers to her
French, male predecessors in Turkey as the experts on the
region, this passage sets up an opposition, which is developed
throughout the diary, between her impressions of Turkey and
those described by earlier male travellers. She finds herself dis-
oriented in Constantinople because she cannot reconcile her
experience of the city with what she has read.

Tinayre, who arrived in Turkey in 1909, is what Ali Behdad (1994) refers to as a 'belated' traveller to the Orient because, though she came expecting to discover the exotic Turkey about which she had read, the country was already undergoing Westernisation. With a first visit in 1876, Pierre Loti had preceded Tinayre in Turkey. This was when he met the young woman Aziyadé, his affair with whom became the subject of a novel named for her and published in 1879. He travelled again to Constantinople in 1903, when he met the three Turkish women whose confined existence he described in *Les Désenchantées* (1906). Although he preceded Tinayre, Loti also came to Turkey too late to find the Orient he dreamed of, free of recent occidental influences. Behdad writes of belated European travellers, like Tinayre and Loti, that they 'could not help but experience a sense of displacement in time and space, an experience that produced either a sense of disorientation and loss or an obsessive urge to discover an "authentic" other' (Behdad 1994: 13). Tinayre experienced disorientation upon her arrival in Constantinople but she soon found her footing and set about researching the conditions of women in Turkey by seeking out women of different social classes and professions. Loti, on the other hand, so desired to discover an authentic Other that was already lost, that he fell into a trap, carefully laid out for him by the woman who inspired the character of Djénane in *Les Désenchantées*, and her friends.[8]

Loti's *Les Désenchantées*

Much to her credit, Marcelle Tinayre came close to discovering the false basis for Loti's novel during her travels to Turkey. Because of the popularity of *Les Désenchantées* in France at the time of her trip, and because of her own interest in the conditions of women in Turkey, Tinayre set out to meet 'the disenchanted', women who were highly educated yet made to suffer a confined and indolent existence. She travelled first to Andrianople (present day Edirne) to visit her brother-in-law and his wife Marguerite living in this provincial town, the last military post before the Bulgarian border (Quella-Villéger 2000: 287). Marguerite Tinayre's social contacts in Andrianople provided her with introductions to many different Turkish women. Tinayre wrote that she preferred to meet the Muslim women of this city early in her trip, as Andrianople had conserved its customs and traditions. She hoped that this would better enable her, later, to understand by comparison the small elite of the 'disenchanted' that she expected to encounter in Constantinople (Tinayre 1910: 160). However, even before returning to Constantinople, Tinayre began to suspect that the 'disenchanted' did not exist. She certainly did not find them in Andrianople:

> And the disenchanted, you ask? ... They exist, do they not? ... Friends, we are in the provinces. There are no disenchanted women in Andrianople ... We will see, later, in Stamboul. Here the Muslim women are satisfied or resigned. They do not complain. If they are unhappy, they are unaware of their unhappiness. I will add that they do not speak French, or very little, and that they have never read a novel.[9]

None of the women she meets later in Constantinople correspond to the picture painted by Loti either, though Tinayre continues to use the type Loti evokes as a way to describe the women that she encounters. She writes of her friend Selma Hanoum, for example, that she admires her and loves her dearly, and that she is not at all 'disenchanted' but rather a woman of action and good sense (ibid.: 316–17, see also 211, 298). Loti himself began to doubt the truth of the stories fed to him by Djénane, Mélek and Zeyneb when he read Tinayre's travel diary in *La Revue des Deux Mondes* (Buisine 1998: 251). Tinayre had written, once again comparing the women she met to Loti's models, that a certain Madame L... pacha reminded her of Djénane:

> The lovely face, the pink dress accented with point-lace and black velvet, the pure, comfortable language, unaccented, makes me think of Pierre Loti's Djénane. But Djénane, it seems, was a half-imaginary creature and the women of Stamboul deny her any real existence ... Madame L... pacha smiles quietly when I speak to her about a physical resemblance with the romantic disenchanted women. – Disenchanted women? There were some in Stamboul, and they were not the most interesting of my compatriots. Loti's book gave birth to dozens of them. Yes, many women learned that they were very unhappy. They had no doubt about it, after having read the novel.[10]

Tinayre's account led Loti to write to his sources in Turkey asking them for the truth. His letter states:

> The attacks continue. Now it is Marcelle Tinayre (a well-known name, this time) who spent the fall in Turkey; she writes in the *Revue des Deux Mondes* that she spoke of *Les Désenchantées* and

of Djénane to some Turkish women (wives of pachas of whom she almost gives the name) and they smiled ironically and said that they did not believe it. In the end, it is exasperating, and I want the truth affirmed ...[11]

One of Loti's two living sources (he believed Djénane to be dead) managed to keep him in the dark, publishing a long article in *Le Figaro* in response to Tinayre's travel narrative, asserting the 'truth' described in *Les Désenchantées* (Hadidje-Zennour 1909).

'Real' Turkish Women

Instead of the 'disenchanted', Tinayre met many very interesting women of whom she left convincing portraits. She consistently attempts to draw parallels between their situation and that of women in France. In this way she de-Orientalises Turkish women and tries to create solidarity between them and her readers at home.

Tinayre began her research by visiting a school for Turkish girls during her stay in Andrianople. She questions the teachers at the school about the curriculum they teach and then asks them about their own experiences as working women, highlighting the similarities between their experience and that of women in France. Tinayre tells the teachers that until recently, even in Europe, a woman from a good family could not work without lowering herself. She notes, however, that a great number of women were currently living independently and, even married, earning a living. The teachers reply that they, too, earn their own living and are proud of it (Tinayre 1910: 172–73). This dialogue demonstrates an effort on Tinayre's part to show that similarities exist between the situations of women in France and in Turkey. She goes on to try to describe these to the teachers in Andrianople but does feel, finally, that there are parts of Frenchwomen's experiences that they are unable to grasp. She wonders how they could understand a situation like that in Europe where women's gains in the workforce are changing their relationships with men who, instead of being their protectors, are becoming competitors and rivals (ibid.: 173). Although very curious about the subject, Tinayre decides not to ask the teachers what their husbands think of their careers, as she feels that they are unlikely to answer her question truthfully. Despite these barriers to their mutual understanding of their relationships with men, this dialogue is the first in a series of meetings with Turkish women in which Tinayre attempts to draw parallels between herself and them.

Later on in the book, in Pera, the European section of Constantinople, Tinayre asks to visit a hospital. According to her, it is in the hospitals and schools that one can see what society does for women and also in what way and to what extent women contribute to social change (ibid.: 255). There she is surprised to discover a Turkish nurse – a heroine of a new kind, Tinayre calls her (ibid.: 262) – who left her harem with her parents' permission to take care of the sick. The conversation she has with the nurse, named Sélika, is similar to the one she had with the teachers described above. She asks how the nurses are recruited and trained, and Sélika replies that they find the women where they can, that they are devoted and obedient, but that they do not have any formal professional training and are thus more like servants than nurses. She tells Tinayre that the nurses work hard yet earn only thirty francs per month and laments how far behind Turkish society is compared to the French (ibid.: 265–66). As she did when she met the teachers, Tinayre again draws parallels between the exercise of the nursing profession by women in Turkey and in France. She tells Sélika that nurses in Parisian hospitals are no better recruited, trained or paid than the Turkish nurses (ibid.: 266). In an effort to show that France is, in fact, at least somewhat ahead of Turkey, Tinayre goes on to describe the progress the women's movement hopes to make in French hospitals to improve the situation of nurses. She tells Sélika of her hope that the French would soon become more organised in respect of nurses, that schools would be founded to train them, that their salaries would be raised, and that an attempt would be made to increase the prestige of their profession in order to recruit bourgeois girls (ibid.: 267). The fact that Tinayre draws parallels between the situations of women entering the professions in Turkey and in France is important and shows that both societies are experiencing similar transformations, if not at the same rate. Equally important is the way she includes the voices of the women she interviews in her text. These transcribed exchanges evoke intimate conversations and give the reader the impression of having access to Turkish women's voices, and of being in dialogue with them.

In her effort to highlight similarities between Turkish and European women, Tinayre downplays issues in relation to

arranged marriages and polygamy that figure prominently in
Loti's *Les Désenchantées*. According to Tinayre, Turks in 1909
rarely have more than one wife and the general rule is a tem-
pered monogamy, much like that of European men. She writes
that it is considered preferable to have one wife and some dis-
creet extramarital affairs with Greek, Armenian or Western
women, who represent pleasure without any obligations and
do not trouble the peace of the home (ibid.: 202). Thus Tinayre
observes, and excuses, the same sexual double standard in
both France and Turkey.

In addition to drawing parallels between the women she
meets in Turkey and those in France, Tinayre also attempts to
de-Orientalise, or demystify Turkish women for her European
readership. There are two topoi in particular that have dominated representations of Eastern women by Western men: the
Oriental dancer and, of course, the harem. Tinayre's descriptions of both dispel the myths, and replace them with her own
eyewitness accounts. She sees an Oriental dancer at a wedding she attends near Andrianople:

> The Oriental dancer, the *almée*, the *bayadère*, the *houri*, the
> voluptuous woman who haunts the dreams of college boys and
> dances in the verses of the poets ... Here she is in her reality,
> without any preparation or tricks to use for the benefit of trav-
> ellers hungry for poetry. Here she is, as the people from over
> there know her and love her, as I saw her with my own eyes [...]
> Oh Hermann Paul! ... Oh Abel Faivre! ... What a model for
> you! ... Castanets on her fingers, she places herself before us,
> the foreign women, and starts frenetically shaking her rump,
> her flabby breasts, her obscene stomach ...[12]

Tinayre explicitly contrasts the typical Orientalist representation of the dancer with what she sees herself, and finds a great
gulf between them. Her references to caricaturists Hermann-
Paul (1864–1940) and Abel Faivre (1867–1945) suggest that
she was conscious of the fact that her own portrait of the
dancer, though reflective of her experience, reads like a caricature of canonical representations of this topos. In the case of
the harem, she again identifies the opposition between its
mythical representation and her own experience of it:

> With what tone of voice they pronounced this word 'harem'!
> They saw a sumptuous and mysterious room, carpets, sofas,
> eunuchs, hookahs and perfume-burners ... And among these
> 'turqueries', fat women, white, a bit stupid, very jealous, wear-

ing gauze and baggy trousers ... My friends, the harem is not
this glorious prison. You can have a harem in your own home
if the lady of the house has a room to herself and a small salon
which is closed to your male friends but in which she entertains
her female guests. The harem is the woman's apartment.[13]

By identifying this opposition, Tinayre follows in a tradition of
female travellers to the Orient who, according to Billie Melman, describe the harem as a 'monogamous, middle-class
abode' and 'understate, or prefer to ignore, altogether, the
obvious political and sexual aspects of seclusion and
polygamy' characteristic of it (Melman 1992: 162). Tinayre's
desire to normalise Turkish women for her French readership
and reduce their alterity clearly leads to absences in her
account of women's lives, particularly in relation to issues
such as arranged marriages, seclusion and polygamy.

What particularly distinguishes *Notes d'une voyageuse en
Turquie* from earlier female travel writing is the impassioned
speech with which Tinayre closes the book, offering solidarity
to her Turkish sisters:

You have for you the sympathy of all European women. Those
who have met you will make you loved by those who do not
know you. We consider you faraway sisters. If we could – and it
is not certain that we can – help you by changing public opinion so that it is favourable to your desires, we will try to do so
with all our skill, all our influence, and all the energy of our
friendship. [...]
    Do not despair, sisters and friends from the Orient. The men
of your race will realise sooner or later that you are indispensable agents in the success of their enterprise. Their conception
of marriage and family will evolve little by little. They will wish
to find companions in you, not servants or dolls of pleasure. In
the interest of their happiness, in the interest of their sons, they
will raise you in dignity and freedom. But this will take time,
much time ...[14]

Tinayre's hopes for Turkish women are cautious but sincere.
The changes that she notes in the relationships between men
and women in Turkey, the attempt to forge unions between
near-equals, are similar to those she has observed in France.
Improvements in women's access to education, and thus to the
professions, are also similar in both Turkey and France. While
male travellers like Loti looked longingly to the past in an
attempt to capture a lost image of Oriental women that per-

haps never existed, Tinayre looks to their future and links the future of women in Turkey with the aspirations for progress of European women of the Belle Epoque.

Notes

1. Tinayre never received the award as, upon hearing of her nomination, she wrote articles for *La Patrie* and *La Liberté* on 7 January 1908, stating that she would not wear the red ribbon of the Legion of Honour: 'I do not wish to be remarked upon by the grocer or the owner of the corner restaurant. I do not want to hear people say as I pass, "There goes a woman who must have been a canteen-keeper or a mid-wife"'. ('Je ne porterai pas ma décoration. Je ne tiens pas du tout à être remarquée par l'épicier ou le restaurateur du coin; je ne veux pas entendre sur mon passage ces mots: Tiens, en voilà une qui a dû être cantinière ou sage-femme') (Quella-Villéger 2000: 269).
2. For more on the feminism, or lack thereof, in Marcelle Tinayre's novels see Waelti-Walters (1990: 31–53) and Holmes (1996: 57–62). See also Juliette Roger's chapter on novels of professional development in this volume.
3. Tinayre's other trips outside Europe were to Algeria in 1911 and to North America in 1937 (Quella-Villéger 2000: 218, 421).
4. When Tinayre arrived in Constantinople in 1909, Turkey was in a period of transition. The Young Turk Revolution had begun the previous year. A constitution had been proclaimed and elections ordered. There was a sense that the dawn of freedom in Turkey had begun, particularly in these early years of the revolution. In April 1909, however, just days after Tinayre arrived in Turkey, armed reactionary uprisings against the Young Turks began to break out and, in response, the policies of the Young Turks became more repressive. The military oligarchy of the Young Turk leaders would end with the defeat of the Ottoman Empire in 1918 (Lewis 2002: 210–11).
5. For more on the book's reception, see Quella-Villéger (2000: 294–96).
6. '[i]ci même, des gens croient encore au harem légendaire, et je constate, une fois de plus, la fascination que la femme orientale exerce sur l'Européen, le prestige du voile ... Toute figure cachée, interdite, est pour cela même supposée belle. [...] Ils voient partout Djénane et Aziyadé ... Quand j'essaie de rectifier cette image trop littéraire de la femme turque, ils sont déçus. Et cependant si le type chimérique, la création idéale a sa beauté, combien la réalité est plus émouvante!' (Tinayre 1910: 374–75). All translations are mine.
7. 'Une ville si compliquée! Le Bosphore, la Marmora, la Corne d'or, la rive d'Europe et la rive d'Asie, Péra, Galata, Stamboul, Scutari, tout cela c'est Constantinople, et dans mon imagination, c'est un chaos. J'ai lu les bons auteurs, les spécialistes de l'Orient, Gautier, Loti, Farrère, et ma mémoire est pleine de phrases et d'images somptueuses ... O mosquées! Ô minarets! Ô caiques! Cyprès d'Eyoub, tombeau d'Aziyadé, petit yali de Beïcos, je vous vois bien ... Mais la topographie, l'arrangement matériel de toutes ces mers, de toutes ces villes, et de tous ces continents qui entrent les uns dans les autres, je ne les ai pas encore saisis' (Tinayre 1910: 6). A 'caique' is a light skiff propelled by two rowers that is characteristic of the Bosphorous and a 'yali' is a water-side residence.

8. For more on the genesis of *Les Désenchantées* see the preceding chapter by Jennifer Yee.
9. 'Et les "désenchantées", me dites-vous? ... Elles existent pourtant! ... Les amis, nous sommes en province. Il n'y a pas de désenchantées à Andrinople ... Nous verrons, plus tard, à Stamboul. Ici les Musulmanes sont satisfaites ou résignés. Elles ne se plaignent pas. Si elles sont malheureuses, elles ignorent leur malheur. J'ajoute qu'elles ne parlent pas le français, ou à peine, et qu'elles n'ont jamais lu un roman (Tinayre 1910: 203–4).
10. 'Le beau visage, la robe d'intérieur rose, garnie de guipure et de velours noir, le langage pur, aisé, sans accent, me font penser à Djénane de Pierre Loti. Mais Djénane, parait-il, était une créature à demi chimérique et les dames de Stamboul lui refusent toute existence réelle ... Madame L... pacha sourit doucement quand je lui parle d'une ressemblance physique avec la romanesque Désenchantée. – Des Désenchantées? Il y en avait quelques unes à Stamboul, et ce n'était pas les plus intéressantes parmi mes compatriotes. Le livre de Loti en a fait éclore des douzaines. Oui, beaucoup de dames ont appris qu'elles étaient fort malheureuses. Elles ne s'en doutaient pas, après avoir lu le roman' (ibid.: 337–38).
11. 'Les attaques continuent. Maintenant, c'est Marcelle Tinayre (un nom connu, cette fois) qui est allée passer l'automne en Turquie; elle raconte dans la *Revue des Deux Mondes* qu'elle a parlé des Désenchantées et de Djénane à des dames turques (femmes de pachas dont elle donne presque le nom) et que celles-ci ont souri ironiquement, disant qu'elles n'y croyaient pas. À la fin, c'est exaspérant, et je veux la vérité affirmée ...' (quoted in Lefêvre 1939: 118).
12. 'La danseuse orientale, l'almée, la bayadère, la houri, la femme-volupté qui hante les rêves des collégiens et dans les strophes des poètes ... La voici, dans sa réalité, sans préparations ni trucs à l'usage des voyageurs affamés de poésie ... La voici, telle que le petit peuple de là-bas la connaît et l'aime, telle que je l'ai vue, de mes yeux [...] O Hermann Paul! ... O Abel Faivre! ... Quel modèle pour vous! ... Castagnettes aux doigts, elle se place devant nous, les étrangères, et elle commence à remuer frénétiquement sa croupe, ses seins flasques, son ventre obscène ...' (Tinayre 1910: 197–99).
13. 'De quel ton, ils prononçaient ce mot « harem »! Ils voyaient une salle somptueuse et mystérieuse, des tapis, des divans, des eunuques, des narghilés, et des brûle-parfums ... Et parmi ces « turqueries », des femmes grasses, blanches, un peu bêtes, très jalouses, vêtues de gaze et de pantalons bouffants ... Mes amis, le harem n'est pas cette prison dorée. Le harem, vous pouvez l'avoir chez vous, si Madame fait chambre à part, et si elle possède un petit salon où n'entrent pas vos camarades, où les dames seules sont reçues. Le harem c'est l'appartement particulier de la femme' (ibid.: 201–2).
14. 'Vous avez pour vous la sympathie de toutes les femmes européennes. Celles qui vous ont entrevues vous feront aimer par celles qui vous ignorent. Nous pensons à vous comme à des sœurs lointaines. Si nous pouvions – ce qui n'est pas sûr – vous aider par un mouvement d'opinion favorable à vos désirs, nous y emploierions toute notre adresse, toute notre influence, toute l'énergie de notre amitié. [...]

Ne désespérez pas, sœurs et amies d'Orient. Les hommes de votre race sentiront tôt ou tard que vous êtes un des agents indispensables au succès de leur entreprise. Leur conception du mariage et de la famille évoluera peu à peu. Ils souhaiteront trouver en vous des compagnes, et non pas des servantes ou des poupées de plaisir. Dans l'intérêt de leur bonheur, dans l'intérêt de leurs fils, ils vous élèveront en dignité et en liberté. Mais il faudra du temps, beaucoup de temps …' (ibid.: 379–80).

CONCLUSION

As the preceding chapters demonstrate, the Belle Epoque was an era of lively, articulate and surprisingly radical feminist activity in France, when new images of women as mobile, assertive and excitingly modern were seeping into popular culture, mingling there with more traditional images of women as mothers and objects of male desire. The 1914–18 war put an end to what had been a vibrant, conflictual, creative period for French women, resolving, as Annelise Maugue puts it, the 'crisis of masculine identity, not by the emergence of new values but by the resurrection of ancient virile myths'.[1] Achievement of the suffrage, which in 1914 had seemed imminent, was delayed until 1944, and many of the other battles fought had to be fought again in a climate embittered by so many male deaths, then by the Depression of the 1930s and the fear of another conflict. But in many ways a radical agenda had been set as the century turned, and although the achievement of equal rights, opportunities and agency in the world would be a long (and still unfinished) struggle, the eloquent articulation of these goals, in feminist and New Woman discourses, in new forms of behaviour, and in art, meant that they could not be forgotten. The altered sense of what it was to be a woman would survive, in the handed-down memories and in the literary and artistic achievements of Belle Epoque women.

1. 'la crise d'identité masculine non pas en favorisant l'émergence de nouvelles valeurs mais en redonnant vie aux anciens mythes virils' (Maugue 2001: 215).

SELECT CHRONOLOGY
1870–1914

1870–71	Franco-Prussian war and siege of Paris.
———	Demise of the Second Empire – birth of the Third Republic.
1871	March-May: the Paris Commune.
———	Moderate feminist journal *Le Droit des femmes* (1869) relaunched as *L'Avenir des femmes* by Léon Richer and Maria Deraismes (returned to original title 1879).
1878	First of the great Expositions (World Fairs) in Paris.
———	International congress on women's rights in Paris.
1880	Law establishing state secondary education for girls.
———	Establishment of the first Ecole normale supérieure (teacher training institute) for women.
———	The Sorbonne admits women (previously only the Medical Faculty and the Collège de France had done so).
———	Hubertine Auclert attempts to register as a voter on local electoral list on the grounds that the Constitution gives the vote to 'tous les Francais'.
1881	Law establishing free, compulsory state education for both sexes aged six to thirteen.
———	Blanche Edwards becomes the first woman to qualify as a doctor – though she was only allowed to proceed to hospital training as an intern in 1887.
———	Laws guaranteeing freedom of assembly and of the press.
———	Hubertine Auclert founds the journal *La Citoyenne*.
———	Auclert refuses to pay taxes to a government for which she cannot vote.

1882	Georges Ohnet: *Le Maître de Forges.*
———	Jeanne Loiseau (Daniel Lesueur) wins the *grand prix de l'Académie française* for poetry.
1883	Zola: *Au Bonheur des Dames.*
1884	Rachilde publishes the scandalous *Monsieur Vénus.*
———	Loi Naquet – law legalising divorce.
1885	Mlle Leblois becomes the first woman to gain a doctorate in science.
1885–6	Freud attends Charcot's clinic at la Salpétrière. Charcot publishes visual studies of hysterical women.
1886	Law entitling married women to open a bank account without their husband's consent.
———	Louise Michel, the 'Red Virgin of the Commune', publishes her memoirs.
1887	Rachilde: *La Marquise de Sade.*
1888	Sarah Bernhardt's play *L'Aveu* staged at the Odéon.
———	Camille Claudel's *Sakountala* shown at the Salon.
1889	Great Exposition in Paris.
1889–1913	Ten feminist congresses held in Paris, seven of them international.
1890–1910	Major rebuilding and expansion of the great Parisian department stores including *La Samaritaine,* the *Grand Bazar,* the *Grands Magasins du Printemps.*
1890	Mlle Chauvin becomes the first woman graduate in law.
1892	Female sugar workers strike in Paris (twenty days).
———	Loïe Fuller arrives in Paris to appear in the Folies-Bergère.
1892–4	Professor Henri Marion's Sorbonne lectures on the psychology of women.
1893	Daniel Lesueur: *Justice de femme.*
1894	Daniel Lesueur: *Haine d'amour.*
———	Marcel Prévost publishes *Les Demi-vierges* (*The Semi-virgins*).
———	Ibsen's *The Doll's House* performed in Paris.
———	Séverine: *Notes d'une frondeuse.*
1894–99	Dreyfus affair.
1895	The first public, paying cinema screening by the Lumière brothers at the Grand Café in Paris.
———	Women corset-makers in Limoges strike for 108 days.
———	Camille Claudel sculpts *Les Causeuses.*
1896	Alice Guy directs her first film, *La fée aux choux* (*The Cabbage Fairy*) at Gaumont.
———	Méliès' first films including *The Vanishing Lady.*

1897	Marguerite Durand founds *La Fronde*.
1898	Marie Curie co-discovers radium with her husband, Pierre Curie.
———	Louise Michel: *La Commune*.
———	Madeleine Pelletier enrols at the Collège de Science.
———	Female sugar workers strike again in Paris.
1899	Marcelle Tinayre: *Hellé*
1900	Great Exposition in Paris.
———	The first woman lawyer is admitted to the bar (*le barreau*).
———	Colette: *Claudine à l'école* (published under Willy's name).
———	Rachilde: *La Jongleuse*.
———	Gabrielle Reval: *Sévriennes*.
———	Hubertine Auclert: *Les Femmes arabes en Algérie*.
———	Opening of the Paris metro.
———	Daniel Lesueur elected to the *Société des gens de lettres*.
1901	Founding of the moderate *Conseil national des femmes françaises*.
———	Anna de Noailles: *Le Coeur innombrable*.
1902	Marcelle Tinayre: *La Maison du péché*.
1903	Marie Curie receives the Nobel prize in physics (jointly with Pierre Curie).
———	*La Fronde* ceases to run as a daily.
———	Charles Maurras publishes his essay on 'le romantisme féminin'.
———	Colette Yver: *Les Cervelines*.
1904	State celebrations of the centenary of the Civil Code. Feminists demonstrate against the Code's discriminatory stance on women. Durand organises an anti-Code banquet.
———	Women writers establish their own literary prize, the *Prix fémina vie heureuse*, with an all-female jury.
———	Madeleine Pelletier joins the freemasons.
———	Renée Vivien: first edition of *Une femme m'apparut*.
1905	The 'sardinières' (sardine workers) of Douarnez strike (ninety days).
———	Mlle Baudy becomes the first woman to be awarded the *agrégation de philosophie*, achieving the second highest mark in this highly competitive examination.
———	Marcelle Tinayre: *La rebelle*.
1905–6	Nelly Roussel delivers her feminist lecture 'L'Eternelle sacrifiée' some fifty times in different venues.
1906	Marie Curie appointed to the chair of general physics at the Sorbonne.
———	Madeleine Pelletier joins the SFIO.
———	Pierre Loti: *Les Désenchantées*.

1907	Law granting married working women control of their own wages.
———	Law giving parental rights to the mother of an illegitimate child.
———	Sarah Bernhardt's play *Adrienne Lecouvreur*.
1907–8	Pelletier founds the journal *La Suffragiste*.
1908	Hubertine Auclert and Madeleine Pelletier arrested for acts of violence at local voting stations.
———	Daniel Lesueur: *Nietzschéenne*.
1909	Natalie Barney's salon started at the rue Jacob.
———	Death of Renée Vivien.
———	Bernhardt's play *Un Coeur d'homme* performed at the Théâtre des Arts.
———	Diaghilev's *Ballets Russes* in Paris, with Anna Pavlova and Nijinsky dancing.
———	Marcelle Tinayre travels to Turkey and publishes her travel diary in *La Revue des deux mondes*.
———	Charles Géniaux: *Les musulmanes*.
1910	Feminists present themselves as candidates at parliamentary elections, including, in Paris, Auclert, Pelletier, Durand and Caroline Kaufmann.
———	Women playwrights' organisation *La Halte* founded.
———	Colette: *La Vagabonde*.
———	Marguerite Audoux: *Marie-Claire*.
———	Marcelle Tinayre: *Notes d'une voyageuse en Turquie*.
1911	Lucienne Heuvelmans wins the prestigious *Grand prix de Rome* for sculpture.
———	Marie Curie awarded a second Nobel Prize for science.
1912	Law allows mothers of illegitimate children to take out paternity suits.
1913	Colette: *L'Envers du music-hall*.
1914	Jean Jaurès, leader of the Socialist Party (SFIO), argues for women's suffrage in Parliament. A referendum organised by *Le Journal* receives a massive response (505,912 forms) from women declaring themselves pro-women's suffrage. A five-thousand-strong pro-suffrage rally is held in Paris.
———	Outbreak of the First World War.

BIBLIOGRAPHY

1900. 2000. Exhibition catalogue. Paris: Réunion des Musées Nationaux.

A. B. 1897. 'Loïe Fuller', *Le Monde illustré*, 6 November 1897.

Abel, R. 1990. 'Booming the Film Business: the Historical Specificity of Early French Cinema', *French Cultural Studies* 1, 2, 79–94.

Accampano, E. A., Fuchs, R. G. and Stewart, M. L. (eds) 1995. *Gender and the Politics of Social Reform in France, 1870–1914.* Baltimore and London: Johns Hopkins University Press.

Adamowicz, E. 2001. 'Bodies Cut and Dissolved: Dada and Surrealist Film' in A. Hughes and J. S. Williams (eds), *Gender and French Cinema.* Oxford: Berg, 19–33.

Agate, M. 1945. *Madame Sarah.* London: Benjamin Blom.

Albistur, M. and Armogathe, D. 1977. *Histoire du féminisme français du moyen-âge à nos jours.* Paris: Editions des femmes.

—— and —— 1978. *Le Grief des femmes: Anthologie de textes féministes du Second Empire à nos jours.* Paris: Editions Hier et Demain.

Allard, O. 1997. *Isadora, la danseuse aux pieds nus, ou la révolution isadorienne.* Paris: Editions des Ecrivains associés.

Allwood, G. and Wadia, K. 2000. *Women and Politics in France 1958–2000.* London: Routledge.

Amory, C. and Bradlee, F. (eds) 1960. 'Nominated for the Hall of Fame: 1923, the Comtesse de Noailles ... Marcel Proust' in *Vanity Fair: Selections from America's Most Memorable Magazine. A Cavalcade of the 1920s and 1930s.* New York: Viking Press.

Angenot, M. 1986. *Le cru et le faisandé: sexe, discours social et littérature à la Belle Epoque.* Brussels: Editions Labor.

Antle, M. 1997. 'Mythologie de la femme à la Belle Epoque', *Esprit Créateur*, 37, 4, 8–16.

Asselain, J.-C. 1984. *Histoire économique de la France du XVIIIe siècle à nos jours. Tome 1: De l'Ancien Régime à la Première Guerre Mondiale; Tome 2: De 1919 à la fin des années 1970.* Paris: Editions du Seuil.

Astruc, G. 1931. 'Le premier feu d'"artifice"', *La Revue musicale*, January 1931, Supplement 1, 426.

Auclert, H. 1879. *Séances du Congrès ouvrier socialiste de France. Troisième Session tenue à Marseille du 20 au 31 octobre 1879 à la salle des Folies Bergères.* Marseille: J. Doucet, 148–58.

────── 1881a. 'La Citoyenne', *La Citoyenne*, 1, 13 February 1881.

────── 1881b. 'Ceci remplacera cela', *La Citoyenne*, 8, 3 April 1881.

────── 1881c. 'Une loi stérile', *La Citoyenne*, 11, 24 April 1881.

────── 1881d. 'Les maris assassins', *La Citoyenne*, 40, 14 November 1881.

────── 1882a. 'La sphère des femmes', *La Citoyenne*, 54, 19 February 1882.

────── 1882b. 'La fête des hommes', *La Citoyenne*, 62, 2 July 1882.

────── 1883. 'La femme vivisectée', *La Citoyenne*, 77, 8 October 1883.

────── 1885. 'Lutte de classes, lutte de sexes', *La Citoyenne*, 96, May 1885.

────── 1886. 'L'homme est trop grand', *La Citoyenne*, 109, June 1886.

────── 1887. 'La Fédération de 1889 et les femmes', *La Citoyenne*, 123, August 1887.

────── 1889. 'Voile et viol', *La Citoyenne*, 140, January 1889.

────── 1890. 'Masculinisme international', *La Citoyenne*, 159, June 1890.

────── 1891. 'Plus de licou', *La Citoyenne*, 178, 1 July 1891.

────── 1897. 'Le Vote des Femmes', *La Fronde*, 13 December 1897.

────── 1900. *Les Femmes arabes en Algérie.* Paris: Lamarre.

────── 1923. *Les Femmes au gouvernail.* Paris: Giard.

Audoux, M. 1958 [1910]. *Marie-Claire.* Preface by Octave Mirbeau. Paris: Fasquelle, collection J'ai lu.

Audoux, M. 1987 [1920]. *L'Atelier de Marie-Claire.* Paris: Grasset et Fasquelle, collection Les Cahiers rouges.

Ayral-Clause, O. 2002. *Camille Claudel: a Life.* New York: Abrams.

Baedeker, K. 1904. *Guide to Paris and its environs.* Leipzig, etc.: Baedeker. Reprinted 1913.

Bakalti, S. 1996. *La Femme tunisienne au temps de la colonisation (1881–1956).* Paris: L'Harmattan.

Banville, T. de. 1888. *Les Belles Poupées.* Paris: G. Charpentier.

Bard, C. 1995. *Les Filles de Marianne, Histoire des féminismes 1914–1940.* Paris: Fayard.

────── 1997. 'Marianne and the Mother Rabbits: Feminism and Natality under the Third Republic' in M. Cross and S. Perry (eds) *Population and Social Policy in France.* London and Washington: Pinter, 34–48.

Bard, C. (ed.) 1999. *Un siècle d'anti-féminisme.* Paris: Fayard.

Barnes, D. 1992 [1928]. *Ladies Almanack*. Elmwood Park, Illinois: Dalkey Archive Press.

Barney, N. C. 1910a. *Actes et Entre'actes*. Paris: Sansot.

—— 1910b. *Je me souviens*. Paris: Sansot.

—— Undated. Unpublished memoirs. Manuscript, Natalie Clifford Barney Collection, Paris.

—— 1929. *Aventures de l'esprit*. Paris: Emile-Paul.

—— 1930. *The One Who is Legion, or A. D.'s After-Life*. London: Eric Partridge. Reprinted 1987. Orono, Maine: Nartional Poetry Foundation.

—— 1960. *Souvenirs indiscrets*. Paris: Flammarion.

—— 1992. *A Perilous Advantage: the Best of Natalie Clifford Barney*. Translated and edited by Anna Livia. Norwich, Vermont: New Victoria Publishers.

—— 2002. *Toujours vôtre d'amitié tendre: Lettres à Jean Chalon, 1963–1969*. Paris: Fayard.

Barrès, M. 1930. *Mes Cahiers*, Vol. 2. Edited by Philippe Barrès. Paris: Plon.

—— 1977 [1889]. 'Complications d'amour' in Rachilde, *Monsieur Vénus*. Paris: Flammarion, 5–21.

—— 1992. 'The Complications of Love' in Rachilde, *Monsieur Vénus*. Translated by Liz Heron. London: Dedalus, 1–8.

—— 2004 [1897]. *Les Déracinés*. Paris: Honoré Champion.

Baubérot, J. 2000. 'Laïcité and its Permutations at the fin(s) de siècle(s)' in K. Chadwick and T. Unwin (eds) *New Perspectives on the Fin de Siècle in Nineteenth- and Twentieth-Century France*. London and New York: Edwin Mellen Press, 21–42.

Baudelaire, C. 1885. 'Eloge du maquillage' in *Le Peintre de la vie moderne, Oeuvres complètes*, Vol. 3. Paris: Calmann Lévy, 99–104.

—— 1965 [1863]. 'Some French Caricaturists' in J. Mayne (ed.) *The Painter of Modern Life*. London: Phaidon, 166–86.

—— 1976. 'Marceline Desbordes-Valmore' in *Oeuvres complètes*. Paris: Gallimard, Bibliothèque de la Pléiade, 145–49.

Beach, C. 1994. *French Women Playwrights before the Twentieth Century – A Checklist*. Westport, Connecticut: Greenwood Press.

Beauvoir, S. de. 1974 [1958]. *Memoirs of a Dutiful Daughter*. Translated by J. Kirkup. New York: Harper & Row.

Behdad, A. 1994. *Belated Travelers: Orientalism in the Age of Colonial Dissolution*. Durham and London: Duke University Press.

Benjamin, W. 1978. 'The Work of Art in the Age of Mechanical Reproduction' in *Illuminations*. Translated by Harry Zohn. New York: Schocken Books, 217–51.

Benstock, S. 1986. *Women of the Left Bank: Paris, 1900–1940*. Austin: University of Texas Press.

Bentley, T. 2002. *Sisters of Salome*. New Haven and London: Yale University Press.

Berger, J. 1972. *Ways of Seeing*. London: BBC; New York: Penguin Books.

Berlanstein, L. 1996. 'Breeches and Breaches: Cross-Dress Theater and the Culture of Gender Ambiguity in Modern France', *Comparative Studies in Society and History* 38, 2, 338–69.
—— 2001. *Daughters of Eve: a Cultural History of French Theater: Women from the Old Régime to the fin de siècle.* Cambridge, Massachusetts: Harvard University Press.
Bernhardt, S. 1888. *L'Aveu.* Paris: P. Ollendorff.
—— 1907. *Adrienne Lecouvreur.* Paris: Charpentier et Fasquelle.
—— 1911. *Un coeur d'homme.* Paris: Charpentier et Fasquelle.
—— 1993. *L'Art du théâtre.* Monaco: Editions Sauret.
Béroud, S. and Régin, T. 2002. *Le Roman social. Littérature, histoire et mouvement ouvrier.* Paris: Les Éditions de l'atelier.
Bertaut, J. 1909. *La Littérature féminine d'aujourd'hui.* Paris: Librairie des Annales Politiques et Littéraires.
Bertrand, A. and Carré, P. A. 1991. *La Fée et la servante: La société française face à l'électricité, XIXe–XXe siècle.* Paris: Edition Belin.
Bibliothèque Marguerite Durand, Paris. Dossier *Daniel Lesueur.*
Bibliothèque Marguerite Durand, Paris. Dossiers *La Fronde.*
Bibliothèque Marguerite Durand, Paris. Dossier *Marguerite Durand.*
Bidelman, P. K. 1982. *Pariahs Stand up! The Founding of the Liberal Feminist Movement in France, 1858–1889.* Westport, Connecticut: Greenwood Press.
Birkett, J. 1986. *The Sins of the Fathers: Decadence in France 1870–1914.* London: Quartet Books
Blankley, E. 1984. 'Return to Mytilène; Renée Vivien and the City of Women' in S. Squier (ed.) *Women Writers and the City: Essays in Feminist Literary Criticism.* Knoxville: University of Tennessee Press, 45–67.
Blin, G., Chapon, F., Prévot, N. and Sieburth, R. (eds) 1976. *Autour de Natalie Clifford Barney: Recueil établi sous la direction de Georges Blin.* Paris: Université de Paris, Bibliothèque littéraire Jacques Doucet.
Blum, L. 1962 [1908] 'L'Oeuvre poétique de Madame de Noailles', *Revue de Paris*, 15 January 1908. In *L'Oeuvre de Léon Blum* (1905–14), Vol. 2. Paris: Albin-Michel, 407–24.
Bongie, C. 1991. *Exotic Memories: Literature, Colonialism and the Fin de Siècle.* Stanford, California: Stanford University Press.
Bourdieu, P. 1979. *La Distinction. Critique sociale du jugement.* Paris: Les Editions de Minuit.
—— 1982. *Ce que parler veut dire: l'économie des échanges linguistiques.* Paris: Fayard.
Bourget, P. 1883. *Essais de psychologie contemporaine.* Paris: Alphonse Lemerre.
Bredbenner, C. L. 1998. *A Nationality of Her Own.* Berkeley and Los Angeles: University of California Press.
Breeskin, A. D. 1986 [1971]. *Romaine Brooks: in the National Museum of American Art.* Washington, D.C.: Smithsonian Institution Press.
Brévannes, R. 1909. 'Le gala russe', *Le Figaro*, 19 May 1909.

Brion, H. 1982. *La voie féministe*, 1917–19. Paris: Syros, Mémoires des femmes.

Brooks, R. n.d. 'No Pleasant Memories'. Unpublished manuscript. Archives of the Smithsonian Institution of American Art.

Browning, R. 1991. 'Meeting at Night' in J. Woolford and D. Karlin (eds) *The Poems of Browning*, Vol. 2. London: Longman, 358.

Buisine, A. 1988. *Tombeau de Loti*. Paris: Aux Amateurs de Livres.

––––––– 1998. *Pierre Loti: l'écrivain et son double*. Paris: Tallandier.

Buisseret, A. 2000. 'Les femmes et l'automobile à la Belle Epoque', *Le Mouvement Social*, 192, 41–64.

Carlson, M. 1972. *The French Stage in the 19th Century*. Metuchen, New Jersey: Scarecrow Press.

Cartwright, L. 1995. *Screening the Body: Tracing Medicine's Visual Culture*. Minneapolis: University of Minnesota Press.

Causse, M. 1980. *Berthe, ou, Un demi-siècle auprès de l'Amazone: Souvenirs de Berthe Cleyrergue*. Paris: Tierce.

Chadwick, K. and Unwin, T. (eds). 2000. *New Perspectives on the Fin de Siècle in Nineteenth- and Twentieth-Century France*. London and New York: Edwin Mellen Press.

Chadwick, W. 1990. *Women, Art, and Society*. New York: Thames and Hudson.

––––––– 2000. *Amazons in the Drawing Room: the Art of Romaine Brooks*. Berkeley and Los Angeles: University of California Press.

Chalon, J. 1979. *Portrait of a Seductress: the World of Natalie Barney*. New York: Crown.

––––––– 1994. *Liane de Pougy*. Paris: Flammarion.

Chapman, R. 1992. *Henry Poulaille and Proletarian Literature*. Amsterdam: Rodopi.

Chapon, F., Prévost, N. and Sieburth, R. 1976. *Autour de Natalie Clifford Barney*. Paris: Universités de Paris.

Charbonnel, R. (Jean Ferval) 1909. 'La Renaissance du paganisme', *Akademos*, 1 (January), 26–33.

Chiba, Y. 1992. 'Sada Yacco and Kawakami: Performers of *Japonisme*', *Modern Drama*, 35, 35–53.

Cim, A. 1891. *Bas-bleus*. Paris: A. Savine.

Citti, P. 1987. *Contre la décadence*. Paris: Presses Universitaires de France.

Cixous, H. 1975. 'Le Rire de la Méduse', *L'Arc*, 39–45.

Clarétie, J. 1907. 'La Vie à Paris', *Le Temps*, 8 November 1907.

Clark, L. 1995. 'Bringing Feminine Qualities into the Public Sphere. The Third Republic's Appointment of Women Inspectors' in E. A. Accampano, R. G. Fuchs and M. L Stewart (eds) *Gender and the Politics of Social Reform in France, 1870–1914*. Baltimore and London: Johns Hopkins University Press, 128–56.

––––––– 2000. *The Rise of Professional Women in France*. Cambridge: Cambridge University Press.

Clover, C. 1987. 'Her Body, Himself: Gender in the Slasher Film', *Representations*, 20 (Fall), 187–228.

Cocteau, J. 1963. *La Comtesse de Noailles oui et non*. Paris: Librairie Académique Perrin.

Cody, M. 1984. *The Women of Montparnasse*. New York: Cornwall Books.

Coindreau, M. E. 1942. *La Farce est jouée: Vingt-cinq ans de théâtre français: 1900–1925*. New York: Editions de la Maison Française.

Colette 1913. *L'Envers du music-hall*. Paris: Flammarion.

—— 1955. *The Vagabond*. Translated by Enid McLeod. New York: Farrar, Straus and Giroux.

—— 1984 [1910]. *La Vagabonde*. In *Oeuvres* Vol. I. Paris: Gallimard, Bibliothèque de la Pléiade, 1065–1232.

—— 1986. *The Vagabond*. Translated by Enid McLeod. Harmondsworth: Penguin.

—— 1991 [1932]. *Le Pur et l'impur*. In *Œuvres* Vol. III. Paris: Gallimard, Bibliothèque de la Pléiade, 551–653.

—— 2002 [1958] *Paysages et portraits*. Paris: Flammarion.

Compain, L.-M. 1903. *L'Un vers l'autre*. Paris: Stock.

Comte, A. 1877. *Cours de philosophie positive*. Paris: Baillère.

Cova, A. 1997. *Maternité et droits des femmes en France (XIXe – XXe siècles)*. Paris: Anthropos.

Cross, M. 2000. 'La Fronde: Feminism at the Dawn of a New Era' in K. Chadwick and T. Unwin (eds) *New Perspectives on the Fin-de-siècle in Nineteenth- and Twentieth-Century France*. London and New York: Edwin Mellen Press, 95–116.

Current, R. N. and Current, M. E. 1997. *Loïe Fuller, Goddess of Light*. Boston: Northeastern University Press.

Daudet, Mme A. 1898. *Journées de femmes*. Paris: Charpentier Fasquelle.

Dauphiné, C. 1982. 'Présentation' in Rachilde, *La Jongleuse*. Paris: Editions des Femmes, 7–23.

—— 1991. *Rachilde*. Paris: Mercure de France.

David, A. 1924. *Rachilde, homme de lettres*. Paris: Editions de la Nouvelle Revue.

DeJean, J. 1989. *Fictions of Sappho 1546–1937*. Chicago: Chicago University Press.

Delly. 1956. *La Biche au Bois* (original date of publication not found). Paris: Tallandier.

Delvaille, B. 2001. 'Gide en voyage'. *Magazine littéraire*, 397 (April 2001), 85–86.

Demolins, E. 1892. 'De Paris à Edimbourg', *Mouvement social* (bound in with *La Science sociale*, 4, 1892), 103.

Depaulis, J. 1995. *Ida Rubinstein: Une inconnue jadis célèbre*. Paris: H. Champion.

Deraismes, M. 1980. *Ce que veulent les femmes. Articles et discours de 1869 à 1894*. Préface, notes et commentaires de Odile Krakovitch. Paris: Syros, Mémoires des femmes.

Dijkstra, B. 1986. *Idols of Perversity: Fantasies of Feminine Evil in Fin-de-siècle Culture*. Oxford: Oxford University Press.

Dissart, C. 1898. 'La grève des batteuses d'or', *La Fronde*, 13 March 1898.

Dizier-Metz, A. 1992. *La Bibliothèque Marguerite Durand: Histoire d'une femme, mémoire des femmes*. Paris: Mairie de Paris.

Doyen, E.-L. 1917. *Surgical Therapeutics and Operative Technique* I. Translated by H. Spencer-Browne. London: Baillière, Tindall and Cox.

Duclaux, A. M. F. 1920 [1913]. 'The Countess of Noailles: "le grand poète"' in *Twentieth-Century French Writers (Reviews and Reminiscences)*. New York: Charles Scribner's Sons, 178–92. First published in *The Times Literary Supplement*, 10 July 1913.

Ducrey, G. 1996. *Corps et graphies. Poétique de la danse et de la danseuse à la fin du XIXe siècle*. Paris: Champion.

———— 1999. 'Introduction: Rachilde' in G. Ducrey (ed.) *Romans fin-de-siècle 1890–1900*. Paris: Robert Laffont, 619–35.

Dumas, A. 1872. *L'Homme-femme*. Paris: Michel Levy Frères, Librairie Nouvelle.

———— 1880. *Les femmes qui tuent et les femmes qui votent*. Paris: Calmann-Lévy.

Duncan, I. 1927. *My Life*. New York: Boni & Liveright.

———— 1932. *Ma Vie*. Translated by J. Allary. Paris: Gallimard.

Durand, M. 1897, 'LA FRONDE', *La Fronde*, 9 December 1897.

Dusein, G. 1982. 'Loïe Fuller: expression chorégraphique de l'art nouveau', *La Recherche en danse* 1, 82–86.

Elliott, B. and Wallace, J.-A. 1994. *Women Artists and Writers: Modernist (im)positionings*. London: Routledge.

Engelking, T. L. 1993. 'Genre and the Mark of Gender: Renée Vivien's "Sonnet féminin"', *Modern Language Studies*, 23, 4 (Fall), 79–92.

———— 2001. '"A la recherché de la pureté": Colette on Women Writers', *Atlantis: A Women's Studies Journal/Revue d'études sur les femmes*, 26, 1, Fall/Automne, 3–12.

Evenson, N. 1979. *Paris, a Century of Change 1878–1978*. New Haven: Yale University Press.

Ezra, E. 2000. *Georges Méliès*. Manchester and New York: Manchester University Press.

Faderman, L. 1981. *Surpassing the Love of Men: Romantic Friendship and Love between Women from the Renaissance to the Present*. New York: William Morrow.

Felski, R. 1989. *Beyond Feminist Aesthetics. Feminist Literature and Social Change*. New York: Hutchinson Radius.

Ferlin, P. 1995. *Femmes d'encrier*. Paris: Editions Christian de Bartillat.

Figuero, J. and Carbonel, M.-H. 2003. *La véritable biographie de la Belle Otero et de la Belle Epoque*. Paris: Fayard.

Finch, A. 2000. *Women's Writing in Nineteenth-Century France*. Cambridge: Cambridge University Press.

Fischer, L. 1996. *Cinematernity*. Princeton: Princeton University Press.

Fortescue, W. 2000. *The Third Republic in France 1870–1940. Conflicts and Continuities*. London and New York: Routledge.

Foster, J. 1985. *Sex Variant Women in Literature*. Tallahassee, Florida: Naiad Press.

Fourastié, J. 1979. *Les Trente glorieuses ou la révolution invisible*. Paris: Fayard.

Frader, L. L. and Rose, S. O. (eds) 1996. *Gender and Class in Modern Europe*. Ithaca and London: Cornell University Press.

Fraisse, G. 1998. *Les Femmes et leur histoire*. Paris: Gallimard.

Fresnois, A. du. 1909. 'Réflexions sur la littérature féminine', *Akademos*, 10 (15 October), 503–13.

Frude, N. 1983. *The Intimate Machine*. London: Century.

Fuchs, R. (ed.). 1996. Forum on 'Population and the State in the Third Republic', Special Issue of *French Historical Studies*, 19, 3, Spring, Whole Issue.

Fuller, L. 1908. *Quinze ans de ma vie*. Paris: Librairie Félix Juven. Reprinted 2002. *Ma vie et la danse*. Paris: L'Œil d'Or.

———— 1913. *Fifteen Years of a Dancer's Life*. Translated by Prince Bojidar Karageorgevitch. Preface by Anatole France. London: Herbert Jenkins Limited; Boston: Small & Maynard & Co.

Garguilo, R. 1989. 'La littérature prolétarienne avant 1920', *La revue des lettres modernes*, 911–24, 5–17.

Garreau, B.-M. 1991. *Marguerite Audoux: La couturière des lettres*. Paris: Tallandier.

———— 1992. 'Marguerite Audoux – l'histoire d'un succès', *La Famille littéraire de Marguerite Audoux. Causeries du 5 juin 1992 à l'Hôtel de Ville d'Aubigny-sur-Nère*. Ennordres: La sève et la feuille.

———— 1997. *Marguerite Audoux: La Famille réinventée*. Paris: INDIGO & Côté-femmes.

———— 1998. *La Famille de Marguerite Audoux*. Villeneuve d'Asq: Presses Universitaires du Septentrion.

Garvey, E. G. 1996. *The Adman in the Parlor: Magazines and the Gendering of Consumer Culture, 1880s to 1910s*. New York: Oxford University Press.

Gaudichon, B., Rivière, A. and Ghanassia, D. 1999. *Camille Claudel Catalogue Raisonné*. Paris: Adam Biro.

Gaultier, J. de. 1924. *La Vie mystique de la nature*. Paris: G. Grès et Cie.

Gautier, J. 1901. '"Sada Yacco" – Le Théâtre et la Femme', *Femina*, 1 October 1901, 324–25.

Genette, G. 1987. *Seuils*. Paris: Editions du Seuil, collection Points.

Géniaux, C. 1909. *Les Musulmanes*. Paris: Editions du 'Monde illustré'.

Gide, A. 1949. *Anthologie de la poésie française; avec une préface*. Paris: Gallimard, Bibliothèque de la Pléiade.

———— 1972 [1902]. *L'Immoraliste*. Paris: Gallimard.

———— 1997. *Journal: 1926–50*, Vol. 2. Edited by E. Marty and M. Sagaert. Paris: Gallimard, Bibliothèque de la Pléiade.

Gordon, F. 1990. *The Integral Feminist. Madeleine Pelletier, 1874–1939*. Cambridge: Polity.

Gordon, F. and Cross, M. 1996. *Early French Feminisms 1830–1940: a Passion for Liberty*. Cheltenham: Edward Edgar.

Gordon, R. B. 2001. *Why the French Love Jerry Lewis*. Stanford: Stanford University Press.

Goujon, J.-P. 1986. *Tes blessures sont plus douces que leurs caresses: Vie de Renée Vivien*. Paris: Régine Desforges.

Gramont, E. de. 1928. *Mémoires*, Vol. 2. Paris: Grasset.

Gregh, F. 1933. *La Comtesse de Noailles*. Paris: Bernard Grasset.

Groult, B. 1978. *Le Féminisme au masculin*. Paris: Denoël.

Gubar, S. 1984. 'Sapphistries', *Signs*, 10, 1 (Autumn), 43–62.

Guide Michelin France. 1900. Reprinted in 2000. Paris: Les Pneus Michelin.

Gulickson, G. L. 1996. *Unruly Women of Paris. Images of the Commune*. Ithaca and London: Cornell University Press.

Hadidje-Zennour 1909. 'La Vérité vraie sur les Désenchantées', *Le Figaro*, 21 December 1909. Reprinted in part in Hélys 1924, 277–79 and Lefèvre 1939, 119.

Hahn, R. 1930. *La Grande Sarah: souvenirs*. Paris: Hachette.

Hardin, J. 1991. 'Introduction' in J. Hardin (ed.) *Reflection and Action: Essays on the Bildungsroman*. Columbia: University of South Carolina Press, i–xvii.

Harris, B. 1973. 'The More Profound Nationality of their Lesbianism: Lesbian Society in Paris in the 1920's' in P. Birkby, B. Harris, J. Johnston, E. Newton and J. O'Wyatt (eds) *Amazon Expedition: a Lesbian Feminist Anthology*. Washington, N.J.: Times Change Press, 77–88.

Hatem, M. 1992. 'Through Each Other's Eyes: the Impact on the Colonial Encounter of the Images of Egyptian, Levantine-Egyptian and European Women, 1862–1920' in N. Chaudhuri and M. Strobel (eds) *Western Women and Imperialism: Complicity and Resistance*. Bloomington: Indiana University Press.

Hause, S. C. 1987. *Hubertine Auclert: the French Suffragette*. New Haven and London: Yale University Press.

Hause, S. C. with Kenney, A. R. 1984. *Women's Suffrage and Social Politics in the French Third Republic*. Princeton, New Jersey: Princeton University Press.

Havercroft, B. 1992. 'Transmission et travestissment: l'entre-genre et le sujet en chiasme dans *Monsieur Vénus* de Rachilde', *Protée*, Winter 1992, 49–55.

Hawthorne, M. C. 1990. 'Introduction', *The Juggler*, by Rachilde. Translated by M. C. Hawthorne. New Brunswick and London: Rutgers University Press, xi–xxvi.

——— 1997. 'Women's Movements: the Gendered Subtext of Anomie' in B. Cooper and M. Donaldson-Evans (eds) *Moving Forward, Holding Fast: the Dynamics of 19th-century French Culture*. Amsterdam and Atlanta: Rodopi.

——— 2001. *Rachilde and French Women's Authorship: from Decadence to Modernism*. Lincoln and London: University of Nebraska Press.

Hellerstein, E. O., Hume, L. P. and Offen, K. (eds) 1981. *Victorian Women: A Documentary Account*. Stanford: Stanford University Press.

Hellerstein, N. 1995. 'Narrative Innovation and the Construction of Self in Marguerite Audoux's *Marie-Claire*', *The French Review*, 69, 2 (December 1995), 246–54.

Hélys, M. 1924. *L'envers d'un roman: le secret des 'Désenchantées' révélé par celle qui fut Djénane*. Paris: Librairie académique Perrin.

Hemmings, F. M. J. 1993. *The Theatre Industry in 19th-Century France*. Cambridge: Cambridge University Press.

Henderson, J. A. 1971. *The First Avant-garde*. London: George Harrap.

Hilden, P. 1986. *Working Women and Socialist Politics in France 1880–1914*. Oxford: Oxford University Press.

Hoeveler, D. L. 1990. *Romantic Androgyny: the Woman Within*. London: Pennsylvania State University Press.

Holmes, D. 1996a. *French Women's Writing, 1848–1994*. London and Atlantic Highlands, New Jersey: Athlone Press.

—— 1996b. 'Monstrous Women: Rachilde's Erotic Fiction' in A. Hughes and K. Ince (eds) *French Erotic Fiction: Desiring Writing, 1880–1990*. Oxford: Berg, 27–48.

—— 2001. *Rachilde. Decadence, Gender and the Woman Writer*. Oxford: Berg.

Horville, R. 1977. 'The Stage Techniques of Sarah Bernhardt' in E. Salmon (ed.) *Bernhardt and the Theatre of Her Time*. Westport, Connecticut: Greenwood Press, 35–66.

Huesca, R. 2001. *Triomphes et scandales. La belle époque des Ballets russes*. Paris: Hermann, collection Savoir sur l'art.

Huysmans, J. K. 1977 [1884]. *A rebours*. Paris: Gallimard.

Ibsen, H. 1965 [1879]. *A Doll's House*. Harmondsworth: Penguin.

Irigaray, L. 1974. *Spéculum de l'autre femme*. Paris: Editions de Minuit.

Iskin, R. E. 2003 'The Pan-European Flâneuse in Fin-de-Siècle Posters: Advertising Modern Women in the City', *Nineteenth-Century Contexts*, 25, 4, 333–56.

—— [forthcoming, 2006] 'The Flâneuse in Fin-de-Siècle French Posters' in A. D'Souza, and T. McDonough (eds) *The Invisible Flâneuse?: Art, Gender and 19th-Century Paris*. Manchester and New York: Manchester University Press.

Jey, M. 1998. *La littérature au lycée: invention d'une discipline 1880–1925*. Paris: Klincksieck.

Johnston, J. 1973. *Lesbian Nation: the Feminist Solution*. New York: Simon and Schuster.

Jordanova, L. 1989. *Sexual Visions*. London: Harvester Wheatsheaf.

Juilliard Beaudan, C. 1994–5. 'Réclusion et exclusion: l'ambiguïté du désir dans la représentation de la femme islamique', *Nineteenth-Century French Studies*, 23, 1–2, 35–41.

Kaplan, R. E. 1995. *The Fin de Siècle Crisis of Democracy in France*. Oxford: Berg.

Kawakami Otojiro to 1900 nen Paris Bankoku Hakurankai (Kawakami Otojiro and the Paris World Fair 1900). 2000. Exhibition catalogue. Fukuoka: City Museum.

Kerber, L. K. 1998. *No Constitutional Right to be Ladies: Women and the Obligations of Citizenship*. New York: Hill and Wang.

Kermode, F. 1961. 'Loïe Fuller and the Dance before Diaghilev', *Partisan Review*, 28, January-February, 48–75.

Klejman, L. and Rochefort, F. 1989. *L'Egalité en marche: le féminisme sous la Troisième République*. Paris: Presses de la FNSP/des femmes.

Koritz, A. 1995. *Gendering Bodies/performing Art: Dance and Literature in Early Twentieth-Century British Culture*. Ann Arbor: University of Michigan Press.

Krakovitch, O. 1980. *Maria Deraismes. Ce que veulent les femmes*. Paris: Syros.

Kuisel, R. F. 1981. *Capitalism and the State in Modern France: Renovation and Economic Management in the Twentieth Century*. Cambridge: Cambridge University Press.

Laity, C. 1990. 'H. D. and A. C. Swinburne: Decadence and Sapphic Modernism' in K. Jay and J. Glasgow (eds) *Lesbian Texts and Contexts: Radical Revisions*. New York: New York University Press, 217–40.

———— 1996. *H.D. and the Victorian Fin de Siècle: Gender, Modernism, Decadence*. Cambridge: Cambridge University Press.

Lanoizelée, L. 1954. *Marguerite Audoux*. Paris: M. Pernette, collection Plaisir du bibliophile.

Laplace-Claverie, H. 2001. 'Construction et déconstruction d'un mythe fin-de-siècle: l'impossible genèse de l'*Essai sur Cléo de Mérode* de Jean de Tinan' in A. Montandon (ed.) *Mythes de la Décadence*. Clermont-Ferrand: Presses Universitaires Blaise Pascal, collection Littératures, 197–204.

Laplagne, J.-F. 1996. 'La femme et la bicyclette à l'affiche' in P. Arnaud and T. Terret (eds) *Histoire du sport féminin*. Paris: L'Harmattan, 83–94.

Larousse, P. 1865. *Grand dictionnaire universel du XIXième siècle*. Tome VIII. Paris.

Lasserre, P. 1909. 'La Littérature féminine', *L'Action Française, organe du nationalisme intégral*, 9 February 1909.

Laurent, M. 1988. *Rodin*. Paris: Chêne-Hachette.

Lavendan, H. 1938. 'Avant l'oubli', *L'Illustration*, 16 July 1938, 1–87.

Lawrence, K. R. (ed.). 1992. *Decolonizing the Canon: New Views of Twentieth-Century 'British' Literary Canons*. Chicago: University of Illinois Press.

Le Dantec, Y.-G. 1933. 'La Place d'Anna de Noailles dans la poésie contemporaine', *Mercure de France*, 244 (1 June), 276–98.

Lefêvre, R. 1939. *Les Désenchantées de Pierre Loti*. Paris: SFELT, Editions Edgar Malfère.

Lemoine, P. 1998. *Droit d'asiles*. Paris: Odile Jacob.

Léo, A. 1990 [1869]. *La Femme et les moeurs. Monarchie ou liberté*. Introduction et notes de Monique Biarnais. Paris: Editions du Lérot.

Lesueur, D. 1883. *L'Amant de Geneviève*. Paris: Calmann Lévy.

———— 1893. *Justice de femme*. Paris: Alphonse Lemerre.

——— 1894. *Haine d'Amour*. Paris: Alphonse Lemerre.

——— 1904. *Le Masque d'Amour*, Vol.1 *Le Marquis de Valcor*, Vol. 2 *Madame de Ferneuse*. Paris: Alphonse Lemerre.

——— 1908. *Nietzschéenne*. Paris: Alphonse Lemerre.

Le Vassor, P. 1912. 'A La Halte.' *Comoedia*, 8 December 1912.

Lever, M. 1987. *Isadora*. Paris: Presses de la Renaissance.

Lewis, B. 2002. *The Emergence of Modern Turkey*. Third edition. Oxford: Oxford University Press.

Leymarie, M. 1999. *De la* Belle Epoque *à la Grande Guerre. 1893–1918. Le triomphe de la République*. Paris: Livre de Poche, La Librairie générale française.

Lista, G. 1994. *Loïe Fuller. Danseuse de la Belle Epoque*. Paris: Stock-Editions d'Art Somogy.

Livia, A. 1995. 'Mario/Marion: Lucie Delarue Mardrus' Hermaphrodite Angel.' Unpublished paper.

Loïe Fuller Danseuse de l'Art Nouveau. 2002. Exhibition Catalogue. Nancy: Réunion des Musées Nationaux.

Loti, P. 1906. *Les Désenchantées: roman des harems turcs contemporains*. Paris: Calmann Lévy. Reprinted 1999. P. Loti, *Romans*, Vol. 1. Paris: Omnibus.

Lucchesi, J. 2001. '"The Dandy in Me": Romaine Brooks's 1923 Portraits' in S. Fillin-Yeh (ed.) *Dandies: Fashion and Finesse in Art and Culture*. New York: New York University Press, 153–84.

Lukacher, M. 1994. *Maternal Fictions: Stendhal, Sand, Rachilde and Bataille*. Durham: Duke University Press.

McMahan, A. 2002. *Alice Guy Blaché: Lost Visionary of the Cinema*. New York: Continuum.

McMillan, J. 1981. *Housewife or Harlot: the Place of Women in French Society 1870–1940*. New York: St Martin's Press.

——— 1985. *Dreyfus to De Gaulle. Politics and Society in France 1898–1969*. London: Edward Arnold.

——— 2000. *France and Women 1789–1914, Gender, Society and Politics*. London: Routledge.

McRobbie, A. 1991. 'Dance Narratives and Fantasies of Achievement', *Feminism and Youth Culture: from 'Jackie' to 'Just Seventeen'*. Boston: Unwin Hyman, 189–219.

Magraw, R. 1983. *France, 1815–1914: the Bourgeois Century*. London: Fontana.

Maignien, C. and Sowerwine, C. 1992. *Madeleine Pelletier, une féministe dans l'arène politique*. Paris: Les Editions ouvrières.

Makward, C. P. and Cottenet-Hage, M. 1996. *Dictionnaire littéraire des femmes de langue française. De Marie de France à Marie Ndiaye*. Paris: Editions Karthala.

Mallarmé, S. 1945a. 'Autre étude de danse: Les fonds dans le ballet d'après une indication récente', *Crayonné au theatre* in *Œuvres complètes*. Paris: Gallimard, Pléiade, 307–9. First published as 'Considérations sur l'art du ballet et la Loïe Fuller', *The National Observer*, 13 March 1893.

—— 1945b. 'Ballets', *Crayonné au theatre* in *Œuvres complètes*. Paris: Gallimard, Pléiade, 303–7. First published in *La Revue indépendante*, December 1886.

—— 1945c. 'Le seul, il le fallait fluide ...', *Crayonné au theatre* in *Œuvres complètes*. Paris: Gallimard, Pléiade, 311–12. Text dates from ca. 1896.

—— 1949. *L'amitié de Stéphane Mallarmé et de Georges Rodenbach, Correspondance 1887–1898*. Geneva: Pierre Cailler.

Margairaz, M. 1989. *Histoire de la RATP*. Paris: Albin Michel.

Margardant, J. B. 1990. *Madame le Professeur: Women Educators in The Third Republic*. Princeton: University of Princeton Press.

Marion, H. 1900. *Psychologie de la femme*. Paris: Armand Colin.

Marival, R. 1902. *Le Çof, mœurs kabyles, roman*. Paris: Société du Mercure de France.

Marks, E. 1979. 'Lesbian Intertextuality' in G. Stambolian and E. Marks (eds) *Homosexualities and French Literature: Cultural Contexts/ Critical Texts*. Ithaca, New York: Cornell University Press, 353–77.

—— 1992. *Sexual Anarchy. Gender and Culture at the Fin de Siècle*. London: Virago.

Martin, H.-J. and Chartier, R. (eds) 1986. *Histoire de l'édition française. IV, Le livre concurrencé, 1900–1950*. Paris: Promodis and Le Centre national des lettres.

Martin-Fugier, A. 2001. *Comédienne: de Mlle Mars à Sarah Bernhardt*. Paris: Seuil.

Martinet, M. 1976. *Culture prolétarienne*. Paris: Maspero.

Marx, R. 1893. 'Chorégraphie: Loïe Fuller', *La Revue encyclopédique*, 1 February 1893, 107–8.

Masson, F. 1921. Speech pronounced on the occasion of the presentation of the 'Grand Prix de l'Académie Française', printed in *Le Temps*, 2 December 1921.

Mathey, M. 1902. *La Traite des blancs: roman de mœurs coloniales*. Paris: Félix Juven.

Mauclair, C. 1900. 'Sada Yacco et Loïe Fuller', *La Revue Blanche*, 15 October 1900, 277–83.

Maugue, A. 2001 [1987]. *L'identité masculine en crise au tournant du siècle*. Paris: Payot et Rivages.

Mauriac, F. 1933. 'Homage to Anna de Noailles', *Les Nouvelles Littéraires*, 6 May 1933.

Maurras, C. 1927 [1903]. 'Le Romantisme féminin: allégorie du sentiment désordonné', *L'Avenir de l'intelligence*, Paris: Flammarion, 145–234. First published in *Minerva*, 1 May 1903.

Melman, B. 1992. *Women's Orients: English Women and the Middle East, 1718–1918*. Ann Arbor: University of Michigan Press.

Mendelson, D. 1989. 'Le "voyage en Orient" et le renouvellement de l'écriture "fin-de-siècle"' in G. Ponnau (ed.) *Fins de siècle*. Toulouse: Presses Universitaires du Mirail, 295–301.

Mendès, C. 1890. *Méphistophéla*. Paris: E. Dentu.

Mérode, C. de, 1955. *Le Ballet de ma vie*. Paris: Editions Pierre Horay.

Meusy, J.-J. 1995. *Paris-Palaces, ou le temps des cinémas (1894–1918)*. Paris: CNRS Editions.

Milligan, J. 1996. *The Forgotten Generation: French Women Writers of the Inter-war Period*. Oxford: Berg.

Mondadon, L. de. 1930. 'Les Inexactitudes de Mme la comtesse de Noailles', *Les Etudes (religieuses, philosophiques, historiques et littéraires)*, 205 (20 December 1930), 706–13.

Monicat, B. 1996. *Itinéraires de l'écriture au féminin: Voyageuses du 19e siècle*. Amsterdam/Atlanta: Rodopi.

Montorgueil, G. 1897. *La Parisienne*. Paris: Librairie Conquet.

Mora, E. 1966. *Sappho, histoire d'un poète et traduction intégrale de l'œuvre*. Paris: Flammarion.

Morand, P. 1981 [1930]. *1900*. In *Œuvres*. Paris: Flammarion, 325–411.

Morel, J.-P. 1977. 'Littérature prolétarienne et transformations du genre romanesque', *Europe*, mars-avril 1977, 15–23.

—— 1985. *Le roman insupportable. L'Internationale littéraire et la France (1920–1932)*. Paris: Gallimard.

Nietzsche, F. 1967. *Ecce Homo*. Edited and translated by W. Kaufmann, *On the Genealogy of Morals and Ecce Homo*. Translated by W. Kaufmann and R. J. Hollingdale. New York: Random House, 1967; Vintage Books, 1969.

Noailles, Anna de. 1901. *Le Coeur innombrable*. Paris: Calmann-Lévy.

—— 1903. Interview by Paul Acker, *L'Echo de Paris*, 1 April 1903.

—— 1920. *Les Forces éternelles*. Paris: Fayard.

—— 1921a. 'Réponse à "Enquête sur le romantisme et le classicisme. A propos de la controverse Raymond de la Tailhède-Charles Maurras"', *La Renaissance, littéraire, politique, artistique*, 8 January 1921, 2–3.

—— 1921b. 'Réponse à Frédéric Masson', *Le Temps*, 3 December 1921.

—— 1926. 'Une heure avec la comtesse de Noailles'. Interview by Frédéric Lefèvre, *Les Nouvelles Littéraires*, 18 September 1926. In Lefèvre, F. 1929. *Une heure avec ...*, Vol. 5. Paris: Gallimard, 26–44.

—— 1927. *L'Honneur de souffrir*. Paris: Bernard Grasset.

Offen, K. 1988. 'Defining Feminism: a Comparative Historical Approach', *Signs*, 14, 119–57.

—— 2000. *European Feminisms 1700–1950*. Stanford, California: Stanford University Press.

Ohnet, G. 1882. *Le Maître de Forges*. Paris: Ollendorff.

Olivier-Martin, Y. 1980. *Histoire du roman populaire en France*. Paris: Albin Michel.

Orenstein, G. 1979. 'The Salon of Natalie Clifford Barney: an Interview with Berthe Cleyrergue.' *Signs*, 4, 484–96.

Ortega y Gasset, J. 1963 [1904]. 'El Rostro maravillado', *Obras completas*, Vol. 1. Madrid: Revista de Occidente, 33–36. First printed in *El Imparcial*, 25 July 1904.

—— 1963 [1923]. 'La Poesía de Ana de Noailles', *Obras completas*, Vol. 3. Madrid: Revista de Occidente, 429–35. First printed in *Revista de Occidente* 1 (July 1923).

Ory, P. (ed.). 1987. *Nouvelle histoire des idées politiques*. Paris: Hachette.

Otero, C. 1926. *Les souvenirs et la vie intime de la Belle Otero*. Paris: Editions le Calame. Reprinted 1993. *Souvenirs et vie intime*. Monaco: Sauret, collection Pages perdues et retrouvées.

Péladin, J. 1979 [1891–2]. *La decadence latine, 9–10. La gynandre, la panthée*. Geneva: Slatkine; Paris: Champion.

Pelletier, M. Undated. *Doctoresse Pelletier: Mémoires d'une féministe*. Manuscript, Bibliothèque Historique de la Ville de Paris.

—— 1900. 'Recherches sur les indices pondéraux du crâne et des principaux os longs d'une série de squelettes japonais', *Bulletins et mémoires de la Société d'anthropologie de Paris*, 1, 514–29.

—— 1902. 'Toujours l'hominisme', *La Fronde*, 2 December 1902.

—— 1904. 'La Prétendue infériorité psycho-physiologique des femmes', *La Vie normale*, 10 December 1904.

—— 1906. 'Les Femmes s'agitent et veulent voter', *L'Humanité*, 22 December 1906.

—— 1907a. 'Les Facteurs sociologiques de la psychologie féminine', *La Revue socialiste*, January 1907.

—— 1907b. 'Féminisme bourgeois', *Le Socialiste*, 5–12 May 1907, 2.

—— 1908a. 'La Tactique féministe', *La Revue socialiste*, April 1908, 318–33. Reprinted in C. Maignien (ed.) 1978. *L'Education féministe des filles et autres textes*. Paris: Syros, 143–56.

—— 1908b. 'La Question du vote des femmes', *La Revue socialiste*, September-October 1908, 193–203, 329–42.

—— 1911a. 'Le Féminisme à la Chambre des Députés', *Les Documents du progrès*, September 1911.

—— 1911b. *L'Emancipation sexuelle de la femme*. Paris: Girard et Brière.

—— 1978 [1914]. *L'Education féministe des filles et autres textes*. Edited by C. Maignien. Paris: Syros, 61–115.

—— 1996 [1933]. *La Femme vierge*. Paris: Indigo & Côté-femmes. First printed 1933, Paris: Valentin Bresle.

Perrot, M. 1998. *Les Femmes ou les silences de l'histoire*. Paris: Flammarion.

—— 1979. 'La Femme populaire rebelle' in P. Werner (ed.) *L'Histoire sans qualités*. Paris: Galilée, 125–56. Also reproduced in Perrot 1998, 153–76.

—— 1986. 'Women, Power and History: the Case of Nineteenth-Century France' in S. Reynolds (ed.) *Women, State and Revolution. Essays on Power and Gender in Europe since 1789*. Brighton: Wheatsheaf, Harvester Press, 44–59.

—— 1991. 'Sortir' in G. Duby and M. Perrot (eds), *Histoire des Femmes, Vol. 4, le XIXe siècle*. Paris: Plon, 467–94. Also reproduced in Perrot 1998, 227–58.

Perry, C. 2003. *Persephone Unbound: Dionysian Aesthetics in the Works of Anna de Noailles.* Lewisburg: Bucknell University Press.

Planté, C. 1989. *La Petite soeur de Balzac.* Paris: Editions du Seuil.

Plott, M. 2002. 'The Rules of the Game: Respectability, Sexuality, and the *Femme Mondaine* in Late Nineteenth-Century Paris', *French Historical Studies*, 25, 3 (Summer), 531–48.

Pougy, L. de. 1898. *L'Insaisissable.* Paris: P. Lamm.

—— 1899. *Myrrhille.* Paris: P. Lamm.

—— 1901. *Idylle saphique.* Paris: Librairie de la Plume. Reprinted 1987. Paris: Editions des femmes.

—— 1903. *Ecce homo.* Paris: Société parisienne d'édition.

—— 1904. *Les Sensations de Mademoiselle de La Bringue.* Paris: A. Michel.

—— 1906. *Yvée Lester.* Paris: Ambert.

—— 1908. *Yvée Jourdan.* Paris: Ambert.

—— 1977. *Mes cahiers bleus.* Paris: Plon.

Poulaille, H. 1937. 'Le dernier roman de Marguerite Audoux', *Marianne*, 2 December 1937, 5.

—— 1986 [1930]. *Nouvel âge littéraire.* Paris: Plein chant.

Praz, M. 1956. *The Romantic Agony.* Translated by A. Davidson. New York: World Publishing.

Prochasson, C. 1999. *Paris 1900, essai d'histoire culturelle.* Paris: Calmann Lévy.

Pronier, E. 1942. *Une vie au théâtre: Sarah Bernhardt.* Genève: Juillien.

Proust, M. 1919. *A l'ombre des jeunes filles en fleurs.* Paris: Nouvelle Revue Française.

—— 1952. 'La Vicomtesse Gaspard de Réveillon' in *Jean Santeuil*, Vol. 2. Preface by André Maurrois. Paris: Gallimard, 304–13.

—— 1954 [1913–27]. *A la recherche du temps perdu.* Paris: Gallimard, Pléiade.

—— 1994 [1907]. 'Les Eblouissements par la comtesse de Noailles' in P. Clarac and Y. Sandre (eds) *Essais et Articles*, Folio Essais, 229–41. Paris: Gallimard. First printed in *Le Figaro*, supplément littéraire, 15 June 1907.

Quella-Villéger, A. 1986. *Pierre Loti l'incompris.* Paris: Presses de la Renaissance.

—— 2000. *Belles et rebelles: Le roman vrai des Chasteau-Tinayre.* Bordeaux: Aubéron.

Quiguer, C. 1979. *Femmes et machines de 1900.* Paris: Klincksiek.

Rabaut, J. 1996. *Marguerite Durand (1864–1936): 'La Fronde' féministe ou 'Le Temps' en jupons.* Paris: L'Harmattan.

Rachilde. 1887. *La Marquise de Sade.* Paris: E. Monnier.

—— 1888. *Madame Adonis.* Paris: E. Monnier.

—— 1977 [1884 and 1889]. *Monsieur Vénus.* Paris: Flammarion.

—— 1982 [1900]. *La Jongleuse.* Paris: Editions des femmes.

—— 1992. *Monsieur Vénus.* Translated by Liz Heron. London: Dedalus.

Ragon, M. 1986 [1974]. *Histoire de la littérature prolétarienne de langue française*. Paris: Albin Michel.

Rapazzini, F. 2001. *Un soir chez l'Amazone*. Paris: Fayard.

Rastignac, 1893. 'Courrier de Paris', *L'Illustration*, 14 January 1893, 26–27.

Rémond, R. 2002. *La République souveraine. La Vie politique en France 1879–1939*. Paris: Fayard.

Rearick, C. 1985. *Pleasures of the Belle Époque: Entertainment & Festivity in Turn-of-the-Century France*. New Haven and London: Yale University Press.

Rendall, J. 1985. *The Origin of Modern Feminism*. Houndmills: Macmillan.

Rennert, J. 1973. *100 Years of Bicycle Posters*. London: Harper and Row.

Reval, G. 1900. *Sèvriennes*. Paris: Ollendorff.

Reyer, G. 1942. *Un Cœur pur: Marguerite Audoux*. Paris: Grasset.

Reynolds, S. 2001. 'Albertine's Bicycle, or: Women and French Identity during the Belle Epoque', *Literature and History*, 10, 1, 28–41.

——— 2002. 'Lateness, Amnesia and Unfinished Business: Gender and Democracy in Twentieth-Century Europe', *European History Quarterly*, 32, 1 (January), 83–97.

Rich, A. 1992 [1980]. 'Compulsory Heterosexuality and Lesbian Existence' in M. Humm (ed.) *Feminisms – A Reader*. Hemel Hempstead: Harvester Wheatsheaf, 175–80.

Richardson, J. 1977. *Sarah Bernhardt and Her World*. New York: Putnam.

Rilke, R. M. 1944. *Les Amantes*. Edited and translated by M. Betz. Paris: Emile-Paul Frères.

Rioux, J.-P. 1991. *Chronique d'une fin de siècle. France 1889–1900*. Paris: Seuil.

Roberts, M. L. 1994. *Civilisation without Sexes: Reconstructing Gender in Post-war France, 1917–1927*. Chicago and London: University of Chicago Press.

——— 2000. 'Acting Up: the Feminist Theatrics of Marguerite Durand' in J. B. Margadant (ed.) *The New Biography: Performing Femininity in Nineteenth-Century France*. Berkeley: University of California Press, 171–217.

——— 2002. *Disruptive Acts: the New Woman in Fin-de-Siècle France*. Berkeley: University of California Press.

Robinson, L. S. 1997. *In the Canon's Mouth: Dispatches from the Culture Wars*. Bloomington: Indiana University Press.

Rochefort, F. 2001. 'La seduction résiste-t-elle au féminisme? 1880–1930' in C. Dauphin and A. Farge (eds) *Séduction et Sociétés: Approches historiques*. Paris: Editions du Seuil, 214–43.

Roe, D. 1983. 'Les premiers écrits de Marguerite Audoux', *Bulletin des Amis de Charles-Louis Philippe*, 41, 48–58.

Rogers, J. 1997. 'Women at Work: the *Femme Nouvelle* in Belle Epoque Fiction', *Esprit Créateur*, Special issue on *Women of the Belle Epoque*, XXXVII, 4 (December), 17–28.

Rogers, N. B. 1998. *Fictions du scandale: corps féminin et réalisme romanesque au dix-neuvième siècle.* West Lafayette: Purdue University Press.

Rolley, K. 1990. 'Cutting a Dash: the Dress of Radclyffe Hall and Una Troubridge.' *Feminist Review*, 35 (Summer), 54–66.

Ronson, F. 1980. *La Grève des ventres: propagande néo-malthusienne et baisse de la natalité en France, XIX–XX siècles.* Paris: Aubier.

Roussel, N. 1979 [1906]. *L'Eternelle sacrifiée.* Edited by D. Armogathe and M. Albistur. Paris: Syros, Mémoires des Femmes.

———— 1994. 'She Who Is Always Sacrificed' in J. Waelti-Walters and S. C. Hause, *Feminisms of the Belle Epoque: A Historical and Literary Anthology.* Translated by J. Kjaer, L. Willis and J. Waelti-Walters. Lincoln: University of Nebraska Press, 17–41.

Royer, C. 1900. 'En 1900 soyons moins bêtes!', *La Fronde*, 3 January 1900.

Rubin, G. 1982. Introduction to *A Woman Appeared to Me* by R. Vivien. Tallahassee, Florida: Naiad Press, iii–xxxi.

Ryan, A. 2002. 'Camille Claudel: the Artist as Heroinic Rhetorician', *Irish Women's Studies Review*, 8, *Making a Difference: Women and the Creative Arts*, 13–28.

Salin, S. 2000. 'The Limits of Difference: a Comparative Study of the Relationship between Women Workers and Trade Unionism in the Tobacco and Hat Industries (France 1890–1914)', unpublished Ph.D. thesis, University of Northumbria.

Salmon, E. (ed.) 1977. *Bernhardt and the Theatre of Her Time.* Westport, Connecticut: Greenwood Press.

Salt, B. 1996. 'Cut and Shuffle' in C. Williams (ed.) *Cinema: the Beginnings and the Future.* London: University of Westminster Press.

Sammons, J. 1991. 'The Bildungsroman for Nonspecialists: an Attempt at a Clarification.' in J. Hardin (ed.) *Reflection and Action: Essays on the Bildungsroman.* Columbia: University of South Carolina Press.

Sartori, E. M. and Zimmerman, D. W. (eds) 1991. *French Women Writers. A Bio-Bibliographical Source Book.* Westport, Connecticut: Greenwood Press.

Sauvé, R. 2000. *De l'éloge à l'exclusion: les femmes auteurs et leurs préfaciers au XIXe siècle.* Paris: Presses Universitaires de Vincennes.

Sauvy, A.-M. 1986. 'La littérature et les femmes' in H.-J. Martin and R. Chartier (eds), *Histoire de l'édition française.* Vol. 4: *Le Livre concurrencé: 1900–1950.* Paris: Promodis.

Schenkar, J. 2000. *Truly Wilde: the Unsettling Story of Dolly Wilde, Oscar's Unusual Niece.* New York: Basic Books.

Schimmel, H. D. and Cate, P. D. 1983. *The Henri de Toulouse-Lautrec W. H. B. Correspondence.* New York: Dodd, Mead, and Co.

Schlumberger, J. 1913. 'Les Vivants et les Morts, par la Comtesse de Noailles', *Nouvelle Revue Française*, 10, 462–65.

Schwarz, H. 1996. *The Culture of the Copy.* New York: Zone Books.

Scott, J. W. 1996. 'The Rights of "the Social": Hubertine Auclert and the Politics of the Third Republic' in *Only Paradoxes to Offer: French Feminists and the Rights of Man*. Cambridge, Massachusetts and London: Harvard University Press, 90–124. (Translated 1998. 'Le "social" et ses droits: Hubertine Auclert et la politique de la Troisième République', *La Citoyenne paradoxale*. Paris: Albin Michel, 127–70.)

Scribe, E. and Legouvé, E. 1917. *Adrienne Lecouvreur*. New York: Oxford University Press.

Secrest, M. 1974. *Between Me and Life: a Biography of Romaine Brooks*. London: Macdonald and Jane's.

Ségur, N. 1926. 'Madame de Noailles' in *Le Génie européen*. Paris: Fasquelle, 145–76.

Serge, V. 1976 [1932]. *Littérature et révolution*. Paris: Maspero.

Shapiro, A.-L. 1996. *Breaking the Codes: Female Criminality in fin-de-siècle Paris*. Stanford, California: Stanford University Press.

Shaw, G. B. 1898. *Mrs Warren's Profession*. In *Plays Pleasant and Unpleasant*. London: Grant Richards.

Showalter, E. 1992. *Sexual Anarchy*. London: Virago.

Silverman, D. L. 1989. *Art Nouveau in fin-de-siècle France: Politiques, Psychology and Styles*. Berkeley: University of California Press.

Smith, P. 1996. *Feminism and the Third Republic: Women's Political and Civil Rights in France, 1918–1945*. Oxford: Clarendon Press.

Sowerwine, C. 1978. *Les Femmes et le socialisme*. Paris: Presses de la FNSP.

—— 1982. *Sisters or Citizens? Women and Socialism in France since 1876*. Cambridge: Cambridge University Press.

—— 1988. 'Madeleine Pelletier (1874–1939): femme, médecin, militante', *L'Information psychiatrique*, 9 November 1988, 1183–93.

—— 2001. *France since 1870. Culture, Politics and Society*. Basingstoke: Palgrave.

Spackman, B. 1998. 'Recycling Baudelaire: the Decadence of Catulle Mendès (1841–1909)' in A. Hustvedt (ed.) *The Decadent Reader: Fiction, Fantasy, and Perversion from Fin-de-Siècle France*. New York: Zone Books, 816–22.

Stamboulian, G. and Marks, E. 1979. *Homosexualities and French Literature: Cultural Contexts/Critical Texts*. Ithaca: Cornell University Press.

Stewart, M. L. 2001. *For Health and Beauty: Physical Culture for Frenchwomen 1880s–1930s*. Baltimore and London: Johns Hopkins University Press.

Stokes, J., Booth, M. and Bassnett, S. 1988. *Bernhardt, Terry, Duse: the Actress in Her Time*. Cambridge: Cambridge University Press.

Stoler, A. 1996. 'Sexual Affronts and Racial Frontiers: European Identities and the Cultural Politics of Exclusion in Colonial Southeast Asia' in G. Eley and R. Grigor Suny (eds) *Becoming National: a Reader*. New York: Oxford University Press, 286–322.

Struve, G. 1972. *Russian Literature under Lenin and Stalin, 1917–1953*. London: Routledge and Kegan Paul.

Suleiman, S. 1977. 'Le récit exemplaire: parabole, fable, roman à thèse', *Poétique*, 8, 32, 468–89.

—— 1983. *Authoritarian Fictions: the Ideological Novel as a Literary Genre*. New York: Columbia University Press.

Szyliowicz, I. L. 1988. *Pierre Loti and the Oriental Woman*. Basingstoke: Macmillan.

Taïeb, E. 1982. *La Citoyenne*. Paris: Syros.

—— 2000. 'Abuses of "Masculinism" in Hubertine Auclert's *La Citoyenne*', *Women seeking expression: France, 1789–1914*. Melbourne: Monash Romance Studies, 6, 101–17.

—— 2001. 'Corps réifiés, corps souffrants: une image du corps des femmes dans le discours d'Hubertine Auclert', *Degré* 105–6, h1–22.

Talva, F. 1982 [1938]. 'La grandeur de Marguerite Audoux', *Bulletin des amis de Charles Louis Philippe*, 40, 53–59. First printed in *La Semaine égyptienne*, 30 June 1938.

Taranow, G. 1972. *Sarah Bernhardt: the Art within the Legend*. Princeton, New Jersey: Princeton University Press.

Terdiman, R. 1985. *Discourse/Counter-Discourse: the Theory and Practice of Symbolic Resistance in Nineteenth-Century France*. Ithaca: Cornell University Press.

Thiesse, A.M. 1984. *Le Roman du quotidien: Lecteurs et lectures à la Belle Epoque*. Paris: Le Chemin vert.

Thompson, C. 2000. 'Un troisième sexe? Les bourgeoises et la bicyclette dans la France fin-de-siècle', *Le Mouvement social*, 192, 9–40.

Tiersten, L. 2001. *Marianne in the Market, Envisioning Consumer Society in Fin-de-Siècle France*. Berkeley: University of California Press.

Tinayre, M. 1902. *La Maison du péché*. Paris: Lévy.

—— 1905. *La Rebelle*. Paris: Lévy.

—— 1909. 'Notes d'une voyageuse en Turquie (avril-mai 1909)', *La Revue des Deux Mondes*, 1 November 1909.

—— 1910. *Notes d'une voyageuse en Turquie*. Paris: Calmann-Lévy.

Todd, C. 1994. *A Century of French Best-sellers 1890–1990*. London: Edwin Mellen.

Tombs, R. 1999. *The Paris commune, 1871*. London: Longman.

Touret, M. 1989. 'Quelle esthétique pour une littérature prolétarienne?', *La Revue des lettres modernes*, 911–24, 63–102.

Valette, A. 1898a. 'Les casseuses de sucre', *La Fronde*, 20 February 1898.

—— 1898b. 'L'hygiène dans l'atelier', *La Fronde*, 10 March 1898.

—— 1898c. 'Sténographie et machine à écrire', *La Fronde*, 6 February1898.

Verneuil, Louis. 1942. *La vie merveilleuse de Sarah Bernhardt*. New York: Brentano's.

Viala, J. 1993. 'Qu'est-ce qu'un classique?', *Littératures classiques*, 19 (Fall), 11–31.

Vivien, R. 1902a. *Brumes de fjords*. Paris: Alphonse Lemerre.
―――― 1902b. *Cendres et poussières*. Paris: Alphonse Lemerre.
―――― 1903. *Sapho, traduction nouvelle avec le texte grec*. Paris: Alphonse Lemerre.
―――― 1905. *Une femme m'apparut*. Paris: Alphonse Lemerre.
―――― 1977 [1904]. *Une femme m'apparut*. Paris: Régine Deforges.
―――― 1975 [1923–4]. Poèmes de Renée Vivien. New York: Arno Press. Original edition Paris: Alphonse Lemerre.
―――― 1982. *A Woman Appeared to Me*. Translated by J. Foster, with introduction by G. Rubin. Tallahassee, Florida: Naiad Press.
―――― 1986. *Œuvre poétique complète de Renée Vivien; 1877–1909*. Edited by J.-P. Goujon. Paris: A. Michel-R. Deforges.
Waelti-Walters, J. 1990. *Feminist Novelists of the Belle Epoque: Love as a Lifestyle*. Bloomington and Indianapolis: Indiana University Press.
Waelti-Walters, J. and Hause, S. C. 1994. *Feminisms of the Belle Epoque: A Historical and Literary Anthology*. Translated by J. Kjaer, L. Willis and J. Waelti-Walters. Lincoln: University of Nebraska Press.
Weber, E. 1986. *France, Fin-de-Siècle*. Cambridge, Massachusetts: Harvard University Press.
Williams, L. 1986. 'Film Body: An Implantation of Perversions' in P. Rosen (ed.) *Narrative, Apparatus, Ideology*. New York: Columbia University Press, 507–34.
Williams, R. H. 1982. *Dream Worlds: Mass Consumption in Late Nineteenth-Century France*. Berkeley; Oxford: University of California Press.
Williamson, J. 1978. *Decoding Advertisements: Ideology and Meaning in Advertising*. London: Marion Boyars.
Woolf, V. 1977 [1938]. *Three Guineas*. Middlesex: Penguin.
XIXième siècle. Paris: Presses Universitaires de Vincennes, 2000.
Yee, J. 2000. *Clichés de la femme exotique*. Paris: L'Harmattan.
Yver, C. 1892. *Mademoiselle Devoir*. Rouen: Mégard.
―――― 1903. *Les Cervelines*. Paris: Calmann-Lévy.
―――― 1920. *Dans le jardin du féminisme*. Paris: Calmann-Lévy.
Zeldin, T. 1977. *France 1848–1945*. Oxford: Oxford University Press.
Zola, E. 1880. *Nana*. Paris: Charpentier.
―――― 1970 [1883]. *Au bonheur des dames*. Paris: Fasquelle.
―――― 1992. *The Ladies Paradise*. Translated by Henry Vizetelly's firm, 1886. Introduction by K. Ross. Berkeley: University of California Press.
Zuber, H. (ed.) 1998. *Guide des sources de l'histoire des transports publics urbains à Paris, XIXe-XXe siècles*. Paris: Publications de la Sorbonne.
Zylberberg-Hocquard, M.-H. and Liszek, S. 2002. 'Marie-Claire ou la voix des couturières: Marguerite Audoux' in S. Béroud and T. Régin (eds) *Le Roman social: Littérature, histoire et mouvement ouvrier*. Paris: Les Éditions de l'atelier, 39–46.

Notes on Contributors

Maggie Allison is Honorary Visiting Senior Lecturer in French Studies at the University of Bradford, UK. Her research is in media analysis with particular emphasis on the representation of women in the political arena in Britain and France. She has published articles on women and the media in *Women in Contemporary France* (A. Gregory and U. Tidd, eds, Berg 2000), on representations of women politicians in *Représentations des femmes de pouvoir: mythes et fantasmes* (O. Krakovitch and G. Sellier, eds, Harmattan 2001), and on Lucie Aubrac in *South Central Review* (Winter 2002–Spring 2003).

Máire Fedelma Cross is Professor of French at the University of Sheffield, UK, and Director of the Centre for European Gender Studies. A specialist on Flora Tristan, she has published widely on feminist politics in France. Among her publications relating to this volume are 'La Fronde and the fin de siècle' in *France: fin(s) de siècle(s)* (K. Chadwick and T. Unwin, eds, 2000) and 'Représentations de l'affaire Dreyfus dans le journal *La Fronde* entre décembre 1897 et septembre 1899' in *Littérature et Nation: Revue d'histoire des représentations littéraires et artistiques* (1996). She is currently writing a book on Flora Tristan's politics.

Tama Lea Engelking is an Associate Professor of French at Cleveland State University, Ohio, USA. Her main area of research is early twentieth-century French women poets and novelists. She has published articles on Renée Vivien, Natalie Clifford Barney, Colette, Rachilde, Anna de Noailles, Gérard d'Houville (Marie de Régnier) and Lucie Delarue-Mardrus. Her most recent publications include 'Renée Vivien and the Ladies of Lake' (*Nineteenth-Century French Studies* 30, 2002) and 'A la recherche de la pureté: Colette on Women Writers' (*Atlantis: A Women's Studies Journal/Revue d'études sur les femmes*, Fall 2001). She is currently working on a book tentatively titled *Belle Epoque Barbarians: Writing the Woman Writer in Turn-of-the-Century France*.

Jeri English is a Ph.D. candidate in the Department of French at the University of Toronto, Canada. She is currently completing a thesis titled *Les stratégies préfacielles au féminin: les métamorphoses des préfaces aux œuvres de femmes au XXe siècle*. Her research areas include French women writers in the nineteenth and twentieth centuries; enunciation and discourse theory; and feminist theories on gender and writing, subjectivity and literary canon formation.

Elizabeth Ezra teaches in the School of Modern Languages at the University of Stirling, Scotland. She is the author of *Georges Méliès* (Manchester University Press 2000) and *The Colonial Unconscious: Race and Culture in Interwar France* (Cornell University Press 2000); co-editor (with Sue Harris) of *France in Focus: Film and National Identity* (Berg 2001); and editor of *European Cinema* (Oxford University Press 2004).

Melanie Hawthorne is Professor of French at Texas A&M University, USA. Her recent book, *Rachilde and French Women's Authorship: From Decadence to Modernism* (University of Nebraska Press 2001), was named best book in French and Francophone Studies by the Modern Languages Association of America in 2001. She has also edited *Contingent Loves: Simone de Beauvoir and Sexuality* (2000), co-edited a volume on gender and fascism, and translated a novel by Rachilde entitled *The Juggler*. Her research concentrates on nineteenth and twentieth-century French women writers, with particular attention to the fin-de-siècle period and to issues of sexual expression.

Diana Holmes is Professor of French at the University of Leeds, UK. She has published extensively on French women writers, including books on *Colette, French Women's Writing 1848–1994* and *Rachilde: Decadence, Gender and the Woman Writer*. Her work includes studies of some of the most popular female novelists of the Belle Epoque period, and she is currently working on a study of French romantic fiction, *Romancing the text: romance and readership in twentieth-century France*.

Margot Irvine is Assistant Professor in French and European Studies at the University of Guelph, Canada. She completed her PhD thesis *'Les récits de voyages des couples dans le dix-neuvième siècle français'* ('Travel Writing by Couples in the French Nineteenth-Century') at the University of Toronto in 2000.

Ruth E. Iskin teaches in the Department of the Arts at Ben Gurion University of the Negev, Israel. She is completing a book on *Impressionism, Modern Women and Parisian Consumer Culture.* Her essays have been published in *The Art Bulletin, Discourse* and *Nineteenth-Century Contexts.* Essays in recent anthologies are: 'The Flâneuse in Fin-de-Siècle French Posters' in *The Invisible Flâneuse? Art, Gender and 19th Century Paris* (Aruna D'Souza, and Tom McDonough, eds., Manchester University Press, 2006) and 'Selling, Seduction and Soliciting the Eye: Manet's *Bar at the Folies-Bergère',* in *Reclaiming Agency: Feminist Art History in the Postmodern Era* (Norma Broude and Mary D. Garrard, eds., The University of California Press, 2005). Her work has been supported by the Mellon Postdoctoral Fellowship in the Humanities at the Penn Humanities Forum, University of Pennsylvania, the Ahmanson-Getty Postdoctoral Fellowship at The Center for 17th & 18th Centuries Studies, UCLA, and the Izaak Walton Killam Memorial Postdoctoral Fellowship at the University of British Columbia.

Angela Kershaw lectures in French at Aston University, UK, where she teaches modern French and European culture, French language and translation studies. Her main research interest is in interwar French literature and politics, and she is currently preparing a monograph on women, politics and fiction in 1930s France. Her research interests encompass French literature of the first half of the twentieth century, women's writing and gender studies.

Hélène Laplace-Claverie is a Lecturer in French Literature at the University of Paris IV-Sorbonne, France. Her main fields of research are the performing arts and, more precisely, the links between literature and dance (especially in the nineteenth century). Her major publications include *Ecrire pour la danse: les livrets de ballet de Théophile Gautier à Jean Cocteau (1870–1914)* (Champion, 2001), and the co-editing (with Claudine Lacoste-Veysseyre) of Théophile Gautier's *Théâtre et ballets* (section III of the *Œuvres complètes,* Champion, 2003).

Naoko Morita is Assistant Professor of Media Studies and French at Tohoku University Graduate School of Information Sciences, Japan. Her main fields of research are popular literature (*romans-feuilletons*, ghost stories) in the nineteenth century, text and image, and dance and literature. Her publications include 'Fantasmagorie: art de faire voir des fantômes' (*Etudes francaises*, University of Waseda 2001) and 'L'écriture et son double dans un conte japonais, suguse no en' (*Textuel*, Université Paris VII 2000).

Kimberly van Noort is an Associate Professor at the University of Texas at Arlington, USA, where she teaches twentieth-century French literature and culture, film theory and women's studies. She is the author of a book on Paul Morand and articles on Marguerite Duras, Jacques Lacan, André Gide and post-war French literature. Her current research centres on women playwrights in France.

Anna Norris teaches contemporary French literature and culture at Michigan State University, USA. She has worked extensively on French women's prison writings, and her most recent publications on this topic include: *L'Ecriture du défi: les textes carcéraux féminins du 19e et du 20e siècles: entre l'aiguille et la plume* (Summa 2003). She is currently working on two projects: the writings of Marie Cappelle Lafarge, and the use of the child in French films about the Second World War.

Catherine Perry is Associate Professor of French and francophone studies at the University of Notre Dame, USA. She specialises in French literature of the nineteenth and early twentieth centuries with a focus on poetry. Her book *Persephone Unbound: Dionysian Aesthetics in the Works of Anna de Noailles* (Bucknell University Press/Associated University Presses 2003) studies Noailles' poetry and prose in relation to philosophical and aesthetic currents in early twentieth-century Europe. She has also published articles on Ronsard, Stendhal, Balzac, Barrès and Wagner, Anna de Noailles, Gérard d'Houville (Marie de Régnier), Valéry, Proust, Nicole Brossard and Malika Oufkir.

Sián Reynolds is Professor of French at the University of Stirling, Scotland. She works on both French and Scottish history, is the author of *France between the Wars: gender and politics* (Routledge 1996), and is currently researching a book on Paris and Edinburgh during the Belle Epoque.

Juliette Rogers is Associate Professor of French at the University of New Hampshire, USA. Her main fields of research include Colette, Belle Epoque women writers, and women writers from French Canada. She has published articles on these topics and, in particular, on representations of women students and professionals in Belle Epoque novels.

Angela Ryan is a Lecturer at University College, Cork, Eire and a Government of Ireland Senior Research Fellow in the Humanities (Irish Research Council for the Humanities and Social Sciences) for research into the heroine in Greek, seventeenth-century and twentieth-century French tragedy. She has published on French and comparative literature and theory, psychoanalysis and philosophy, myth and subjectivity, art, traductology, the heroine, Irish women's writing, Sand, Barthes, Belghoul, Bourdieu, Cixous, Kristeva and Compagnon, and has translated Strong, Yeats and Gaelic poetry into French. She received the 2001 *Prix de l'Ambassade* for translation.

Edith Taïeb is Assistant Professor of French at the American University of Paris, having previously taught at Paris III (La Sorbonne Nouvelle), France. A specialist in Hubertine Auclert, her doctorate in language sciences was on 'Le discours politique d'Hubertine Auclert dans *La Citoyenne* (1881–1891)'. Her publications include a monograph on Auclert (*La Citoyenne*, Syros 1982) and various articles.

Carrie Tarr is a Research Fellow in the Faculty of Arts and Social Sciences, Kingston University, UK, and Visiting Research Fellow at Leeds University. She has published widely on gender and ethnicity in French cinema. Recent publications include *Diane Kurys* (1999), *Women, Immigration and Identities in France* (co-edited with Jane Freedman, 2000) and *Cinema and the Second Sex: Women's Filmmaking in France in the 1980s and 1990s* (with Brigitte Rollet, 2001). She is currently preparing a book entitled *Reframing Difference:* beur *and* banlieue *cinema in France*.

Jennifer Yee is a Lecturer and Fellow at the University of Oxford (Christ Church), UK. She has worked mainly on the late nineteenth century and is particularly interested in the construction of national, racial and gender identity through narrative. Her publications include *Clichés de la femme exotique: un regard sur la littérature coloniale française entre 1871 et 1914* (L'Harmattan 2000) and articles in *The Australian Journal* *of French Studies, L'Esprit créateur, French Studies, Literature and Medicine, Textual Practice* and *Tulsa Studies in Women's Literature,* among others.

INDEX